ADVANCE PRAISE FOR *GENERATION ZERO*

"Hal Phillips has written a uniquely important and highly original book that simply represents a MUST read for all soccer fans in the United States and beyond. Using his own personal experience of growing up in the location (white suburbia) and the time (1970s) where and when soccer emerged from its dormant if not moribund state in American history, Phillips offers a most vivid and learned account of how soccer congealed into a structure and force in the 1980s which, in turn, formed the basis for its most diversified flowering in contemporary America. I learned so much from this evocative work that I found enriching as well as entertaining!"

— **Andrei S. Markovits,** professor of Comparative Politics and German Studies, University of Michigan; author of *Offside: Soccer and American Exceptionalism*, and the 2021 memoir, *The Passport as Home: Comfort in Rootlessness*

"Hal Phillips has done a masterly job of celebrating the players and '80s era that laid the foundation for today's American soccer culture. He has produced a valuable history of the players, who despite no pro league and myriad frustrations kept the game alive, and he pulls back the curtains on how they came together to create a national team that today ranks among the world's most noteworthy."

— **Jim Trecker,** National Soccer Hall of Fame Colin Jose Media Award Winner, World Cup '94 senior vice president/communications, co-editor, *100 Years of Soccer in America*

"It's taken my entire lifetime for soccer in this country to move from obscurity to the status of big-time sport, and over those decades, Hal Phillips was the journalist I knew who stuck it out and followed that fascinating ascent. Now he is ready to share the story with sports fan everywhere."

— **Larry Olmsted,** NY Times bestselling author of *FANS: How Watching Sports Makes US Happier, Healthier and More Understanding*

"Hal Phillips parlays stylish prose, magnificently obsessive legwork, and hands-on (okay, feet-on) experience into an authoritative and highly entertaining account of how a generation of players decisively moved soccer from niche to mainstream in American sporting culture."

— **Carlo Rotella,** author of *Cut Time: An Education at the Fights*

———————

"My good friend Hal Phillips is one of those gifted modern Renaissance writers who can write engagingly about anything from gourmet food trucks to football – or, to be more precise, futbol, the world's most popular team sport. Can four billion delirious soccer fans possibly be wrong? Brother Hal thinks not, and skillfully reveals in his delightful new book, **Generation Zero,** why American sports fans might have been absurdly slow to join the party but are finally catching Futbol Fever from the playing fields of suburbia to the posh professional stadiums of Major League Soccer. In the process, he tells a charming tale of his own soccer awakening shaped by an unlikely generation of early stars who transformed America's indifferent view of the game into a robustly growing passion that threatens to rival baseball as the nation's third most popular spectator sport. A must read for your sports bookshelf – and the budding soccer star you're driving to practice twice a week."

— **James Dodson,** bestselling author of *Final Rounds, American Triumvirate* and *Ben Hogan: An American Life*

———————

"Hal Phillips has buried it in the upper right corner with **Generation Zero,** his modern history of soccer in the U.S. There's not a futbol fan or Sunday striker or Soccer Mom who won't enjoy the mastery he displays in telling the story of the beautiful game, in a country that came to it late. This is both a compelling, comprehensive history and a heartfelt account of one man's passion for something that many Americans didn't even notice was sweeping the nation and burrowing into its culture."

— **Jeff Wallach,** Sunday striker and author of the novels *Mr. Wizard* and *Everyone Here Is From Somewhere Else*

———————

GENERATION ZERO

FOUNDING FATHERS, HIDDEN HISTORIES & THE MAKING OF SOCCER IN AMERICA

HAL PHILLIPS

dickinson-moses press

Nantucket, Massachusetts

dickinson-moses press

Dickinson-Moses Press
109 Old South Road
Nantucket, MA 02554
www.dickinsonmoses.com

Ordering Information:
Quantity sales. Special discounts are available on quantity purchases by corporations, associations, and others. For details, contact the publisher at the address above.

Publisher's Cataloging-in-Publication Data:

Names: Phillips, Hal, author.

Title: Generation zero : founding fathers , hidden histories and the making of soccer in America / Hal Phillips.

Description: Includes index. | Nantucket, MA: Dickinson-Moses Press, 2022.

Identifiers: LCCN: 2022907832 | ISBN: 979-8-9860198-0-2 (paperback) | 979-8-9860198-1-9 (ebook)

Subjects: LCSH Soccer. | Soccer--United States--History--19th century. | Soccer--United States--History--20th century. | Sports--History. | BISAC SPORTS & RECREATION / Soccer | BIOGRAPHY & AUTOBIOGRAPHY / Sports

Classification: LCC GV944.U5 .P45 2022 | DDC 796.3340973--dc23

Printed in the United States of America

FOR SHARON

TABLE OF CONTENTS

Members of the U.S. Men's National Team celebrate their historic World Cup berth in Port of Spain, Trinidad, on the day everything changed: Nov. 19, 1989. *(Jon van Woerden photo)*

PROLOGUE

January 2022

This book was born over a pint of imperial stout in the spring of 2012. My family had been vacationing through Montana and the Pacific Northwest. After an obligatory up-and-down at the Space Needle, we lit out for Seattle's Pioneer Square neighborhood, where my wife and two kids located a lunch spot. I found a pub. For once, my priority was not food but rather a Champions League semifinal: Barcelona-Chelsea, second leg, live from the *Camp Nou*. Having spent much of the sepia-tinged 1990s seeking out satellite-delivered soccer programming in drinking establishments coast to coast, I was pleased but not surprised to find a suitable venue there in the Emerald City. On my first attempt, no less. By 2012, one had come to expect such modern conveniences in this country. I didn't even have to sweet-talk the barman into switching the channel. The game was already on. At halftime, a couple pints to the good, I scrutinized my surroundings with more acuity: At 47 years of age (b. 1964), I was clearly the oldest guy in the bar.

During my 20s and 30s, such footballing fare had not been broadcast in America. By 2012, the game arrived via three separate cable networks. Today, half a dozen portals deliver eight to 10 matches of quality nearly every day of the week. What's more, take a good look around your preferred, public-soccer-watching whereabouts — a tavern or sports bar, or perhaps the next time you're part of an MLS match crowd. What you'll discover is a community dominated by fans *born* in the Eighties and Nineties, alongside a healthy sprinkling of my peers. If my elders from the Baby Boom (b. 1943-60) are represented in such settings, they quite probably grew up elsewhere, in foreign, futbol-loving cultures of long-standing. Sitting there in Seattle, nursing my beer, urged on by insistent notes of caramel, this generational segmentation intrigued me. Thinking back, that was the first time I sat back and asked myself, *How did we get here?*

Later that same April of 2012, Fox and its affiliate portals broadcast all 10 season-ending Premier League matches at once, a veritable bacchanal of soccer programming, even by modern standards. Just the week before, Millennial American striker Clint Dempsey (b. 1983) had notched his 50th goal for the English club Fulham FC. Fellow Yank Michael Bradley (b. 1987) was starting in midfield for Chievo in Italy's *Serie A*. Their countryman Jozy Altidore (b. 1989) netted 19 times for AZ Alkmaar in the Dutch *Eredivisie*. When Yanks first crashed top European leagues, our goalies went first. In 2012, after starting out with Manchester United, Everton's Tim Howard (b. 1979) stood as the finest keeper in England. German-born Jermaine Jones (b. 1981), Fabian Johnson (b. 1987) and Timmy Chandler (b. 1990), all starters for their respective *Bundesliga* clubs, had recently sought and obtained American citizenship, so as to represent *this* country at the 2014 World Cup. Similarly, across the Atlantic, two products of U.S.-Mexican parentage who both played their club soccer in *LigaMX* — Jose Francisco Torres (b. 1987) and Edgar Castillo (b. 1986) — also cast their lot with Jurgen Klinsmann's national team. In the U.S. itself, Major League Soccer had evolved into something respectable and lasting.

If that last nugget comes across as faint praise, I ask you: Please consider the messenger. My specific American cohort, Generation X, well remembers the woebegone period when no first-division soccer existed in this country. None. We remember when the idea of U.S.-bred players competing in foreign first divisions was considered absurd, almost laughable. U.S. soccer used to be an oxymoron, like Jamaican bobsledding. Then, seemingly in the blink of an eye, our players proved world class — and Americans watched the game on TV, in bars and stadia, with genuine interest. Passion, even.

Date ranges for specific American generations tend to vary slightly at the margins. William Strauss and Neil Howe, the distinguished demographers I rely upon in this book, define Generation X as those Americans born between 1961 and 1981. As such, we in Gen X place a special value on MLS because, unlike Millennials (a designation coined by Strauss and Howe) and even younger Americans, we grew up alongside the North American Soccer League (NASL), only to witness its tragic, tawdry shuttering in 1984. We value this country's World Cup participation in a similar way because we remember a time before routine qualifications. We intimately recall the period when most Americans did not know we had a national soccer team — and did not want to know.

TWO YEARS LATER, IN THE IMMEDIATE run-up to World Cup 2014, I watched a collection of pundits hold forth in Rio de Janeiro while lounging in an open-air, purpose-built studio overlooking Copacabana beach. The U.S. Soccer Federation had sent to Brazil a squad that commanded an unprecedented level of traveling support. No country had more fans in South America — or so Michael Ballack and Alexi Lalas and Roberto Martinez informed us, from a sleek, overtly contemporary couch. Back in Connecticut, ESPN and its sister network in the Disney imperium, ABC, expected for this World Cup the next in a series of record-setting television audiences.

I turned 50 years old in 2014. My peers and I had traditionally approached soccer programming the way we had approached booze in high school or dope in college: from a position of extreme scarcity. Accordingly, we luxuriated in all that World Cup content — first and foremost because we had lived through *The Before Time*. The massive media coverage from Brazil 2014, the hordes of Americans traveling to Brazil to watch in person, illustrated and emphasized again the tectonic shifts that had taken place in the country of our birth. Once upon a time, long ago, in a galaxy far, far away, we had resided in a famously soccer-indifferent country. Somewhere along the time/space continuum, the situation had radically changed.

Watching the 2014 studio show from Rio, cognizant of these generational and cultural transitions, I wanted Ballack, Martinez and especially Lalas to weigh in on this full-blown American-soccer metamorphosis. How and when exactly did all this happen? They never addressed these questions. It seemed as though no one had. So I began to take up the mantle myself.

When I started asking knowledgeable, engaged U.S. soccer folk about this fulcrum-like phenomenon, they invariably pointed to World Cup 1994, held right here in the good ol' US of A. That tournament was indeed a revelation, very much a coming-out party: record in-stadium attendance; surprisingly strong television ratings; a sun-splashed, well administered soccer orgy that impressed even our skeptical European cousins. The host nation qualified automatically but nevertheless advanced to the knockout stage, where it fell (on Independence Day) to eventual champion *Brasil.* MLS launched two years later. That's a rock-solid record of legacy-leaving. What's more, durable public reputations were forged in 1994. In 2014, when ESPN sought American pundits for its conspicuously casual studio tableau, they tapped '94 alumni Lalas and Cobi Jones.

"We wanted to leave something behind, a legacy — and I think it was the mullet. We tore it up on the mullet front."

—Marcelo Balboa (b. 1967)

However, as I continued to loose my journalistic training on this subject matter, my reporting and the historical record began to tell a different, more cogent and compelling story. For reasons I'll make plain, the Modern American Soccer Movement officially took root Nov. 19, 1989, on the island of Trinidad. *That* was the moment it all changed. *That* was the U.S. Men's National Team (USMNT) whose victory first qualified this nation for a World Cup, after 40 long years of trying. Six months later, the Italian World Cup of 1990 — not World Cup 1994 — first mainstreamed soccer in America. In fact, had this specific generation of national team players not succeeded in qualifying for *Italia* '90, there might not have been a USA '94. "From a soccer and historical standpoint," U.S. striker Bruce Murray (b. 1966) attests, "you'd have to go with 1990. The team that went to the Olympics in '88, then the World Cup: That team changed everything. We showed this country what soccer was all about. We even got the TV people at ESPN and TNT to care."

Admittedly, Murray might possess a bias. He went the full 90 in Port of Spain. He started all three matches at *Italia* '90. Along with all his colleagues on the 1990 USMNT, he's also a member of Generation X. As my research progressed, his case and this generational connection only grew wider, stronger and more credible, however. The American Youth Soccer Organization had been formed in 1964. When youth soccer leagues exploded across suburbia during the second Nixon administration, they introduced the game to each and every member of that pivotal 1990 national team. To all of us in Gen X. From this point forward, I refer to this proto-American cohort as *Generation Zero*, because it all started with them/us. They/we were the first authentically indigenous soccer players and fans this country produced, the first Americans effectively born to the game. Generation Zero grew up with the sport and fell in love with it, as kids do. It's logical, ultimately even unsurprising, that this generation of futbol natives definitively delivered the nation from its century-long, footballing dark age.

IN ITALY THAT SUMMER OF 1990, Murray and his teammates did not presume such a grandiose role in U.S. soccer history. In fact, while they remained very young men, fresh out of college, they were already jaded, all too accustomed to professional disillusion: NASL had folded the moment they were poised to make their living in it. Such a cataclysm should have stunted their careers and American professional soccer in general for another generation, maybe two. The game's longtime critics had predicted something approaching extermination, and the mid-Eighties did become a pro soccer wasteland here, a real step backward. Nonetheless, a mere five years later, the players most disadvantaged by the collapse of NASL instead claimed U.S. soccer's seminal victory, effectively resurrecting the game in this country. Six months later, at *Italia* '90 itself, competing on surprisingly equal footing against the host country and tournament favorite, they found the mountaintop experience exhilarating — and a bit dizzying.

"I remember Chris Sullivan [b. 1965] got subbed on for Bruce Murray late in the Italy game," striker Peter Vermes (b. 1966) recalls. "We had a defensive corner kick. So we're going back to mark up. I'm running back and I turn to Chris and I'm like, 'Sully, I got Baresi.' And he's like, 'I got Vialli.' And we both look at each other like, Oh really? We got *these* guys? Who are we to have *these* two guys — Franco Baresi and Luca Vialli! Because, you know, on the other side, I don't think they were saying, 'Yo, I got Vermes.' They had no idea who we were."

"They were probably saying, 'You take the dude with the blond mullet and I'll take the dude over there with the dark mullet,'" adds Vermes' teammate in Italy, Marcelo Balboa (b. 1967). "We wanted to leave something behind, a legacy — and I think it was the mullet. We tore it up on the mullet front."

No amount of cultural cachet could save the mullet. Happily, the legacies of Generation Zero have proved more numerous and sweeping than "business in front, party in the back."

Beginning that unlikely summer of 1990, soccer's haphazard, indeterminate expansion in the U.S. instantly became inevitable, headlong growth. MLS launched in 1996 but was announced in 1993; today it boasts the sixth highest attendance among futbol leagues worldwide. Seven consecutive World Cup qualifications ensued. Soccer had long before buried all comers on the youth-participation front — everyone knows *that*. What you may not realize: A December 2017 Gallup poll revealed a game poised to overtake baseball as the country's third most popular spectator sport. Seem dubious? Go ahead and attend a Major League Baseball game. Then attend an MLS match. Judge for yourself which sport is poised to win the demographic battle — the generational fight for hearts, minds and wallets — over the long term. Today in America, the international nature and scope of *The Beautiful Game*, along with our abiding, unfettered jingoism, have only served to further soccer's formidable evolution here.

The norm-shattering, expectation-defying, mullet-wreathed, history-making story of Generation Zero is little known or appreciated today. The facts of the matter have fallen into a historical crevasse. What's more, they have been held hostage there all these years by a distinctly American algebra of feckless Boomer indifference, tweet-short media memories, lingering xenophobia, historiographical sloth, and surprisingly potent brand politics. In attempting to crack this proof, I have sought to set the record straight. In the process, as a bonus, I stumbled upon something I believe to be more meaningful, irresistible and mythic: U.S. soccer's modern Creation Story. A collective epic not before told, but sorely in need of telling.

The 1989 USMNT on November 19, in Port of Spain, two hours before the celebration, 90 minutes before it changed the course of American soccer, a few seconds prior to the opening whistle. We continue to turn the clock backward... *(Jon van Woerden photo)*

The one and only Pelé lets loose with a free kick the night of June 20, 1975, at Nickerson Field in Boston. In the wall stand Minutemen (from left) Jorge Calado, Wolfgang Suhnholz, Eusébio, Axel Neumann and Bill Wilkinson. *(Boston Globe photo/Getty Images)*

1.   *HOTBEDS*

(1970 to '75)

When they came for Pelé that brisk June night, the locals ripped the shirt from his back. They absconded with one of his shoes, too, and tore his vintage, Seventies-era short shorts. Global sporting icons deserve far more solicitous treatment, we can agree. But those American soccer fans of pitch-invasion age (let's call it 18 to 25) didn't know from matters of soccer etiquette, not back then, not halfway through the ever-so-brief Ford administration, not so early in the game's modern evolution upon these shores. When, in its misplaced excitement, the crowd had finished with the 34-year-old Brazilian and some semblance of on-field order had been restored, Pelé was not seriously hurt. But he did lie prostrate for a time — and a bit freaked out, surely — on the weirdly verdant AstroTurf at Nickerson Field. His tying goal, late and dramatic, was exactly what we'd all come to see, or hoped to see. That's precisely why and when folks stormed the field in communal spasms of ecstasy and adulation. That's what happens, we the faithful discovered that night, when a flesh-and-blood savior comes to town and overdelivers.

The year was 1975. I was 10 and three-quarters years of age. My father had chaperoned a few youth soccer teammates and me to our first-ever professional match: our Boston Minutemen home to Pelé's New York Cosmos. Up and out way past our bedtimes, we innocents bore witness to this madcap scene, to its confusing aftermath, to the new era it signaled.

Capacity had been greatly exceeded that evening. This was obvious in the moment. Next morning, the crowd situation formed the basis of hand-wringing accounts from a variety of Boston-area journalists — "a security problem just waiting to happen," they tut-tutted. To my friends and me, this judgment felt tone-deaf and priggish. The good-natured mauling of soccer's most august ambassador was, in fact, just one of several equally important, electrifying takeaways. First, don't bury the lead: Our Minutemen won this game, 2-1. Next, we watched American-born left back Benny Brewster help them do so, firsthand. Yes, Pelé was carried from the field, not to return — but we soon saw the man, with our own wide eyes, get up and walk the earth again, right there on the sideline below. Finally, it was the broader tableau inclusive of all this stimuli — almost cinematic in scope and shock value — that made our hair stand on end. It seemed to our impressionable, pre-pubescent brains that most of metropolitan Boston had flooded these modest premises to experience something truly massive and historic, something uproarious and unpredictable. Something almost holy.

We stood the full 90. Our serendipitous place in this passion play was a mere causeway, an interstitial place between places: a featureless concrete thoroughfare raised up in Brutalist fashion behind the west goal. Before and below us the action unfolded unobstructed, the spillover crowd enveloping the field in a picture frame of living, breathing, hooting and hollering humanity. During the match this pending security issue moved and morphed like a gargantuan amoeba, fattening in places only to thin back out, shifting sideways and backward but never losing its interior, rectangular integrity where it met the field of play — that is, until Pelé struck from just outside the box some 20 minutes from full time. Behind us loomed a trio of high-rise Boston University dormitories. I remember craning my neck to see their many windows all filled with ticketless spectators. Beyond the opposite goal, the city skyline twinkled in dark repose over the monolithic, man-made horizon that was the Massachusetts Turnpike. For a soccer-mad kid like myself, this was the stuff of some baroque fantasy become real, for I could never have conjured such a scene without having observed it with my own waking eyes.

With no seats to complicate our spectating experience, we did indeed stand — our flat chests pressed against a low, rounded bit of industrial railing. When Edson Arantes do Nascimento — the semi-mythical Pelé, his highness *O Rei* — tied the score with 20 minutes still to play, that's when the invisible rectangular barrier gave way and they came for him. The masses. To lay hands on the man, the same jubilant, numinous fellow they'd seen jumping into the arms of teammates, in slow motion, every Saturday afternoon during the opening montage to ABC's *Wide World of Sports*. That night at Nickerson Field, these would-be soccer fans acted (out) as any newly minted devotees might have: by touching the hem of his garment. Several garments, in fact.

Tucked unobtrusively off Commonwealth Avenue, Nickerson Field had been pieced together slapdashedly, seemingly in sections, starting in the 1960s. It first took shape on the site of Braves Field, formerly home to the city's National League baseball franchise, which had decamped for Milwaukee back in '53. Despite this big-league heritage, and because The Hub has never been a college sports town, Nickerson would always play second fiddle in a city of philharmonics (Fenway Park, Boston Garden). For the breadth of their meager three-year existence, the expansion Minutemen proved fitting tenants for this second-rank stadium that, after all its evolutions, still seemed only half-finished in 1975. The single formalized stand, the old right-field grandstand, was located south of the playing surface. Across the way stood a skimpy, metallic, seemingly provisional bleacher. Official capacity: 12,500. There was nothing at all on either end of the pitch, and, in this regard, a healthy, well lubricated portion of the 20,000 on hand that June evening in 1975 could not believe their good fortune. They had arrived there, one imagines, to root for the home team — but also to get a real-deal, up-close glimpse of the visiting celebrity striker, the celebrated savior of American soccer. Pelé had joined his new teammates on the Cosmos only a few months before. Together they had arrived in Boston to take on our gallant Minutemen, whose fortunes rested largely on the aging shoulders of another imported megastar, a still-luminous figure named Eusébio da Silva Ferreira.

Many futbol aficionados during the 1960s placed Eusébio beside, if not above, Pelé in the pantheon of transcendent footballers. He was indisputably a giant in his own right — and the two icons knew each other well. Nine years prior, at the 1966 World Cup, Eusébio and Portugal didn't merely defeat Pelé and Brazil in the final group-stage match. They roughed up *O Rei* and denied the defending champions a place in the quarterfinals.

The great Eusébio, the original Black Panther (born in Mozambique), would best his South American rival in this NASL rematch, as well — though he wouldn't finish the game either. One wonders what Eusébio thought of Pelé's tying goal and the intoxicated mob it inspired. The Portuguese had scored first that portentous night at Nickerson Field, to put the Minutemen ahead — his team, the home team. No one had invaded the pitch to celebrate *his* goal.

Just nine years *later*, this very same match and all its attendant pageantry — even the mauling of Pelé himself — had been more or less expunged from the public consciousness. The North American Soccer League (NASL) would abruptly collapse in late 1984. Thereafter, Pelé's narrow escape from the Boston mob would register as but a footnote alongside all the other slices of U.S. soccer ephemera: the rock-hard synthetic playing surfaces, the head-spinning franchise shifts, the startling array of period pornstaches, all the imported talent, and the native-born drones who served them, literally and figuratively. Come 1985, outside the mind's eye of young fans like myself, all of these memories lay buried somewhere in the rubble.

For 17 years, the professional game *had* flourished here, or so it appeared in the moment. Hadn't NASL cheekily made off with top international players from all points across the civilized futbol world? Not just Pelé and Eusébio but glittering global icons like Johan Cruyff, Franz Beckenbauer, Carlos Alberto and George Best, as well? Yes. It had.

It wasn't just an extended fever dream. They had *all* competed here, in the flesh, before large crowds, on American soils.

When the league folded its tent, however, there was no slow fizzling out, no lingering soccer fandom to support a successor. NASL's final Soccer Bowl was held in October 1984. By the following January, professional outdoor soccer lay comatose in the U.S. from sea to shining sea. In the immediate aftermath, the league seemed to many observers a sort of social experiment gone sadly and unforgivingly awry. They viewed NASL's short tenure as an awkward sporting dalliance from which players and fans had quickly moved on. Within weeks, the foreign luminaries got straight out of Dodge — retired or moved back to Europe and South America. Without the skill or connections to follow them, native players found themselves immediately unemployed — or underemployed by random, low-budget indoor clubs.

Also alone and abandoned were all the young soccer fans minted during the league's heyday. Few of *them* ever moved on, however. Starting in 1985, as young adults, they would produce from this forbidding void what American soccer had failed to create in a century of trying: a golden generation of native-born players *and* an audience that would care — the nation's first legitimate futbol fan base. This epic transformation, however, was ultimately forged on the field of play: down in the Caribbean, on the Korean Peninsula, in the Eternal City of Rome. Just five short years after professional soccer imploded here, these children of the Seventies did the impossible: They climbed out of the resulting crater, covered in primordial ooze, to redeem the U.S. game at a stroke — *and* to show that NASL had not died in vain.

The folks who stormed the field that late-spring night at Nickerson Field weren't little kids. They were impetuous-but-consenting young adults who had arrived under their own power, not in the back seat of their dad's station wagon. They were mostly young men, late-stage Baby Boomers, and they were caught up in something impassioned but fleeting, something quite apart from what we 10-year-olds experienced.

Our next elders had not been raised on the game, as we had been. They had not partaken of the youth leagues in full flower across the country by 1975. Boomers came to their soccer fandom a bit later in life. Too late. And so their interest in the sport would prove merely episodic. By May 1985, when everything went pear-shaped — when NASL vanished and the U.S. Men's National Team failed to qualify for yet another World Cup — they, too, had moved on.

Timing is everything. My friends Tom Wadlington, Dave Goganian and I experienced that Minutemen match, the presence of Pelé and Eusébio, NASL, and the game generally in a completely different fashion from those Americans only a decade our seniors. That dynamic begins to explain why our generation still loves and supports soccer today, while Baby Boomers generally couldn't care less. Among our younger suburban cohort in Greater Boston, for example, Minutemen keeper Shep Messing and outside back Benny Brewster weren't just token Americans. They were living *gods*. In metropolitan New York, where Franz Beckenbauer himself arrived in 1976 to join Pelé and Carlos Alberto on the Cosmos, Queens native Mike Windischmann didn't just rejoice at the news. He and *his* 10-year-old teammates met *Der Kaiser*'s plane.

Windischmann would grow up to captain the U.S. Men's National Team (USMNT), the outfit that finally qualified this country for a World Cup — after 40 long years of trying. All of Windischmann's teammates on that team developed their own youthful, similarly worshipful relationships with NASL and its stars, domestic and foreign-born. Golden generations of talent require a professional model to which they can aspire. Like Wad, Gogo and me, these future World Cuppers all developed those attachments and aspirations during the 1970s, as ball boys (Marcelo Balboa, at L.A. Aztecs games), as trainees (Bruce Murray's club coach was Washington Diplomat midfielder John Kerr Sr.), or as plain ol' Star-struck fans (Steve Trittschuh never got over the fact that NASL folded before he could play for his hometown St. Louis Stars).

From their pre-adolescent points of view, back in 1975, soccer and NASL had *always* been a part of their lives, and always would be. Wasn't this America's game of the future, the *wave* of the future, as we'd all been told? All those matches we attended, all the heroes we worshipped — were they not real? As 10-year-olds, the league's disintegration come the mid-1980s was inconceivable. But that is exactly what happened: NASL vanished just when Windischmann and Murray and Trittschuh were old enough to compete in it.

Even more fantastical was the idea that U.S. soccer would regather itself so quickly — on the field, behind these same 10-year-old boys, now young professionals in their own right — to score the most pivotal, demonstrably foundational victories in the sport's U.S. history. And here we begin to see the first hints of logic in our storybook narrative. For if the United States were to finally qualify for the World Cup, and make soccer in this country a lasting, meaningful, modern cultural force, naturally the break-through generation would be composed of soccer natives — the first-ever cohort of red-blooded American boys and girls who truly immersed themselves in the game.

No one in those NASL crowds back in 1975, none of those 9- and 10-year-old kids therein, could have anticipated their starring roles in this drama to come — not standing there beneath the klieg lights of Nickerson Field, not chasing down balls on the sidelines of Anaheim Stadium, not crowding the reception hall at J.F.K., holding up a sign that read, *Herzlich Willkommen!* All we knew back then was that Pelé and Eusébio and Beckenbauer and Trevor Francis and Rodney Marsh were charismatic international superstars, and NASL was our only chance to see them playing the same game we did, at the highest continental level, in the flesh.

To mark the sheer gravity of our first NASL experience, Wad, Gogo and I had donned our most impressive game jerseys — because pride is more powerful than self-consciousness when you're 10 and three-quarters. We wore our uniforms to NASL games, but to play block tag and whiffle ball in the neighborhood, too. We wore them on errands with our parents — but never to school, for whatever reason. In the Fifties and Sixties, young boys wore baseball and football jerseys in the same way, for the same reason. Come the Seventies, soccer jerseys joined the sartorial mix.

That night the late-stage Boomers ran down Pelé, we slipped on the glorious red and white of Wellesley Hotspur. Full marks to our coach, Vince Harackiewicz, for co-opting such a cool British team name some 40 years before Major League Soccer (MLS) made such things fashionable. Lesser marks for his perverse choice of Arsenal red over proper Tottenham blue.

By 1975, my teammates and I on Hotspur had developed a wholehearted relationship with the game. Not in any sophisticated, zonalmarking sense. We didn't yet know our team's name and colors were at odds, for example. But we *had* played the game nearly every day for two or three years by that time — on club teams, in our suburban rec leagues, in our respective neighborhoods, and every day at recess from Hunnewell School. The prospect of any pro match, much less the spectacle that was Minutemen vs. Cosmos, would have been pure unadulterated stimulus for any fifth grader growing up outside of Boston. But this was Pelé vs. Eusébio, The King vs. The Black Pearl, under the lights at B.U.! This was *our sport* — and so it meant more than any Patriots or Red Sox game could.

While paying due homage to the imports, we also passionately marked the every move of someone else that night — someone less skilled, not nearly so famous, and entirely local. NASL rules required that each team field at least two North Americans during every match, at all times. This strategy would eventually prove a fateful misstep for the league and all of American soccer, frankly — but we didn't care about any of that. Not back then. This quota, this league directive, put Benny Brewster on the pitch for the Minutemen that night and every night, and we mighty Spurs cared ever so deeply about *that*. Brewster started for Boston at left back. Did he deserve that place? Did his fellow Yank Shep Messing deserve his starting spot in goal? We kids didn't yet know from "affirmative actions" like these. We could not have known how they might disrupt merit-based team selection — or hinder U.S. player development in the long term. To be fair, no one did.

All we sons of the suburbs could discern were grown American men playing *our* game beside and against all those exotic celebrity athletes, in the floodlit crucible of Nickerson Field. And it thrilled us.

The North American Soccer League had instituted this quota system for two reasons: to better develop native U.S. and Canadian players; and to engage continent-wide support by stirring aspiration in young fans like Wad, Windischmann, Gogo, Trittschuh, Balboa and myself. Tactic #1 didn't work out particularly well, but tactic #2 proved an unqualified success. The league made it clear to kids like me, to kids like future national team stars Paul Caligiuri, John Stollmeyer, Brian Bliss and John Harkes: *This could be you someday.* Harkes served as a Cosmos ball boy during a period when Santiago Formoso, who hailed from Harkes' north Jersey hometown, played for the Cosmos. "He was like a rock star for us," Harkes recalls. "From the moment I knew what the Cosmos were, playing for them was all I wanted to do."

As many NASL clubs did, the Minutemen had smartly deployed Brewster, this native of Newton, Massachusetts (by way of Brown University), to clinics and youth soccer events all over Greater Boston. Benny wasn't just local. He was wicked local, and this expedient bit of community outreach worked its aspirational magic on young soccer players across New England, in their thousands. My friends and I flocked to Brewster's clinics. We channeled him during our club practices. We cheered him after the Minutemen folded and NASL promptly (though briefly) returned to our region in the form of the New England Tea Men, whose brain trust cannily signed Brewster for his final season, in 1978. Benny never really left. His presence was felt in eastern Massachusetts soccer circles for a good long time — as the owner of his own Brewster-branded camps, then as men's head coach at Boston College.

I struggle to remember a whole host of crucial American moments from 1975 — the surrender of Saigon and the end of the Vietnam War, for example. I've since seen the iconic photographs of embassy staff being plucked from that downtown rooftop, of course. I've read the detailed historical accounts by Stanley Karnow and Neil Sheehan, among others. But I don't *remember* any of those scenes being broadcast on television, not as a 10-year-old, not in the moment. The Weather Underground's bombing of the U.S. State Department, Jimmy Hoffa's disappearance, Margaret Thatcher's rise to power, Generalissimo Francisco Franco's enduring death... Of all these things, I cannot claim firsthand, in-the-moment recollections. But I do recall and can still picture, with unnerving clarity, the sight of Benny Brewster heroically humping it up and down the left sideline at Nickerson Field, his straight, blond, shoulder-length hair gyrating wildly around an ever more prominent bald patch on the back of his head.

SOCCER IN AMERICA DIDN'T COME OF AGE during the 1970s. When *All in the Family* debuted (1971), that transformation remained some 20 years off. However, during this markedly strident and disaffected socio-political period, ushered in by the Kent State shootings and Manhattan's Hard Hat Riot, soccer did for the first time establish a toehold in the larger culture. And it just so happens that the legions of 10-, 11- and 12-year-olds who attached themselves to the game in various ways during the Nixon, Ford and Carter administrations were the same kids who would grow into the adult players and fans who *would* bring about that critical transformation circa 1989-90.

On one level, this is exactly what we might expect. American children of the Seventies were the first to be beguiled by the glamour of NASL — by homegrown talents like Brewster and striker Kyle Rote Jr. — and by the prospect of playing a sport that, unlike American football, basketball and baseball, allowed for such lightly coached, unfettered, highly aerobic competition. At our schools, in community rec leagues rapidly multiplying in every nook and cranny of suburbia, we took soccer into our bosom as American boys (and girls) never had before.

Every member of that breakthrough 1990 World Cup squad was first exposed to the game during this time, under similar cultural circumstances. Millions of our suburban contemporaries did likewise. Most kids never developed such elite talent, of course, but even the mere mortals carried forward a lasting attachment to the game, a widespread affection this country had not yet witnessed. Soccer had been played in the U.S. since the late 19th century. It had attracted steady participation through the decades — but never so broadly until the early 1970s.

Today, we casually refer to this nationwide proliferation of suburban leagues as the "Youth Soccer Revolution." What was it about America during this era — and those children of the Seventies — that enabled and fed such dramatic recreational change? Moreover, what enabled this particular generation, as it grew to adulthood, to succeed in making the U.S. a viable soccer nation, where previous generations had *all* failed? That's what this book is about: the demonstrable, epochal transformation all those sons and daughters of the suburbs engendered.

Today, we tend to think of the Youth Soccer Revolution and the sport's subsequent growth as an inevitability, a force majeure. It was not. The North American Soccer League is often linked with the explosion of youth soccer, historically and chronologically, but NASL disappeared in 1984, never to return. Until our subjects qualified this country for a World Cup in November 1989, no American national team had ever done so. The U.S. had been a futbol backwater for a century. Suddenly, come 1990, it was not. Then, four years after qualifying for our first World Cup, we hosted one. Where no first-division league had existed from 1984-1995, these same sons of the revolution enabled Major League Soccer (MLS) to form, in 1996.

So what *was* it about America in the Seventies that produced these founders and framers, U.S. soccer's Generation Zero? What rendered such fertile footballing ground? We can't begin to answer these questions until we unpack the evolutions, legitimacies and formative backdrops that composed the Me Decade.

The game had not been strategically dropped on these United States from the sky on Jan. 1, 1970. It had been a sporting presence in large-ly *urban* pockets across the country for decades. Until the Age of Nixon, however, it had largely been restricted to those pockets — from met-ropolitan areas as sprawling as New York City, San Francisco, St. Louis and Philadelphia to communities as modest as Fall River, Bethlehem and Bridgeport. These were the ethnic/urban "hotbeds" to which immigrants had first brought the game from Europe and points south.

In the 1970s, however, American soccer started to develop an entirely new and wildly enthusiastic hotbed variety: white-bread/suburban. Only thereafter did the breadth of middle-class America start getting wise to the game's charms — because so many urban families were rapidly vacating cities for all those suburbs. For all the slow-moving socioeco-nomics behind America's postwar demographic shift, soccer's suburban migration happened relatively quickly and would fundamentally change both the American game and the larger sports landscape, for keeps.

———·•·———

"Everyone played soccer when I was growing up. My older brother played before me, so the leagues weren't all that new. It certainly wasn't new to us," recalls national team defender Steve Trittschuh, born in 1965 and reared just across the Mississippi River from St. Louis in suburban Granite City, Illinois. Trittschuh's dad never played the game. "He was more of a baseball guy. He actually wanted me to pursue baseball and I had a chance out of high school to play professionally, but I just played [baseball] for the fun of it. Soccer was always my passion."

St. Louis was a classic urban hotbed throughout the 1940s, Fifties and Sixties, chockablock with immigrant populations from Germany, Ireland, Mexico, Italy, Serbia, Lebanon and Greece. Post-World War II, once these populations had prospered and assimilated for a time, they would relo-cate west to Missouri suburbs like Fenton or St. Charles, or they'd cross the river to southern Illinois and help fertilize this new category of hotbed in places like Belleville and Granite City. This formula was replicated in dozens of metropolitan areas throughout the decade. My family just happened to arrive in one of these, the lily-white Boston suburb of Wellesley, in 1973. I had never touched a soccer ball until that time, but in Wellesley, like Trittschuh in suburban St. Louis, I found the game everywhere — thanks to Ray Copeland, an English transplant who helped found and nurture the town's youth soccer system starting in the late 1960s. If the Wellesley United Soccer Club had a framer, it was Mr. Copeland.

America's urban/ethnic populations had existed for decades in metropolitan areas famous for their diverse, soccer-loving populations. Large cities like Los Angeles and Chicago stand out, of course, but there were smaller population centers like St. Louis where immigrant groups would eventually earn "hotbed" status for their cities. Take Milwaukee and its suburbs, for example, with their formidable German and Hungarian populations. Bob Gansler, U.S. national team coach from 1989-90, grew up there during the 1950s and starred for the local Bavarian Club team early in the 1960s. He would eventually play in the nascent NASL for the Chicago Mustangs, alongside the Argentinian Luis Balboa, father of Marcelo Balboa, the USMNT defender who grew up in the sprawling hotbed of Greater Los Angeles. Generations are woven tightly together in this story: Gansler would coach Marcelo at the Italian World Cup of 1990.

St. Louis had earned an even more pronounced soccer reputation by the time Trittschuh came along. Saint Louis University was one of the country's early collegiate soccer powers. The St. Louis-based Missouri Athletic Club annually bestows the Hermann Trophy, college soccer's equivalent of the Heisman Trophy. What's more, it had been home to Harry Keough, hero of America's shocking 1-0 win over England at the 1950 World Cup in Brazil. (To be clear, all three of America's FIFA World Cup appearances prior to 1990 — including Brazil '50 — had been secured by invitation, or via regional qualification tournaments featuring but a handful of countries. The inaugural 1930 World Cup was entirely invitational. In 1934, a worldwide total of 32 teams entered the qualification process and 16 advanced to the finals in Italy. In North America, Cuba eliminated Haiti; Mexico eliminated Cuba; and the U.S. beat Mexico, 4-2, to secure the lone regional place. Only three North American countries attempted to qualify for the 1950 World Cup. Mexico won the group, the U.S. finished second, and both advanced to Brazil. Cuba stayed home. The system of global qualification via the game's various regional Confederations was instituted prior to the 1954 tournament in Switzerland. Until Generation Zero showed up, these U.S. qualification efforts had gone 0 for 9.)

"I was like five when I started with soccer. That's what you did in St. Louis," Trittschuh recollects. "A lot of the Catholic schools had teams, too. We had the St. Louis Stars in the NASL; we went and watched their games. Eventually the Steamers were around [competing in the Major Indoor Soccer League]. There was always soccer in St. Louis."

In the same way that Bostonians knew and revered Benny Brewster, Trittschuh paid special attention to his fellow Americans on the Stars and Steamers.

"Most of them were St. Louis guys: Don Ebert, Greg Makowski . . . A lot of them went to SIU [Southern Illinois University in Edwardsville, where Trittschuh would later star] or Saint Louis University," he says. "We knew exactly who they were. It's funny: Cruyff played here in St. Louis. Rinus Michels [architect of the Ajax and Dutch national team juggernauts] coached here. It's amazing to think that all that happened *here* — in the 1970s! You knew about these foreign players, of course, but you paid special attention to the Americans because they were local and playing right there in front of you, alongside these legends."

In the late 1980s, when ESPN first started televising the occasional World Cup qualification match, I was confused as to why the U.S. Soccer Federation (USSF) often staged them at an insignificant, modestly bleachered facility in Fenton, Missouri. Honestly, the place appeared no bigger than a high school football stadium. Here's the sobering truth: The St. Louis

Soccer Park — also known throughout this period as Big Arch Stadium; today known as World Wide Technology Soccer Park — was one of the few places the Federation could expect to sell out *and* ensure a majority of U.S.-backing spectators. Did these fans create an American Soccer Fortress in suburban Fenton? Hardly. But whatever home-field advantage there was at the Soccer Park is owed to the region's hotbed status: the long-standing population of soccer-loving natives in Greater St. Louis.

Over the years, Federation pooh-bahs were slow to deploy this kind of match-siting strategy. It wasn't in place by May 1985, for example, when the U.S. crashed out of qualifying at the hands of Costa Rica — the final World Cup failure before these fated children of the Seventies finally broke through in 1989. That specific loss to the *Ticos* proved the swan song for an entire generation of U.S. players that preceded Generation Zero, and the 0-1 result well illustrated our country's prevailing match-siting naïveté. The second leg of this two-game, home-and-home series (a "tie" in soccer parlance) was contested in Torrance, California, where supporters of Costa Rica overran Murdock Stadium. The outsized Costa Rican population in Southern California effectively wiped out any home-field advantage for the Americans. This is what *never* happened in Fenton.

Up to and including this crucial and ultimately disastrous 1985 qualifier, USSF executives cared as much about gate receipts as they did about on-field results — results they were accustomed to surrendering. Well, that's not entirely fair. But they did care a bit too much about the gate: Halftime festivities that day in Torrance, for example, featured not a high school band playing Sousa marches but rather a display of Chicano folk dancing. In this quasi-hostile atmosphere, the Americans — featuring a 20-year-old Paul Caligiuri in midfield and a 19-year-old Mike Windischmann at center-back — failed to score and went down in flames.

Was Southern California not a soccer hotbed? It certainly was, but one wielding a double-edged sword for the national team, even today. The futbol culture in Greater Los Angeles — four seasons long and brimming with Central American influence — develops more than its share of talent (and futbol-savvy fans). But its immigrant populations are newer than those in St. Louis or Milwaukee or Philadelphia. They may support the U.S., but they are just as likely to support one of the 41 nations represented by the Confederation of North, Central America and Caribbean Association Football (CONCACAF), the Miami-based body that organizes regional soccer matters here, including qualifying for the World Cup.

The American game gathers a great deal of strength from the demographic mix in SoCal. Just don't schedule a meaningful USMNT qualifier there, lest the precious home-field advantage be squandered.

"I remember playing Mexico one time in the Santa Ana Bowl," remembers Paul Krumpe, who grew up in Torrance and debuted for the U.S. national team in 1986. "I had my whole family there, and my wife's family had not seen a lot of soccer. They were completely surrounded by Mexican fans! The only other time I played Mexico was at the Coliseum in Los Angeles. Again, 60,000 people there, and 55,000 were cheering for Mexico. That's what U.S. Soccer did at the time because they needed to sell tickets, to make it viable. American fans had not bought in yet."

Even as the U.S. has today caught and overtaken most of its regional rivals — all but Mexico, really — this issue of how and where exactly to best assert a home-field advantage has not gone away. The tensions relating to where one's family came from, and how long those identities should linger here in the American melting pot, will always be with us. The Federation is more savvy today: In the late 1990s, it began to schedule key winter qualifiers in places like Columbus, Ohio — especially those fixtures against our neighbors to the south. In 2010, however, more than 100,000 fans packed the Rose Bowl in Pasadena, California, for a Gold Cup Final — the biennial CONCACAF championship — pitting the U.S. against Mexico. Some 75,000 showed up to support *El Tri*, and the Americans went down, 4-2. Venue matters, and it will always complicate issues of fan support in a nation so large and diverse as this one.

———————

"My dad actually coached my brother, who is two years older than me — that's how it was back then. Even in St. Louis. Who exactly was gonna step up and coach the team? It was just dads mainly," Trittschuh explains. "When I got to be about 12, though, I had an ex-professional who knew the game, and he was my coach. His name was Ruben Mendoza. He kinda brought proper soccer to Granite City, Illinois."

Mendoza would prove a hugely influential figure in St. Louis soccer circles. His story illustrates the process by which an urban/ethnic game proliferated across America's more homogenous, populous, expanding suburbs during the 1970s.

Mendoza's bio also shows how tangled and varied the "immigrant" story can be in the U.S. His parents were Mexican nationals, but he was born in St. Louis in 1931. When he was eight, the family moved to the Mexican state of Durango, only to return stateside in Ruben's teens. He starred for his club team, St. Louis Kutis SC, throughout the 1950s; he made four appearances for the U.S. Men's National Team and played on two separate U.S. Olympic squads. Later, as Trittschuh attests, Mendoza moved his family from city to suburb, affording the youth leagues of Granite City a preposterously high level of coaching acumen throughout the 1970s.

The coaching bounty didn't stop there. When Trittschuh got to high school, his head coach was Bob Kehoe, who had played in NASL for the Stars and coached the USMNT in 1972. Thereafter, with Mendoza as his assistant, the two established a high school soccer dynasty at Granite City North. "I was fortunate in that I had a lot of good coaching," Trittschuh says.

And how. During the 1960s, even in an established hotbed like Greater St. Louis, young suburban players did not enjoy access to guys like Mendoza and Kehoe. By the 1970s, they did. It was exactly this sort of accessible coaching expertise — combined with soccer's move to more populous, upscale suburbs like Granite City, Wellesley and Bethesda, Maryland — that made all the difference when it came to producing Generation Zero, America's first generation of elite players.

However, the impact ran deeper and was felt even more broadly than that. Think of the hundreds of kids who played beside Trittschuh and his brother at the youth levels in Granite City. They *all* got the same expert, highly nuanced coaching from Ruben Mendoza. Think of all the Granite City kids who played on teams not coached by Kehoe. These children of the 1970s joined similar cohorts, from suburban communities across the country, to form America's very first, nationwide, truly homegrown soccer fan base.

Once my family had moved to Wellesley that winter of 1973, and once the snow had melted, I discovered that two kids next door, Peter and Rebecca Borden, would often kick a soccer ball around their front yard. In time, I was invited to join them. At our K-5 Hunnewell School, where latent-hippie choir teachers forced us to sing selections of Cat Stevens and Karen Carpenter (interspersed with healthy, almost ecstatic doses of *Godspell* and *Jesus Christ Superstar*), we played soccer every single day at recess. It was an unwieldy match pitting 20 to 30 third- and fourth-graders against 15 to 20 fifth-graders. Running scores were carefully kept over the course of each week, with the winner often decided just before the bell rang on Friday.

Like Trittschuh, I found all of this soccer culture firmly in place. If my family had arrived in Wellesley during the winter of 1963 or even 1968, it would not have been there.

"So, my family is originally from Germany. We moved to Texas in 1967," says Mike Woitalla, executive editor at *Soccer America*, a magazine founded, not coincidentally, in 1971. "By the time I was 10, in 1974, we were back to Germany and I watched the World Cup there, on TV. When we came back to Dallas, I wanted to play soccer. *Had* to play soccer, actually. By that time, the youth leagues had just started in North Dallas. By the next year, it was everywhere across Dallas. Later we moved to Hawaii, and they had a league *there* I could play in."

The structure given to all this Seventies futbol ferment would be familiar to anyone playing or coaching youth soccer today: Kids introduced to the game via entry-level, all-inclusive recreation or "house" leagues segmented by age groups (U-10, U-12, etc.) and competing intramurally, within a specific community. From there, interested and capable players graduated to "club" programs segmented in the same fashion, where teams competed with counterparts from nearby communities. In either case, largely clueless Soccer Dads invariably presided at midweek practices. My first house-league team played five forwards and two fullbacks — a formation devised in the late 19th century and adapted through the years but farcically out of date by 1973. We relied on Soccer Dads more intrinsically for prosaic matters like driving the honkin' big, fake-wood-paneled station wagons to weekend games. Yes, folks carpooled quite routinely back then.

Youth soccer today, as embodied by the so-called "premier" system, has moved light-years ahead in many ways. Crucially, there are far more qualified coaches to go around — many of whom first learned the game during the 1970s. Year-round soccer can foster extraordinary skill development. For the money they charge — roster places on premier sides today can cost thousands of dollars each year — one might well expect such development. But think about it: Elite clubs today, these premier clubs, are businesses. They're small and scrappy. They aren't in the habit of cutting from team rosters *anyone* whose parents will shell out that sort of money, which sorta takes the shine off the whole "premier" thing.

Folks valued participation in the 1970s, naturally. But that's what house leagues were for. Early in the Youth Soccer Revolution, *club* soccer meant no-nonsense tryouts, actual roster cuts and comparatively kick-ass uniforms. The club system that took shape during the 1970s proved far more merit-based, frankly, except for the occasional kid who got his roster spot because his dad coached the team. And the cost? "Nothing much," my mom reports. "Maybe 25 dollars?" Nevertheless, tryouts were make or break — a serious business that did not waver to spare anyone's feelings. They resulted in "A" teams (for all the best players), "B" teams (for the next best) and perhaps "C" teams for those left over — if and only if another game-but-under-qualified father made himself, and his station wagon, available.

In the spring of 1974, my very first club team, Ajax, was assembled as Wellesley's "B" team in U-10. We were coached by Eric Krause, a great luxury — for us — in that he was a German national. He knew what he was doing and had the accent to prove it. What's more, his son Dirk debunked or at least tempered the whole "coach's son" stereotype: He was our star midfielder, who made sure his best friend, the fleet and skilled G.T. Wright, played for Ajax as well.

Mr. Krause's keen grasp of futbol was a godsend. He was the cosmopolitan force behind our canny team name, for example. This was the heyday of Dutch soccer: the Amsterdam super club Ajax, its bitter rival Feyenoord of Rotterdam, of Cruyff and Michels, of Total Football and Clockwork Orange, of European Cups and near misses at the World Cup itself. Much of this homage was lost on us kids, at the time, perhaps because our uniforms did not in any way recall the famous Ajax kit: white jerseys with a thick, red, vertical bar down the middle of the shirt. Instead we wore still-pretty-damned-cool jerseys of vertical green-and-white stripes — with not-so-cool baseball-style stirrup socks of green-and-white horizontal bands. This unfortunate hosiery had probably been salvaged from some Little League storage locker. Mr. Krause dropped the ball there. I've looked into it: Ajax never wore anything like our green striped uniforms — even as some sort of obscure alternate kit. I don't know what he was thinking.

But we never complained about such sartorial matters to Mr. Krause, who proved a genial dude, a welcome window on the wider soccer world, and a fine coach. He was exactly the foreign influence young American players needed — more than we perhaps knew at the time. In naming us for a Dutch team, he opened our eyes to the internationalism of the game we were just beginning to discover. Dirk would often goof around in goal; throwing his body this way and that to make some save, he would simultaneously yell "Sepp!" — a shout-out to Sepp Maier, West Germany's World Cup-winning goalkeeper in 1974. On later teams, we'd follow Dirk's lead but instead yell "Shep!" — referring to Herr Messing, the flamboyant American keeper on the Minutemen and later, more famously, on Pelé's Cosmos.

Most on-field participants in America's Youth Soccer Revolution did not progress from house to club soccer. Even fewer went on to play in high school or college. Today, however, nearly all of them — house or club players, male or female — can nevertheless distinguish an English Premier League match from the MLS variety, Chelsea from Schalke, a dangerous tackle from a cynical act of simulation. Likewise, while most Americans never played baseball or softball beyond Little League or Legion, they carry their enthusiasm for and understanding of the game into adulthood. Such grassroots ultimately produce lifelong fans. This is how it works.

IT'S IMPOSSIBLE FOR ANY PIECE OF WRITING to depict a particular time and place down to the last detail. However, because the sport of soccer was played on these shores for a full century before the 1970s, to no foundational effect, surely there was *something* pivotal about Nixon's America that triggered and fostered the game's unlikely growth.

Journalist Tom Wolfe did his best to flesh out this period — and slap a sticky label on it — with his 1976 *New York* magazine essay, "The 'Me' Decade and the Third Great Awakening." Wolfe had already demonstrated this penchant for sweeping, if sometimes facile and over-generalized encapsulations of entire eras. He started with *The Electric Kool-Aid Acid Test*, an attempt to sum up the 1960s. Later, with *The Bonfire of the Vanities*, he took on the Eighties. "The 'Me' Decade" has enjoyed more lasting impact than these full-length books, perhaps because it was a magazine piece — brevity being the soul of wit and wisdom — and perhaps because the transitional, unmoored, atomized nature of the 1970s is somehow more conducive to attempts at grand retrospection.

"Anyone old enough to have lived through the 1970s knew them as a long and often embarrassing anticlimax — a shapeless, burned-out interregnum between the high dramas of the Sixties and the bright, hard edges of the Reagan era," wrote *The New Yorker*'s George Packer in 2014. "Unlike the decades that preceded and followed, the Seventies seemed to have no plot: a mishmash of musical styles and fads, a blur of failed presidents, a series of international fiascoes, a mood of cynicism and farce."

This was adult America, of course — Ruben Mendoza's America, my parents' America. And it surely was a mishmash. The same day President Ford pardoned Nixon for his Watergate transgressions (Sept. 8, 1974), Evel Knievel attempted, and failed, to jump the Snake River Canyon. Such cynicism and farce were symptoms of a broader cultural anxiety. It stemmed from Baby Boomers in open conflict with their elders, who were old and wise enough to suspect the wheels were coming off.

The pervasive nature of Seventies-style economic, cultural and geopolitical anxiety has been lost over time, even to those who were there. But hindsight brings focus. Today, we better recognize the larger issues then coming to a head. It was the Arab oil embargo (1973-74) that first introduced to Americans the idea of "energy insecurity." There's a reason we still affix "gate" to anything that rises toward the level of scandal. After 30 years of steady expansion, the U.S. economy and its bedrock job security had begun to unravel, alongside the union movement — some people make a connection there. The Cold War raged unabated. *Roe v. Wade*, the 1973 Supreme Court decision that gave women the right to an abortion and buoyed a growing feminist movement, concluded the decade as the ultimate political wedge — something an emerging conservative crusade would deploy, as a cudgel, to divide the nation.

These long-term ideological confrontations, these new but still tectonic domestic shifts, both economic and cultural, resulted in a destabilization that hinted — for the first time since the Civil War, perhaps — that the United States might not prevail in all her struggles. The deteriorating situation in Vietnam only underlined the fragility of our standing as a hegemon.

With this multi-pronged anxiety spilling over into paranoia, tens of millions deployed popular culture as an escape hatch or decompression chamber. In prime time, a first-run episode of *Phyllis* drew more eyeballs than a World Series game does today. Alas, the monoculture also raised up cultural refuse such as *Donnie & Marie,* an insipid variety show that dominated Friday night ratings. Meanwhile, sentimental goo on the order of *Little House on the Prairie* passed for prestige drama.

In theaters, the mass culture served up a relentless series of disaster films: *The Poseidon Adventure, Towering Inferno*, the *Airport* series, *Earthquake* (in Sensurround!), *The Swarm* and *The China Syndrome.* The last feature should perhaps be listed separately. It was a serious, well-wrought, topical film — whereas the others were mainly schlock that invited needless anxiety about taking a cruise, closing the door on an elevator, or boarding a 747. Released 12 days before the Three Mile Island nuclear power plant accident, *The China Syndrome* was pretty classy cinema and damned prescient. Yet it was clearly a *disaster* film — one that leveraged the nation's fears and delivered an even more bracing brand of existential dread.

There *was* a momentum to the 1970s. It was driven not by economic or electoral factors, but rather by a cultural anxiety that stemmed from a lack of concerted, communal direction. This was Wolfe's thesis: The Sixties were intense and chaotic, but they featured large, identifiable forces pushing the country in discernable directions, however offensive they may have been to the young or the old, the right or the left, the black or the white. The Seventies featured little such directional certainty. According to Wolfe, this later brand of upheaval was a reckoning, whereby an "atomized individualism" was slowly taking over from two competing and ultimately doomed theories of community — one that idealized the 1950s and another that idealized the 1960s.

Apprehensive cultures romanticize the past. *The Waltons* and *Little House* both idealized bygone eras, but most TV nostalgia from the 1970s fixated on Eisenhower's America, the 1950s. *American Graffiti* (1973) stands out, but this George Lucas film spawned a whole raft of derivative, television imitations: *Happy Days, Laverne & Shirley, Joanie Loves Chachi.* Lucas himself was an über-Boomer, born in 1944, a cultural product of the Sixties. Yet he was no bomb-throwing radical. He was a sentimentalist — and the creative force behind *Star Wars*, another iconic piece of Seventies cinema that riffed on a raft of throwback themes (westerns, Joseph Campbell-type heroic archetypes) and launched myriad sequels, all of them high-gloss metaphors for how American life *ought* to be conducted, according to long-standing traditions.

When I got home from school in 1975, UHF channels brimmed with yet more outdated, syndicated paeans to early New Frontier-era conformity: *Leave It to Beaver, The Adventures of Ozzie & Harriet, Father Knows Best, Gunsmoke* and *Bonanza*. This pervasive, clearly obsolete content represented a stubborn refusal by certain cultural minders — mainly TV executives much older than Lucas and his peers — to truly synthesize and reckon with what had happened in the meantime, during the 1960s.

Vestiges of Sixties-style communitarianism remained potent and present in Seventies culture, but they were continually in conflict with Fifties-style conformity and attempts at order-keeping. As one of this country's preeminent chroniclers of disorder, author Joan Didion detected the brewing of all this cultural chaos before anyone else. In the title essay of her 1968 book *Slouching Towards Bethlehem*, she observed that America's late-Sixties youth movements, which had purported to be about community and coming together, were instead symptoms of a shared society in the process of unraveling, mainly on account of a breakdown in public communication and myth-sharing between factions. "It was the first time I had dealt directly and flatly with the evidence of atomization," she would later explain.

Atomization is a key concept in her work from the late 1960s and Seventies. Another is what she called sentimentality — what we here refer to as nostalgia. In either case, we're talking about the shared, glorified belief in cultural fairy tales with preordained shape and emotional logic. However, atomization and sentimentality are incompatible. They aggravate each other. We well recognize today what can happen when national narratives are no longer broadly shared, when communication breaks down and bubbles develop. Didion was interested in how that happens. So was Wolfe. And so am I.

As kids, Generation Zero reveled in the freedoms created by the atomization Wolfe and Didion identified. Economic recession and the feminist movement led to a marked increase in two-income homes during the 1970s. The middle class was getting a taste of what the working class had known for some time: It took two salaries to get by in America. As a result, we who fought and won the Youth Soccer Revolution did so as the first suburban cohort of so-called "latchkey kids." So many moms had gone back to work by mid-decade that there was little stigma attached. Not so far as we could tell. We reveled in the run of our houses, the autonomy of our afternoons.

Precisely such liberties from authority also attracted some of us to soccer itself — the one game where parents and coaches weren't continually ordering kids around, calling plays and formations on their behalf, micromanaging and otherwise intruding on the run of play.

Yet we did sense the broader chaos animating our American lives. We witnessed all the hijackings and hostage-takings on TV. (More than 150 U.S. airline flights were hijacked between 1970 and 1974, when Congress effectively revised the Federal Aviation Act to require the screening of carry-on baggage.) We saw and felt the resulting anxieties in our own homes, as our parents watched Baby Boomers leave behind their Sixties-style communitarianism and barrel ahead to uncertain places of cultural, political and economic power, without any appearance of a plan. This ascent of the Boomer — not necessarily the Self — played out as the most meaningful cultural phenomenon of the decade, and perhaps of America's entire post-WWII period.

Historians and demographers William Strauss and Neil Howe cover this cultural ground with enormous insight in their 1991 book, *Generations: The History of America's Future, 1584-2069.* Their brand of generational theory tracks the country's history in a completely original way: by comprehensively dissecting and rigorously classifying 20 distinct American generations, one following another, each lasting some two decades. All 20 generations fit neatly into four archetypes — Civic (Hero), Adaptive (Artist), Idealist (Prophet), and Reactive (Nomad) — that repeat, in that specific order, throughout the history of this nation.

It turns out the Baby Boom generation, a sterling example of the Idealist archetype, wasn't some one-off. Idealist cohorts, Strauss and Howe argue, are *always* the privileged offspring of hypersuccessful Civic or Hero cohorts, of which the WWII or "Greatest Generation" is an archetypical example. The Transcendental strain of Idealist — born between 1792 and 1821 and typified by Henry David Thoreau, Ralph Waldo Emerson and their peers of the pre-Civil War era — was the spawn of another Civic/Hero cohort, the founding and framing cohort the authors dub the Republican Generation.

Over the long arc of U.S. history, Strauss and Howe explain, these four generational archetypes take shape and fit together with alarming consistency, according to predictable patterns, essentially in reaction/relation to one another. For example, throughout U.S. history, Idealists have routinely co-opted cultural and political power from the Adaptive generation that is invariably sandwiched between those Idealists and their Civic parents. During the 1970s, this eclipsed Adaptive cohort proved to be the parents of Generation Zero. Smaller in number than the generations that came before (Greatest) and afterward (Boom), they comprise what Strauss and Howe (and many others) call the *Silent Generation*.

Strauss and Howe refer to Generation Zero (b. 1961-1981) as *The 13th Generation*. Other demographers refer to our cohort as *Generation X*. Regardless of the label, we exhibit the classic traits of the Reactive/Nomad archetype. Our generational destiny means we invariably follow and live in the shadow of Idealists. We are shaped, in fact, by virtue of our reactions to our next elders, these utopian Boomers. Whereas my parents and their generational peers were largely denied their turn at cultural stewardship — by these same hyperpopulous and rapaciously romantic Boomers — my own generation, as predicted by Strauss and Howe, has been similarly dominated by those same navel-gazing Idealists.

Here's the connective, narrative point: This awkward generational situation came to a head — like a massive highway pileup — during the 1970s, when Boomers fully ascended into the workplace and commandeered control of the culture, en masse. They ended the draft. They eagerly staffed the nation's bureaucracy, its media establishment and its public schools. This last assertion is buttressed by the cold, hard fact that my peers sang "Moonshadow" at the behest of 20-something choral directors each academic year from 1973 through 1977.

From our first moments of consciousness, Generation Zero has listened to Boomers' music and been subjected to their political and cultural whims. We would watch with not insignificant horror during the 1980s, as they sold out many of the *ideals* they had so loudly exalted, starting in the Sixties. That was an eye-opener — a sign of hypocrisies to come. Even when they're all gone, we will damn the Boom posthumously for having exhausted our share of the Social Security Trust Fund, for having enabled the Tea Party and Donald Trump, for having willfully remade this country in their Self-obsessed image.

As prickly and nettlesome as Boomers have proved to be over time, it was our Silent Generation parents who felt this cultural ambivalence first and perhaps most acutely, beginning in the 1960s (see the stellar television drama *Mad Men* for a lush, fictionalized but spot-on case study), but especially during the 1970s. Our parents were aggrieved twice over: first by being pushed aside, then again by watching this unsettling cultural transformation wash over their young children, who absorbed the conflicted nuances of this messy, anxious era by osmosis.

Today, students of American soccer history can muster no coherent understanding of Generation Zero, or the pivotal 1970s, without recognizing the power and influence of our next elders in the culture at that time — not *just* Boomers, but our mothers and fathers as well. Already middle-aged during the age of Nixon, these were the Silent Generation Americans who parented us, coached us, and tried to help us make sense of what this country was becoming during the Seventies. While trying to make sense of it themselves.

———•————

It's perfectly reasonable to ask why these cultural dynamics matter to the making of soccer in the United States. Here's why: We must recognize that the modern presentation of the game to Americans — primarily via formation of the North American Soccer League in 1967 — was aimed not at Generation Zero, or the Silent Generation, but at the Baby Boom. This glut of humanity was expected to grow into the largest pool of high-class consumers the world economy had yet seen. Everyone saw it coming. Any fool impresario pimping any organized sport would have attempted the identical target marketing.

And yet this plan backfired. Boomers would prove surprisingly indifferent to the best efforts of such influencers. Backers of NASL had expected such a self-styled "counterculture" to welcome a new, interloping sport. Instead, young adults in the 1970s were contented to support other, more conventional sports with the sheer volume of their viewing habits and buying power. Had our next elders been playing youth soccer as 10-year-olds, as we in Generation Zero had, things might have played out differently. But youth leagues and the critical mass of soccer culture did not yet exist outside enclaves like San Francisco or St. Louis back in 1965, or 1955. Timing is everything. Only a smattering of Baby Boomers played the game as kids.

This Boomer ambivalence toward U.S. soccer had major consequences. Developmental matters were left to Gen Zero, to those of us who came of age in the Boom's considerable undertow. We *reacted* to the opportunity then before us. Against considerable odds, we founded a first-world soccer nation from the scraps our next elders left hanging off the bone. Once the fate of American soccer had been dropped in our laps, it would take 20 years, roughly a generation, to produce from this void a critical mass of world-class footballers — and a critical mass of fans to support them. But this transformation did, in fact, come to pass.

Behold the demographic irony: In their 1997 book *The Fourth Turning*, Strauss and Howe confess that, "Compared to any other generation born in this century, [Generation Zero] is less cohesive, its experiences wider and its culture more splintery." Agreed, and I would attribute a great deal of this atomization to the splintery nature of the 1970s, in which we'd been reared.

And yet, if the Seventies had been more effectively tied to American traditions and uniformly held ideals of community, soccer might *never* have taken such firm hold with so many of us across the country. Boys my age might never have abandoned American football and baseball for something so foreign, so nontraditional.

Let us agree that cultural memory detailed so broadly and ambitiously can sometimes produce unreliable, retrospective understandings. In order to make the past more understandable or palatable, we *sapiens* fill things in after the fact, often without firsthand recollection, the way a child might link a specific time and place to a family photo — even if he or she has no primary recollection of the Polaroid being taken. However, in their fudging of scope and context, such broad-brushed snapshots, such "mediated" memories, are not entirely false, just as a child's memory is not false. For 10- and 11-year-olds, cultural absorption often occurs impressionistically, in dribs and drabs, accented by the odd smear perhaps, over the course of succeeding years.

For those of us who were 10, 11 or 12 in 1975, this is how we captured and today hold the 1970s in our minds: by aggregating and stitching together stories and memories. In these pages, we aim to fashion from these disparate but contemporaneous perspectives a coherent mosaic, a story of beauty and triumph, a story of culture but also of players, coaches and fans, those protagonists who make up Generation Zero, who dared to journey from fledgling youth leagues to the capitals of Europe, from mere hotbeds to the World Cup, the game's ultimate stage. After a century of false starts, these journeys transformed this country into a first-world soccer nation. Today, they represent the collective story and lost legacy of Generation Zero.

Future USMNT captain Mike Windischmann (bottom left) greets Franz Beckenbauer in the terminal at JFK International Airport, upon the German star's arrival in New York, spring 1977. *(Image courtesy of Mike Windischmann)*

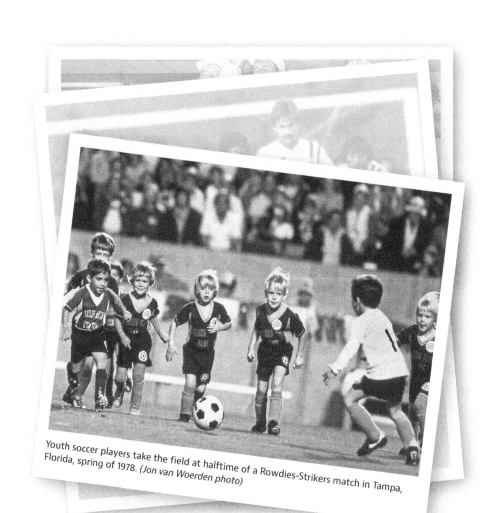

Youth soccer players take the field at halftime of a Rowdies-Strikers match in Tampa, Florida, spring of 1978. *(Jon van Woerden photo)*

2. PUSHBACK

When American soccer went suburban, "hotbed" went along for the ride. In a literal sense, the term has always meant "a bed of earth heated by fermenting manure, for raising or forcing plants." When deployed in the soccer context, "hotbed" proved equally apt when describing the game's regional, urban popularity prior to the 1970s, and its suburban incarnation thereafter. Unfortunately, the word also came pre-freighted with a dumpster-load of subtler, more unflattering baggage. Secondary definitions include "an environment promoting the growth of something, *esp. something unwelcome.*" (The italics are mine; definitions from Merriam Webster.) Neighborhoods or cities or entire regions are routinely described today as "hotbeds" of vaguely foreign or sinister attributes: unrest, political agitation, even terrorism. In the parochial hands of sports media and other self-appointed cultural guardians during the Seventies, this particular expression would prove wantonly double-edged. While the Youth Soccer Revolution was a demonstrable phenomenon, the label simultaneously served as a sort of backhanded shorthand for the game's suspect interloper status on these shores. After all, throughout the 1950s and Sixties, American soccer hotbeds had in fact been almost exclusively urban and ethnic in nature.

The mainstreaming of soccer across the nation's Rockwellian suburbs unnerved old school media in particular. Then Pelé showed up, and the North American Soccer League started making actual headlines. Come

1976, the once-struggling league even signed a network television contract with ABC. All this growth and attention further augmented prevailing negative views of and anxieties about the game. Rather than evaporating over time, the country's thinly veiled xenophobia with regard to futbol — and immigrants, and city folk generally — lingered, festered, then continually bubbled up in print, in schools, on playgrounds. Anywhere the sport bumped up against the status quo.

That June '75 match at Nickerson Field remains a vivid case in point. The match was not, to be clear, Pelé's Boston debut. He had toured the U.S. with his former club side, Santos FC, seven years prior. (His Brazilian squad easily dismantled the semipro Boston Beacons, 7-1, at Fenway Park on July 9, 1968; the Red Sox were off on the All-Star break.) Santos would return to Greater Boston two years later and meet Italian club AC Milan in another exhibition, at Everett Stadium, on June 17, 1970 — but Pelé was not there. He was competing for his country that summer in Mexico, at the World Cup.

I share these minutiae to illustrate two matters of interest: First, there was, at this time, clearly an emerging appetite/market for soccer outside NASL and suburban youth leagues. It was precisely this sort of broader interest that made the sporting establishment, working press included, resentful and dismissive by turn. Second, and more to the point, when *The Boston Globe* reported on the 1970 Santos-AC Milan match in Everett, the four-paragraph story indicated an attendance of 4,500. Former *Globe* staffer Frank Dell'Apa believes this figure to be wildly inaccurate — and not by accident. Or so he reported via his eponymous blog in 2019:

[T]here was more to the crowd, as well, according to Frank Mirisola, former supervisor of referees for Boston Public Schools, who acted as a linesman (assistant referee) in the game.

"There were 18,000 at the game," Mirisola said in a recent interview. "Everett Stadium was a big horseshoe, with bleacher seats, and it held 20,000 at the time. There was a long line at the ticket booth."

What about the discrepancy in crowd numbers in news reports?

"That happened a lot, because they didn't want soccer to make it,"
Mirisola said. "When we played Liverpool (in 1964) they said the crowd
was 10,000. But it was 15,000 – I saw the ticket receipts."

Further disclosure on that 1975 Minutemen-Cosmos match: While the
game did end 2-1, Pelé did not score — not officially. After the Brazilian
potted his goal and fans rushed the field, play would not resume for fully
15 minutes. When it did, the referee called a foul and waved off Pelé's goal.
I was there that night, but somehow did not recall this quite salient fact.
Until consulting the *Globe* archives, neither did I remember that New York's
Mark Liveric would tie the match anyway, before Wolfgang Suhnholz won
it for Boston in overtime. In the end, *none* of these results proved official,
as Cosmos general manager Clive Toye successfully appealed the result,
citing the home team's obvious security failures. The match was replayed,
back at Nickerson, in August 1975. Both Pelé and Eusébio watched from
the stands — a 5-0 Minutemen blowout, before a crowd of just 4,445, or so
the *Globe* reported.

Forty years on, it's instructive to read these archival press clippings.
They are full of revealing details, anachronistic observations and sub-
tle digs. When the *Globe* reported on that original June 1975 match,
for instance, the paper concentrated not on the spectacle, the overflow
crowd it drew, or the condition of world futbol's most celebrated citizen.
Instead, the staff writer fretted openly about how the event had "turned
Nickerson Field into a shoving, marginally controlled maelstrom, and ru-
ined what could have been a wondrous piece of nostalgia." A colleague
wrote, "What resulted last night was a chaotic and nearly tragic nightmare that never would have happened anywhere the game of soccer is
taken seriously." That's some peculiar and petty reporting. Journalists
in the 1950s wrote similarly about Elvis Presley and the prurient movement of his hips. Come the Nineties, mainstream media similarly derided
hip-hop culture for its *dangerous* low-riding jeans.

As a rule, sportswriters are more often taken to task for their cheer-
leading. From 1974-78, Boston was home to a brand-new, ultimately
ill-fated World TeamTennis franchise, the Lobsters. Go rifle through the

Globe stacks for those game stories. They were downright celebratory — and probably *inflated* attendance! Because tennis was familiar and "American" enough to worry no one.

Professional soccer in the 1970s remained but a minor feature in America's exceedingly crowded sporting landscape. The league had formed in 1967, nearly went under in 1969, rebounded thereafter, yet remained some distance below the mainstream sporting radar — even after Pelé arrived. By 1984, the entire enterprise had disappeared. But these realities were largely lost on contemporary mainstream media. Because soccer was perceived as something "other," coverage routinely attacked, held down and/or minimized it. Not all, but most sports writers felt it was their obdurate patriotic duty to protect the country's economic and cultural status quo. American soccer would battle this closed-shop media mentality for many decades to come, and this prejudice was not the territory of sports writers alone. Their cause was aided and abetted by gym teachers, Little League coaches, high school athletic directors and police officers alike.

Two days after the fact, Pelé's mauling at Nickerson Field was front-page news in his hometown paper, *The New York Times*: "Cosmos Demand More Security for Pele," the headline blared. According to the story: "The Minutemen had assured the Cosmos they would have at least 200 policemen at the game. Toye said he had counted only 14 Boston policemen and eight Boston University guards at Nickerson Field, the B.U. stadium. Rafael de la Sierra, a vice president for Warner Communications, which owns the Cosmos, said he went to the nearest police station at halftime to ask for help. 'They told me soccer attracts only 2,000,' he said."

———•———

In the broader scheme of the 1970s, soccer's potential popularity, acceptance and success encountered de facto obstructions more daunting than conservative, middle-aged sports writers in loud blazers: namely, the credible bandwidth issues of American sports fans themselves. For while soccer had made considerable inroads on the grassroots level by 1975, mainstream American sports were all growing in reach, revenue and cultural impact — on a scale that frankly dwarfed anything NASL could hope to muster.

The National Football League had just doubled its strength and reach by virtue of its 1969 merger with its former competitor, the American Football League. In the decade to follow, it would assert the extraordinary cultural dominance we recognize today. Pro football's growth and appeal were such that yet another competitor emerged just five years post-merger: the World Football League, which launched in 1974, only to fold a year later. The WFL and NASL were, in fact, subject to very similar media and cultural skepticism, for the same hidebound reasons.

During the Me Decade, Major League Baseball could still lay claim to the mantle of America's "national pastime." The National Basketball Association dealt with similar startup competition throughout the first half of the Seventies, only to follow the NFL's acquisitive precedent: The NBA absorbed the American Basketball Association in 1976 — more evidence that pro hoops and its collegiate incarnation were surging in popularity and scope. In 1967, the National Hockey League first expanded beyond its Original Six into a host of American cities. By 1979, 15 new teams had joined the NHL.

Even boxing, horse racing, tennis and golf — sports that periodically claimed "major" status through the first half of the 20th century — still commanded episodic but widespread attention of media and fans. These individual sports were further buoyed by a steady stream of charismatic, thoroughly American personalities: Muhammad Ali, a healthy chunk of the entire heavyweight boxing division, Secretariat, Jack Nicklaus, Johnny Miller, Jimmy Connors, John McEnroe and Chris Evert. Two sporting events that made the biggest impressions on me during this period were the 1972 and '76 Summer Olympic Games.

Despite these headwinds, youth soccer went from strength to strength during the Seventies. Professional soccer put a dent in this bloated sporting landscape, but NASL and American pro soccer didn't manage to break through. That hurdle would not be cleared until the mid-1990s, when all those youth soccer players raised in the 1970s had grown up to populate rosters and fill stadiums in support of Major League Soccer.

————•+•————

I subscribe to no fewer than five dedicated soccer podcasts. Hundreds are available today in America's mature footballing culture, but I have a particular soft spot for the always jaunty, periodically compelling *Men in Blazers*. Hosts Michael Davies and Roger Bennett have carved for themselves a clever niche. Both are native Britons and yet, because they have lived here since the 1980s, each is well equipped to observe and assess the U.S. game's fascinating evolution — never more wryly than when they refer to soccer as "America's Sport of the Future, since 1972!" It's a good line, equal parts bouquet and brickbat. Soccer has indeed been this country's pastime-in-waiting for decades — always with the sense that despite its verifiably laudable qualities, here was a game that, in the States, amid all this sporting competition, needed selling.

From a media perspective and from a wider cultural perspective, soccer had clearly failed to penetrate our robust and stubbornly parochial *sports culture* over the first three-quarters of the 20th century. Authors Andrei Markovits and Steven Hellerman detail the context of this failure — and the fascinating nature of U.S. sporting insularity — in their 2001 book *Offside: Soccer and American Exceptionalism* (Princeton Press):

It's important to emphasize that what we mean by "sports culture" is what people breathe, read, discuss, analyze, compare, and historicize; what they discuss at the office watercooler; and what comprises a significant quantity of barroom (or pub) talk; in short, what people follow as opposed to what people do. In other words, while activity (doing) and culture (following) overlap to a certain crucial degree ... they are separate entities in which we view the "following" as more essential for our conceptualization of a society's sports culture. To be more precise, we are more interested in what we call "hegemonic sports culture," meaning the sports culture that dominates a country's emotional attachments rather than its calisthenic activities.

Markovits and Hellerman assert that each of America's hegemonic sports — what they call the Big 3.5: baseball, football, basketball and hockey — all developed their footholds in U.S. sports culture during the country's industrialization at the turn of the 19th century. The historical timing here is important because industrialization led to what they call "bourgeoisification," which made this country quite different from those in the Old World.

In short, bourgeois America created a new liberal identity, priding itself on being of European origin, yet also on transcending — and bettering — this origin's old aristocratic framework by a new republican virtue in a new world. Or, to paraphrase Alexis de Tocqueville . . . America had the luxury of being born bourgeois without having to become so.

Here's the takeaway: As a sporting pursuit of such obvious and contemporaneous European strain, soccer would always be at a disadvantage when seeking hegemonic status in the U.S. This is the battle Major League Soccer, for all its successes, still fights today.

Baseball and what became formalized in the late 19th century as American football had the distinct advantage of being perceived as homegrown "American" games — despite their clear connections to cricket/ rounders and British rugby/soccer, respectively. Basketball, created in 1888, was verifiably homegrown, as ice hockey had been in neighboring and not-all-that-foreign Canada. Once these hegemons are established, they are very difficult to unseat, assert Markovits and Hellerman, who further argue that once a critical mass of sporting hegemons is achieved, there isn't necessarily room for any more:

The story is pretty much the same in all advanced industrial societies. Once a nation's "sports space" is filled, there are very few changes in this space. . . Indeed, all established sports prolifically utilize a constant appeal to history to discredit their potential rivals.

In a nutshell, soccer had a window of daylight in the 1870s to establish itself in the American sporting space. For reasons detailed above (and others we'll relate in Chapter 5), it missed that chance. Once baseball,

American football, then basketball and hockey managed to occupy that space, unseating one of them was always going to be tough sledding — especially for soccer, an athletic pursuit so closely identified with European sports culture, not red-blooded U.S. sporting culture.

After nearly 100 years of anemic, futile efforts to advance its cultural standing, soccer finally managed to break through during the 1970s — *calisthenically*, in terms of participation. So it is written: "Train up a child in the way he should go: and when he is old, he will not depart from it" (Proverbs 22:6). So it *was* legislated: Title IX, the 1972 federal statute mandating equal sporting and educational opportunities for women, would result in thousands of girls' soccer programs at the high school and college levels across America. All of these soccer-friendly ingredients came together early in the decade, just as the Boom came of age, as adults. They were too old to effectively "train up," these Boomers. For kids in Generation Zero, however, the timing proved impeccable.

Incidentally, 1972 was about the time that the English disowned the word "soccer." They did so in specific response to all this footballing activity then taking place across the Atlantic, in their formerly soccer-indifferent colonies. There was no act of Parliament, but British linguistic prejudice in this regard has proved uniform and lasting. Even today, otherwise soccer-supporting Brits, like Bennett and Davies, continue to deride this specific locution. They should know better. The word is thoroughly English and quite venerable.

Our cousins first coined *soccer* in the mid- to late-19th century to distinguish between so-called association football and rugby-style football. The English Football Association, known as The FA, had been formalized and its rules first written down in 1863. The Rugby Football Union followed suit in 1871. So yes, "soccer" is shorthand for *association* — British shorthand. The sport's international governing body, *Federation Internationale de Football Association*, formed in 1904. We know this organization best by its acronym, FIFA. The lesser-known English translation of its name — the International Federation of Association Football

— speaks volumes as to the broad, longstanding acceptance of this specific phraseology.

Among U.K. types, the term "soccer" remained perfectly respectable, uncontroversial and interchangeable with "football" for more than a century — until the mid-1970s, when the upstart NASL started poaching British stars in earnest. Two Manchester boys arrived first: George Best from United and Rodney Marsh from City. Two years later, NASL had signed Alan Ball, Geoff Hurst, Bobby Moore and Gordon Banks — all of them members of the fabled '66 World Cup champions. That was galling, surely, as were the AstroTurf, the cheerleaders and NASL's garish, Technicolor uniforms. It seemed to many Britons that America was threatening to colonize *their* game in reverse. Some nations might have been flattered. The English especially were not amused. They have yet to get over it.

———•———

Young men and women today are strongly encouraged to specialize in a single sporting discipline. This practice was nearly unheard of during the Seventies, when the three-sport athletic ideal — for most boys, typically football, basketball and baseball — still held cultural primacy. In that sense, back then soccer didn't threaten other sports the way that it might today, when playing soccer 10 months out of 12 for a premier club might mean dumping rival activities altogether.

Even so, throughout the 1970s and well into the 1980s, soccer was perceived as a further disruptor of the domestic status quo because it infringed upon this triangulated dominion. Its obvious growth prompted significant, open dissent from the organizers of and participants in more established youth sports — especially American football — as soccer began to pull kids and resources its way. This pushback, this "appeal to history," Markovits and Hellerman also call "contestation." It's a universal phenomenon, they make clear, one not particular to the U.S. However, during the Seventies, in America, even 10-year-old kids couldn't miss it. Growing up in Wellesley, I participated in organized and pickup versions of basketball, baseball, hockey, football, golf, volleyball, and track and field. No one in the culture at large gave two shits about these choices. But a whole host of guys, big and small — and they were all guys — sure seemed mighty put off that I played soccer.

The socioeconomic context of the game's growth during this period is important: Suburbs tend to be more conservative and affluent than urban areas full of first- and second-generation Americans. There's more disposable household income in the suburbs, too, and more competition for that money when it comes to recreational choices. There are only so many kids in any one town. The more boys opt for soccer, the fewer opt for football in the autumn or baseball come the spring. Not surprisingly, this zero-sum reality didn't sit well with the adults who organized and coached those "traditional" sports. In the Seventies, these folks found themselves competing not merely for warm bodies, but also for access to local playing fields and funding, be it public or participant-raised.

Remember one of Markovits and Hellerman's theses: *All established sports prolifically utilize a constant appeal to history to discredit their potential rivals.* In the 1970s, it sounded like this: "Why don't you play an American sport?"

I recognize this suggestion sounds a bit paranoid, or possibly grandiose, but the verbal battle for hearts and minds was real and acute. The loudest grumbles came from American football quarters. This much was made very clear to my teammates and me: Soccer wasn't just un-American. It was the very embodiment of a "pussy sport." We heard this slander, directly and more obliquely, over and over again. It came mainly from football players but also from their coaches, many of whom were our gym teachers, too.

The evidence for this deliberately provocative, faux macho, verifiably misogynistic label? Well, wasn't it obvious? Here was a sport played in shorts and *knee socks*. Here was a game with only a modicum of physical contact — or so they thought. Here was a sport played by smaller guys who couldn't succeed at American football. Here was a sport played by girls as well! Here was a sport that embraced the 0-0 draw — all draws!!

It all sounds a bit ridiculous today, especially in light of soccer's continued mainstreaming — not to mention the dire concussion issues American football is confronting. What's more, many of these assertions were issued by children wearing jean shorts. In retrospect, it's hard to take them seriously. Nevertheless, this cultural resentment of soccer and its less-than-manly, less-than-American qualities — this threat to America's precious bodily fluids, as Stanley Kubrick's mad general, Jack D. Ripper, might have put it — was unmistakable.

"I used to get teased *all* the time about playing soccer," recalls Marcelo Balboa, a member of the U.S. Men's National Team at *Italia* '90, who grew up in Southern California, where soccer participation wasn't even that new and the ethnic ethos was strong. "'Why don't you play an American sport?' That's what they said! Man, how do you answer that, as a kid? This was still a country that barely knew what soccer was."

Balboa could be talking about almost every gym teacher at my junior high school: male, conservative, schooled only in the arts of football, basketball and baseball, a bit doughy and often corseted into those stretchy coaching shorts purveyed at the time by Russell Athletic. I was big for my age. I could run. These guys could not understand why I wasn't playing football and said so, publicly, over and over again. They mostly *appealed to history,* in the way Balboa describes. They didn't use the pejorative vernacular. That was left mainly to my peers.

"They called us pussies and shit like that," Tom Wadlington remembers. "I remember that football players themselves were the most aggressive about that sort of thing. They were threatened, I guess? Maybe they'd heard it from their coaches? You'd get that talk walking from school out to practice. I remember that sort of thing starting early but lasting through high school."

During the 1970s, the choice to play and stay with soccer required, then engendered, a certain level of self-possession and iconoclasm. Luckily, that mishmash of a decade was also a period as rebellious and countercultural as the 1960s. The "other" was derided and accommodated by turn. Flower children weren't meeting armed troops with posies, but millions did mass in the streets to challenge the draft, to build a modern environmental movement ("Give a hoot, don't pollute!"), and to support an equal rights amendment. People were grappling for the first time publicly with the idea of legal protections for aboriginal Americans, gay men and women, Hispanics and other increasingly segmented people of color. In the Seventies, something as new and solemn as identity politics could gather popular steam, alongside something as new and frivolous as disco or platform shoes. In 1973, *Mad* magazine, the voice of weird and transgressive American youth, reached its peak circulation of 2.8 million.

The counterculture was very much alive during the Seventies — as were the subsequent forces of reaction. Soccer was but one source of this friction. Lucky for us, the dads coaching our teams were Silent Generation guys who, while largely clueless about futbol, were open to new things in ways men from the Greatest Generation were not. In ways Boomers should have been but were not. It wouldn't be the last time our next elders would disappoint us.

YOUTHFUL SOCCER PIONEERS OF THE MID-SEVENTIES answered reactionary attacks on our manhood, incipient though it was, in myriad ways. There were physical confrontations. There was gym class, and various other sporting arenas where we could demonstrate the actual athleticism of soccer players. What's more, the fact that luminous figures like Pelé, Eusébio and other international stars were flocking to NASL certainly helped legitimize the act of playing this world game. But no figure during the 1970s did more to quell the debate than one of American soccer's truly unsung heroes, Kyle Rote, Jr.

In a different time and place, Rote would have been a great story for his on-field prowess alone. Somewhat forgotten today, Rote was the NASL's first American-born "skill player" of consequence. Most of the league's quota-filling, U.S.-born players were grunts: goalies (like Messing), wingbacks (Brewster), or fit, hardworking, under-skilled midfielders like the Cosmos' young phenom, Ricky Davis. By contrast, Rote — the son of New

York Football Giants star Kyle Rote — was a striker, and a prolific one. In 1973, his rookie season with the Dallas Tornado, he led the NASL in scoring.

While Rote was a legit offensive sensation, it would take a trashy bit of mass-market, sports-entertainment programming to convey his obvious physical gifts, and those of all soccer players, to the wider culture.

Superstars first burst into the American sporting consciousness during the winter of 1973, when ABC collected prominent athletes to compete in a sort of nontraditional, made-for-TV decathlon. Its popularity would trigger an avalanche of even schlockier competitions: *Battle of the Network Stars* (hosted by none other than Howard Cosell), for example, and *Team Superstars*, which pitted World Series champions and Super Bowl champions in competitions like outrigger canoe races, tug of war on the beach, and obstacle courses. It was *Superstars*, however, that unleashed this particular torrent. The idea had been hatched by figure-skating commentator and former Olympian Dick Button, of all people. The show grew into a phenomenon that captured the imagination of adolescent boys from coast to coast. Fittingly, the inaugural competition was claimed by a former Olympian: pole-vaulter Bob Seagren, who would later cross over into acting by playing Billy Crystal's gay lover on the quite-racy-for-its-time sitcom *Soap*.

We soccer players paid particular attention starting in 1974, when Kyle Rote Jr. struck a blow for alleged pussies in knee socks everywhere by winning the first of his three *Superstars* "titles" in four years. Put that in your contestation pipes and smoke it, futbol naysayers.

"Yeah, that was big for me," reports *Soccer America* editor Mike Woitalla (b. 1964). "When I was playing in the Seventies, soccer was still considered a foreign sport. I can't really overstate that, or how happy the *Superstars* thing made me, made all of us — because we were playing when people didn't really know what soccer was. It was not a sport certainly that got a lot of respect. To have him win the *Superstars* was just a huge affirmation.

"I can remember Kyle Rote from the Tornado games I went to, as well. So I looked up to him in the way other kids latched onto Americans in NASL.

But yeah, the *Superstars* thing was huge. Kyle Rote was already famous in Dallas because of his father. He wasn't a great player, but Ron Newman [Rote's British-born Tornado teammate] was brilliant. He figured out that if he hit him a good cross, Rote could score on headers."

It's hard to pin down the actual popularity of anything on television in the pre-cable Seventies, a period featuring just three network channels and a bunch of UHF stations showing reruns of Fifties sitcoms alongside even more archaic content like *Little Rascals, The Three Stooges, Felix the Cat* and *The Bowery Boys.* The paucity of viewing options resulted in massive Nielsen ratings that stemmed from having literally nothing else to watch.

Bearing in mind the suspect nature of the era's television-entertainment universe, perhaps it is less surprising that *Superstars* resonated so hugely with our pre-pubescent demographic. God help us, but my friends and I would have watched it religiously even if Kyle Rote Jr. had not won three out of four. As it happens, however, he *did.* This proved conclusively and for all time what superb all-around athletes soccer players truly are, and how recognizably *American* soccer players could be.

———•·•———

Kyle Rote, magnificent though he was in our eyes, represented an exception to the rule in NASL. From the moment of its inception, international players and coaches dominated league proceedings. And yet, despite these manifold foreign influences, we, the young members of Generation Zero, knew practically nothing of international futbol itself. Few native-born Americans did. Day to day, there was no news to be had regarding any of the major European leagues. None. World Cup qualifying in Europe or South America? Nothing. Not on TV, not in the newspapers, not in the agate — the fine print where sports sections detail the least significant news.

In important ways, Rote solidified our love for the game and our rightful American place in it. But the fact that we gathered this revelation through such a cockeyed media lens as *Superstars* underlines just how primitive and insular the U.S. soccer universe remained during the 1970s.

Such insularity never did American football or basketball any harm, but for soccer there were major consequences. National soccer teams, for example, exist to compete internationally. Yet American attempts to participate in and otherwise qualify for the World Cup, the ultimate international setting, routinely lay in ruins before the public even had the chance to take notice. As a result of this simple lack of familiarity and exposure, the biggest competition in the sport — in all of global sport — was devalued and largely ignored by U.S. soccer culture, American media and the general public.

The 1966 World Cup final had been shown here on two-hour tape delay. It was the first time soccer had *ever* been broadcast in the U.S. as stand-alone programming. More often the game was covered, to the extent it was covered at all, via highlights on sports variety shows like *Wide World of Sports*, which is how the 1970 final — and only the final — was delivered to American households from Mexico City. Not a single match from West Germany was broadcast live on American television. Highlights of the '74 final were eventually shown the following weekend on a program called *CBS Sports Spectacular*.

"I used to watch *Wide World of Sports* just to watch the Pelé goal in the introduction montage," Woitalla admits. "My family is German, and my dad had a shortwave radio with an antenna on the roof. He'd get up in the morning and listen to the *Bundesliga* scores — and we subscribed to *Soccer America*! But it was hard to get news about the games, really hard. My grandfather would send me clippings from German newspapers."

Clive Toye had been a sports writer in his native England before moving across the pond to become general manager of the Baltimore Bays in 1967, NASL's inaugural season. He would later serve as general manager of the Cosmos; many credit him for engineering Pelé's move to the club in 1975. It was Toye — along with former U.S. Men's National Team coach and NASL commissioner Phil Woosnam — who secured American TV rights to the Mexican *Mundial* in 1970. They paid a whopping $1,500 ($11,000 in 2022 dollars) for the privilege.

"We couldn't find anybody to televise a single game," Toye told *The Guardian* in 2015. "We had to put it on closed circuit at Madison Square Garden, a place in Chicago, and a place in Los Angeles — the only places in the United States where you could watch that World Cup live. Now you can't even *say* 'World Cup' without paying $1,500 to somebody, for God's sake."

By 1975, the grassroots and professional soccer landscapes in the United States would appear to have changed considerably. The American game had made its fateful move from city to suburbs, where youth league rosters did spilleth over. NASL, now eight years old, was beginning to look like a goer. "Growing up in Queens," says Mike Windischmann, "I'm like 10 years old, and all of a sudden Pelé is coming to the Cosmos and we're watching him at Downing Stadium — then Beckenbauer shows up!"

Windischmann really did travel to JFK with his mates to meet Beckenbauer's plane. "Two months later I opened up the mailbox and there's an autographed picture that Beckenbauer had sent me," the future USMNT captain recollects. "I still have the envelope and the card . . . When Beckenbauer and Pelé were your heroes, and you're able to go to the games and *see* them in person — plus all these great international players? It drove all the young guys to play soccer."

One by one, these future members of the U.S. national team were drawn into the youth soccer vortex, intrigued not only by what their peers were doing, but by what NASL professionals were doing. "The Cosmos — that was the dream for us," remembers John Harkes, Windischmann's future national team colleague in midfield, who grew up across the river in Kearny, New Jersey. "That had a massive influence on me. Because I thought that one day: 'I want to do this.'"

The entirety of this aspiration, however, was concentrated on the NASL and its stars. There remained negligible domestic interest in the game's marquee event, the World Cup — in large part because the U.S. Men's National Team couldn't manage to qualify for one. Kyle Rote Jr. may have starred in NASL, but over his entire competitive career, he played only five times for his country. Why so few? American attempts to qualify in 1974,

'78, '82 and '86 all failed — and quickly. None of these efforts progressed past the preliminary stages of CONCACAF qualifying.

There *had* been one near miss, however, and it came halfway through this country's 40-year World Cup drought, in 1969, during the run-up to Mexico's first *Mundial*. It was the closest the U.S. would ever come to qualifying before it finally did, five quadrennials later.

———•◆•———

Because they hosted *Mundial* 1970, the Mexicans qualified automatically. With that, the most formidable impediment to U.S. quali- fication — the Mexican national team itself — was removed. Indeed, the Americans breezed through a multitiered qualifying tournament that winnowed CONCACAF's spotty field to just three combatants. Haiti and the United States would play a home-and-home tie in April 1969 for the right to play El Salvador for the Confederation's single qualifying spot. The left back on that U.S. squad? None other than Bob Gansler, the man who would manage his country's long-awaited, history-making qualifi- cation for World Cup 1990 in Italy, two decades later.

"Phil Woosnam was the coach. Gordon Jago, who was still with us and respected highly, was his assistant," Gansler explains. "That was 1968. We were almost exclusively players from the early years of NASL. A handful of us were from my club, Chicago Mustangs, and from all over the coun- try, of course."

First-division soccer had been resuscitated in the U.S. only in 1967, some 44 years after the Great Depression crushed the old American Soccer League in 1933. Fully professional futbol naturally proved a boon to young, aspiring players like Gansler. But its emergence signaled the onset of something else important to our story: pro soccer's outsized influence on and intermingling with the U.S. Men's National Team. That dynamic is best illustrated by the league's peculiar genesis story.

Two separate and competing league entities were born that Summer of Love: the National Professional Soccer League and the United Soccer Association, both vying for the attention of a broader public that from all accounts could not have cared less. FIFA had not yet sanctioned the NPSL, which nevertheless got underway first — a decision that obliged the USA to move up its launch a full 12 months. In order to make possible that premature launch, the USA imported entire sides of foreign players to compete that first summer — the offseason for most European leagues. The entirety of the Washington Whips roster, for example, came courtesy of the Scottish club Aberdeen FC. The L.A. Wolves were imported en masse from the Birmingham, England, club, Wolverhampton Wanderers.

The NPSL — led by president Robert Hermann, the fellow for whom collegiate soccer's Hermann Trophy is named — made more of an effort to deploy North American players. It was the NPSL, in fact, that first hatched the on-field quota policy, requiring two North Americans on the field at all times. The NPSL also had the advantage of a two-year national television contract with CBS. That agreement obliged referees to whistle fouls and delay play — counseling injured players to linger on the ground awhile longer — to allow the insertion of commercials. It mattered little. The ratings were so moribund that CBS backed out after the inaugural season, whereupon the two leagues threw their lots in together, on Dec. 7, 1967. Gansler and his fellow Americans — some native-born, some naturalized citizens — didn't view the merger as infamous. Not at all. The newly combined entity, the North American Soccer League, began the 1968 season with 17 of the 22 teams that had participated in the competing 1967 campaigns. It folded only five redundant teams in cities where the USA and NPSL had overlapped.

Consolidated, renamed and seemingly reenergized, the new NASL was initially viewed as a godsend to the U.S. national team and its hopes to qualify for World Cup 1970, to be held right next door, two summers hence.

"We had Gerry Baker on that national team, who was playing in England someplace at the time. He was Scottish but had been born in America. So we had a little bit of a foreign flavor," Gansler reports. "From NASL we had [Adolph] Bachmeier, Willy Roy, Eddie Murphy — names that only the really old-timers remember probably. We had a good group. We went through the first round of things pretty confidently and competently.

"What happened then? Well . . ."

Gansler doesn't normally mince words, but here his voice trails off and he shakes his head. Haiti claimed both legs of the CONCACAF playoff that spring of 1969. The home team prevailed 2-0 in Port-au-Prince, then 1-0 in San Diego before a crowd of 6,500. No contemporaneous news reports tell us how many in attendance might have been Haitian — not that media-reported attendance figures could be trusted . . . For Gansler and his fellow Yanks, yet another World Cup had proved beyond their capabilities.

Even in the late 1960s, the urgency of World Cup qualification was obvious. It was, in fact, central to the mantra repeated over and over again in NASL and U.S. Soccer Federation circles throughout the Seventies and Eighties: *If we can just qualify the USMNT for a World Cup, the event will be on national TV for two weeks and Americans, finally in the position to mobilize their signature jingoism, will take — or begin to take — soccer into their hearts.*

In 1969, despite the enormous stakes at hand, the minds of U.S. players had been elsewhere during the Haitian tie. There had been pay disputes prior to the first leg: These newly professionalized players wanted to be treated like true internationals, Gansler contends. Equally unsettling had been Woosnam's departure as national team manager. The Welshman had decamped just before the first Haiti encounter to become executive director of the NASL, then teetering on the edge of financial collapse.

"Not that we want to dwell on the history, but people don't remember it," Gansler says, letting out another world-weary sigh. "In 1968, we had 17 teams in NASL. After we went through the first round of qualification, about November, we found out the next year there were going to be just five teams — in the *league* — which meant a lot of us had to rearrange our lives. With that in our backpacks, we went to the next stage, the home-and-home with Haiti: a team we had beaten in friendly situations before, the previous two years in fact. We didn't survive that, so we didn't make it. Obviously, and this is a personal opinion, I think we were good enough to get it done. We had an awfully good group of players. But it wasn't to be, not at that time."

The 1969 Haitian national team was not a bad side. It would prove the lead edge of the country's own golden generation. While El Salvador would earn the sole CONCACAF berth at Mexico '70, Haiti would qualify — at Mexico's direct expense — for the next World Cup, in West Germany.

But Gansler is correct: The playoff defeat proved a massive opportunity lost, a crushing blow for U.S. soccer competitively, organizationally, and commercially, in terms of marketing the game to the broader public. After the failure in San Diego, the national team would not play a single competitive match, not even a friendly — a free-standing international fixture, one not attached to any official tournament or qualifying campaign — for nearly two years.

———•———

The remainder of the 1970s should have markedly improved Team USA, for these were prime NASL years. Under Woosnam, the league would survive its 1969 wobble and furnish American players with professional experience in numbers never before seen in this country. During the 1971 season, thanks to the quota, a record 42 Americans (including 30 native-born players) held spots on NASL rosters.

However, by the next World Cup quadrennial, little had changed. Or not nearly enough. The qualifying campaign for West Germany '74 came to a crashing halt in September 1972, when the U.S. suffered a 3-1 defeat to Mexico following a loss and draw with Canada. Note the timing: The Americans bowed out during the preliminary stage of CONCACAF qualifying. If the 1969 attempt had represented two steps forward, this result walked the Yanks three steps back.

The same deflating footsteps were retraced during qualification for World Cup '78, on which the U.S. Soccer Federation reportedly spent $200,000 ($855,000 in 2022 dollars) — a vast sum compared to previous efforts. In November of 1976, the Americans looked poised to advance to the final CONCACAF stage, but an unlikely draw between Mexico and Canada left the U.S. and its northern neighbor tied behind Mexico. Only the top two sides would go through, and goal difference was not yet used to break ties. So the Americans and Canadians played a single, decisive playoff match on neutral ground in Port-au-Prince, Haiti.

We don't know precisely how many Haitians attended *this* match either, but a capacity crowd of 32,869 did pack the *Stade Sylvio Cator* on Dec. 22, 1976. Haiti had already qualified, so the crowd was eager to scope out the competition to come. They didn't see much of a contest. Canada's Brian Budd scored an early goal when his errant shot deflected off the knee of U.S. midfielder Al Trost. It was a mighty forgettable day for Mr. Trost, who, stricken with food poisoning, was subbed off at halftime. American defender Steve Pecher was red-carded after the break, the Canadians scored twice more, and another World Cup had gone by the boards.

By the end of 1976, American ineptitude in CONCACAF had undermined any gains that six solid years of NASL play — including two Pelé years — might have brought to the overall quality of U.S. soccer at the professional, domestic level. More important, the continuing lack of American involvement in the World Cup finals conspired to keep the tournament and the sport's international profile utterly remote from U.S. fans and would-be soccer enthusiasts alike.

VIDEO EVIDENCE OF THE 1974 WORLD CUP was not made available to me until July 1977. That was the summer I first attended soccer camp, a veritable rite of passage for so many members of Generation Zero, elite players and otherwise. The Puma All-Star Soccer Camp was owned and operated by Hubert Vogelsinger, then a 39-year-old Austrian émigré who'd coached the Minutemen that June night in 1975 when Pelé came calling. Hubie deserves a digression, because few did more to promote the game in the United States during the 1970s than he did.

Among Puma campers, legend had it that Vogelsinger arrived in the U.S. only after the Austrian *Bundesliga* banned him for head-butting a referee. The story seemed plausible to us: Blond and buff, the man was super-intense, bristling with manic energy. Vogelsinger was indeed an Austrian national. But the facts of his stateside arrival were quite different — and far more romantic. While at university during the early 1960s in Vienna, he met, courted and ultimately married an American exchange student, the former Lois Smith. He followed her back to Boston, where he played in the semiprofessional American Soccer League (the second of four separate ASL incarnations). Thereafter he took up a succession of coaching positions: first at the Middlesex School in suburban Concord, then at nearby Brandeis University, and finally at Yale — before making the leap to the professional ranks with the expansion Minutemen in 1974.

For a guy whose only playing credentials were six years with the provincial Austrian club Allentsteig, an outfit he left at 18, that's a pretty meteoric rise. Hubie knew how to market himself. He also sensed the passion for soccer then bubbling up in the U.S. sporting zeitgeist and cannily made for himself a place in it. At Yale, he broadened his North American reputation with a succession of books — *How to Star in Soccer*, 1968; *Winning Soccer Skills and Techniques*, 1970; *The Challenge of Soccer: A Handbook of Skills, Techniques, and Strategy*, 1973. Between the writing, the coaching and his camps, Hubie would prove a hugely influential figure to thousands if not millions in the burgeoning U.S. soccer culture.

The man was not selling snake oil, after all. Soccer camps proliferated during the 1970s because participation boomed while competent coaching remained at a premium. Soccer camp also proved a sanctuary for Generation Zero — an immersive, cosmopolitan place where the emphasis was skill development. It also proved a safe space where the game never required defending, where American national team failures were not dwelled upon, where the coaching staff included not a single Soccer Dad.

Hubie's staff of foreign-born counselors put us through the paces each day, all day. In the evenings we'd gobble down cafeteria provisions before retiring to various lounges to watch films. It was there, sitting on a lightly stuffed, mass-produced dorm couch, that I first beheld an authentic international football match — a full-length reel-to-reel of the '74 World Cup final between West Germany and Holland, the famous encounter where the Dutch kicked off and strung together 16 passes before Cruyff was taken down in the penalty area. Johan Neeskens converted, and the Dutch led 1-0 — before their vaunted opponents even got a touch! Naturally, the

Germans fought back and won the match, 2-1, as German teams are wont to do. Following on the European Championship they'd claimed in 1972, Beckenbauer, Gerd Mueller, Paul Breitner & Co. removed all doubt as to who ruled world futbol during the mid-1970s — in no small part because of who'd been in goal the whole time: "Sepp!"

Back in Wellesley, meanwhile, *someone* had been paying attention. In 1977, the town formalized its club soccer system. My team remained unchanged — the Pilgrims would stay and play together for the better part of 10 straight years — but we became part of a newly unified and rebranded Wellesley United Soccer Club. Accordingly, all the travel teams regardless of age group or gender wore the same uniforms, exact replicas of those worn by the vaunted West Germans: white, long-sleeved jerseys with black piping, black shorts and white socks. In the tie-dyed, wide-collared, flower-power Seventies, we stood out — even if our Teutonic homage wafted over 90 percent of the heads on either sideline.

We looked good, even though our new jerseys were made of a ghastly acrylic fabric meant to mimic the piqué cotton Lacoste deployed on its signature "alligator" tennis shirts, then very much the rage. We made do because Puma and its rival German outfitter, Adidas, hadn't identified America's youth soccer market as worth their time and effort. Not yet. Neither had Umbro nor Admiral, two more brand names then in vogue. Nike remained content to concentrate on niche track and field footwear. Accordingly, for Generation Zero, brand loyalty and awareness were dominated not by shirts and shorts, but cleats. In 1976, the shoe most everyone coveted was Adidas' World Cup model, though I aspired to Puma's King Pelé — "Puma Kings," we called them. I would always be a Puma guy — a nod to what I perceived to be fashion, perhaps to Hubie Vogelsinger, and to the fact that Pumas ran wide. They were always a much better fit for my Flintstone-esque feet. "I was *definitely* an Adidas guy," Marcelo Balboa reveals. "That was *the* shoe when I was coming up. Even when I was just a young pup on the national team, I was thrilled that Adidas was giving us free shoes. You walk into camp, and every damn trip you got a new pair of shoes!"

The vast majority of American kids who latched onto futbol during the 1970s learned the game while playing for Soccer Dads: solid Silent Generation types who were open-minded and giving of their time, but who had never played the game a day in their lives. Had we examined these situations more closely, we might have noticed an obvious disconnect: Our basketball, baseball and football coaches on fields adjacent had *all* played those sports before. Eleven-year-old boys, though, do not examine anything with much rigor. On some level, we recognized that soccer was new. As such, we found it unremarkable and somehow logical that the parents who coached us — these demonstrably geriatric dads, who were clueless about so many things — were ignorant of soccer, too.

That was the slack we cut Vince Harackiewicz, the man we called H ("Aitch"). Despite his "foreign" sounding surname, he'd been born in the U.S. and possessed no firsthand knowledge of this game we played and he "coached." H was a Soccer Dad of the first order: no technical understanding to speak of, but full of enthusiasm for the sport. He eventually assembled and administered a fine club team, took on college-age assistants who *did* know the game, and, over the course of seven to eight years, squired Pilgrims all over the East Coast, Quebec, England and Holland.

Our very first team photo, the one in my parents' scrapbook, illustrates our fearless attitude, born of the early success and sheer anarchy H enabled. Picture a bunch of 9- and 10-year-olds, some casually defiant, arms folded across our chests, others giggling and mugging for the camera. Several of us are clearly yelling something, our mouths rounded to form the soft "a" and hard "o" sounds. H smiles benignly, aware of nothing taking place around him — his gaze fixed not on the camera but somewhere off in the distance.

It was Tom Wadlington who introduced our teammate Mike "Mini" Mooradian to GAPO, an acronym for *Gorilla Arm-Pit Odor*. For decades, our specific local legend held that GAPO had originated as a bogus deodorant product depicted in Wacky Packs. These were cards and stickers sold in a baseball-card format (meaning they came with gum) and featuring fake, often gross-out spoofs of household products, some of which were sendups of actual brands. Like *Hostage* cupcakes. Others were complete fabrications, like GAPO, the preferred deodorant of larger primates. Only the 1970s could have produced consumer novelty products so ridiculous, trashy and widely popular.

GAPO, as shorthand for serious body odor, has survived into the 21st century, but no trace of its foundational faux product exists in the Wacky Pack online archive, which, readers may be alarmed to learn, is not administered by the Library of Congress. Yet the fact remains: It was Mooradian who ran with the GAPO concept. He dreamed up "The GAPO Stick," a stray branch that purportedly conferred Gorilla Arm-Pit Odor on whomever it touched. By the time we gathered for this team picture, in May of 1975, the antic power of The GAPO Stick had coursed through our team for weeks. When the photographer suggested we say "cheese," Mini instead started yelling "GAPO!" and the rest of us eagerly chimed in.

As 9- and 10-year-old delinquents in the making, we found Wacky Packs altogether hilarious and attractively subversive. They were much the rage among preteen consumers during a brief period mid-decade — an era of notable junk food innovation: Pringles, Starburst and Skittles all debuted or otherwise became available at this time. Doritos were just six years old as the decade dawned. They were considered highly exotic in my suburban town — and truly scrumptious. When Frito-Lay introduced the nacho cheese variety (1972), it blew our white-bread minds. Bubble Yum, a massive step forward in gum technology for its long-lasting flavor and durable mass, created a minor sensation circa 1974, when its uneven commercial release and distribution prompted us to bike all over town in search of this highly prized confection.

In spring 1976, our second season under H, we Pilgrims won another state title. As we cut an ever-wider swath through Massachusetts, we came to learn that we could pretty much have our way with H, as well. He was kindly and cerebral (a helluva bridge player apparently), but never raised his voice. Mainly he drove us to games, offered praise in barely audible tones, and passed out sticks of Juicy Fruit at halftime. Sometimes there were oranges, too, but a spotty rotation of moms was responsible for those. (During the 1970s, no one felt so strongly about hydration.) At practice, on afternoons when there was no organizing activity like a scrimmage, H simply could not or would not assert anything resembling adult authority. Not when GAPO undermined our portrait-sitting. Not even when a 12-year-old Chuck Christoforo absconded with H's Vista Cruiser — an absolute whale of a station wagon — and drove it all over the practice fields at Sprague Elementary School. There were no repercussions.

What's more, my teammates and I were largely nonplussed by H's light supervisory hand. Those of us who grew up in the 1970s expected — and, in the end, required — far less parental supervision, direction and encouragement than 11-year-olds do today, I daresay. This observation likely smacks of generational bias. But I contend it is a demographic fact. We didn't just pioneer the youth soccer leagues, or buy and consume enough Skittles to enable their lasting success. Generation Zero — what most demographers call Generation X — proudly comprised America's first crop of suburban latchkey kids. What's more, my friends and I never viewed this state of affairs as any sort of predicament, then or now.

We were bike mavens, too, fearless explorers who went to school and returned home completely on our own. Thereafter we traveled in packs and routinely transported ourselves to and from soccer practice, several miles across town, often at rush hour, without helmets. Nixon-era suburbia, with its bike-friendly sidewalks, and the 1970s generally, with its free-range parenting ethic born in part from the rise of double-income households, afforded Generation Zero glorious and empowering freedom of movement and athletic expression. These liberties shaped us as individuals in the long term. They informed who we'd become as adults, long after they informed us as youthful consumers of sport.

Those liberties, and H's lack of authority, also meant that we could hit up Gubellini's Market whenever we pleased. Guba's was an idiosyncratic, throwback establishment located near Sprague, inside what appeared to be someone's home. The front parlor featured candy for sale, a soda case, and a small ice cream freezer. For we cheeky, intrepid Pilgrims, it was de rigueur to show up at soccer practice with Giant Pixy Stix, maybe some Yodels or something else from the era's robust universe of snack-cake purveyors: Hostess, Drake's, Little Debbie, even Dolly Madison, the brand mysteriously advertised only on Charlie Brown holiday specials. If we arrived at practice empty-handed, H might look up in the middle of some drill gone awry only to realize half his team had gone rogue — off to Gubellini's for a fresh supply of Charleston Chew and Pop Rocks.

————•————

While Soccer Dads are not held up as paragons of futbol acumen in these pages, I don't relate these memories to make fun. We loved and appreciated H in our own way. He made a great many truly indelible things happen for Pilgrims, for me personally, and for soccer in our town. H and his like introduced Generation Zero to the game, for better and for worse. They were pioneers, too. They did the best they could, enabling their sons and daughters to learn a sport they probably would not have chosen for them. The Modern American Soccer Movement had to start somewhere. In many important ways, it started with them.

The period covered in this book extends from that moment early in the 1970s, when American youth soccer culture achieved critical mass, to the arrival of those youth soccer *products* at the 1990 World Cup as adult competitors. That's a period of roughly 20 years, a full Strauss and Howe generation. This interval is useful in measuring the influence of Generation Zero beyond *Italia* '90, as well. For example, H formed our team in 1975, and we took on the Pilgrims name in 1976. The "Soccer Mom" coinage entered the U.S. pop lexicon in 1996, during a presidential electoral cycle in which young, female, suburban voters were judged to have represented a critical, balance-tipping demographic. We'd be hard-pressed to identify a stronger cultural indicator of the game's newly established familiarity, acceptance and pervasiveness.

Such historical gestation is never orderly, linear or preordained. The seeds of NASL first germinated in 1966. Twenty years later, U.S. professional soccer had disintegrated. NASL was gone, as was the second-division

ASL. The 1966 World Cup final was the first soccer programming ever presented on American television. The only futbol on American TV in 1986 was the indoor variety, aired very late at night, on a content-starved ESPN, right after competitive bull riding.

By 1986, however, FIFA had grown impatient with mere gestation. The game's global power broker didn't care about sanguine suburban demographics. It wanted to know why the U.S. couldn't take part in its showcase event. It wanted to know when NASL would be replaced. America's serial bungling in these areas — specifically, its inability to bring the professional game before its hundreds of millions of well-heeled consumers — was costing FIFA and its corporate partners a fortune.

On July 4, 1988, FIFA finally took a flier and simply awarded the U.S. the 1994 World Cup. Getting to that moment is central to our narrative, as is FIFA's unspoken caveat: The Yanks were obliged to qualify for *Italia* '90 or the deal was off, and the '94 tournament would be contested elsewhere. Few national teams, representing any country, have ever been asked to sing for so much supper. As late as Nov. 18, 1989, it appeared as though Generation Zero had kicked it *all* away. "We were well aware of the situation of hosting the World Cup and the potential of it being moved, so the situation was very clear," remembers Paul Caligiuri, whose goal on Nov. 19, 1989, freed his teammates of all these burdens and, at a stroke, recast the U.S. as a modern, capable, first-world soccer nation. "We controlled our destiny," he told *The Guardian* in 2015. "It became monumental."

The narrative connection between Caligiuri's so-called "Shot Heard 'Round the World" and the embryonic 1970s remains clear and unbroken. The Seventies launched a collective Hero's Journey, one we will follow in succeeding chapters, through all the nonlinear triumphs and pitfalls, all the way to World Cup 1990.

Twenty-year gestation periods are neat and clean, but American soccer's coming-of-age wasn't supposed to take that long. Nor was it supposed to involve Generation Zero at all. The Baby Boomers, our next elders in the culture, were supposed to found and foster a modern soccer nation here. Instead, they left the game for dead. And so the mantle fell to the next cohort in line. Raised on the game and tempered by hard-won successes, we made the game stick. In fact, GZ has done for U.S. soccer what government scientists did for Steve Austin, fictional fulcrum of *The Six Million Dollar Man*. After the crash and burn, we took to our bosom a sport that was barely alive. We had the technology, so we rebuilt it. We made the American game better than it was.

"Superstar" Kyle Rote Jr. on the November 1974 cover of *Soccer Monthly*, a magazine published privately until 1978, when the U.S. Soccer Federation acquired it. SM ceased publication in February 1982. Rote made 142 NASL appearances during his career, but only five for the USMNT. *(Image courtesy of the USSF)*

Ray Hudson turns away from keeper Shep Messing during a Stompers-Strikers match in Fort Lauderdale on June 10, 1978. Neither club maintained a youth development academy to identify and nurture local talent. No NASL club ever did. *(Jon van Woerden photo)*

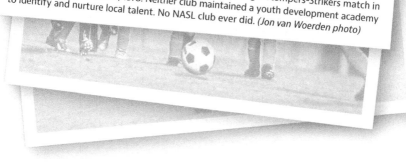

3.   THE GREAT MAN THEORY OF DEVELOPMENT

(1977 to '79)

Webster, New York, hometown of former national team midfielder Brian Bliss, is a suburb of Rochester, a community founded on the shores of Lake Ontario by late 18th-century New Englanders. Over the next century, buoyed by construction of the Erie Canal, the city attracted a mix of German immigrants and former slaves, many of whom had traveled north via the Underground Railroad. Today, Rochester's population is more than 15 percent Hispanic. A minor league outpost when it came to baseball (the AAA Red Wings) and hockey (the AHL Americans), Rochester proved eager to stake its claim as a *major* league soccer town. The Lancers joined the North American Soccer League in 1970 and promptly won the title. Throughout the decade, they played their games before consistently enthusiastic crowds at Holleder Memorial Stadium, named for a local lad who'd played American football at Army and died in Vietnam. The club flourished throughout much of the NASL era, fueled by the Youth Soccer Revolution taking place all around them in Webster, Irondequoit, Pittsford, Greece and Henrietta.

Greater Rochester is a textbook example of a Seventies-era hotbed, born of suburban demographics and top-down NASL influence. However, this obvious success never produced the sort of coaching that elite players like Bliss required. How could it? "We grew up still playing with a parent/coach, a dad or some guy who was interested to help out, not because he ever *played* the game but because he was a volunteer," Bliss explains. "I think a lack of proper coaching played a role in the slow evolution of soccer in this country, up through that period for sure. You don't want to blame coaching, but that was the evolution of our game."

If such a coaching deficit prevailed in 1976, when Brian Bliss was a kid, imagine the state of youth coaching in 1966, or 1956. Suddenly, the slow maturation of U.S. soccer becomes much easier to grasp. Even as the Lancers enjoyed peak popularity, in a hotbed they helped create, they never went the youth academy route. They never sought to funnel regional talent to the club and expose that talent to Lancer-sponsored, professional coaching acumen over the long term. At the time, this academy structure was the established European model for player development at the club level. It's the model Major League Soccer has since deployed. Some NASL clubs may have *contemplated* such a system during the 1970s. But none of them ever implemented one. As a result, the teenage Bliss was obliged to leave Greater Rochester to find the top-level coaching his futbol development required. Downstate, in the borough of Queens, Mike Windischmann followed the same path for the same reasons.

"I had good coaches. Well, some. Others were just parent coaches, you know?" Windy recalls. "We had some German families there in Queens. *Those* dads knew what they were doing. Lenny Roitman and Tim Demyriac. At the same time, growing up, I had quite a few who were just parents. I think it was a pretty simple formula: If you had some good coaches, you developed. But you had to get yourself onto the New York state team, the Eastern Regional team with George Tarantini. That's where you got the quality technical instruction from guys who could really get you going in your career."

As teens, Bliss and Windischmann each managed to find the advanced coaching they needed — not in Greater Rochester or Queens, but via the Olympic Development Program, a scouting and coaching apparatus founded in 1978. However, they were outliers among their teammates on the 1990 World Cup team, most of whom were fortunate enough to find elite coaching in their hometowns, as 12-year-olds. A remarkable number found it in their own backyards.

Compare Bliss' soccer upbringing with that of Peter Vermes, who grew up in south Jersey, the son and protégé of an accomplished Hungarian-born player. Michael Vermes was a so-called 56er, a refugee who fled the danger and madness of Hungary's armed resistance to Soviet Russia, in 1956. He and his wife Magdalena got out, emigrated to the U.S. and settled in Philadelphia.

"He was a professional player. He played for Honved," says Peter Vermes, referring to Budapest Honved FC. "He played at the time of [Ferenc] Puskas, [Sandor] Kocsis and all those guys who were there. He was a young guy. He was coming up through the system. He escaped Hungary when he was just 23 years old. But he was playing first team football at 19, 20, 21. Obviously, my dad was not one of the impact guys, but he did play with those stars and was a part of that group. He talked about it all the time. He talked about Puskas forever!"

And why not? Puskas was nearly superhuman, the finest player on perhaps the finest team of the 20th century. For six years, starting in May 1950, the Hungarian national side lost but one match: the 1954 World Cup final. The Mighty Magyars fell to West Germany that afternoon, 3-2 — after having trounced the same team during the first round, 8-3.

"It got to the point where my two brothers and I used to be like, 'OK, yeah right, Dad — like you really knew Puskas . . .' But many years ago, Puskas came and did a tour through the United States and supposedly, he was coming to the Hungarian Club in Philadelphia," Vermes says. "So, my dad got us all in the car, we drove over, we come walking through the door . . . and there he was: Ferenc Puskas himself. He saw my father and called him by his nickname! My brothers and I were like, 'Holy cow! He was actually telling the truth.'"

Once Michael Vermes' playing days were over, in the early 1970s, he did as Ruben Mendoza had done in Greater St. Louis at exactly the same time: He left the city and moved his family across the river to the suburbs. The Vermes clan settled in Delran, New Jersey. That's where Peter Vermes received his European soccer tutelage. Michael also coached at the Hungarian Club, which supported a spectrum of youth teams that functioned all over suburban Philly as a sort of proto-premier system.

"My father didn't really coach me when I first started," Vermes remembers. "He coached my older brothers and then took on my U-9 team when I was 6 years old. I had been playing 'up' for years. At that time, back in those days, there were a lot of ethnic clubs, especially in New York and Philadelphia. In Philly, there was the Hungarian club, the German-Hungarian club, a Yugoslav club. Dynamo was another club. They had Inter, the Italian club. They had a Polish club. All these teams had ex-international players who had left those countries — but there was no national league for them to play in here. The ethnic league in Philly was basically a men's league, if you will, but at a high, high level. Within those systems, clubs had their first team, a reserve team, then almost something like an academy — one team for every age group, U-18, U-16, U-14 and all the way down. Each one coached by a guy who really knew the game.

"So I played at the Hungarian club and also the German-Hungarian club. Werner Fricker, who was president of U.S. Soccer during the 1980s, was also president of the German-Hungarian club. My dad knew him, but I was just a little tyke at the time."

During the 1970s, not all youth soccer hotbeds were created equal. In terms of access to skilled coaching, suburban Delran was the exception — thanks to one man, Michael Vermes, who coached up his son, of course, but dozens and dozens of Peter's teammates, as well. Mendoza similarly transformed the soccer education of Steve Trittschuh and all his teammates. He made an exception of Granite City, Illinois. But Greater Rochester and most suburban soccer communities across the country remained the rule.

Trittschuh agrees with Bliss: More than anything else, a dearth of sophisticated coaching kept U.S. soccer in its mediocre-at-best holding pattern throughout most of the 20th century: "You're always going to have the American players who are athletically gifted, hardworking and will never quit," he says. "But eventually they need coaches who know what they are doing to create technically skilled players. Even today, it's amazing how many coaches don't."

Parent coaches tend to fall short in the expectation realm, as well.

"Having a dad who played pro soccer was a big leg up," observes Marcelo Balboa, whose father, Luis, played in the early days of NASL. "It wasn't just his *example*. I think my dad, being an ex-professional, demanded that much more from us — and had a lot more to offer, in terms of technique and the mindset. He never let us get complacent, either. No matter what, it was never good enough... My goal was always to be better than my dad. I wanted that, and I wanted it more than most guys, I think."

———•·•———

All it took was a single soccer-savvy, foreign-bred coach or father to tip the balance or get the ball rolling toward the development of a truly productive hotbed — one that turned out superior, technically proficient individuals, sides, entire clubs. During the 1970s, enough able coaches finally came into contact with enough young American players of quality to produce a golden generation of talent. Our run-of-the-mill hotbed of Wellesley, Massachusetts, never did acquire such a transformative coaching figure. However, midway through 1976, we *did* get our first taste of just what we were missing, and how potent the uber hotbed formula could be.

The Pilgrims had won the state under-12 championship that spring and traveled west along Interstate 90 to play the New York state champs from Irondequoit, a north Rochester suburb that sits directly across Irondequoit Bay from Bliss' hometown of Webster. Our 3-1 victory earned us a date with the Montgomery County Pintos, a collection of Maryland boys from suburban D.C. They were coached by a pair of Brits, John Kerr Sr. — then a player/coach with the NASL's Washington Diplomats — and Gordon Murray, the Scottish-born father of future national team striker Bruce Murray. The Pintos visited Wellesley for a July match and fairly well dismantled us, 4-1. They were, by far, the best side we had ever seen. Young Mr. Murray — only 10, half our size but already a precocious talent — scored twice.

As it happened, Bruce Murray and his older brother Sterling billeted with my family, in our chocolate-brown Victorian on Dover Road. John

Kerr Jr. — the first American to play in the English first division, who made 16 appearances for the U.S. Men's National Team — billeted half a mile away on Weston Road, with Tom Wadlington's family.

"Those teams we had were ridiculous," Murray asserts today, looking back. "We had guys who ended up playing at UNC and Duke, guys who played professionally. I loved the way they used to billet kids at tournaments. Those were the good ol' days. We'd go up to Massapequa [Long Island] and stay with families there, too. It was great."

We Pilgrims had never encountered a true footballing phenom before. Once the match got underway, however, we recognized this kid didn't earn his place because his dad coached the team. Murray and Kerr would eventually team with two more Greater D.C.-bred future USMNTers, John Stollmeyer and Desmond Armstrong, to lead the Fairfax (Virginia) Spartans to a National Amateur Cup title in 1986. John Kerr Sr. coached that team, as well.

Stollmeyer got repeated doses of serious coaching, starting at a very young age. "My dad, who's from Trinidad and really knows the game, coached me all through rec soccer until I tried out for the Redwings, at the Annandale Boys Club," he explains. Annandale is a D.C. suburb, too, part of Fairfax County, Virginia, which borders on Montgomery County, Maryland. "As it turned out, my stepfather, who's French, was coach of the Redwings. I won't go back through all *that* history, but I played for the Redwings a couple years, then went back down to my own age group and my dad coached me again. Then, when I was older, I played for John Kerr Sr."

Outside the U.S. Soccer Federation and its coaching network, few men had more impact on the elite fortunes of Generation Zero than John Kerr Sr. He sired one U.S. international player and coached up another half-dozen from young ages. Come 1987, under Kerr's direction, that same Fairfax Spartans team would enter the newly reconstituted American Soccer League, the "A-League," as the professional Washington Stars. Before passing away in 2011, he also served a long stint as head of the Major League Soccer Players Association.

As a player — and a symbol of what could be aspired to in North America — John Kerr Sr. proved no less influential. A Scot by birth, he emigrated to Canada and signed with NASL's Detroit Cougars in 1968, though his star would truly rise with the Washington Darts. This gig brought him to Greater D.C. He reared a family there and never left. In 1972, he caught on as a midfielder with the pre-Pelé Cosmos, earning all-star standing and, eventually, five caps for Canada ("cap" meaning a full international appearance for one's country; the English term is derived from the actual headgear national team participants were presented, starting in the late 1800s, to mark such occasions). By the time he arrived in Wellesley with his Pintos that July of '76, Kerr Sr. had turned 33. He retired from the Diplomats a year later. Thereafter he concentrated on the youth team his son and Bruce Murray were quickly turning into a juggernaut. Montgomery United, under Kerr Sr.'s direction, would win national titles at the U-16 (1981) and U-19 levels (1983).

"John Kerr was a second father to me," Murray says. "My dad and he were best friends. Me and John Jr. were best friends, and still are. He really knew the game, obviously, but his philosophy was simple: Keep it moving, get stuck in. Very simple and very Scottish in that way. But he loved skill and wanted us to be technical and creative and take people on, so he wasn't Scottish at all in that respect!"

———————

The billeting tradition that delivered Bruce Murray to my house included an informal rule of reciprocity. Accordingly, after we hosted his Pintos in July 1976, the Pilgrims were invited to Maryland for a big tournament the Pintos organized and hosted that October. To complete the circle, I stayed with the Murrays down in Bethesda.

I remember both Murray lads to have been nice kids and lovely house-guests, always a please and thank you. At one point, before our July match in Wellesley, my younger brother, Matthew, ventured into our den holding the two or three trophies I had claimed as a member of the Pilgrims. He admired them — and me, I suppose. This move embarrassed me slightly at the time. Not nearly so much, however, as the moment that fall when I walked into the Murray household and encountered entire walls and massive bookcases stocked to the gills with soccer trophies — dozens and dozens of them. One in particular caught my eye and stayed with me: *Bruce Murray, 1976 Orange Bowl Juggling Champion.* The kid could juggle the ball indefinitely. I convinced him to demonstrate in his own backyard. He proceeded to casually but deftly keep the ball up for five or 10 minutes, chatting with me all the while and pointing at things in the distance. Eventually we got bored and moved on to something else.

During that October 1976 tournament down in Maryland, the scales fell from our eyes completely. We Pilgrims were eviscerated — much as we'd been competitively disemboweled three months earlier, in Wellesley. We did put up a good fight against the Pintos' great rival, Annandale Boys Club, earning shocked praise from the Murray boys. But there's no sense in sugarcoating it: We were *way* out of our league.

As 12-year-olds, we did not yet understand the impact expert coaching could have. We only knew that south of New England, for whatever reason, there were teams and players operating on a much higher level. We reckoned it was something to do with the warmer weather allowing for year-round play. Perhaps the players in Florida were better still!

Six years later, in 1982, we won the state title, a competition conducted as part of the James P. McGuire Cup, America's U-19 national club championship. We drew Annandale again and fared somewhat better, losing 2-1. Annandale went on to win the whole kit and caboodle. For those keeping score at home: Pilgrims fell to the eventual McGuire Cup national champions, Annandale Boys Club, in 1982. Six years prior, we got shellacked by the eventual 1983 McGuire Cup champions, Montgomery United. "We knew how to lose — only to the very best teams," Wadlington said to me recently. Quite rightly.

It wasn't the climate, of course. Nor was it relevant that the Pintos and Annandale had drawn broadly from entire counties — whereas our player pool was limited to a single suburban town. No. Clearly there were hotbeds and there were *hotbeds*. What made *actual* hotbeds so damned fertile was not temperate climes, nor sheer numbers, but rather the availability of first-class coaching.

IF THERE EXISTED A GROUND ZERO for Generation Zero, however, it was not Montgomery County, Maryland or the suburbs of northern Virginia. That honor goes to Kearny, New Jersey, a place fairly well devoid of Soccer Dads during the 1970s. Pronounced like a circus *carney*, this north Jersey suburb of New York City, hard by the Meadowlands Sports Complex, possessed its own distinct and potent stew of the ethnic and white bread during the Me Decade. That goulash is the reason Bob Gansler still refers to Tony Meola, John Harkes and Tab Ramos as "The Jersey Mafia." Gansler tends to lump them all in with Peter Vermes, who hails from more southerly Delran. Accordingly, "The Kearny Mafia" would be more accurate, as this single, middle-class town of 25,000 produced three cornerstone players on four World Cup teams in the space of a single generation.

Kearny stood apart from the nascent suburban hotbeds that blossomed throughout the Seventies, not just for the stars it produced — nor for the ethnic mix that fueled a dependable stream of soccer-savvy parent coaches — but instead for a soccer history that made urban-American seedbeds of the Fifties and Sixties look positively arriviste.

Formed in 1867 from bits of neighboring Harrison, the township of Kearny developed its soccer reputation a full century before Harkes, Ramos and Meola came along. During the 1870s, Scots and Irish immigrants settled there in the thousands, many to work in a pair of thriving manufacturing operations, Nairn Linoleum and the Clark Thread Co. Upon expanding its operations in Kearny, Clark in particular would lure across the Atlantic hundreds of workers from its plant in Paisley, Scotland, just west of Glasgow. This importation of able-bodied persons and soccer heritage, straight from the old country, proved seamless and robust. What's more, the influx arrived roughly at the same time the British formalized "association" football (as opposed to rugby). Soccer was already hugely popular among working men in Britain's industrialized north. These sons of the north delivered the game directly to Kearny.

"Oh yeah. When I grew up, it was *still* a completely Scottish and English town," Tony Meola reports. "There were three of us — myself, Tab Ramos and my best friend Sal Rosamilia — and it seemed like we were the only ones in Kearny who *weren't* English, Irish or Scottish."

Contemplating organized American soccer from the 19th-century perspective is a bit mind-bending, but Kearny shows how quickly and easily the game transferred to and thrived on these shores. Check this out, courtesy of the website NJsportsheroes.com:

In 1885, the American Football Challenge Cup tournament began. The first champion was the Clark-backed ONT of Kearny (ONT was short for Our New Thread, Clark's new product). The Kearny club defeated New York FC in the title game, and then went on a tour of Canada, winning 9 of 11 matches and drawing one. A team of Canadian stars returned the favor, touring the New York Metro area in the fall of that year. On November 25, the Canadian stars met a hand-picked team of American stars at the Clark field in Kearny. The Canadians won, 1–0. It was the first international soc-cer match played by a U.S. team. The Clark factory club won the next two "American Cups." They beat the cross-town Kearny Rangers both times. In the years that followed, soccer continued to grow in popularity in New Jersey. However, control of the Challenge Cup shifted to the great teams from Massachusetts and Rhode Island. Not until 1896, when the Paterson True Blues won, did the American Cup return to the Garden State.

When I first read this account, part of me thought, *Well, of course au-thentic association-style football traveled to the U.S. during this period of unparalleled European immigration.* However, I was astonished to learn of something so formal and organized as the American Football Challenge Cup, whose very name also indicates that, during the 1880s, there was no reason to mistake this brand of football for any other kind.

What I'm detailing in these pages is a history of the *Modern* American Soccer Movement, however, so we shan't go into the incredibly broad impact Kearny, along with neighboring Harrison and Paterson, had on early 20th-century soccer in the United States. (For more on that subject, check out the 2019 documentary *Soccertown, USA*.) The futbol culture that evolved there, into the 1970s, speaks for itself.

"We had a place called The Courts; you went there every night. That's what you did," Meola reports, noting that The Courts were located just over the Kearny town line in Harrison, a 10-minute walk from what became Red Bull Arena in 2010. "I was probably 12 when I started going there. It didn't matter what time you got there: Your opponent could have been another 12-year-old kid, coulda been a 52-year-old man — coulda been Irish or Italian. But that's where we learned the game, my friends and me. If your friend was on the other team somehow, he had to get kicked.

"Look, we do a better job of training and developing kids today, but I still think we're missing something in this country. We've sort of skipped that free-form part of the development process: playing on your own, with older guys, more or less in the street. Win or go home. I mean, we stood around all night to get a game at The Courts. Until the cops would come and kick us out."

Meola's dad, Vincenzo, had been a second-division professional in his native Italy before emigrating in the 1960s. He owned a barber shop in Kearny, and that vocation kept him from coaching, his son explains. Anywhere else in the nation, a father with *that* sort of resume would have been invaluable — perhaps the difference between building a successful soccer program, or not. In Kearny, however, Vincenzo's absence mattered not a whit. There were plenty of soccer-savvy coaches around, a luxury afforded very few communities back then — and very few premier clubs even today. A century of soccer culture will do that for a town. It was John Harkes' Scottish-born father, Jimmy, who coached Meola, Harkes and Ramos throughout the 1970s — along with hundreds more Kearny boys. He did so as part of Thistle United FC, a club sponsored by the local Scots American Club.

"Kearny was a strange sort of hotbed at the time, in a period where soccer everywhere else wasn't that mainstream at all," Meola maintains.

"But if you didn't play soccer in Kearny, you weren't cool. That's the way we all looked at it. It validated you in town — if you had a state championship jacket on, or not. Very, very unique in that way. Still that way."

———•◦•———

World Cup 1978 would prove another nonevent for this country's swelling ranks of young soccer players. The tournament was, of course, contested — in Argentina. However, America's long-standing insularity from and disinterest in the international game, combined with State Department pressures (a brutal and conniving military junta then controlled the government in Buenos Aires) conspired to keep the entire competition something of a secret. No live matches were televised in the U.S. No week-old highlights of the final. Nothing. All the same, the summer of '78 would prove busy and broadening for our young squad of Pilgrims. Coach H, never the tactician but ever the impresario, had arranged for our U-14 team to make a pilgrimage in reverse — to England and Holland. On some abstract level, my teammates and I had begun to recognize our status as soccer pioneers. Our overseas tour only confirmed this trailblazing cred.

However, Generation Zero was bigger and broader and more accomplished than we knew at the time. The historical record makes that clear: John Stollmeyer and his mates from Annandale Boys Club, for example, were touring Holland fully seven years earlier, as 9-year-olds! You don't make that sort of trip so early in the modern story of U.S. soccer without a cosmopolitan outlook born of foreign stock, and Stollmeyer's lineage — in addition to his formative soccer environment — fairly well embodied this ideal.

"Because my dad was from Trinidad, I grew up with cricket and soccer. He really did know the game; he was a student of it," Stollmeyer says. "A lot of what was going on in Dutch soccer at that time was a huge thing we mimicked back then — two men toward the ball and all that. And we did get around. The first time I went overseas with a club team, I was in the fourth grade. Went to Holland. That was 1971. Went there with the Red Wings and we played against the Ajax youth team. Lost 3-0."

Of the 22 guys chosen to represent the U.S. at *Italia '90*, Stollmeyer occupied the role of elder statesman. Born in 1962, he was fully 27 years of age when Paul Caligiuri let loose with the "Shot Heard 'Round the World" on the ever-consequential island of Trinidad. "I was the oldest guy on the team," Stolly confirms. "Krumpe just acted the oldest."

Everything his younger teammates went through, Stollmeyer invariably experienced first. He was, in fact, the proto-denizen of Generation Zero. As such, his developmental experience was something of a template, all of it built in suburbia, on the shoulders of those born elsewhere.

"All the coaches at that club, down through the system, had some type of ethnic background... We traveled a lot. I mean, I've got patches like you wouldn't believe! My dad let us all be exposed to all these different styles of play."

—*John Stollmeyer*

"Mr. White, who helped coach the Rebels [the "Born in 1962" team at Annandale Boys Club], was from Scotland," he says. "All the coaches at that club, down through the system, had some type of ethnic background. It was a hotbed of soccer back then. You know how it goes on the East Coast — we traveled to tournaments everywhere. I also went to Mexico the summer between fifth and sixth grade. Bermuda, England, Canada. We traveled *a lot*. I mean, I've got patches like you wouldn't believe! My dad let us all be exposed to all these different styles of play. John Ellis — my dad brought him over from England to help us train. He moved over eventually and is still involved with soccer in northern Virginia."

Ellis arrived, at Mr. Stollmeyer's behest, with an Advanced Full Badge Coaching License from the English Football Association and a boundless enthusiasm for the nascent American game. He would lead multiple youth teams — boys and girls, representing various D.C.-area clubs — to multiple national age-group championships. In 2000, he joined the full-time staff of U.S. Women's National Team coach April Heinrichs. Fifteen years later, his daughter, Jill Ellis, led the women to a third World Cup title, followed by their fourth in 2019.

It's instructive to spend a little time really studying the **1990 World Cup Roster**, one that includes hometowns. Go ahead. I'll wait.

1990 U.S. World Cup Roster

D	Steve Trittschuh	1965	Granite City, Illinois
D	John Doyle	1966	Fremont, California
D	Jimmy Banks	1964	Milwaukee, Wisconsin
D	Desmond Armstrong	1964	Washington, D.C.
D	Mike Windischmann	1965	New York City
D	Marcelo Balboa	1967	Cerritos, California
M	John Harkes	1967	Kearny, New Jersey
M	Tab Ramos	1966	Kearny, New Jersey
M	Brian Bliss	1965	Webster, New York
M	Chris Henderson	1970	Everett, Washington
M	Paul Caligiuri	1964	Walnut, California
M	Neil Covone	1969	Hialeah, Florida
M	John Stollmeyer	1962	Annandale, Virginia
F	Christopher Sullivan	1965	San Jose, California
F	Peter Vermes	1966	Delran, New Jersey
F	Eric Wynalda	1969	Westlake, California
F	Paul Krumpe	1963	Torrance, California
F	Eric Eichmann	1965	Margate, Florida
F	Bruce Murray	1966	Bethesda, Maryland
G	David Vanole	1963	Redondo Beach, California
G	Tony Meola	1969	Kearny, New Jersey
G	Kasey Keller	1969	Olympia, Washington

Now, compare these players (and their respective youth-soccer petri dishes) to those on the **2002 World Cup roster.**

2002 U.S. World Cup roster

D	Gregg Berhalter	1973	Tenafly, New Jersey
D	Pablo Mastroeni	1976	Mendoza, Argentina (Phoenix, Arizona)
D	David Regis	1968	La Trinité, Martinique
D	Carlos Llamosa	1969	Palmira, Colombia
D	Jeff Agoos	1968	Geneva, Switzerland (Richardson, Texas)
D	Steve Cherundolo	1979	San Diego, California
D	Tony Sanneh	1971	St. Paul, Minnesota
D	Eddie Pope	1973	Greensboro, North Carolina
M	Eddie Lewis	1974	Cerritos, California
M	Frankie Hedjuk	1974	La Mesa, California
M	John O'Brien	1977	Playa del Rey, California
M	Claudio Reyna	1973	Livingston, New Jersey
M	DaMarcus Beasley	1982	Fort Wayne, Indiana
M	Cobi Jones	1970	Westlake Village, California
F	Josh Wolff	1977	Stone Mountain, Georgia
F	Clint Mathis	1976	Conyers, Georgia
F	Earnie Stewart	1969	Veghel, Netherlands
F	Joe-Max Moore	1971	Tulsa, Oklahoma
F	Brian McBride	1972	Arlington Heights, Illinois
F	Landon Donovan	1982	Ontario, California
G	Brad Friedel	1971	Lakewood, Ohio
G	Kasey Keller	1969	Olympia, Washington
G	Tony Meola	1969	Kearny, New Jersey

Note the striking differences in the columns at far right. In 1990, World Cup roster representation came largely from three overarching hotbeds — New Jersey/New York City, Greater D.C., and California — with traditional urban enclaves St. Louis and Milwaukee supplying one player apiece. There were only four true outliers: two from Florida (Neil Covone and Eric Eichmann) and two from Washington (state, 19-year-olds Kasey Keller and Chris Henderson). None of these four played a minute at *Italia* '90.

Uber hotbeds were rare in the 1970s because first-class coaching was hard to find, especially at the youth level. If one lumps D.C. in with NYC/NJ to form a single Mid-Atlantic breeding ground, this super-region would account for eight of the 22 players Bob Gansler took to Italy in 1990 — all of them starters or key reserves. In 2002, just 12 years down the evolutionary road, the national team roster indicates the marked geographic spread of soccer development capabilities — due to the continued spread of more sophisticated coaching talent into a wider array of suburban hotbeds. Naturalized players must be considered separately, but look at all these "new" sources of World Cup-caliber talent: Ohio, Oklahoma, Illinois, Georgia, Indiana, Minnesota, North Carolina, Arizona, Texas.

"With the 1990 team, you had a generation of kids who were all products of the soccer boom. That was new. They had soccer culture at home, and organized soccer outside of that home," confirms *Soccer America*'s Mike Woitalla. "Some of that was NASL. I think you can say this was a generation of kids who really grew up with the sport and aspired to NASL and grew up in a soccer culture in a way their predecessors did not. But think of all immigrant-parent influences, too. I think of Marcelo Balboa, whose dad was Argentinian. Guys like Murray, Kerr and Harkes, whose dads were all Scottish guys who played the game and coached their sons."

CLOSE OBSERVERS OF THE U.S. SOCCER scene might have noticed a notable news item released by Sporting Kansas City, the Major League Soccer franchise, in January of 2014. The requisite press-conference image showed SKC manager Peter Vermes standing alongside young Erik Palmer-Brown. The accompanying verbiage was as startling as it was brief:

Sporting Kansas City has turned down a $1 million bid from Italian giant Juventus for 16-year-old defender Erik Palmer-Brown ... Palmer-Brown, a member of the U.S. Under-18 national team, was a homegrown signing for the MLS club last August. A resident of Lee's Summit, Mo., he had been a member of the SKC youth academy since the age of 11.

Palmer-Brown's spurning of Juventus, his academy involvement with a professional soccer franchise, the *existence* of a league-sponsored academy: These are the realities of 21st-century American soccer. They were all unimaginable in the late 1970s, when the elite talents composing Generation Zero had just started to get noticed beyond their home states and regions. That Vermes stood beside Palmer-Brown at this 2014 press event, that Vermes would essentially be overseeing his development in Kansas City, as opposed to Turin, slathered on another layer of irony. And progress.

"You're absolutely right, and it shows the evolution not only of the American game but also of the club structure here, the academy system, the homegrown players," Vermes tells me. "All that means we're at least moving in the right direction today."

As the Me Decade drew to a close and most members of Generation Zero were approaching high school age, a range of outwardly sanguine soccer developments all pointed toward progress. In 1977, NASL had reached peak popularity. Pelé's farewell season culminated with title-winning and tribute games that each drew capacity crowds in excess of 70,000 at the Meadowlands in East Rutherford, New Jersey (a six-mile ride north from Kearny, on Schuyler Avenue). The Cosmos would repeat as champions in 1978, beating the Tampa Bay Rowdies in the season-ending Soccer Bowl, before another sellout crowd of 75,000, on national television.

However, for all this wider cultural exposure and success, no NASL franchise supported a bona fide academy system to develop a young American talent like Eric Palmer-Brown, who, at this writing, in January of 2022, plays for Troyes, in the French first division, on loan from mighty Manchester City. Up to 1978, such development responsibilities were left to youth coaches, meaning a handful of capable immigrants and thousands of Soccer Dads. In the end, they did the job NASL declined to do. Indeed, its stubborn refusal to invest in the development of young North American talent ultimately doomed the entire league enterprise.

The obvious solution, then and now, was an academy system attached to each NASL franchise. Every European club maintains one, a practice dating back to the 1950s. Every MLS team operates at least one today, often more than one. In the competitive, cash-poor atmosphere of 1977, however, there was little incentive for NASL clubs to take unnecessary competitive chances on *mature* American or Canadian players. Spending in the long term on developing homegrown, North American talent via youth academies? A complete non-starter.

This last point is perhaps the most galling, in retrospect, because most NASL teams employed foreign-born general managers and coaches whose native futbol cultures were built on *precisely* this sort of club-sponsored academy system! They should have known better.

"Look, I was a massive fan of NASL," declares Marcelo Balboa, who grew up in Cerritos, California, only 20 miles from each of the two home fields occupied by the L.A. Aztecs during this period: the L.A. Coliseum and the infamous Murdock Stadium, in Torrance. "This was back in the old days of NASL. I remember going to California Surf games, too. They played in Anaheim. I was happy to see the Johan Cruyffs and Pelés of the world, and George Best. But I don't think they were looking to develop American players back then. Having those two Americans on the field was more an attempt to get noticed. It was marketing. The fact we put so many people in stadiums during the Seventies — that was awesome. But let's just say this attitude toward player development was why the national team was where it was, back then.

"Look where the national team is today, once we started a national league [MLS] that developed its own players. Two courtesy spots? You know what the quota meant: It was token — and they were putting those guys in spots on the field where they would not affect the team too much, too adversely. They weren't developing players. Compare that to what we're doing now. We're developing *players* today."

By the time they were 14, 15 and 16 years old, future members of the 1990 USMNT were all developing their skills more or less ad hoc. Yes, they did so mainly in uber hotbed communities, under some skilled coaches; these veritable unicorns looked after them quite well. But that's not a system. John Kerr Sr. or Luis Balboa or Jimmy Harkes could not begin to meet the needs of suburban-bred talent in all 50 states. What's more, 15-year-old kids across Generation Zero, elite and otherwise, were poised to enter a high school soccer system where capable coaches were even fewer and farther between.

Into this void stepped an unlikely savior: the U.S. Olympic Committee, on whose coattails the U.S. Soccer Federation would ride for the next decade.

The National Sports Festival debuted in 1978, in response to the fear — yet another broad cultural anxiety — that the Soviet Union had developed a sporting edge on the free/western world. According to Olympic journalist Phil Hersh, the U.S. Olympic Committee launched the Festival to be "a U.S. equivalent to the communist Spartakiade, held on a quadrennial basis by the former Soviet Union and its former satellite in East Germany. As the competitive position of U.S. athletes in the Olympics slipped relative to that of the Soviets and East Germans, it was felt the U.S. needed some kind of multi-sports event to simulate the Olympic experience."

Soccer is a prominent Olympic sport. The U.S. was scheduled to host the Summer Olympiad in Los Angeles, come 1984. In the absence of a club-sponsored academy system administered by NASL clubs, and 28 years into its World Cup drought, the U.S. Soccer Federation eagerly bought into the Festival model — along with what came to be known as the Olympic Development Program (ODP) — as an act of practical desperation.

"People thought it was the USOC trying to graduate kids to the 'next level' and become Olympic-caliber athletes, but I beg to differ," Peter Vermes explains. "We didn't have enough good coaches around the country. At that time, the better players were not being selected out to train and get some time and opportunities with really good coaches. ODP was meant to address *that* issue specifically."

Just one member of the 1990 national team, proto-Gen Zero midfielder John Stollmeyer, took advantage of the first two Festivals, each held in Colorado Springs during the summers of 1978 and '79. (The National Sports Festival would rebrand as the U.S. Olympic Festival in 1985.) Each and every guy who went to *Italia* '90 would eventually partake of ODP, however. For the first time, the amateur soccer community in America had developed, or been handed, a means of gathering the best talent from across the nation, in a single place, under the watchful eyes of qualified coaches. The Olympic Development Program changed U.S. soccer forever.

Brian Bliss entered Webster Schroeder High School in suburban Rochester during the fall of 1977. He didn't participate in ODP until the early 1980s, yet his experience was typical and well illustrates how the process worked. Because Webster didn't feature any unicorn, foreign-born coaching, ODP in many ways made the career of Brian Bliss.

"You needed to perform in a five-day window, at ODP camp, in order to be recognized — in order to be brought into the next elite camp for regional or national sides. You had to string together four to five good days, or maybe three to four good games, to make it happen, to catch the eye of coaches, to make the regional teams and get more coaching. It was intense."

—Brian Bliss

"The whole system," he explains, "boiled down to this: Try out for your local team, make that. Then participate in the state cup or state tryout process, and hopefully you represent your state on that team of 20 guys. Then go to the regional event with that state team, showcasing your talent there in front of national team coaches. At some point, those coaches say, 'We'll take these nine to 12 guys from this region, and mix them with nine to 12 from the other three regions, and have another camp.'"

Bliss and every one of his teammates at World Cup 1990 broke through to regional/national prominence in precisely this fashion. "Back then you set your calendar as a soccer player not to your club stuff," Bliss recounts.

"If you were an elite player, you set your calendar to what was happening at the ODP camps. That was your way to break through."

In the absence of a traditional, professional club-driven academy culture — which would not emerge until MLS emerged — ODP nevertheless developed top native talent better than the U.S. Soccer Federation ever had before. Developing a competitive Olympic squad was the nominal priority, not a U-20 team that would target success in FIFA competitions going forward. However, the Federation *did* end up relying on ODP and the Festivals to develop those youth national teams through the 1980s.

What's more, the pressure to perform at this rarefied level tempered players by fire. The stakes were real — and recognizable. ODP provided their first real exposure to high-level performance, on demand.

"You needed to perform in a five-day window, at ODP camp, in order to be recognized — in order to be brought into the next elite camp for regional or national sides," Bliss asserts. "You had to string together four to five good days, or maybe three to four good games, to make it happen, to catch the eye of coaches, to make the regional teams and get more coaching. It was intense. Today you're being monitored day to day, week to week — in an academy setting, over the long term. With the ODP system, you get there on a Tuesday and by Sunday, if you didn't put together three good games, you didn't have the chance to move on to another camp nationally."

Bliss knows his way around the player development subject. After serving as technical director for the Chicago Fire in MLS, he joined Sporting KC in 2016. Today he serves the club as technical director and vice president of player personnel. He works alongside another beneficiary of the ODP system, Peter Vermes, the manager and sporting director at SKC.

"It was a privilege to be invited and play on the state or regional team," Vermes insists, looking back. "And I don't mean this as any disrespect to the program, but the ODP is almost insignificant today — because all the best coaches are in club soccer now. The roles have reversed. We had the ODP program back then, because we didn't have the club coaches at the time. U.S. Soccer put all their eggs into this one basket, bringing all the best players through ODP, to hopefully put a team together and hopefully find success. Today, compared to the pre-1990 era, we have fewer national and regional team camps and all those other things, because now we have a league and academies to help prepare players."

————————

John Stollmeyer went straight from Annandale, Virginia, to the 1978 National Sports Festival, thanks to the Olympic Development program. As the most senior member of Generation Zero, Stollmeyer proved just old enough to take advantage of the elite coaching on offer via this brand-new camp/tryout system. Every other member of Gen Zero would eventually follow suit, but no one did so with such precocity — as a 15-year-old playing in a pool of U-19s.

"So I get to this national camp, in Colorado, and I still remember those guys out there: Erhardt Kapp from UConn, Charlie Stillitano, Billy Morrone," he says. "I'm 15, and these guys are in their first and second years of college! All of a sudden, here I am and playing with Stevie McLean out of Philadelphia Textile and [Craig] Scarpelli, the goalie from University of Tampa, a Jersey guy.

"So, I don't start the first game, but we're down 2-0 and Lito Zabala out of Wisconsin-Milwaukee has scored both goals. So the coach says to me, 'Stollmeyer, can you play defense?' And I said, 'Yeah.' 'I want you to mark Zabala. Wherever he goes, you mark him tight.' So I get on the field and someone passes him the ball and, you know, Zabala just barely misses scoring again. McLean comes over to me and says, 'If he touches that ball again, *I'm* gonna kick you.' I cleaned him out on the sideline after that, and he wanted nothing to do with the game anymore. We ended up winning, 3-2."

This national-camp performance made *Stollmeyer's* career. A month prior, he'd been a virtual unknown playing club and high school soccer in northern Virginia. No one at the Federation knew who he was. ODP funneled him straight to Colorado Springs, where his coaches were senior national team manager Walt Chyzowych and his assistant, Bob Gansler.

The abiding revelation of that first Festival camp, however, was not Stollmeyer, nor any of the other talented players gathered there. The revelation was the gathering itself, and the ODP process that delivered everyone to Colorado Springs. Over the next 10 years, the Olympic Development Program would prove a staple in developing rosters for both the World Youth Championship — what FIFA would eventually rebrand as the U-20 World Cup, in 2006 — and senior national team squads. ODP did what NASL should have been doing all along.

The young, elite U.S. players preceding Generation Zero did not represent some primitive, retrograde cohort. In the late Seventies and early Eighties, for example, while Harkes, Ramos and Meola were still coming of age, Greater Kearny alone could boast *four* local products playing in NASL: Spanish-born Santiago Formoso for the Cosmos; Hugh O'Neill with the Hartford Bicentennials and Memphis Rogues; Eddie Austin of the Tampa Bay Rowdies; and Harrison's David D'Errico, who played all over NASL — including with my hometown Tea Men, in 1978. The U.S. Soccer Federation saw fit to cap D'Errico 21 times.

There had been youth leagues to serve these guys and their generation of players during the late 1960s — just not so many as would come later. There were foreign-born coaches to take over from Soccer Dads in the more elite context — just not so many as would come later. There were even youth national team camps that gathered elite regional talent in one place — just not so often, or ever so comprehensively, as the ODP system would, starting in 1978, precisely when Gen Zero emerged.

THE FIRST OBLIGATION OF THE NORTH American Soccer League, from its meager beginnings in 1967 to its sad disintegration in 1984, was survival. This it managed to do. Yet that act of survival proved so all-absorbing and chaotic that two additional but no-less-vital functions never developed: 1) the grooming of quality senior players for contemporary club and national team play; and 2) the development of young talent for future club and national team duty. The latter function would have required club-administered academies. NASL franchises made an economic, elective decision not to invest in those. Myopic? Of course. But that's what eventuates when unstable clubs spend 100 percent of their efforts just keeping the lights on.

By contrast, the failure of clubs to effectively groom the mature U.S. pros already on their respective rosters was structural. Individual franchises had no choice in this matter because, sadly, the quota arrangement had been baked into the North American Soccer League from the outset.

The quota is often discussed as an NASL curiosity, but the reality is more stark: It systematically *discouraged and disincentivized* clubs from developing U.S. and Canadian pros. It discouraged and disincentivized clubs from fielding more than two North Americans at once and from playing them in central positions. Many had predicted the quota system would eventually fade away. It *never* went away, despite having backfired in these and other respects, over and over again, for 17 years.

"I remember they asked me back then about going to college or the NASL," Stollmeyer recollects. "This would have been 1982 or '83. But back then the NASL had so many washed-up, second-rate European pros just coming over and taking the money. It was always that way. I think that stifled the growth of American players because they wouldn't put Americans on the field, in the middle of the field — they wouldn't let us grow. And if you might have been good enough, they hid you at left back."

As a Benny Brewster fanboy, that hurts. But Stolly's assessment is accurate. NASL clubs never embraced meaningful North American player development because they never embraced *any* long-term goals. Struggling franchises tend to avoid those. They focus on the "now": Win games. Put butts in seats. Sell more beer. Meet payroll. Avoid moving the team to Calgary.

NASL founders conceived the North American minimum to improve existing native players, by virtue of training and playing next to established, talented, foreign-born players. Marketing played a role, of course: We loved Brewster because he was an American, one of us. However, the quota never did its primary job: It never developed a critical mass of native talent for NASL clubs, the USMNT, or the Canadian national team.

Yet the quota didn't merely fail in this regard. It also produced a host of entirely negative side effects. For example, those North American players it did groom were almost exclusively bit players. "At that stage," confirms Woitalla, "all the Americans were role players on their NASL teams. So, when they went to the national team, they didn't really have the orchestrators you would need to form successful teams."

Foreign-born players were frequently naturalized as a workaround to satisfy the league quota — a cynical dodge that *could* have served U.S. national team prospects in the near term, but did not. Here is a list of noteworthy Team USA field players, those singled out in contemporary press reports as having scored or otherwise stood out for their NASL and/or international performances during 1975 and 1976, when the U.S. crashed out of qualifying for Argentina '78. Those in bold were naturalized citizens:

Boris Bandov	**Miro Rys**	Bobby Smith
Alex Skotarek	Steve Pecher	**Fred Grgurev**
Mike Flater	**Mark Liveric**	Al Trost
Peter Chandler	**Santiago Formoso**	David D'Errico
	Juli Veee	

We know how poorly these players performed for the USMNT. In the NASL context, few made anything resembling a mark. Trost captained the 1976 USMNT. He was the only American, naturalized or native born, among the NASL's top 20 scorers that year, converting 12 times for his hometown St. Louis Stars. Defender Steve Pecher, the 1976 NASL Rookie of the Year, made the first of 17 career national team appearances that year. The American most elevated by his NASL experience, Denver-born Ricky Davis, did not debut for the USMNT until 1977, as a 17-year-old.

One might reasonably ask why Kyle Rote Jr. is not on this list. Well, he didn't play for the U.S. national team after 1975. Why not? His club, the Dallas Tornado, had invested top dollar in this rare U.S-born skilled player. Obliged to field two North Americans for every minute of every match, the club had little incentive to release such a talented, token American for national team duty — and risk his injury there. Here again we observe how the quota system actually worked directly against Federation and national team interests. Clubs often treated their naturalized American players in similar fashion. In truth, many were naturalized not to bolster the U.S. national team but to meet the NASL quota. As such, clubs had even less incentive to release such players for international duty.

Gene Chyzowych served as USMNT coach from 1973-75 before passing the baton to his brother Walt, who served in that lead role through 1980. "There were times we would be putting our hands over our faces and would want to cry," Gene told *The Seattle Times* in 2013. "We'd say: 'Why did the professional league feel like that? Why can't they release some players?'"

Spare a moment to pity the poor Chyzowych brothers, whose family fled oncoming Nazis in Ukraine during the 1940s, only to have their sons bang their heads against wall after wall, trying to whip their adopted national team (and Federation) into some sort of fighting shape. Gene went first, doubling as U.S. Soccer's director of coaching. Eventually, he couldn't afford to take any more time off from his high school teaching position in New Jersey. Enter brother Walt, whom Gene assisted going forward.

Still, dedication is one thing. Results are another. From 1973 to 1976, the USMNT suffered 12 defeats and posted zero international victories. One wonders how many American NASL players, native born or naturalized, truly wanted to participate in such a derelict, underfunded, hapless national team program. Hungarian-born Juli Veee (born Gyula Visnyei) today lives in San Diego, where he coaches and works as an artist. He starred for the Sockers, indoor and out, through the Seventies and well into the 1980s. Veee was officially capped just four times by his adopted country; he made many more appearances on various U.S. Olympic teams. He told *The San Diego Tribune* that, despite the post-match tradition of swapping shirts with opponents, he doesn't have a single jersey from his Team USA experience. American internationals from that era only got one jersey each, he explained. It was impractical to give it up.

> "Soccer Made in Germany? Oh my god. We loved that show! We lived for those highlights. Growing up, I remember wanting to be Gerd Mueller. Der Bomber! It was on PBS, and we'd tune in once a week on Sundays, I believe. It was the only soccer we could get!"
>
> —*Bruce Murray*

In the summer of 1976, the U.S. played host to the Bicentennial Cup, an international exhibition staged to celebrate the nation's 200th birthday. National team contingents from Brazil, England and Italy participated alongside "Team America," whose name belied its actual roots. Just four native-born Americans were included on the roster: Arnie Mausser and Bob Rigby (both goalkeepers), Bobby Smith, and Hartford Bicentennials defender Peter Chandler, who entered this tournament with three career caps. The remainder included NASL stars of various international extractions. Englishmen Rodney Marsh and George Best committed to play for the home side but pulled out when they weren't guaranteed starting spots. Team America dropped all three matches.

If the World Cup stood strangely aloof from a curious but isolated American soccer public during the 1970s, international club soccer flew even further below the radar. U.S. fans may have known these exotic league competitions existed; they produced the talent that occasionally washed up on NASL shores. But there existed precious few sources of world soccer information, save the odd bar-owned satellite dish, late-arriving subscriptions to *The Sunday Times*, or used copies of the *International Herald Tribune* scooped up in airport lounges. That dire situation changed starting in 1976, with weekly syndication of *All Star Soccer*, a highlight program showcasing the English first division, and *Soccer Made in Germany* (SMG), a similar production focused on the West German *Bundesliga*. Both shows aired on select PBS affiliates nationwide.

"*Soccer Made in Germany*? Oh my god. We loved that show!" Bruce Murray remembers. "We lived for those highlights. Growing up, I remember wanting to *be* Gerd Mueller. *Der Bomber*! It was on PBS, and we'd tune in once a week on Sundays, I believe. It was the only soccer we could get!"

In the Greater Boston market, SMG didn't arrive until the early 1980s, but *All Star Soccer* my family enjoyed from the outset. Each episode delivered a 30-minute highlight package from a single match played a week before, with the inimitable Mario Machado providing oddly detached commentary from a remote studio somewhere in Los Angeles. Wolverhampton Wanderers and their Halloween kits seemed to feature every other week, but we also saw plenty of Nottingham Forest, then at the height of their powers, in England and Europe, under Brian Clough. We luxuriated in the splendid standard of play, the packed stadiums (smartly roofed to protect standing supporters from the ceaseless English rain), the muddy winter pitches, the chanting and singing! Even in low-definition, the television spectacle of English football thrilled us in ways a weekend NASL match did not.

Machado, I've come to learn, was one of the unsung heroes of the Modern American Soccer Movement. He briefly served as the "voice" of NASL coverage on CBS, back in 1968. Through his friend Hans Stierle, Machado helped organize and formalize the American Youth Soccer Organization. Founded in 1964, AYSO eventually grew into the first youth soccer system to operate strictly in the suburbs, and apart from the associations serving urban/ethnic clubs. In 1971, Machado and Stierle prevailed upon AYSO to include girls — beating Title IX legislation to the punch by a full year. From 1976-84, Machado published *Soccer Corner* magazine. In 1981, he served as commissioner of the American Soccer League, the nation's once-and-future second division; he succeeded Bob Cousy, the former Boston Celtic who served rather improbably in that role from 1974-79.

Outside the *All Star Soccer* gig, which Machado produced, we knew nothing of the man's wider involvement in futbol. We did notice that he kept showing up in films, playing the role of a TV broadcaster — in *Brian's Song*, for example. Then in *Oh, God!* He appeared as the newsman Casey

Wong in the original *RoboCop* films. He even did a guest spot on *The Brady Bunch*. His hosting of this soccer show seemed to us oddly meta. In retrospect, however, his career met the moment, as Hubie Vogelsinger's had. Machado passed away in 2013, at the age of 78.

Many in Gen Zero maintain an even softer spot for *Soccer Made in Germany* and its own idiosyncratic host, Toby "Oh, he could have done more with that one!" Charles. Indeed, the charming, retired Welsh futbol commentator enjoys a lasting renown: At last check, his fan club on Facebook boasts 192 followers. Mere mention of the show spurred Tony Meola to blurt out, "Toby Charles! On PBS every Saturday morning! I remember it really well. We couldn't get enough of it. We had the English highlights, too, but *Soccer Made in Germany* was on for a whole hour — that was the only time I came in the house on a Saturday."

Distributed by the German Educational Television Network (GETV), *Soccer Made in Germany* ran stateside for 12 full years and innovated, in this country at least, by highlighting several games each week, even the odd European Cup match. In 1981, Charles & Co. presented the women's German Cup final from Frankfurt, surely the first Americans had seen of organized women's club soccer. A year later, from its New York City studios, GETV produced a daily highlight package from *Espana* 1982. It also sourced the live international feed for that summer's final, the first World Cup final shown live to a U.S. audience. ABC relayed that feed to the populace, periodically abandoning live action to air commercials.

"The '82 World Cup was big because we got to see a few games, and the final. It was pretty exciting to watch all that stuff," Meola reports. "That was my first real exposure to the World Cup. Of course I'd *heard* about it, but we'd never had the chance to *watch* it."

———

As the 1970s drew to a close, American soccer had succeeded in moving beyond the niche, to a distinct, ever-widening, increasingly accommodated space in the U.S. sporting culture. This modest but obvious rise had been fueled by supportive demographics and just enough shrewd organizational moves to outweigh those that fell flat. To paraphrase the immortal Chico Escuela, the decade had been very, very good to U.S. soccer. "The Seventies were a pretty amazing time," Woitalla observes. "I was so fortunate that all this coincided with me being a 6-year-old who just *had* to play soccer. It was fantastic. Then there started being some NASL games on TV, but the ones I recall best were *Soccer Made in Germany*, with Toby Charles — that was the greatest thing ever. A lot of the kids on the '90 team watched those games, too. I moved to Hawaii in '74 and we got *Soccer Made in Germany* there! In my household, that was huge."

My girlfriend and I watched the 1982 final live from her household. As late as 1978, the idea of watching any World Cup match live, on a U.S. network, would have been fanciful to the point of absurdity — as fantastical as Jim McKay calling that game, or the idea that I'd *have* a girlfriend. Two quadrennials later, the no-longer-absurd had given way to several more fantasies made real: a place at *Italia* '90 for the U.S. Men's National Team itself, a squad populated by my peers, with most every tournament match broadcast live in the United States.

In the longer term, however, the ceaseless churn of American culture rarely rewards the niche. We prefer long, inevitable arcs toward preeminence. When the U.S. fails to lead the medal count at any Olympic games, we wonder, *Why the hell not?* Accordingly, as the Reagan era loomed, some were tempted to paint soccer's decade-long ascension as yet another sporting extension of our Manifest Destiny. The demographics were there. High schools and colleges had already mobilized; surely they would effectively serve soccer as informal farm systems, as they already did for other sports. *What could possibly go wrong?*

Only everything, and we should have seen it coming: In August 1979, Farrah Fawcett revealed that she had formally separated from her husband, Lee Majors, *The Six Million Dollar Man* himself. He would never bring that sort of price again. Pelé left the building to great fanfare in late 1977, and his departure hollowed out the league's media presence and fan support in ways that slowly but surely proved disastrous. Franchises picked up and moved with increasing regularity. When the stalwart Rochester Lancers folded in late 1980, its demise sent shudders through the hallways of NASL headquarters in New York City. Average attendance leaguewide wouldn't fall off the table until 1983. However, when just 254 souls showed up to watch my New England Tea Men host the Memphis Rogues on April 28, 1980, the slow ebb had begun. Nearly everything American professional soccer had gained during the 1970s, it would surrender by the spring of 1985.

For the elite players in Gen Zero specifically, this series of failures — competitive, organizational and cultural — engendered a special brand of disillusionment. We rightly exalt these guys today for their perseverance. They graduated directly into this shit storm, weathered it, and still managed to create a new birth of soccer in the United States. Nevertheless, taking them back to the early 1980s to discuss the darkness before the nadir proved, for them, a rather dispiriting task: a bit like discussing the concept of Manifest Destiny with survivors of the Donner Party.

Future USMNT member Chris Henderson confers with a North County United teammate during a Washington State Premier League match, 1981. *(Image courtesy of Chris Henderson)*

Inside *Estadio Azteca*, Nov. 9, 1980: This CONCACAF qualifier — a 5-1 cakewalk for the Mexicans — eliminated their northern neighbors from yet another World Cup. The U.S. starters, from left: Captain Steve Pecher, Winston DuBose, Perry Van der Beck, Ringo Cantillo, Greg Villa, Louie Nanchoff, Angelo DiBernardo, Colin Fowles, Ty Keough, Ricky Davis and Greg Makowski. *(Jon van Woerden photo)*

4. THE PRICE OF EXCEPTIONALISM

(1980 to '83)

In the mind's eye, there exist almost too many on-field images of Marcelo Balboa to synthesize into a single overarching impression. The man played in three World Cups, after all. He debuted at *Italia* '90, at 21, coming on for John Stollmeyer during the first group game. Balboa started the next two matches and would not relinquish his starting place for nine years. When foreign footballing media derided the 1990 U.S. Men's National Team as a collection of "college kids," Balboa would have been Exhibit A. He had left San Diego State only the year before. Even at this tender stage, however, his game exhibited a certain dynamism. Some defenders win the ball because they're stronger in the tackle — Balboa came at opposing attackers with speed as well as strength. He was crazy good in the air. Most centerbacks use the velocity of the oncoming ball to power it back the other way; they don't have the hang time to cock the body back and snap through it — like a striker does, in the box. Balboa had the ups and the timing to perform this duty in his own box, in the opposing box, in the middle of the field, in traffic, on balls served from 60 yards away. I always found it amusing to watch opposing strikers recoil when they sensed Balboa's rising torso bumping up against the back of their heads.

"As defenders, our job is often described as destroying things," notes Bob Gansler, a former defender himself, who just happened to play beside Balboa's dad in the early days of NASL. "Unlike defenders at the time,

Marcelo became very comfortable on ball. He could stop an opponent, but he was as good on the outlet, a good long passer, and could also come forward offensively on a restart."

Luis Balboa played professionally in his native Argentina before conferring upon his American-born son this more technical approach to the art of defending. "His dad didn't move much," Gansler recollects, "but the ball moved for him. His father was an out-and-out midfielder, a ball distributor. And given his druthers, 'Celo probably would have liked to stand at midfield, too, directing things from the center."

Balboa the Younger scored 13 times for his country. However, it's a goal he failed to score that we remember best: his bicycle kick from a corner against Colombia at USA 1994. That volley grazed the near post as it whistled wide. The U.S. won the match anyway, its best-ever World Cup performance, some would argue. But *jeezum crow!* Who knew back in 1994 that an American, a central defender for chrissakes, possessed such technical acumen, bravura and flair?

That moment in particular opened the eyes of the world to what U.S. soccer could be, and what it could already do. It opened American eyes, too. All through the 1990s, Balboa brought this combination of skill, grit, speed and aggression to USMNT back fours, to defensive shapes in the Mexican first division, at Club Leon, and Major League Soccer. And wherever he went, the signature, jet-black mane went with him, in styles from unabashed mullets to simple ponytails to Latin-style fades — but always long and flowing, with some kind of Van Dyke thing going on around the chin. Where had this guy come from, and where had he been all our lives? That's what I remember asking myself in 1990, when Balboa first emerged into the broader American soccer consciousness.

Balboa came from exactly where we'd expect: the uber hotbed of Southern California, where his dad Luis coached his club team, Fram-Culver, until his son graduated from high school in 1985. From 15 to 17, however, Marcelo spent four months out of 12 playing retrograde, kick-and-run soccer amid the largely unskilled player pool at Cerritos High School, where he dodged elbows; where he sat at the knee of coaching figures who knew less about soccer than his aunties back in Argentina; where he attempted to manage the ungainliness endemic to all teenagers.

"I was so socially awkward in high school," Balboa says. "I had a little Pepe le Pew mustache and greased-back hair. I was *not* one of the cool kids wearing the O.P. shorts . . . As for the soccer, it was still the dark ages. No disrespect, but that was true. It's easy to forget this was still a country that barely knew what soccer was."

It's no scandal that Balboa and his peers in Generation Zero did not avail themselves of development infrastructures that did not exist in 1982. Here's the scandal: The international paradigm for how to professionally develop first-rate soccer players, deployed worldwide since the 1950s, would not take hold in America for another 30 years, not until 2012. That's when the U.S. Soccer Federation formalized a sea change in the development model for 15- and 16-year-olds. With its sanctioning of year-round academies, typically but not exclusively attached to Major League Soccer franchises, the Federation finally rescued this country from the developmental dark ages.

———

This slow pace of change, our nearly willful ignorance of what works elsewhere, and our developmental templates born of competing interests and American exceptionalism are part of a long-term pattern. We celebrate American soccer in these pages, but so much of the U.S. soccer experience has flown in the face of established, effective international norms that it's hard to decide exactly which bits have most retarded our progress as a footballing nation. For example, while the rest of the world plays its soccer from August through April, the two national leagues established here during the latter half of the 20th century — including the one we still rely upon — both opted to begin play in the spring and conclude in the fall, primarily to avoid competing with American football. This alternative scheduling, however, has left our soccer culture out of sync with prevailing global systems of transfers, contracts, academy training and tournament planning/participation. The issues persist to this day.

League membership determined by promotion and relegation, a given in so many leagues worldwide, has never caught on in the United States. This system essentially demotes the lowest finishers from upper divisions and promotes top finishers from lower divisions, and so on down through a country's soccer pyramid. Despite being a study in meritocracy, something Americans purport to support, P&R has proved a nonstarter on these shores.

While most of the global futbol community refused to play official matches on artificial turf following its emergence in the early 1970s (FIFA, for many years, did not recognize as "official" any match played on the rug), U.S. futbol culture went for it whole hog.

Because Americans have a reputation for despising draws (though it's actually our mainstream media that most disdains them), NASL refused to allow them. Instead, the league relied on a shootout format, whereby attackers bore in on the goal from 35 yards. MLS did likewise throughout the 1990s, before wisely abandoning this tired, impractical, stubbornly contrary idea.

Finally, and most important, instead of sending 15- and 16-year-old talents to apprentice themselves at academies staffed by professional coaches, American soccer prospects throughout the 1980s were instead shuffled off to high schools, where the game was played only four months out of 12 under the supervision of glorified Soccer Dads. From this entirely suboptimal environment, Generation Zero went off to college, where another substandard developmental system — devised to serve the completely different sports of football and basketball — prevailed.

U.S. soccer's consistent disinterest in what has worked internationally goes a long way toward explaining why this country didn't qualify for a single World Cup between 1950 and 1990. This delinquent attitude toward the state of the art also helps explain what befell U.S. soccer in the early 1980s, when good ol' American exceptionalism met the harsh realities of competing in a world game. We did things our own way, and we paid a bitter price for it.

While grassroots America continued to turn out players in record numbers throughout the Reagan Era, professional soccer in this country disappeared just as members of Generation Zero were embarking on their careers. The expiration of NASL in fall 1984 constitutes yet another bit of exceptionalism that blew up in our faces: In most countries, first-division soccer leagues may blunder or lose money or fail to produce enough quality players for their national teams. But rarely do they simply vanish en masse. Here's where promotion and relegation might have played a pivotal, ameliorative role: First-division clubs may overextend, but ambitious clubs from lower divisions are always ready to replace them.

The collapse of NASL in the mid-1980s, and our inability to effectively replace it for 12 long years, should have doomed U.S. soccer for a generation or two. Instead, the cohort of players most adversely affected by the complete absence of professional outdoor soccer in this country punctuated this impoverished footballing decade by representing their country at *Italia '90.*

In one important respect, the model for elite American youth players today does not differ much from Balboa's day. Just as in 1982, 16-year-olds in 2022 mainly seek the attention of college coaches. "High school soccer back then was the only way that college coaches could see us play," Balboa explains. "They wouldn't go to club games, not back then. It was mostly high school games, so it was very important."

In every other respect, however, player development in the 1980s, outside the Olympic Development Program, proved alarmingly random, even for the cream of the crop.

Consider the case of Balboa's contemporary Tom Dooley. Born in Germany in 1961 to an American military father and a German mother, he became an American citizen in time to play for the U.S. at World Cup 1994, beside Balboa. At age 13, however, Dooley had entered the youth system of Bavarian club TuS Bechhofen. At 20, after seven years of foot-balling apprenticeship, he moved to the amateur side of FK Pirmasens before catching on with third division FC Homburg in 1983. With this decade of institutional, formalized training onboard, and no college de-gree, Dooley would go on to play a decade of first-team football in the *Bundesliga* for Kaiserslautern, Bayer Leverkusen and Schalke 04.

Born in 1967, to immigrant parents in Cerritos, California, Balboa enjoyed a leg up on Dooley, developmentally: His father had been a professional footballer. What's more, Marcelo could play year-round, out-door soccer in sunny Southern California. Try doing *that* in Bechhofen. Yet that's where the advantages fall away, because 'Celo's apprentice-ship consisted of club soccer in his immediate community, four years of high school soccer, and three years of college soccer. As a student at San Diego State, he moonlighted for the San Diego Nomads in the semi-professional Western Soccer Alliance. Prior to joining the San Francisco Bay Blackhawks in the American Professional Soccer League, *after* World Cup 1990, the closest Marcelo Balboa ever got to a professional soccer setting was his stint as ball boy for the NASL's L.A. Aztecs.

"Listen, I didn't even make ODP until I was 18," says Balboa, who today coaches high school and elite club teams in Louisville, Colorado. "At 10 or 11, I had just started AYSO [the American Youth Soccer Organization], like everyone else did in California back then. We were into club soccer, but there wasn't much *travel* soccer — you played in the local area. Like, I have a game tonight in Greeley [Colorado] with my U-17s — that's an hour away. That we did not do in California, not back when I played. Not until we were old enough to play in the State Cup, where you got thrown into a pool and played anywhere you had to go."

The Federation first identified every last man on the *Italia* '90 roster via ODP. That discovery process, however, didn't begin until high school, when a player turned 15, 16, 17 or even 18 years old. Prior to these in-terventions, players were "groomed" on parallel tracks: in a privately administered club environment, and in a clearly substandard, deliberately nonconforming high school environment watered down by competing athletic pursuits, in the American tradition.

"I played club soccer for Fullerton Rangers, then moved over to Fram-Culver, and that's when I think we realized what we were into. That's where things got more serious," Balboa explains. "But I played baseball, too. In California, I could play high school football in the fall, soccer in winter, and baseball in the spring. I was encouraged to play every sport imaginable, to develop as an *all-around athlete*."

The emphasis is mine. Tom Dooley escaped this kind of encouragement. He got the same advice in the 1980s that elite American soccer players get today: *If you're serious about your futbol, forsake the all-around athlete archetype and get thee to a reputable academy setting, post haste.* Indeed, that's the advice Taylor Booth followed, nearly 40 years later. The Eden, Utah, native joined the Real Salt Lake Academy at 15; in January 2019, the young midfielder signed with German super club Bayern Munich. *That* is how aspiring 15- and 16-year-old U.S. soccer prospects should be spending their high school years.

With few exceptions, the elite players of Generation Zero don't place much emphasis on their high school experience, not from a developmental perspective. During those years, the Class of 1990 played concurrently on club teams, and then ODP teams, that offered far more in the way of consistently good competition and coaching. However, each of these elite players *did* play high school soccer for three to four months each fall, to the effective exclusion of all other soccer activities. If they played another high school sport as well, that decision took yet more time away from their futbol-specific maturation. Meanwhile, their contemporaries in mature soccer nations were playing for established coaches at professionalized clubs and academies, all year long.

This state of affairs stunted American soccer development throughout the 1980s and ensuing decades — until 2012, when the USSF finally followed the MLS lead and committed to the formalized academy model. The evolution continues. The current crop of U.S. internationals has taken this apparatus to a more European level — Konrad de la Fuente was 12 when he entered *La Masia*, Barcelona's youth academy. Timmy Weah was 14 when he moved from Queens to join Paris Saint-Germain. Christian Pulisic and Gio Reyna were both 16 when they turned pro with Borussia Dortmund. Brenden Aaronson was 16 when he began playing professionally, with the United Soccer League affiliate of Major League Soccer's Philadelphia Union; at 20, he moved to the Austrian club FC Red Bull Salzburg.

High school soccer simply isn't something that elite prospects bother with today. Ironically, even as high school soccer in the early Eighties starved the nation's elite prospects of suitable coaching and competition, it effectively nurtured the broader soccer culture. Participation in high school soccer boomed during the first Reagan administration, formalizing a vital link in U.S. soccer's broader evolutionary chain.

AS THE DECADE TURNED, THE UNITED STATES soccer establishment found itself going on 30 years without a World Cup appearance. The nation's one reliable source of soccer succor appeared to be the domestic professional game, headlined by the North American Soccer League and buttressed by a youth soccer culture still growing by leaps and bounds. NASL opened Season 13 in the spring of 1980 with 32 teams and, atypically, a plausible veneer of stability. Not one franchise shift had taken place since the 1979 Soccer Bowl.

League attendance in 1980 reached its 17-year high-water mark: an average of more than 15,000 per game. Long accused of representing a pasture for imported has-beens, NASL had nevertheless attracted a host of exciting new foreign talents in their primes for the upcoming season:

✦ Julio Cesar Romero, 21, joined the Cosmos along with fellow Paraguayan international Roberto Cabanas, suggesting, as we've observed in the MLS era, that when the U.S. manages to cobble together a decent domestic league, Central and South Americans tend to benefit asymmetrically.

+ Mexican striker Hugo Sanchez, just 21, joined the San Diego Sockers in 1980, on loan from his native club, UNAM Pumas. He would eventually sign with Atletico Madrid, and then across town at Real, where he'd earn his reputation as the greatest Mexican player in Europe. Sanchez finished his career back in North America with the newly formed MLS in 1996 — but getting Sanchez at 21? A major coup for NASL.

+ Future England striker Mark Hateley, then just 19 years old, played the 1980 season with the Detroit Express, and Peter Beardsley — who would later feature for Newcastle, Liverpool and Everton, and star for England at Mexico '86 — spent 1981-83 with the Vancouver Whitecaps.

According to plan, NASL had also produced for the U.S. Soccer Federation a collection of native and naturalized players to stock USMNT rosters, among them Perry Van der Beck, Boris Bandov, Ricky Davis, Larry Hulcer, Angelo DiBernardo, Mark Liveric, Ringo Cantillo, Winston DuBose, Steve Moyers, Ty Keough and Bobby Smith. With a World Cup two years hence and an Olympic tournament scheduled for the summer of 1980 in the Soviet Union, American expectations were again raised in anticipation of The Breakthrough.

One might fairly ask if any of these names, aside from Keough and Davis, ring a bell. Here's one reason why they probably don't: Both qualifying campaigns came to nothing.

To be fair, this cohort of American soccer talent did in fact qualify for the Olympic tournament — under terribly dodgy circumstances. What happened to the old rival Mexico? It's a long story, but a juicy one: When the Mexicans thumped the U.S. in a home-and-home series to open the final qualifying stage, all seemed lost. Again. But the *Yanquis* successfully petitioned CONCACAF, claiming Mexico had fielded several professionals, still a no-no in Olympic competition until 1984. What were all these American NASL players if not professionals? Well, NASL players appearing for the United States were technically paid only a "stipend" by their respective NASL clubs, a practice then allowed under Olympic rules. Bottom line: The U.S. advanced from the group stage in Mexico's place.

(This episode and dozens more, all of them fomented by long-standing geopolitical and socioeconomic dynamics, peg U.S.-Mexico as world football's Most Fraught Derby — "derby" being an English term denoting a rivalry between neighbors, within a city, or anywhere a border is shared. USA vs. Mexico is not the "best" derby, in terms of quality of play or major tournament impact. But for all the sprawling contexts in which it's been so hotly contested over the past 50 years, it's hard to beat and would make a great book subject someday.)

A pair of subsequent wins over Bermuda presaged rather convincing Team USA performances against Suriname and Costa Rica, including a 1-0 win at the latter's Saprissa Stadium. *Presto and behold*: The Americans had secured their first Olympic berth since 1972.

In the spring of 1980, however, President Jimmy Carter banned U.S. participation at the Moscow Games to protest the Soviet invasion of Afghanistan. Ty Keough, the son of 1950s U.S. soccer legend Harry Keough, had naturally hoped to follow in his dad's footsteps and represent his country at *some* international level, on some stage of consequence. He never got that chance.

"It was a bitter disappointment to not be allowed to go to Moscow," he told journalist Michael Lewis in 2010. Although best known today for his game commentary on ESPN, Ty Keough could play a bit: four-time All-American under dad Harry at Saint Louis University; three years outdoors with the San Diego Sockers; then several more indoors with his hometown Steamers. "Competing at the Olympics," Keough continued, "could have tested and solidified a generation of players already benefiting from the NASL, and perhaps given that group a better level of confidence and cohesion to go into qualifying later that year."

———•◆•———

Alas and alack, the confidence and cohesion of which Keough spoke never materialized during CONCACAF World Cup qualifying staged later in 1980. Rather than building on its shady, fortuitous Olympic near miss, the U.S. wrote yet another shambling, disharmonious, ultimately futile chapter in its long history of tournament disqualification.

Where to begin? Playing once more under Walt Chyzowych, lieutenant Bob Gansler at his side, the U.S. opened final qualifying for *Espana '82* by drawing at home with the Canadians, 1-1, in Fort Lauderdale. With the away fixture and a home-and-home with Mexico still to play, this result proved fairly crushing in itself.

Yet festering internal disputes — over how much U.S. players would/should be paid for international duty — immediately overshadowed the Americans' on-field mediocrity. This impasse had been a recurring theme since the late 1960s, when the formation of NASL recast U.S. footballers as genuine "professionals." This evolution engendered a change in self-image among U.S. players: No matter how badly qualifying might be going, guys representing their country wanted to be paid and treated as "internationals." Considering how demoralizing these qualification campaigns could be, perhaps they considered it a form of combat pay.

By 1980, when the players sought $50 more in their weekly allowance, the Federation countered with a mere $35 bump. Ricky Davis offered to cover the difference by donating the money to the Federation. This offer was declined, and team solidarity grew ever more strained, the rifts allegedly falling along native-born (suck it up and play) and naturalized (we deserve to be paid like full and proper internationals) lines.

A bizarre intervention by Cosmos general manager Krikor Yepremian accented this ill-timed cluster-fuck. Immediately following the draw with Canada, Yepremian showed up in the Fort Lauderdale locker room, demanding that three Cosmos players leave the national team and join the club's exhibition tour of Europe.

(Yes, *that* Yepremian. Krikor, older brother of Miami Dolphins placekicker Garo Yepremian, had arrived on the American sports scene alongside his more famous sibling. He negotiated Garo's first NFL contract with the Detroit Lions. Controversy then followed the colorful, impetuous Cyprian wherever he went. After joining the Cosmos, Krikor once got himself ejected from a media vs. management exhibition match — not for tugging on an opponent's jersey, but for pulling an opponent *to the ground* by his jersey. The source of this info: Cosmos striker Giorgio Chinaglia, writing in *New York* magazine during the summer of 1979.)

In any event, the Cosmos players stayed on with the national team, only to participate in dropping the return leg in Vancouver, 2-1.

But wait, there's more! Awaiting the Yanks in the final home-and-home: a highly motivated Mexican side, still smarting from the Olympic-disqualification episode. *El Tri* ended American hopes with a 5-1 thrashing on Nov. 9, 1980, at *Estadio Azteca*. The U.S. won the return leg 2-1 in Fort Lauderdale two weeks later, a rare but meaningless result. Chyzowych took this opportunity, yet another early dismissal from World Cup consideration, to spill his guts on the dire state of USMNT affairs.

"The whole administration needs to be revamped," he vented to the *Fort Lauderdale News.* "The authoritative body which runs soccer in the country in theory must start doing so in practice. The USSF must start laying down mandates and establishing policies in every league in the United States. If it doesn't do that, we will remain behind the eight ball. We've got to start asserting ourselves, and we need full-time professionals. They can't do this as a sideline and expect the coaches to work miracles."

As 1980 drew to a close, the gears of change were engaged. John Lennon and punk icon Darby Crash died on consecutive days in December. A new U.S. president was inaugurated in January 1981, and 52 Iranian hostages arrived home a few days later. Chyzowych's indelicate remarks effectively closed the book on his Federation career. He'd had enough of this quadrennial exercise in hope-raising, followed by anguished hope-deflation. Conveniently for all parties, the USSF had had enough of him, as well.

This now-familiar cycle of promise and failure would strongly inform the way the USMNT stumbled through a big hunk of the Eighties. Eventually, in spring 1985, the U.S. national team program suffered a complete nervous breakdown, got divorced and moved back in with its parents.

———

Right on cue, late in the 1980 campaign, NASL began to list. That first season of the new decade had been billed as "The Year of the North American Player." This renewed emphasis brought with it immediate change: Three North Americans were now required on the field at all times, not two. Demand for U.S. and Canadian players went up. When Seattle Sounders defender Jimmy McAlister, a former NASL rookie of the year, moved to the Toronto Blizzard, his signing set a record for the transfer of an American player ($200,000). But the new quota only highlighted how few North Americans were fit to play first-division soccer and justify that type of money. Disillusioned, a portion of the league's foreign-born talent went home. The on-field product suffered.

The season-ending Soccer Bowl drew 50,000 to RFK Stadium in Washington, D.C., but TV ratings disappointed the league's broadcast partner. ABC announced it would limit the league's 1981 broadcast schedule to the Soccer Bowl only — a move that signaled the network's clear lack of interest in renewing its contract, set to expire at the close of 1981. With that, the Washington, Rochester and Houston franchises threw in the sponge. The New England Tea Men — my hometown boys, including Mike Flanagan, Gerry Daly, Salif "King" Keita and Kevin "The Cat" Keelan — decamped for Jacksonville, while the Memphis Rogues pulled up stakes and headed for that noted soccer hotbed, Calgary, Alberta, Canada.

The only bright spot in this *annus ridiculus*: the CONCACAF U-20 Cup, from which two Confederation teams would qualify for the 1981 World Youth Championship in Australia. Led by young John Stollmeyer and other ODP alumni, the U.S. hosted this event and rode its home-field advantage all the way to the final, losing to Mexico, 2-0. The squad nevertheless earned one of two Confederation tickets Down Under. Several members of that 1981 U-20 USMNT would go on to professional careers: Mike Menendez and Darryl Gee, for example. But aside from Stolly, they remain largely forgotten among modern American soccer fans. The Breakthrough remained a full generation away.

SOCCER CHANGED THE STATUS QUO AT U.S. high schools during the early 1980s, just as the game and Title IX together had changed the youth sports equation a decade before. In both cases, Generation Zero stood astride the transformation. Its sheer numbers in many ways *created* the tipping point. According to Andrei Markovits and Steven Hellerman in *Offside: Soccer and American Exceptionalism*, 115,811 boys registered to play in soccer programs at American high schools in 1976-77. Complemented by 11,534 registered girls, the total came to 127,345. By 1980-81 — just five years later, but exactly when children of the Seventies arrived in high school — the combined total had climbed to 190,495. By 1996-97, the figure had grown to 523,223.

Simply put, Markovits and Hellerman write, *by the end of the 20th century, soccer had become an integral part of the athletic scene of American high school life, transforming itself from an exotic and marginal activity to a normal option on an increasingly diversified menu. Perhaps the most significant of all the data for the game's immense growth … pertains to the number of registered soccer coaches in the country: In 1941 there were the 10 who founded the National Soccer Coaches Association of America. By 1960 their number had increased to 400; in 1980, it was 2,300, and by 1997 it had ballooned to 14,650.*

Not all coaches join national associations like the NSCAA. So those figures were likely to be much higher. Not that anyone would want to play for 90 percent of those coaches.

"High school soccer? A total wasteland," Bruce Murray opines. "The coach at my high school would only play seniors. I was like, 'You're kidding me, right? I'm banging in goals for Montgomery United and we're winning national championships. And you're playing this guy ahead of me?' Look, I was young and hotheaded. This was my first experience with a 'political' situation and I didn't handle it great. But I did quit. I was getting great coaching from John Kerr Sr."

Like Murray, we Pilgrims showed up at Wellesley Senior High School and couldn't quite believe the varsity team was led by "Physical" Phil Davis, an ornery, soccer-ignorant, 65-year-old gym teacher. Davis hailed from another era — another planet. When he took over the brand-new Wellesley High soccer program, in 1969, he'd never played the game in his life. Assisting Physical Phil and serving as junior varsity coach: a younger, more reasonable fellow named Peter Loiter, who'd come to the Wellesley schools in 1969, directly from Springfield College, a place well known for turning out qualified coaches of all stripes.

"I student-taught in Wellesley and I'm there, the first day, and Bud Hines, the athletic director, comes to me and says, 'We need a JV soccer coach.' I had never played soccer," Loiter recalls, "but Hines could not have cared less about soccer. He was a hockey and football guy. He thought soccer was for little pantywaists and such. This was 1969. So, he said to me, 'I'll pay you 450 bucks.' So I said, 'I'm in!'

"At the very beginning I took this soccer coaching course because, you know, I didn't know anything. When I first started with the JVs, I had a book in my hand. My first soccer practice ever! It was actually a wonderful book written by this guy who'd been an English national team coach." Loiter is referring to Charles Hughes, author of *Soccer Tactics and Teamwork* and *The Football Association Book of Soccer Tactics and Skills*.

"So, none of us knew anything. The kid who took our penalty shots that first year hit them with his toe. He was a junior, a really good athlete — he may have been the hockey captain — and every one of his PKs were side panel. I wasn't going to try and change him because I didn't have the skill set to even *try* and change him. At that time, most of the high schools in our Bay State League didn't have enough actual soccer players to have decent varsity teams throughout the league. Not even close. Well, thanks to the Ray Copelands of the world, Wellesley did. Soon enough, Wellesley had hundreds of kids who had started playing soccer when they were little kids."

After my year with Loiter on the JV, Davis retired and Loiter graduated to the varsity — alongside myself and all the Pilgrims who didn't go off to private school. This group hadn't just played soccer before: We were legit soccer natives. We had toured multiple continents, kicking ass and taking names. (That is, until we ran into those juggernauts from Maryland and Virginia.) Along with three senior luminaries from the class ahead of ours, we won a state championship my junior year. The Wellesley High girls won it all the following year. As it had done at the club level during the 1970s, the Wellesley chapter of Generation Zero cemented our suburban high school as a state soccer power.

"We made the transition in your era. We went from having kids who wanted to play but just weren't there yet to your group," Loiter says. "You really were soccer players when you showed up in high school. Today, of course, they're at a higher level still. Of all the eras I was there, though, I think your group played well into adulthood more than any other. I just think it was a group that really loved the game. It actually became part of the fabric of who you guys were. I think it's part of what made the team good and made the game advance so greatly in those years."

Our collective Wellesley experience proved a microcosm of what eventually transpired at high schools all across the country. By 1982, soccer had started to matter because, by that time, suburban schools especially were overflowing with youth soccer revolutionaries. With every passing year, it mattered more. We in Generation Zero weren't just the tipping point. We were the tip of the spear.

———

Today, Peter Loiter lives on Cape Cod. He retired in 1992, after winning a second state soccer title for Wellesley High. Were it not for that $450 coaching stipend in 1969, and pure generational happenstance, Loiter might never have had any real contact with the game. Such was the haphazard circumstance of coaching placement and caliber when Generation Zero arrived in American high schools.

"I think I was a good coach," Loiter says today, "but I don't know that I could succeed today without a background in soccer. At the beginning I wasn't a good soccer coach. And there were a lot of guys like me who, when it came to soccer, didn't know their ass from a hole in the ground. But they had started teaching and some school needed a soccer coach. Then it's like a lot of things: You get the job and some guys work hard at it and others don't. I like to think I did work hard, and I did OK. But not everyone was lucky enough to have a job in a town like Wellesley where soccer was important."

We can reasonably attach relevant zero-sum qualities to Markovits and Hellerman's high school coaching numbers above. When players and coaches choose soccer, they choose *not* to participate in another sport that season. This redistribution of high school athletes (and coaches), starting in the 1980s, incited yet another backlash from the establishment. As broadly popular as soccer had become during the 1970s, pressure from peers and adults to abandon the game for more traditionally American sports had not abated.

"Forget the Eighties: I get people *today* saying soccer players are a bunch of pussies," Balboa maintains. "I remember one girl I was dating in high school basically told me I should just give up on soccer because it wasn't cool, and I was never going to be able to make a living playing soccer anyway. And that was powerful because in a way, that was the same thing everyone *else* was saying at the time. It was normal behavior. They'd say, 'Why you playing soccer? You dribble the ball with your damned feet? Why aren't you playing football, or baseball? Those are *American* sports!' People just didn't get it."

In California, American football (a fall sport) didn't even compete directly for athletes with futbol, a winter sport. But it made not the slightest difference. In most places, including my own hometown, football remained top cultural dog.

According to *Soccer America*'s Mike Woitalla, "It wasn't just that soccer was still new in the Eighties. It was *other*. When I played soccer in high school, in Hawaii, we got a bit of attention. But when I became the kicker on the football team? All of a sudden I was a minor celebrity! Thirty thousand people at these football games — in Hawaii! Soccer was getting there, you know . . . but there were still a lot of people who didn't understand it or even know about it."

Kent James, a lifelong player and fan (b. 1961), got hooked on the game in a Winston-Salem, North Carolina, rec league, but he didn't play organized soccer until his family moved and enrolled him at a private high school in Louisville, Kentucky: "My father always thought soccer was a 'sissy sport,'" he says. "He was disappointed I was not playing football, but he finally came to one of our games. I got knocked out. Took an inadvertent elbow to the face, though I have no recall of the event. My father was a surgeon, and he came down to examine me. Thought I was fine. No concussion protocols then! I got back into the game and scored the winning goal. The next day the newspaper had a picture of me lying on the ground with blood streaming down my face. My father never called it a sissy sport again."

Well into the 1980s, high school boys required an element of independence to stay with soccer as their fall sport. This dynamic was especially true in the country's northern tier, where soccer and football went head-to-head for athletic talent. In the spring, it took a certain independence of spirit to prioritize club soccer over Babe Ruth or American Legion baseball.

What allowed Gen Zero boys to choose soccer in the 1970s and stay with it during the early 1980s, through this negatively reinforcing high school atmosphere? Iconoclasm played outsized roles. What's more, the game *kept* nonconforming kids, often permanently, on account of the *freedom* individuals felt on the field of play. Soccer is a maverick's dream. No other team sport is played so free of in-game coaching and/ or adult supervision — supervision that, in the experience of Generation Zero, could often prove hostile, indifferent or ignorant. For an already self-selected group of recusants, this brand of on-field autonomy only reinforced the urge to thumb our noses at the establishment.

———•———

Those reactionaries who derided soccer in the Seventies and Eighties did possess one unassailable point: Soccer was indeed played by girls and boys alike. Rarely on the same teams back then, but this coeducational reality, along with our short pants and knee socks, proved central to their attempts to peg our sport as unmanly and suspect. Their attempts failed: "Shaming" us into eschewing soccer, so as to protect our pending manhood, only produced the opposite effect. Under such conditions, the embattled, rebellious, immediately post-pubescent American male typically digs his heels in deeper. What's more, the fact that girls were so integral to our nascent soccer culture — they had started out right there beside us, on their own U-10 teams — turned out to be a social boon, the likes of which many of us could not have otherwise engineered.

For the socially stunted, soccer provided our only meaningful contact with the female species, up to and including high school. When we walked out to soccer practice, there they were. When we emerged from the locker room afterward, voila! There they were again. By the dozen. We even had something in common to chat about, something most of them found far more interesting than geeky stuff like Star Wars or video games (*The Empire Strikes Back* was released and *Pac-Man* first focus-group-tested on consecutive days in May 1980.) These synergies produced a fairly elegant social equation: boys' soccer team + girls' soccer team = party. Not just a party, but a near-perfect 1:1 party composition with at least one surefire, default subject of mutual interest.

Because this book focuses relentlessly and unapologetically on the boys' and ultimately the men's game — how and why the USMNT finally matured after decades of international futility — it doesn't devote much space to the women's game. There are reasonable explanations for this narrative choice.

Because the Youth Soccer Revolution took hold in the early 1970s, its initial impact predated the ongoing impact of Title IX, the landmark 1972 legislation mandating equal access to federally funded amenities. As a result, to cite just one example, while Wellesley High founded the boys' varsity soccer program in 1969, it did not offer girls' varsity soccer until the fall of 1977. Lauren Gregg, a U.S. Women's National Team pioneer and the sister of fellow Pilgrim David Gregg, graduated from WHS in spring 1978, so she didn't have a chance to play high school soccer until her senior year. Nearly every aspect of the women's game was similarly later in coming: The NCAA did not conduct a women's collegiate championship until 1982 (the first men's championship was held in 1959). The University of North Carolina claimed that very first national title, with Lauren Gregg at left back. She had first gone off to Lehigh University in Bethlehem, Pennsylvania, in the fall of 1978, only to discover there was no women's soccer program there. At all. She played on the men's JV for two years before transferring to Chapel Hill. The women's national team program didn't get started until 1985, when the U.S. Soccer Federation hired Mike Ryan to field and train a roster of collegiate players to represent the U.S. at the *Mundialito*, a tournament event held in Italy and not sanctioned by FIFA. Six years later, under former UNC coach Anson Dorrance, the U.S. won the first FIFA Women's World Cup.

Laurie Gregg was formally capped just once by her country, in 1986. By then, she was the varsity coach at the University of Virginia. She would also assist in coaching the USWNT from 1989-2000, so she witnessed and influenced the program's storied run to preeminence. And that is the point: From their belated beginnings, American women claimed a place among the world futbol elite almost immediately. It is a position they have not relinquished. Compared to that of the men's national team, theirs is a different kind of story altogether, a more triumphant one, a story of immediate, world-beating success. It's also a book that has been written already, several times over.

———•·•·———

The arrival and maturity of premier and academy systems, along with their like in other sports (AAU basketball, for example), have all contributed to the deconstruction of America's traditional three-sport model. Indeed, if the academy approach works as it's intended to work, elite soccer players today don't play high school soccer at all. In the 21st century, the failure to specialize would feel developmentally primitive. Back in the early 1980s, however, our thoroughly American, multi-sport mindset didn't seem backward — not to us. The U.S. turned out the best athletes in the world, or so we were told. That was the American exceptionalist conceit. All those Jack Armstrong types who won Olympic decathlon medals or played professional football or basketball or baseball: They had *all* grown up playing multiple sports. What's more, the high-school-to-college-to-professional route seemed to be working just fine in every other sporting context we knew. Accordingly, talented athletes played multiple high school sports throughout the 1980s. Steve Trittschuh entertained the idea of professional baseball. Tony Meola attended the University of Virginia on a dual soccer and baseball scholarship.

"I played American football along with soccer," says Marcelo Balboa. "My brother was the kicker and I was the punter. He played his first year on the varsity and I guess I played JV. It was there that I realized I wasn't really a football player.

"The coach said we had to play two positions. I said, cool: punter and kicker. He said, 'No. What position do you play in soccer?' I said, sweeper. He said, 'That's kinda like free safety. Why don't you try that?' One of the first few games we played, I intercepted the ball, ran it down the sideline and got lit up like there is no tomorrow. I mean, lit UP! Didn't see the guy. I was sitting on the ground saying, 'What the hell am I doing?' So I intercepted another one, didn't see the guy again, and got hit even worse! This was back in 1983, and those helmets were huge and bulky and you couldn't see anything. I told the coach I was not into it after that. And he said, 'Well, I think punter and kicker is two positions.'

"In a lot of ways, high school soccer was awesome for me. My brother played with me. He was more technical than I was. He would find a way around a wall and I would run through the wall to get the ball. So, the coach decided to play me at forward. He says, your brother and Enrique — we had another guy with some skill, Enrique — they're gonna knock it past and you're gonna run after it. That was our level of sophistication, the sophistication of our coaching. I didn't care. I was gone! Scoring goals left and right. I thought, *Damn, I'm a forward now!* I had a great time.

"But I remember one game in particular, against our big rival, Gahr High School. I had scored already, and the [Gahr] coach sends out this kind of enforcer dude. You could see the coach say, 'Go mark him.' So I go up to head a ball and he waits for me on the ground. Doesn't jump, just waits there and plants an elbow — just throws it *upward* and smashes my whole jaw. Broke it, fractured everything. So, that was my high school experience. That sums it up right there."

BORN IN FEBRUARY 1969, GOALKEEPER TONY Meola is one of the youngest members of the 1990 USMNT. By the time he entered high school, most of his future teammates had already made themselves known to Federation talent scouts via the Olympic Development Program. Some Kearny boys had even played in a U-20 World Cup. "Early on we had guys like Harkes, Tab [Ramos] and Kris Peat — another goalkeeper at the time — who all of a sudden got called into youth national teams," Meola recalls. "Right away, *that* became everybody's goal."

Most of Gen Zero graduated from high school in the early to mid-1980s. They "finished" their schoolboy soccer educations by making the leap from state teams, organized under ODP, to regional teams competing at the U.S. Olympic Festival. The Federation chose its U-20 national teams from this specific player pool.

"The first time I became aware of all these guys in our age group was the Olympic Festival my sophomore year, like 1984-85 — somewhere in there," recalls Trittschuh, by then enrolled at Southern Illinois University at Edwardsville. "In that era, in the Midwest, we had some good players, but the South team had Windischmann, Tommy Kain and Bruce Murray. The West team had [David] Vanole and Paul Caligiuri. I had *heard* of some of these guys and played against a few of them in college, but that's when I first saw them up close, in one place. I was impressed. But at the same time, I was like, 'Hey, I'm on the same level.'"

"I met the majority at the 1983 U.S. Olympic Festival," says defender Paul Krumpe. "So, that would have been Colorado Springs, the first one I was invited to. We played against each other as regional teams, and the national team coach at the time would pick his best players from each of those regional teams to form national youth teams. So, we played with and against each other in a lot of those situations, way prior to our joining the senior national team in '86 and '87."

Having eschewed the high school game altogether, Bruce Murray luxuriated in the coaching he received while playing for Montgomery United, what amounted to an academy/premier club 20 years ahead of its time. But he happily availed himself of ODP and the Festivals as well.

"With John Kerr Sr. at the controls, we knew we were getting great coaching," Murray says. "We'd go play UNC, the University of Tampa, Clemson — as a club team. And we'd get results! But I was an ODP player in Maryland, too. My mom and dad would drive us over to ODP practice in Baltimore or Columbia [Maryland] with John Ellinger, the first coach of the Nike training academy that produced Landon Donovan and Freddy Adu. That's how I got my start. Then I got invited to some regional events where I met Tab [Ramos], [John] Harkes, Windischmann and Sadri Gjonbalaj — now *there's* a name some folks might remember.

George Tarantini was our coach. That's where the core of our group all started playing together."

⸻

As it happened, the rise of the ODP and the Festival movements paralleled the rise of international youth football competitions globally. Various U-19 and U-20 tournaments had been organized by individual football confederations since the 1950s. CONCACAF followed suit in 1962. But full-on, intercontinental competitions were not conceived and executed until the late 1970s, during the reign of FIFA president Joao Havelange. The Brazilian had his faults — clear tendencies toward autocratic and corrupt behavior among them — but he proved a dedicated and effective expansionist. Havelange enlarged the senior World Cup from 16 to 32 teams. Later, he would lay a foundation for the Women's World Cup and Confederations Cup. Just three years into his term, in 1977, he saw to the launch of a biennial FIFA World Youth Championship.

The inaugural competition, in Tunisia, proved something of a sun-baked debacle. Take heed: Do not fight a land war in Asia, and don't schedule a summer futbol tournament in North Africa. The next event, however, proved a sensation, as it pulled the curtain back on an 18-year-old Argentine phenom named Diego Armando Maradona. Not since Pelé dominated the 1958 World Cup at age 17 had such a young player seized the attention of world football.

Prior to 1977, the USSF maintained a U-20 national team, but aside from participating in the CONCACAF youth competition, the Federation didn't quite know what to do with it. The biennial nature of Havelange's new creation provided national federations something to continually point to and prepare for — precisely what national player development requires. The tournaments themselves gathered all the best young players from around the world in one place. Talent scouts at rich clubs especially could not contain their excitement.

These global initiatives also introduced the USSF to a young Scot named Angus McAlpine, whom the Federation hired in 1975 to coach the U-20s. McAlpine had played in the Scottish first and second divisions, to no particular distinction, but upon earning his coaching license from the Scottish F.A., he decamped for Atlanta in 1968. Three years later he was coaching director at Georgia Soccer, a new umbrella group organizing amateur activities across the state. By '73 he'd earned his C-, B- and A-level coaching licenses from the Federation. He'd also signed on to coach the Atlanta Metros in the second-division American Soccer League.

In time, McAlpine and his thick Glaswegian burr would make themselves intimately known to Generation Zero, but there remained many rivers to cross. His first two attempts to qualify the U.S. for the U-20 World Cup ended in elimination losses to Honduras. From 1980 to 1981, he served as the NASL's director of player development — a position that probably left him twiddling his thumbs much of the time, given the league's low-grade emphasis on grooming young talent. Meanwhile, it was senior national team coach Walt Chyzowych who qualified the junior national team for its first U-20 World Cup, the 1981 edition in Australia. Stollmeyer and his teammates earned a point against Qatar there, but dropped lopsided decisions to Poland and Uruguay.

By 1982, McAlpine had returned to the Federation in the same role. This time, bolstered by the likes of Paul Caligiuri, Kris Peat, Hugo Perez, Tab Ramos, Jeff Duback and Jeff Hooker (all of whom had earned national team places by virtue of their eye-catching performances on state, regional and Olympic Festival teams), McAlpine qualified the Americans for the 1983 U-20 World Cup finals in Mexico.

Safe passage had not come easily. After the U.S. defeated host Guatemala in the Confederation semifinal, a security detail assigned to the Americans never showed up, for perfectly innocent reasons, of course. Local fans rushed and rocked, but never breached, the team bus. The Yanks again fell to Honduras, 1-0, but *Los Catrachos* were subsequently disqualified for using overage players. The U.S. advanced, and Generation Zero prepared to represent its country at a FIFA event for the first time.

However messily it may have been procured, this event proved a massive breakthrough for this young cohort of players, for McAlpine himself, and for the U.S. Soccer Federation. The qualification further validated the ODP approach, while the nervy match and post-match experience in

Guatemala blooded a bunch of Gen Zero lads in the vagaries of away fixtures in the wild and wooly confines of CONCACAF. Allow me to create and define here an apt coinage that shall come in handy as our story continues:

CONCACAFkaesque, adj., *bewilderingly dodgy, corrupt or otherwise substandard; slightly embarrassing but nevertheless compelling; descriptive of match management, field conditions, stadium security and/or administrative ethics as rendered by game officials, futbol fans, federations and/or confederations in Central America and the Caribbean; as in,* The U.S. U-20 experience in Guatemala was predictably CONCACAFkaesque.

———••——

Twenty-first-century types may struggle to grasp just how modestly the USSF operated at this time. When McAlpine led his U-20 charges to Mexico, he was one of only three coaches employed by the Federation. Manfred Schellscheidt was hired earlier in 1983 to coach the U.S. Olympic team, a group of 20-something amateurs that included John Stollmeyer. Alex Panagoulias had also been hired in 1983. He served as the ostensible USMNT coach, though he spent most of his time leading Team America, an all-U.S. professional side then competing in NASL.

McAlpine made three. With such a small staff, however, he also showed up in Princeton, New Jersey, when Tom Wadlington and several other Wellesley Pilgrims arrived at the 1983 Olympic Development Program camp for Region 1, which stretched from Maine to Virginia. For Wad, Peter Geddes, Alex Carrillo and Tom Beckedorff, this weeklong adventure would prove a brush with greatness. For the likes of Bruce Murray and Tab Ramos, it initiated a collaboration that would peak eight years later in Italy.

"The Mass U-19 team we all played on for two seasons ranked only behind the teams from Maryland and Virginia in Region 1," Wad recalls. "One of our best showings was taking the Region 1 select team with Tab Ramos, Bruce Murray and John Kerr Jr. into halftime 1-1. Their coach, Angus McAlpine, gave them a proper bollocking for being outhustled. We could hear his thick accent all the way across the field. They came out fired up and beat us, 3-1."

Wadlington was a first-rate player, as were Geddes and Beckedorff. Carrillo might have been the finest player that Wellesley ever produced. "That summer at Princeton, Alex got picked for the Region 1 camp with some guys who made the U.S. National Team," Wad reports. "But he was blackballed for being one of two guys who went from cabin to cabin spraying some fire extinguisher — as a prank." What about the other guy? "It was George Gelnovatch, already a well known commodity. He was *excused*." Good thing: Gelnovatch would score a crucial goal for his country in Mexico, only a couple months later.

When the elite players of Gen Zero first came together at ODP regional camps like these, each brought to the party a hometown experience, a club experience, a high school and college experience, and a particular regional perspective.

"That first ODP season, when I was 18," Balboa remembers, "we went and made regionals, then went to Colorado Springs to play the Festival. The national team coach was supposed to be there — the U-20 coach. Well, he didn't show up! They ended up videotaping all the games and picking the U-20 national team off that video! Well, they didn't pick the team *off the video*; they picked the team they knew already, a bunch of guys from the East Coast."

"The phrase I remember hearing was 'East Coast Mafia,'" Brian Bliss reports. "[Bob] Gansler and Walt Chyzowych coined it, because we had such a good core of guys coming up through the system, a core that ended up forming the bulk of the national team, as well."

"I was surprised they didn't pick me," Balboa continues, "because, as a defender, I scored three goals in that tournament — and we [the West Regional team] *won* the tournament. But they didn't know who I was. Then they switched the U-20 coach, brought in Derek Armstrong. Being a West Coast, SoCal guy, Derek knew me, saw me play and gave me a chance. From that day, I was a starter with the U-20s — captain eventually, with Lucas Martin, another guy from UCLA. That kind of made my career. We had Danny Pena on that team. Who else: Tony Meola, Jeff Agoos. I got a picture on my wall. Let me go look at it . . . Eddie Henderson!"

Balboa had just turned 22 when he arrived at the World Cup in 1990. He and his teammates Meola and Eric Wynalda were the youngest members of Generation Zero who played in Italy. By the time they filtered through ODP, the program was better established, more comprehensive in scope, and more competitive than it had been in 1982-83, when most of the *Italia* '90 roster got discovered.

"The first time I got noticed was at New Jersey ODP, back when ODP was really the *only* pathway to the national team. I got cut," Meola recollects. "Next time I made it all the way to national camp in Colorado; that was the goal. But I got cut from that team, too. Then I got cut from the U-17s, then from the U-19s going to the U-20 World Cup in Chile [1987]. I was the last cut for the 1988 Olympic team, and by that time I'd had enough. I was on the verge of pursuing the baseball thing. Then Bruce Arena came down and saw me play and I went to UVA on a dual scholarship — and that's when things took off for good.

"But it was never easy, none of it. I think growing up in Kearny prepared me for it, though. I learned, we all learned, a lot of lessons from that town — lessons that we took all the way to Italy."

"Growing up," Trittschuh says, "I never played ODP because I was always playing baseball in the spring. I was a sophomore in college before I met any of the guys at the Festival. You know, I was fortunate because I went to Southern Illinois and we used to play Wisconsin-Milwaukee every year. [Bob] Gansler coached that team. So he sort of knew me already. I'm sure he had a lot to do with bringing me into the Olympic Festival my sophomore year. That would have been 1984-85, in Baton Rouge. That's when I started seeing these guys up close."

First impressions, upon being dropped into the petri dish with a bunch of similarly elite players from across the country? "Honestly, I guess that's when I thought I could really make a living at this," Trittschuh says. "At the time, just starting college, you're just thinking, 'Maybe I can go play for the Steamers indoors'! I didn't think of it in terms of 'The National Team,' not at that time. As things progressed, you raised your sights."

Preconceived notions based on regional reps and college pedigrees eventually gave way to athletic and communal realities. Ever so slowly, a team identity took shape. According to Balboa, "It was a good mix actually. The East Coast guys, well, you know what? It was the way those guys handled themselves. That's what I remember. Their personalities, their confidence in who they were. I think that was the difference between us California guys: We were more laid-back. But the Jersey guys, the East Coast guys, were just so confident, so outspoken.

"You want your midfielders, Harkes and Ramos, to be a little more vocal because they're on the ball, moving, trying to organize. The West Coast boys were a bit more laid-back in comparison. It wasn't a different style of play necessarily. I think every person, in every position, had a different way of playing. If you look at the group over time, little by little, the way it meshed — we all ended up playing the same style.

"But it did start out being divided at the Festivals, not just because of the regional thing but because you're there on one of four different teams. You tend to eat and sit and hang out together with your own team."

———•———

At the 1983 World Youth Championship finals in Mexico, playing for U-20 national team coach Angus McAlpine, Gen Zero took these inchoate kernels of team identity and cohesion to the international stage. The squad impressed where very little had been expected, as would become its custom. The experience also served to forge a single team from disparate, regional parts. In the opener against a strong Uruguayan side, the Americans dropped a 3-2 heartbreaker — after falling behind 2-0. Two days later in Puebla, the Yanks stunned a favored Ivory Coast team 1-0, posting the first U.S. victory at a FIFA competition since the famous 1-0 decision over England in 1950.

Defender George Gelnovatch — he who escaped culpability following the Princeton fire extinguisher incident, and who succeeded Bruce Arena in 1996 as coach at the University of Virginia — netted the winner against the Africans. He tucked home a rebound on 79 minutes, following a Hugo Perez free kick. What had been a tetchy encounter up to that point soon became downright ugly. This match proved the coming-out party for Tab Ramos, then just 16 but something of a revelation as a possessive, attacking, creative force in the center of midfield. Such players tend to draw malevolent attention at the international level. He soon went down with a broken nose. Later, the ref himself got punched in the face. The Ivorians finished with nine men.

Impressively, Ramos still played the full 90 but missed the final group fixture, again in Puebla, where a point against Poland would have seen the Yanks through to the knockout phase. As we'll see in later chapters, it's mighty difficult to advance at the international, tournament level when only a draw is required. Absent their newly minted midfield general, an inert American side surrendered a pair of late goals and bowed out, 2-0.

Unlike senior World Cups, the U-20 championship is held every two years. In 1985, the U.S. team failed to qualify. By that time, much of Gen Zero had aged out of ODP and left the youth national team behind. Mike Windischmann had already been integrated into Alex Panagoulias' senior national team. Rangy, unflappable, precociously comfortable playing inside or outside — in the diamond back four then in vogue — Windy earned his first senior cap as a 17-year-old in the spring of 1984. When Gansler named him captain of the USMNT in 1989, prior to *Italia* '90 qualification, the move surprised no one. It had been coming for five years.

Paul Caligiuri, David Vanole and Paul Krumpe were all enrolled at UCLA in the fall of 1983. This trio supplied the laid-back West Coast vibe to which Balboa referred — but only to a point. Vanole, a big man with a personality to match, would hold down No. 1 national team goalkeeping duties from 1986-1989. By the spring of 1985, Caligiuri, too, was playing alongside Windischmann and John Kerr Jr. under Panagoulias.

"I remember Sigi being frustrated with Paul during that time because he was clearly a defender of some kind," Krumpe recalls, referring to Siegfried Schmid, their coach at UCLA. "But at the start of our senior year, Cal made a point of saying he didn't want to play defense any more. Basically Sigi put him up top and let him go — it didn't work out very well. Sort of a turning point for Cal, I think. He kinda realized, 'I'm a good player but I need to play in the back.' He was such a talent, but he needed to accept the fact that he wasn't gonna be the guy scoring all the goals. He could see how effective he was with truly skilled midfielders playing in front of him. Guys like Harkes and Tab."

Of course, Caligiuri remains pretty famous for at least one goal he *did* score.

For the elite core of Generation Zero, the path during the early 1980s was clear and obvious: college ball, followed by a career in the NASL. Stollmeyer was already a force at Indiana, while Bruce Murray headed further south, to Clemson. Steve Trittschuh stayed close to home, choosing SIU, while Peter Vermes did a year at Loyola in Baltimore, before returning home to Rutgers. Brian Bliss settled in at Division II heavyweight Southern Connecticut State.

Among the Kearny boys, Tab Ramos and John Harkes had each forced their way into the national player pool at precisely the same time, participating in several Festivals before heading to college with the rest of their new cohort. Ramos left for N.C. State in the fall of 1984. He was obliged to reassess his career path almost immediately: NASL closed its doors that November, never to reopen them. Harkes observed this disruption as a senior in high school and then lit out for the University of Virginia in the fall of 1985.

College quickly came to dominate the young lives of this golden generation, on field and off. Save for summer camps and tournaments, they largely went their separate ways. When Generation Zero next formally reassembled, in early 1986, fate and another World Cup qualification failure conspired to drop the U.S. senior national team in their collective lap. This abrupt torch passing had not been planned. Luckily, in many important ways, the squad had already been formed, back in 1983. On field and off.

"I was known as a *bit* of a wise guy, but Harkes, Murray and Bliss? Always clowning around," Windischmann says. "We had all become good friends, but every time you got good news, you had to confirm it because you didn't know if it was Harkes or Bliss on the other end of the phone. When I got the phone call about the National Soccer Hall of Fame, I made three more phone calls — just to make sure it was true . . . In 1985, that *happened* to Jeff Hooker. They called him up and told him he'd been drafted in the first round of MISL [Major Indoor Soccer League], and Jeff told his whole family! Turned out it wasn't true. Jeff had to call them all back. That was ongoing, stuff like that.

"Harkes actually got busted pretty good one time by Angus. John used to do the accent, because Harkes is Scottish himself. Angus had a thick, thick accent. So, Harkes went to the restroom and he thought I was in one of the other stalls. In this thick Scottish brogue, he was like, 'Mikey, are you in there?' But it wasn't me in the stall. It was Angus. Coach gave him some serious running after that."

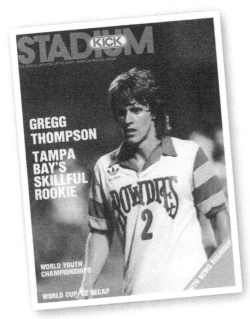

U.S. defender Gregg Thompson, too old to participate in the 1983 World Youth Championships, was NASL Rookie of the Year for 1983. By the middle of 1985, he played exclusively indoors. *KICK Magazine* was the official NASL game program. It published as *Stadium KICK* for the 1983-84 season. *(Jon van Woerden photo)*

Team America midfielder Pedro DeBrito tangles with Fort Lauderdale's Brian Kidd at RFK Stadium in Washington, D.C., June 1983. *(Jon van Woerden photo)*

5.   COLLEGE BOYS & OTHER BRIGHT IDEAS

(1983 to '84)

The North American Soccer League and the U.S. Soccer Federation had, from the league's birth in 1967, coexisted as partners. This arrangement remains quite standard in soccer-serious countries around the world, which is to say, most everywhere in the world. There are 195 sovereign, United Nations-recognized states on planet Earth; FIFA recognizes 211 states and otherwise autonomous regions as members. In any case, from country to country, domestic first-division leagues and futbol associations routinely rely upon and navigate the symbiotic relationships between club and country together. In the spring of 1983, NASL and the Federation stood side by side at a major crossroads. In 18 months, the Summer Olympics would visit Los Angeles, California. The U.S. qualified automatically as host, but who exactly would represent the United States on that team? Directly following the L.A. games, qualification for World Cup 1986 would begin. How should NASL and the Federation best prepare that squad to compete for the coveted, long-elusive CONCACAF berth?

Everyone in the American soccer establishment recognized the shaky financial ground on which NASL stood in 1983. They also recognized how poorly NASL-fed national teams had fared in previous international competitions and qualification tournaments. Despite consecutive strong showings from the American U-20 national team at World Youth Championships in 1981 and 1983, neither the Federation nor interested parties at NASL were prepared to hand the fate of American soccer to a bunch of kids just finishing high school and headed off to college. Not yet. Instead, they quite reasonably focused their hopes, dreams and day-to-day efforts on the more mature Americans then coming into their professional primes in the North American Soccer League.

Still, how could they best prepare this generation of players for the high-stakes challenges that lay ahead? More conservative members of the USSF rightly recognized the improvement in the number and quality of young American players, thanks to the advent of the Olympic Development Program (from 1978) and an overall upgrade in the sophistication of American college soccer. NASL had produced and/or naturalized several players of quality since the last quadrennial. Stay the course, they argued.

A more radical faction within the Federation and NASL was determined to change the way young players were professionalized in NASL itself. The league had developed several stalwart pros — but not nearly enough to field a national team capable of qualifying for a World Cup, even out of a weak confederation like CONCACAF. In fact, these skeptics contended, the NASL quota had demonstrably restricted North American talent development away from the central, skill positions predominantly occupied by imports. They argued it was, in fact, time to double down on the quota.

One agreement *had* been reached once the U.S. failed to qualify for *Espana* '82, once the U.S. Men's National Team had again failed to reach even the final stage of CONCACAF qualifying: Walt Chyzowych had run his course as leader of the senior national team. His chaotic final weeks on the job and the squad's unseemly collapse in November 1980 made that reality clear enough. Chyz was out, along with his assistant Bob Gansler.

Now 40 years old and eager to steer his own ship, Gansler returned to his hometown, where he built a regional power at the University of Wisconsin-Milwaukee. He remained involved in assessing/coaching U.S. talent, albeit primarily at the Olympic Festival level.

Chyzowych moved straight to the Philadelphia Fever (1981-82) in the Major Indoor Soccer League. He got himself fired after 25 games and then returned to the college ranks, where he revived the program at Wake Forest University in Winston-Salem, North Carolina. From 1986-94, he led the Demon Deacons to four NCAA tournament bids. Chyzowych died in September 1994, just six weeks after the American World Cup had concluded. He was 57. His posthumous election to the National Soccer Hall of Fame arrived in 1997. Chyzowych proved a stalwart, versatile product of the urban/ethnic game that prevailed across this country prior to the 1970s. He led an extraordinary soccer life here in the States, starring at striker for the Philadelphia Ukrainian Nationals during the Fifties and Sixties, and then building a collegiate soccer power at Philadelphia Textile (1961-75), now Thomas Jefferson University. He experienced wild success everywhere he played or coached — save for his brief MISL experience and his five-year stint as USMNT coach. Sadly and not at all fairly, it is the latter position for which he'll best be remembered.

While the USSF was convinced its senior national team no longer required the services of Chyzowych, that was the extent of its certainty through the first few months of 1983. With no senior national team camps or matches scheduled, the national team program essentially went dormant again for two years — pretty extraordinary, considering the pending Olympic tournament. However, prior to 1988, the U.S. Soccer Federation did experience chronic difficulties in scheduling international friendlies — a fact many struggle to process today, when the men's and women's national teams play 15-20 full internationals apiece each calendar year without fail. Today, foreign federations are eager to avail themselves of the Grade-A facilities here in the United States, and a healthy cut of its large and lucrative television market. In the early 1980s, however, neither of these factors obtained. "The national team at that time really was a traveling gypsy circus," according to U.S. defensive midfielder Brian Bliss. "Back then it was very difficult to get another national team to even give us a game — because they didn't respect the U.S.

enough to waste a FIFA date, an international date. There was nothing in it for them."

Between the final qualifier under Chyz in November 1980 and an international against Haiti in April 1983, the USMNT played exactly one match: a friendly in Port of Spain against Trinidad and Tobago on March 21, 1982.

Instead, senior American players busied themselves by fighting for a diminished slate of roster spots in the increasingly rickety NASL. Come November 1983, 10 league clubs had thrown in the towel, including the franchise that had debuted in 1975 as the Hartford Bicentennials. By the close of 1979, this outfit had moved and morphed into the Connecticut Bicentennials, Oakland Stompers and Edmonton Drillers. It was Peter Pocklington, chairman of the NHL's Edmonton Oilers, who purchased the Stompers and delivered them to northern Alberta. He folded NASL's northernmost franchise following the 1982 season, deciding that he owned enough professional sports teams named for resource extraction.

NASL players also plied their trade on various indoor circuits, another destabilizing threat to the outdoor league's financial stability and talent pool. Meanwhile, the Federation dithered on subjects ranging from a new senior national team coach to the experimental placement of a U.S. team in NASL itself. There even surfaced, at this time, the fanciful notion that America might capitalize on FIFA's potential removal of the 1986 World Cup from Colombia, where stadia were apparently lacking and, *oh by the way*, a cocaine-fueled civil war raged.

———•••———

With nine successive qualification failures behind them, the Federation prevailed upon NASL and its players' union to swing for the fences. Radical thinking had prevailed: Team America, a group of elite young professionals, would play together all year round, not merely in friendlies and World Cup qualifiers, but in the North American Soccer League itself. Club and country were merged.

Over the winter of 1982-83, the logic in this nontraditional developmental plan was perhaps easier to divine. Eastern European soccer federations had, by the mid-Seventies, established the practice of loaning out groups of young, amateur talent to domestic clubs, where they would be seasoned but not paid. Allegedly. In 1981, the national team of Antigua and Barbuda had played together for a full season in the American Soccer League, what amounted to the second division of U.S. professional soccer at the time. A U.S. junior national hockey team had more recently played as a unit in the minor-league East Coast Hockey League, as preparation for an upcoming World Championship tournament.

Following these examples, Team America would conceivably address multiple shortcomings at once. This approach would guarantee 11 starting spots, central/playmaking roles and serious minutes to U.S. players. A full league schedule, went the thinking, would also promote cohesion within said team, better preparing it for both the Olympic competition and World Cup qualifying, set to begin in 1984.

What's more, Team America would demonstrate to FIFA a new, perhaps innovative, certainly more serious approach to developing a U.S. Men's National Team, one that met international standards — one worthy of hosting and earning automatic qualification for a World Cup in 1986.

As 1983 dawned, the Federation had secured the cooperation of NASL, the MISL and the ASL to release on loan all the players Team America would need. The Federation had finagled the funds to pay those players with assistance from former Washington Diplomats owner Robert Lifton, NASL commissioner Phil Woosnam and league president Howard Samuels. They further wangled a home field for Team America: RFK Stadium, as the Dips had dissolved following the 1980 season. All that remained? To identify and hire a charismatic, capable national team coach to lead it.

———•———

Enter the cigar-chomping, enigmatic, eminently qualified but altogether mercurial Alketas Panagoulias, who went by Alex and whose stamp on the USMNT would be indelible for the next two years. In the colorful Greek, Federation leaders reckoned they had surely found their man — for the princely annual salary of $100,000 (approximately $280,000 in

2022 dollars). Fresh off his stint managing Olympiacos to consecutive league titles in his native Greece, Panagoulias boasted big-time European club *and* international experience: He coached his countrymen from 1973-81, leading the Greeks to their first ever European Championships appearance, in 1980. (The *Galanolefki*, "The Blue & White," would not qualify again until 2004, when they left Portugal as shock champions.) Panagoulias boasted knowledge of the American game as well, playing for NYC's Greek American Atlas throughout the mid-1960s and then coaching the Cosmopolitan League club to three consecutive U.S. Open Cup titles starting in 1967.

Regrettably, right out of the gate, the Team America concept proved half-baked in one important respect: The Federation and NASL had failed to *fully* consult the players regarding this out-of-the-box plan of action. Come January 1983, many U.S. internationals declined to risk their individual careers by joining the experiment. This proved a position of some irony, given the tottering fortunes of NASL, which would fold outright at the close of 1984. Nonetheless, Ricky Davis, the most recognizable U.S. "star," chose not to leave his club, the Cosmos. Tampa Bay Rowdies goalkeeper Winston DuBose — who enjoyed a few cups of coffee, but never anything more than a reserve place, with several English clubs during the late 1970s — wasn't interested either. Neither was naturalized national team veteran Juli Veee.

One Cosmos player who did participate was defender Jeff Durgan, whose relationship with Davis never recovered. "The devil was in the details," Durgan told *The New York Times* in 2013. "The league was in serious jeopardy. It was a last-ditch effort to try to feature American players and energize the national team program. I was 20 years old and had a good situation with the Cosmos, but I wanted to see soccer survive."

Davis, Dubose and Veee were not alone. Team America failed to secure the services of striker Steve Moyers, who showed up for the first two weeks of training and then left for camp Cosmos, never to return. Mark Peterson also bailed, leaving a gaping hole up top, in attack. But Panagoulias *did* have at his disposal a host of good players already in the national team pool: Durgan, Perry Van der Beck, Greg Villa, Dan Canter, Hernan "Chico" Borja, Tony Bellinger, Arnie Mausser. Four solid, natural-ized Americans joined them: Ringo Cantillo, Alan Green, Pedro DeBrito and Alan Merrick.

Merrick in particular, a newly minted U.S. citizen, brought with him a British on-field pedigree, courtesy of his tenure at West Bromwich Albion, and a sincere interest in making Team America and the USMNT work.

"As a player I was very interested in what was happening with the game," he told the US Soccer Players website in 2007. "I was in the players' union in the NASL, trying to make sure that more American players could get a position. I'd played in the country long enough to get my status as a citizen, so as soon as I got that, I was offered a position on Team America."

Panagoulias and his new squad broke well from the gate, going 8-5 and drawing some credible crowds at RFK. Soon thereafter, however, the side fell apart competitively, finishing the '83 season in a 2-15 freefall. The coach consistently blamed the demise of Team America on holdout talent—those top-class American players whose clubs, he claimed, had pressured them not to participate. This assessment doesn't exactly jibe with the team's strong start and feeble second-half performance.

Merrick provides a different take.

"We organized ourselves pretty well initially and had some great leadership from within the playing staff," he said. "Then there were some power struggles — I know that I was chastised for giving my opinions on what I thought should happen, and actually putting in a couple of free kicks and components of the game that would help us.

"The conversation [with Panagoulias] was: 'Cease and desist. You're undermining my coaching ability.' Although I was trying to supplement it, and also assist, because we'd only got a short time to get things right. I think some of the man-management skills were lacking, and people got a little disenchanted, thinking, 'Hey, we're making all of this commitment, but we're not seeing anything back from the USSF or the coaching staff.'

"It was a very good concept. I was not particularly enamored by the coaching selection. The USSF was in total disarray at that point. They were going through growing pains and hadn't put people in place who'd had worldwide experience in the game. They had administrators and personnel making decisions that were way above their heads."

In retrospect, Team America is widely viewed as a fiasco, but Durgan and Merrick are right. There were several objectives in play here, not all of them competing. The plan all along hinged on this group staying together through the offseason and training together — as the national team — something the Federation had failed to foster during the previous two years in any way, shape or form. In fairness, this level of cohesion had been difficult to sustain throughout the 1970s and Eighties.

Team America was supposed to have reentered NASL in 1984. Because FIFA was hinting that professionals might be eligible in Los Angeles, Team America would leverage the league's regular-season schedule as sustained preparation for the Olympic tournament late that summer. Thereafter, it would seamlessly and cohesively take up the matter of World Cup qualifying. This plan, as Merrick suggested, made sense on multiple levels.

But none of it came off. Team America was summarily disbanded when the 1983 NASL season drew to a close, as elements within the Federation got cold feet and its partner, NASL, was admittedly fighting for its very existence. Yes, the last half of the season had been a competitive disaster. But in terminating the trial, players felt their career-altering commitments had been more or less betrayed.

"It was sort of a shock to everybody," Merrick recalls. "We were all thinking that it was going quite well, we'd been respectable, so the experiment was not a total disaster. We'd shown a good skill level and had done a decent job. At the end of the season we thought we were going on tour — to start to have some international matches: 'We're going to play as the U.S. national team and the Olympic team in training.' And we were going to bring in some of the other guys who hadn't joined us for the domestic year, like Ricky Davis and a couple of other players. That would have really bolstered the squad that we had and put us on a very, very good road to producing some good results and turning some heads.

"But the doors were just completely slammed. It was right at the end of the season: 'Here's your last paycheck, bye-bye.' We had an hour's notice, and we were told the doors would be shutting as soon as we'd left, never to be opened again . . . It was a little surreal."

TEAM AMERICA'S ON-FIELD PERFORMANCE and abrupt dissolution proved disappointing and embarrassing to the Federation. Surely the venture did not prove remunerative, either. Nothing in NASL did, at this late stage. But the fall of 1983 brought with it two additional developments that argued for Team America's continued support.

First, the International Olympic Committee *did* vote to lift its conditional ban on professional soccer players, starting with the 1984 Games in Los Angeles. The IOC and FIFA agreed that players from Europe and South America *who had performed at previous World Cups* could not partake in the Olympic futbol competition — but anyone else could. This decision rendered the '84 Games a "youth" tournament for perennial soccer powers and "open enrollment" for everyone else. Because of its decades-long World Cup drought, the U.S. was thus at liberty to bring its best professionals to L.A. Another season of Team America, in 1984, would have served this Olympic effort well.

Second, it became clear that FIFA had no real intention of delivering its marquee event to the United States, not in 1986. The tournament would in fact be shifted from Colombia to Mexico. Nevertheless, ceding the event to Mexico came with a silver lining: To the delight of big-dreaming minnows across CONCACAF, Mexico would qualify automatically as host, thereby eliminating the region's dominant force from the upcoming qualification tournament. In other words, another season of Team America in NASL would have benefited the next WCQ campaign, too.

Taken together, these and Merrick's points make a strong case for Team America's continued presence within NASL. Instead, the experiment was consigned to the dustbin of history. "In hindsight," Durgan told the *NY Times*, "I understand that very few efforts that try to serve multiple masters succeed. There were two goals at odds: trying to secure stability for the NASL by putting together a show and wrapping it in the flag — versus trying to develop players for the national team. We were focused on the moment, rather than looking at the long road ahead."

One important vestige of the Team America experiment did manage to stick, though: Panagoulias himself. His champion in the hallways at NASL, Englishman Phil Woosnam, had been relieved of his commissioner duties during the 1983 season, but the Greek somehow managed to preserve his influence and paycheck. As national team coach, he would preside over the Olympic team in 1984 *and* the next World Cup qualifiers, scheduled to begin as soon as the Olympic flame had been doused.

"It is amazing how this sport found success in spite of itself on so many different levels," Peter Vermes says, letting out a long, rueful sigh. "It was all fiefdoms back then and, well . . . there were a lot of mistakes."

———

Panagoulias remained a controversial figure in American soccer circles throughout 1984 and '85 — for the reasons Merrick describes, for the perception that he was Woosnam's lapdog, for never being American enough, for carrying with him the stink of Team America's collapse. But this much can be said in his defense: He smartly integrated promising, young, still-amateur talent into his USMNT all through 1984 and thereafter, once NASL had shut down. It would have been far easier, more logical, and personally more expedient for the Greek to bring in as many professionals as possible in preparation for the Olympic and World Cup qualifying tournaments. Instead, recognizing talent when he saw it, he gave Generation Zero its first senior caps. Paul Caligiuri, Mike Windischmann, John Kerr Jr. and Brian Bliss all debuted during Panagoulias' fitful reign. Stollmeyer did, too, though he can't be sure exactly when: "You'd think I'd remember that . . . *Shoot*. I don't even think that's on Wikipedia! Truly, I don't know."

Even an established, successful national team cannot risk stagnation through overreliance on veteran talent. Up-and-coming players must be continually sifted in. For once, the Federation seemed to benefit here from some well laid plans. These five players had all been identified through ODP and then further groomed by their resulting places on youth national team rosters. When Panagoulias judged them to be ready, they found their way into the senior national team player pool.

There was just one problem, an issue particular to the ever-anomalous U.S. soccer experience: Elsewhere in the developed soccer world, players of tender age but high footballing IQ and caliber conclude similar national team cameos and then depart for their various professional club sides. There, day-to-day competition against senior players and other up-and-comers from rival clubs weed out lesser talents and temper survivors for the highest levels of competition.

When members of Gen Zero completed their Festival and U-20 stints under watchful Federation eyes, or finished their training with Panagoulias and the senior national team, they all headed back to college. Every single one.

———•—•———

Today, 30 years into the modern American soccer era, collegiate soccer is routinely held up as *the* persistent flaw in the way U.S. national team programs and American professional clubs developed talent — through the lean years, all the way up to 1990 and into the 21st century. As we've detailed, there were several major, longstanding obstacles. However, no other nation in the world sent elite players off to college at 17 or 18 to spend a mere three or four months out of 12 honing their games in ostensibly amateur settings, under the tutelage of coaches often completely unfamiliar with the professional game.

Americans, at their egalitarian best, honestly do believe that everyone, including athletes, should have the opportunity to receive a university education. However, as an effective vocational prospect, college does not serve would-be professional soccer players particularly well. Anywhere.

There are so many nuanced contradictions baked into American collegiate athletics that it's frankly difficult to know where to begin. Our soccer example only adds to the complexity.

This much remains clear: The U.S. is the only country that has ever intentionally attempted to groom international-standard soccer talent via the university model, a fact that continues to confound futbol observers around the world. They are additionally and more broadly confused by America's bizarre-but-insistent confluence of higher education and big-time sports, full stop. Neither does this model — where elite athletic teams, doubling as professional farm systems, are attached to universities — exist outside the United States. Make no mistake: College-age professional athletes are admired the world over; their training and careers are fostered in myriad ways from country to country. Outside the U.S., however, the university-level education apparatus has absolutely nothing to do with those processes.

I played soccer for the University of London during a spring 1985 semester abroad. Americans are often impressed by this, but I'm obliged to tell them that playing university soccer in Britain indicates that one is not terribly good. Not elite certainly, not good enough to be playing in some British club's developmental system. That's where 18- to 22-year-old footballers of actual quality are found in Britain. Not at some posh institute of higher learning.

The British and most of the world look upon American interest in and emphasis on "college sports" as yet another example of our cultural maladjustment. University soccer abroad exists as something of a lark, an extraneous activity like drama club or Vegan House. Nothing that might attract campuswide interest or national TV coverage. "Who," they reasonably enquire, "would care to watch such a thing?" Well, Americans would, because here collegiate athletics perform a multifaceted role unique to this vast, sui generis country: that of an unpaid farm system, which also serves as a revenue generator for the university. Even at smaller, Division III institutions, successful sports programs constitute a stimulant to alumni giving. Please take note of the common denominator here: money.

When the USMNT showed up at World Cup 1990, European football media were fascinated by the idea that Bob Gansler's roster had been stocked with a bunch of "college kids." Only a few had actually left college to join the team, but all *had* attended university: a completely alien concept to the European press. No club team, much less an all-star national team, relied on college-trained players. This plain and simple fact was as true for European giants like Italy, Germany or France as it was for small-fry soccer nations like South Korea or the United Arab Emirates. The phenomenon was peculiarly American.

If the preponderance of world football is any judge, the verdict remains unambiguous: The structural limitations of American college soccer retarded our progress as a soccer nation for decades.

———•◦•———

And yet, every elite player representing Generation Zero — America's golden generation, its breakthrough cohort — participated in college soccer. The collapse of NASL in 1984 didn't move U.S. player development or media coverage away from the college model. On the contrary, the death of first-division outdoor soccer in America placed *more* emphasis, and shined a brighter light, on those few domestic institutions left standing.

"In that era between pro leagues, college soccer became a bigger deal, that much *more* important," Mike Woitalla explains. "At *Soccer America*, we actually had a 'Budweiser Player of the Week' during that period! We can't do that sort of thing anymore, but that was a big deal for the magazine. It kept us going, that deal with Budweiser. And we really did cover college closely. We covered everything — but that became the heart of it. With no real [outdoor] pro league, we covered indoor, we covered international. But yeah, you had that period when college soccer was the highest level of American soccer in a way."

College soccer also brought Woitalla into sports journalism. He played at Cal Berkeley alongside Wellesley's own Tom Wadlington, who was there in the East Bay, playing on the fringes of Cal's formidable program, as well. "What happened was, I thought I was gonna make the Cal team," Woitalla remembers, "and I did end up making it, thanks to some injuries. But before I knew that, I had contacted *The Daily Californian* [the campus newspaper] about covering the soccer team. I ended up doing both."

Like Woitalla, I covered Wesleyan University soccer for our campus paper, *The Argus*, while also playing for the varsity. However, budding journalists weren't the only ones double-dipping at this time.

"Back then, as soon as the college season was over, we were jumping into the winter leagues or the ethnic leagues, always jumping into the next league come the spring," reports Peter Vermes, who started his collegiate career at Loyola University in Baltimore before transferring to Rutgers. "We played constantly."

The NCAA enforcement infrastructure during this period was not nearly the Big Brother that presides with such impudence today. It had yet to fully monetize one of its enduring cash cows: the Division I men's basketball tournament. It didn't have the money to fund effective enforcement across the universe of intercollegiate athletics. The NCAA was but a minor scourge, on the whole, and it focused mainly on high-profile pursuits like big-time collegiate football and basketball programs.

About soccer, it did not give a fig. As a result, talented players could participate in Division I, II or III soccer and essentially moonlight for ethnic clubs with impunity during the offseason — as Vermes describes — and sometimes during the NCAA season itself. That behavior would technically have represented a violation of NCAA rules, even if players weren't paid under the table. Which, of course, they were. But the NCAA turned, if not a blind eye, then an accommodating one.

"It was much easier in the college game back then, because the rules were not as stringent as they are today," Vermes confirms. "You could play for the Brooklyn Italians and the Hungarian club there in New York when the college season was over. I played for Atlas in the Greek League.

Wherever I could find soccer, I was playing it. Today, these young guys can't do that."

And so, on the college front circa 1984, we are obliged to keep two conflicting facts in our heads simultaneously: 1) The U.S. relied on college soccer to feed its national team during those crucial years when the country finally *did* produce enough international-quality talent to qualify for a World Cup; and 2) Collegiate soccer has never produced international quality talent, to any meaningful degree, anywhere else in the developed soccer world. We must reckon with this disconnect to fully understand Generation Zero, and to fully understand where we've been as a footballing nation, where we are today, and why it took so very long to get here.

———·—·———

Authors Andrei Markovits and Steven Hellerman grudgingly acknowledge the first point above but place far more emphasis on the second: "It is universally accepted," they write, "that the years of age between 18 and 22 are totally critical in the development of skills necessary for playing soccer at its highest level. Spending those years in NCAA soccer simply does not suffice for establishing those skills." They take the matter a step further, however, arguing that because association-style football never established itself as a collegiate sport of broad popularity during the late 19th century, soccer was destined *never* to evolve into a major American sport — and so it never had the chance of evolving into a professional feeder system on the model of gridiron, basketball and baseball.

"These are distinguished academics. (Markovits taught at Wesleyan while I was there, though I never met him.) Thus they eschew the word "major" when describing American sports, opting instead for the more magisterial and intellectually hefty "hegemonic," which, to be fair, is also perfectly apt. As Markovits has explained elsewhere, their use of hegemonic in this context cleverly refers to Marxist philosopher and linguist Antonio Gramsci's "path-breaking work on a form of domination which is in some ways consensual, and to which both the dominator and the dominated agree and consent. Clearly, there is a power relationship that is profoundly unequal but what makes a hegemon so effective is that it exerts its power by creating a cocoon of consent from which the dominated does not even feel the need to exit."

M&H argue persuasively that two of the nation's Big Three sports, football and basketball, owe their hegemonic status in the larger culture to their collegiate roots. Both games first became broadly popular at the college level — gridiron in the 1880s, roundball in the 1930s — decades before professional teams were even conceived. In this specific regard, baseball, the country's original sporting hegemon, is the outlier. Its breakout period, professional and collegiate, took place at about the same time, during the 1870s and Eighties.

The irony? Scholarship argues just as persuasively that association football, or soccer, actually beat rugby football and gridiron to the American college scene — only to squander this cultural inside track due to the whims of a dozen capricious blue bloods in Cambridge, Massachusetts.

Conventional wisdom recognizes the first, organized American football game took place Nov. 6, 1869, between host Princeton University and nearby Rutgers University. According to M&H, that encounter should be classified as both the first organized football game *and* the first organized soccer game in American history:

The game was played according to rules somewhere between those of association and rugby football. Columbia joined the original two in 1870, and by 1872 the group included Rutgers, Princeton, Yale and Stevens. These schools played an association-type kicking game. Even though local differences in rules persisted, all participants agreed that the ball could not be picked up with the hands, caught, thrown or carried. Soccer, in its rudimentary form, seemed to have assumed an important foothold among leading American colleges.

Unfortunately for university advocates of this kicking game, Harvard was not on board, and as the Crimson went — in the 19th century at least — so went the rest of America's colleges. At that time, undergraduates in Cambridge played an intramural sport known as the Boston Game, a kick-catch-and-carry hybrid that more closely resembled British rugby. Despite repeated invitations to come play the kicking game in league with its collegiate neighbors to the south and west, the patrician set in Cambridge stood aloof from this game that differed so markedly from their own Boston Game.

Enter McGill University in Montreal, which, true to its Commonwealth standing, played a game even closer to British rugby. In search of an opponent, Harvard hosted the Canadians for two matches in May of 1874, the first according to Boston Game rules, the second according to McGill's rules. The Cantabrigians won the first match, as one might expect. But the Crimson also managed a scoreless tie in the second match, something in which students — and even the broader Boston press — took overweening pride. When Harvard won a rematch in Montreal the following October, beating McGill at its own game, the die was cast.

If American colleges at the time paid outsized attention to what Harvard did (the games its students played, how they dressed, what curricula they pursued), the Crimson placed a similarly skewed importance on what archrival Yale did. Their competition in all things cemented the future course of these two diverging approaches to 19th-century football.

Barely one year later, in 1875, the desire of Harvard and Yale to meet at football became so keen that in October two delegates from each university met in Springfield, Massachusetts, to set the so-called Concessionary Rules that were to govern their first game . . . The Springfield Agreement paved the way for Harvard and Yale to play their very first contest in football on Saturday, 13 November, at Hamilton Field in New Haven, an event that eventually became an annual ritual known for years in American sport culture as simply "The Game." . . . Yale's well-established rivalry with Harvard proved much stronger than its membership in the loose association with Columbia, Princeton and other schools then playing the "kicking game." Yale still fulfilled its "soccer obligations" that year to Columbia and Wesleyan, but by 1876 Yale had dropped soccer and replaced it with rugby. The other universities soon followed, Princeton succumbing last in 1877.

From 1869 to 1875, it wasn't at all clear that American colleges — so crucial to the formation of hegemonic sports, according to M&H — would choose rugby over soccer. Once *The Game* had been played and established, no argument remained. The kicking incarnation of football soon disappeared entirely from the college-sporting scene, not to reappear until 1902. The NCAA would not stage a national soccer championship until 1959.

Once Harvard and Yale put the kibosh on soccer's ascent, a full century would pass before college soccer would again play a central role in building the sport in America. Even in renewing its impact, however, the college game came with enormous strings attached.

LET'S REVIEW THE UNITED STATES ROSTER for *Italia* '90, including where exactly all 20 players received their respective collegiate soccer training:

D	Steve Trittschuh	Southern Illinois University
D	John Doyle	University of San Francisco
D	Jimmy Banks	University of Wisconsin-Milwaukee
D	Desmond Armstrong	University of Maryland
D	Mike Windischmann	Adelphi University
D	Marcelo Balboa	San Diego State University
M	John Harkes	University of Virginia
M	Tab Ramos	North Carolina State University
M	Brian Bliss	Southern Connecticut State University
M	Chris Henderson	University of California, Los Angeles
M	Paul Caligiuri	University of California, Los Angeles
M	Neil Covone	Wake Forest University
M	John Stollmeyer	Indiana University
F	Chris Sullivan	University of Tampa
F	Peter Vermes	Loyola University/Rutgers University
F	Eric Wynalda	San Diego State University
F	Paul Krumpe	University of California, Los Angeles
F	Eric Eichmann	Clemson University

F	Bruce Murray	Clemson University
G	David Vanole	University of California, Los Angeles
G	Tony Meola	University of Virginia
G	Kasey Keller	University of Portland

As we've touched upon, defending the college game in the context of elite, international player development is tough sledding. History and evidence from around the world make it damned clear: College is not an effective petri dish. Markovits and Hellerman are crystal clear on this matter:

We believe that college-level soccer actively hinders instead of fosters the experience and playing competence necessary to perform at the game's premier level. After graduating high school, high-caliber soccer players faced with the choice between a free college education or rolling the dice on a career in professional soccer have, for reasons of pragmatic self-interest, opted for the former. Until there is enough bonus money available to make the latter choice worthwhile for much of the best young American soccer talent – as has been the case with professional baseball, football, basketball and hockey — as well as the creation of organized venues similar to baseball's farm system, hockey's junior club system, or the intricate and deliberate pyramid-like network of the European clubs (that weans players from their childhood onto the professional level), elevating the skills of a large number of American players to "first-division levels" will remain an elusive endeavor.

M&H published *Offside* in 2001. Nearly two decades down the road, these observations and proposals remain spot-on and relevant today. Major League Soccer *has* created junior club systems that foster elites from amateurism to professionalism. Eventually, financial incentives do keep players engaged with this path forward.

In 1990, every single national team player who traveled to Italy had played college soccer: 100 percent. By 2008, just 68.8 percent of USMNT participants had played college soccer. By 2018, it was down to 39.6 percent. In other words, by 2018, Team USA selected about 20 percent more players from youth programs/academies than from colleges, compared to a decade prior. Increasingly, the academies that feed Federation and

MLS teams aren't entirely domestic. In 2008, four of the 48 players who played at least one game for the senior national squad had come through a youth academy abroad — two in England and two in Mexico. In 2018, 20 of the 53 players who played at least one game for the USMNT had done apprenticeships outside the United States.

The mid-1980s obviously preceded all this evolution, but some things never change. World Cup 2018 was the first tournament Team USA missed since 1986. When the Americans crashed out, having failed to secure a point at lowly Trinidad and Tobago in October 2017, college soccer was still being blamed for the ills of U.S professional soccer.

"I honestly believe the college system for basketball and American football and maybe baseball is probably as good a setup as you can have anywhere in the world to prepare people to play professionally," Minnesota United FC manager Adrian Heath, an Englishman, told the *Minneapolis Star Tribune* in June 2018. "It's probably the worst for soccer. We can't have kids going to college at 18, staying for two, three years playing three months of competitive football a year. Everywhere else in the world, it's getting more [games]. Here, it's getting less at a really important time."

———·•·———

Heath is not wrong, but the early 1980s were a different time. Four distinctly American, college soccer realities from this period informed the options then available to members of Generation Zero. They also explain to 21st-century types how something as backward as college soccer produced this country's golden generation of talent.

1. With NASL so precariously placed during the early Eighties — soon to join the choir invisible, in fact — college was the *only* viable option for elite U.S. soccer players coming out of high school.

Older members of Gen Zero might have felt otherwise when they graduated from high school, or decided to leave college in 1981 or '82, when NASL remained a viable if unstable professional option. For everyone else on the *Italia '90* roster, NASL went away just as their professional and senior national team careers commenced. The remaining futbol landscape proved extraordinarily bleak — no outdoor leagues that rose above the semiprofessional level; fully professional soccer limited to MISL; no residency program or even a prototype from the Federation; no overseas league prospects at all. College soccer was the only game in town, the best possible hedge.

"Even in this day and age, look at how few guys go through the academy system and make it as pros. It's so few, and even fewer really make any money. You better have something like college to fall back on," declares John Stollmeyer, who arrived at Indiana University in the fall of 1981. "I almost left IU to go pro. I was sick of school and I would've gone pro — if NASL had still been around. And not been such a mess! I could have come out at the end of 1985, but come out to what?"

For the few first-rate players the U.S. had developed, college soccer was acknowledged to be something of a holding pattern. Marcelo Balboa is six years younger than Stollmeyer, but his decision-making process was much the same: "You had to play college. I think that was the only way we could get where we wanted to get," he says. "I think back then it was a holding pattern — only because we had nowhere else to go! You had to play all four years somewhere, in order to open up the next door.

"Nowadays, kids are leaving college at the Generation Adidas level" — the competition run by Major League Soccer for players not yet eligible for MLS SuperDraft early entry. "We're talking sophomores and juniors, so I think today it's not a holding pattern; college *can* be that next-stage progression. Can I go from high school and show in two years what I can do — so I can get drafted by my junior year? Yes.

"It's still a huge step between college and the MLS, but look at all the other steps you can take now. You can still play in PDL" — the third-division Professional Development League, which was replaced in 2022 by MLS Next Pro. "You can play USL Pro [the nation's second division], NPSL [the National Premier Soccer League, fourth division], and then you've got MLS. So many steps on your way to the ultimate goal, the highest level, Major League Soccer. Compare that to back in the 1980s, when all we had was the Western Alliance, which *no one* was looking at."

To be clear, the Western Soccer Alliance didn't form until 1986. Accordingly, Balboa and other, younger members of Gen Zero — Tony Meola, Eric Wynalda, Kasey Keller and Peter Vermes — could perhaps have availed themselves of the Alliance exclusively, in lieu of college. They could have forgone college soccer and played in the A-League, which formed in 1988. But they did not. They all went the four-year college route and, during that time, merely dabbled in these new leagues as amateurs.

———•◆•———

2. Division I college soccer in the Eighties wasn't so terrible on the technical development front. It was actually a marked upgrade from Seventies-era college soccer in that respect.

The youth soccer explosion of the 1970s poured hundreds of thousands of players into high school soccer programs by the end of the Me Decade. The best of that lot similarly swamped college programs during the 1980s with more competent, native-born players than coaches had ever seen before.

"College soccer at that point had kind of taken off a little bit," observes Paul Krumpe, for 24 years the head coach at Loyola Marymount University in Los Angeles. He stepped down in the spring of 2022. "I think back to the Seventies, when the best program was USF [University of San Francisco], but they didn't have a lot of Americans on that team. There were a lot of Ethiopians and Nigerians who came over and went to school there."

According to *Soccer America* editor Paul Kennedy, writing for the magazine in 2020, "The 1977 Hartwick team was one of the greatest college teams ever assembled, with players recruited from two main sources: New Jersey (Billy Gazonas and Art Napolitano from Trenton, Joey Ryan from Harrison, Tom Maresca from Bloomfield, and Khyen Ivanchukov and Zeren Ombadykow from the Kalmyk-American community in Howell) and the Merseyside area of England (Aly Anderson, Jeff Tipping and Stephen Long from Liverpool and Duncan MacDonald from Southport)."

At the highest levels of college soccer, the issue prior to 1980 was the same issue that dogged NASL: Foreign players took too many minutes, in too many crucial positions on the field. The foreign influence never completely went away, Krumpe says, "but when we won the national championship at UCLA in 1985, it was all Californian kids. Not just all Americans, but all *Californians*. You finally got to the point at the college level where you got a sense that American soccer players were starting to develop. Prior to that, it was mainly foreign players coming over and making that impact."

In sum, relying on the college game to provide viable U.S. national team prospects in the 1960s and Seventies was a dead-end fantasy. In the 1980s, not so much.

3. Division I college soccer in the 1980s was greatly improved because the coaching had greatly improved.

A quick scan of the college coaches for whom future USMNTers played during the Eighties makes this argument pretty compelling. Bruce Arena is the headliner here. He coached John Harkes and Tony Meola, and then Claudio Reyna, at the University of Virginia before graduating to MLS. Arena's D.C. United teams dominated the league during the late Nineties. Then he led the U.S. to its only World Cup quarterfinal, in 2002.

Bob Gansler was Jimmy Banks' coach at the University of Wisconsin-Milwaukee before taking over the USMNT in 1990, with only a short stint as U.S. U-20 skipper in between. Gansler went on to enjoy a long and successful run in Major League Soccer.

Sigi Schmid's decorated career in MLS was preceded by two decades at UCLA, where he won three national championships between 1980-99. He groomed a succession of top talents there: Caligiuri, Krumpe, Cobi Jones, Brad Friedel, David Vanole, Frankie Hejduk, Carlos Bocanegra, Eddie Lewis, Joe-Max Moore, Chris Henderson and Nick Rimando. Schmid was born in Germany, but his soccer development was pretty darned American: His émigré family landed in Torrance, California, when Sigi was just four years old. He was among the first players to participate in AYSO, in fact, and later

starred in midfield at UCLA from 1972-75. (When his protégé Krumpe relinquished head coaching duties at Loyola Marymount, in 2022, Sigi's son
Kyle Schmid succeeded him.)

These college skippers all got famous in MLS. There were dozens of
collegiate colleagues who never made that leap, who never even sought
it, but who nevertheless served to upgrade the overall quality of college
coaching during the 1980s.

Markovits and Hellerman are generally dismissive of U.S. college
coaching acumen: "Very few college coaches have hailed from the world
of professional soccer, and fewer still have played the game at a level performed by the top leagues and teams in the world. Indeed, signaling the
college game's insularity has been that very few of the NCAA-licensed
coaches have hailed from Europe and Latin America . . . So it is not surprising that most American college coaches compensate their deficient
cultural feel for the game with excessive emphasis on 'playbook' soccer
dominated by athleticism and learned mechanics."

This argument, published in 2001, is based upon indisputable truths.
Yet it's also true that the situation was rapidly changing and evolving
during the 1980s. Stollmeyer would certainly push back on M&H. He
played for the legendary Jerry Yeagley at Indiana, whose resume adds
nuance to our perceptions of an evolving college game. Yeagley won six
national championships in Bloomington between 1973 and 2003. He
won another as a player with West Chester University, in 1961! His understanding of the game extended well beyond any playbook. To Krumpe's
point, the Indiana program Yeagley led had matured on a very fast track:
Until 1973, soccer at IU had been a mere club sport.

"I think if I'd gone to a real program like they have available today, I'd
definitely have been better as a pro," Stollmeyer admits. "But I learned a
ton at IU. I learned how to defend properly. I mean, I learned that in my
first year. I recognized that defending is pure will. There's no right way to
attack, but there is a right way to defend, and a lot of guys still don't do it.
At IU, in our time, under Coach Yeagley, we learned how to defend because
he taught us how."

4. College soccer wasn't exclusionary during the Eighties when it came to skill development. Translation: There was plenty of productive moonlighting going on at this time.

This last point is perhaps the most pivotal. Yes, the coaching could have been better. From a development standpoint, U.S. college players traditionally spend too much time *not* playing soccer. But a light touch from NCAA enforcement arms during the 1980s allowed motivated, skilled players to further hone their games in the nation's many urban/ethnic leagues, where the best soccer in North America was being played post-NASL. I played semipro soccer in these ethnic leagues, but not till after college. Many members of the *Italia '90* squad saw no need to wait.

"Oh yeah. I played for a team called the Hollywood Stars and an indoor team called Newport Beach Breakers in a league when I was at UCLA," Krumpe recollects. "That was in the winter and spring, when we weren't playing in college. We'd drive down and play in what were essentially Sunday league games, in semiprofessional leagues. Everybody did. It was certainly to supplement the college season. For guys who needed and wanted to play all year round, you could.

"It was $60 a game — if your team won. You could say it was what college soccer now refers to as 'actual and necessary or needed expenses.' You weren't making money over the top. Obviously there were some guys who got paid more under the table, but you got paid to travel to the game. You got meal money, a per diem if you like. It wasn't a lot of money. Of course, we didn't make a lot of money with the national team either!"

There is very little enthusiasm on the part of these former national team players to trash the system that produced them, of course. They all played college soccer prior to qualifying this country for the World Cup. The results, in their quite reasonable view, speak for themselves. Moreover, many work as college coaches and professional club technical directors today. They have seen the college system progress still further, *alongside* the club- and federation-sponsored academy systems now operating across the country.

Vermes, for one, still sees a place for the college system in the 21st century: "As much as the college game has improved, it still has the same type of structure and schedule as it did," he says. "When you add it all up, they're playing only one year of soccer in four years. In that sense, nothing has changed: I can't say it's *the* place to get your development. It's one of many. But it still provides us with players who can play in MLS because a lot of them are late bloomers. Sometimes those guys really mature in college and get on the right path. It's not a dead zone by any means, but there's no doubt that the academies are the wave of the future. We're already seeing that, right before our eyes."

Some elite college programs now conform, or make better efforts to conform, to the model that Markovits and Hellerman prescribed. Vermes and I spoke on this topic in 2017, just prior to formation of the first College Development Program. This collaboration between USSF and participating NCAA men's soccer programs allowed college teams, starting in 2018, to play a spring schedule against each other, following what the Federation terms its "technical framework of best practices for elite youth development." In short, matches operated the way US Soccer Development Academy matches did, with traditional FIFA timekeeping, maximum game-day rosters of 18 players, and three substitution moments with no reentry. Unfortunately, the Federation discontinued the CDP, along with all its Development Academy programs, in April 2020, citing COVID-19 restrictions. As of March 2022, they had not been revived.

"Look, the college option was the best thing we had at the time," Krumpe says. "NASL had folded, so there *was* no outdoor pro league. The reality was, college represented the highest-level soccer American guys could play at the time, outdoors. But I gotta say, the level of soccer has so greatly increased over the 25 years since we qualified. That's not *all* on the academies. College has played a role. It's just progress. We're getting there."

For Brian Bliss, who juggled USMNT and national U-20 duties throughout the second Reagan administration, going back to college meant returning to Southern Connecticut State University in New Haven. His four seasons with the Owls included deep runs into the Division II NCAA Tournament, three titanic battles with Division III also-ran Wesleyan University, just up the Merritt Parkway, and numerous trips *down* the Merritt for off-the-books appearances in New York City's semiprofessional Cosmopolitan League.

Because Wes played Southern in each of my four seasons, Bliss and I crossed paths several times. He and I featured in the center of the pitch during this fixture my sophomore, junior and senior years, though only we D3 darlings would have circled those games on the schedule. We never came that close to getting a result, save a 1-0 loss my junior year. Still, it was a thrill to play a top-class team like Southern, and we all knew who Bliss was. By 1985, he had already appeared for the USMNT, for fuck's sake — a 2-2 draw with Ecuador in Miami on Dec. 2, 1984. To be honest, during my last two years at Wesleyan (as a stopper in a diamond back four), I spent more time against SCSU worrying about Marvin Etienne, a naturalized Haitian striker who played some U-20 games for the U.S. later in the 1980s. Marvin is the uncle of Columbus Crew star Derrick Etienne Jr. and Fritz Etienne, Marvin's father, had been part of Haiti's golden generation, which qualified for the 1974 World Cup, having also eliminated Bob Gansler & Co. from the 1970 field. I well remember chasing Marvin's ass all over North Field, our home ground, and troubling him not in the slightest.

Southern was a very, very good side. Six times national Division II champions. And lest you be thrown by that Roman numeral, consider that the University of Connecticut — a Division I national power throughout the 1980s and Nineties, under coach and prickly American soccer icon Joe Morrone — refused to schedule the Owls, not even in preseason. "Those would have been interesting matches," Bliss contends. "But they didn't want any part of us. When Joe was there, I remember someone tried to put together a match, a 'made-for' match, for charity. But he still wouldn't do it."

Morrone had nothing to gain by playing Southern. The Owls had nothing to gain by playing Wesleyan, but in the latter case regionalism prevailed. Geography prevailed each winter, too, in the Hartford suburb of Glastonbury, home to the biggest, most centrally located indoor facility in the Nutmeg State. Southern, Wesleyan, Central Connecticut State, UConn, the University of Hartford, Conn College, Trinity and Yale all fielded teams there annually. The cream of the Connecticut talent pool circa 1985 included Bliss, Etienne, Connecticut-born USMNTer Jim Gabarra, plus Yale keeper Jeff Duback, his midfield teammate Kevin Maher (the 1983-84 MISL Rookie of the Year), and a few UConn guys. They were all good enough to keep going — to chase the next level. The rest of us were not good enough, despite the fact that we played in college and might log a few semipro seasons before the Eighties expired.

Strict hierarchies of skill always prevail in the athletic world. Some wannabes self-identify and peel off in the eighth grade, others after high school or college. There are two factors to bear in mind about how these decisions were reached — in this sport, in America, during the 1980s: First, never had so many young American men arrived at college expecting to play soccer, a direct result of the Youth Soccer Revolution that Gen Zero launched. At Wesleyan my freshman year, 50 guys showed up for double sessions that August of 1982. Down at Duke University two years earlier, Kent James reports that he was one of 75 to 100 who tried out — for the junior varsity! Behold the sanguine demographic power of GZ, vanguard of the modern American soccer boom. All these newcomers, at both schools and hundreds more across the country, had played the game all their lives — in youth leagues, on club teams, in high school. They figured they'd try their luck and see what college soccer was really about. I guarantee that 10 years prior, in 1972, 50 young men did not show up, in Middletown or Durham, for the first day of soccer tryouts. Varsity soccer hadn't even debuted at Wes until 1968.

Second, college rosters are limited in size. Most of these prospective players got cut, or labored in JV obscurity for a year before finding something better to do. But never did they forget or forsake soccer. James transferred to and played at Swarthmore. Others stayed put and played intramurals. Later, they competed in men's leagues until such time that their hamstrings said, *Stop!*

Many American men wax sentimental their entire lives about their organized baseball experiences, some of which concluded by the age of 12. Ditto for their glory days playing basketball, hockey or football. It doesn't matter *when* one stops physically competing in a given sport. Men, by the millions, fall in love with this ongoing nostalgia even before they stop competing and then carry a richly romanticized, personally informed fandom through the entirety of their adult lives. Part of that dynamic is the lure and soothing comfort of the pack. Yet another part of this sentimental journey is surely down to the sport itself. Soccer had never gone mainstream enough to grab American kids on such a broad, visceral level until the early 1970s. Once it did, however, the game held and beguiled them, boys and girls, for life.

Westwood on Nakdong: UCLA products Paul Caligiuri, David Vanole and Paul Krumpe following the 1988 Olympic opener in Daegu, South Korea. *(Image courtesy of Paul Krumpe)*

An NASL exhibit case at the National Soccer Hall of Fame in Frisco, Texas — and yes, that is suede fringe hanging from the Caribous of Colorado jersey. The league passed to history the evening of Oct. 3, 1984. (*Jon van Woerden photo*)

6.   GATEWAY TO THE ABYSS

(1984 to '85)

Late on the afternoon of Aug. 11, 1984, the largest crowd ever gathered to watch a soccer match on American soil filed into the Rose Bowl in Pasadena, California. Those 101,799 souls arrived to witness Brazil vs. France in a gold medal match, the denouement of the men's soccer competition at the Los Angeles Summer Olympiad. Had the contest taken place 18 months earlier, it would have amounted to a splendid argument supporting America's not-yet-realistic, half-baked, and ultimately ill-fated bid to host what became the Mexican World Cup of 1986. In the immortal words of then-U.S. Soccer Federation president Gene Edwards, when FIFA rejected that bid: "What would have happened if we got it? We could easily have messed it up."

As it happened, the '84 Olympic experience nevertheless proved crucial in several difference-making, foundation-laying respects. The sold-out final indicated there was no shortage of fan support for soccer in this country — something that concerned FIFA even 10 years later, when the U.S. *did* host the World Cup. The 1984 competition also represented the most prestigious, largest-scale tournament ever conducted in the United States to that point. Administratively, it exceeded every expectation. The three-week competition proved a five-ring showcase spotlighting the international game, America's potentially viable place in it, the country's ready-made stadium infrastructure, and the domestic first division that supplied every player on the Team USA roster.

The Olympic soccer crucible would also serve as prep and prelude to the national team's most critical period since spring 1969, the last time the USMNT came within spitting distance of World Cup participation. As host, Mexico had automatically qualified in 1970. For Mexico '86, the host nation was again exempt from the qualification process. The lone CONCACAF bid was wide open. Right there for the taking.

History tells us pretty much everything that could have gone wrong for the U.S. on the road to Mexico '86 did, in fact, go wrong. But national team players, coaches and administrators could not have known that future reality, not as those 100,000 U.S. fans filed out of the Rose Bowl. All they saw before them was the opportunity of their collective soccer lifetimes.

The IOC's decision in late 1983 to allow professionals to participate resulted in the reshuffling of several Olympic rosters, but none so dramatically as the United States'. Prior to this shift in player eligibility, the U.S. Olympic Committee and the U.S. Soccer Federation had organized an amateur squad of 20-somethings led by Manfred Schellscheidt, who, prior to accepting the Olympic gig, had taken over the Philadelphia Fever when Walt Chyzowych was fired halfway through the 1981-82 MISL season. When pro participation was suddenly confirmed, the Federation severed relations with the German, turned all those amateurs loose (most went back to college), stocked the team with pros from the North American Soccer League, and handed the reins to Alex Panagoulias. The Greek was the USMNT coach, after all, though he hadn't done much since Team America missed out on the NASL playoffs and then disbanded in November 1983.

Shellscheidt was not happy with the new arrangement. "We were competitive in 34 games around the world," he told *The New York Times* in March 1984. His team of amateurs had won nine games, lost 14 and tied 11. "I was happy with the team, and I think the players would have done well in the Olympics. But Gene Edwards told me they couldn't afford two coaches. That's funny, because they hadn't been paying me recently — but they had a $100,000-a-year coach doing nothing. I hadn't figured that Edwards would let things go so far and then make a change."

Edwards, who served as U.S. Soccer Federation president from 1974-84, told the *Times* that Schellscheidt had been "paid on a per-diem basis for a special project. He was paid for all the work he did." Whatever the case, Schellscheidt and the college kids, among them Gen Zero senior statesman John Stollmeyer, were out. Panagoulias and NASL's best American pros were in.

The Soviet Union led a tit-for-tat boycott of the 1984 Los Angeles Summer Games, in response to the U.S. failing to show up in Moscow four years earlier. This pullout engendered its own reshuffling, just weeks before the opening ceremonies. The USSR stayed home, as did Czechoslovakia and East Germany, each members of the Soviet-dominated Warsaw Pact. In their place were inserted West Germany, Norway and reigning World Cup champion Italy. Only Norway fielded something resembling an "A" squad in Los Angeles, however. France's "B" team ultimately topped a "B" team from Brazil in the gold medal match, 2-0, before that record-setting crowd in Pasadena.

———•———

Off the field, the U.S. Federation made lasting impressions and forged key relationships during the 1984 Olympic tournament. FIFA came away thoroughly impressed with its potential stadium venues, to say nothing of the enthusiasm and sheer number of American soccer supporters. Combined futbol attendance at the four venues — the Rose Bowl; Stanford Stadium in Stanford, California; Harvard Stadium in Allston, Massachusetts; and Navy-Marine Corps Memorial Stadium in Annapolis, Maryland — more or less equaled the combined attendance of *all* the other events staged at these Olympics. What's more, a little-known Los Angeles attorney named Alan Rothenberg had administered the tournament with considerable aplomb. His skills, first made evident on this broader stage, would later enable him, with FIFA's support, to win the U.S. Soccer Federation presidency in August 1990. He went on to play a pivotal role in organizing USA '94, and in the launch of MLS two years later.

On the field, the American performance that summer of '84 proved decidedly less convincing. The U.S. did send a top-choice team of professionals — precisely what the Federation and NASL had envisioned for Team America the previous summer. It included Ricky Davis, whose presence was surely ironic, if not a bit annoying, to his fellow squad members. After refusing to leave his club to participate in Team America, the holding midfielder ended up bolting from the Cosmos anyway, in late 1983, to join the St. Louis Steamers in MISL.

With Davis playing centrally, in a creative role that didn't exactly suit his attack-dog skills, Panagoulias' charges did not embarrass themselves that Olympic Summer. They tuned up with a surprising 0-0 result against Italy on May 30 and then opened the tournament with an impressive 3-0 dispatch of Costa Rica before 78,000 at Stanford Stadium — to that point, the largest crowd ever to gather for a soccer game in the United States. It was mainly downhill from there, however, as the Yanks fell 1-0 to Italy and drew 1-1 with Egypt, which also sent its "A" team, for what that's worth. The Pharaohs advanced on goal difference, at the Americans' direct expense, and reached the quarterfinals — as did the Canadians, whose senior national team was then grooming and deploying its own golden generation of talent.

A win in the final group game against Egypt might well have changed the way we view this particular generation of American footballers, what I call the Ricky Davis/NASL Cohort. But "goals change games," as the saying goes. Scoring once more against the Egyptians might have changed *history*. Reaching the knockout stages and perhaps playing for an Olympic medal might have given the squad and the U.S. soccer community something to hang their hats upon — a ripe prize NBC could have spent meaningful time showcasing on television as well. As it was, the '84 Games proved just another middling-to-poor, anonymous international performance, this time on home soil. NBC televised next to nothing of the soccer competition, opting instead for taped excerpts that, early in the competition, fixated on the U.S. team and its failure to advance. As a domestic profile-builder for American soccer, the 1984 Games were a dud.

"I think everything for U.S. soccer has been a learning experience, and you can add the '84 Olympics right in there with everything else. They tried it this way, with professionals in '84, and it didn't work. The next logical step was the college kids: us."

—*Marcelo Balboa*

"I didn't go to those games," says Marcelo Balboa, who was 17 that summer and lived nearby. "We didn't have any way of getting there. I was still in high school. I remember watching the Olympic team play, or practice, or maybe play some exhibition at Gahr High School? I don't remember. But I do remember seeing Ricky Davis, Kevin Crow. Maybe Jeff Hooker was on that team . . ."

Hooker was indeed on the team. John Stollmeyer was not. Still a collegiate, Stolly had been in the development pool for these Olympic games, but was released when FIFA announced that professionals who had not participated in previous World Cups would be eligible. "They released all us amateurs and went all professional," he remembers. "That was the Mike Fox and Ricky Davis group, and, you know, my time with them and with Alex [Panagoulias] was pretty short. Alex seemed just a little bit *odd* to us, I have to say. I came from Chyzowych and went to Panagoulias — then to Lothar [Osiander] and Gansler after that. Alex was always just a little . . . different."

———•———

International soccer is a game of generations. When one fails or ages out, a younger generation takes its place. Balboa rightly sees the Federation's later decision — to throw young, collegiate-groomed Generation Zero into the competitive international fires — as stemming directly from the inert, on-field Olympic experience in 1984.

"I think everything for U.S. soccer has been a learning experience, and you can add the '84 Olympics right in there with everything else," he contends. "They tried it this way, with professionals in '84, and it didn't work.

The next logical step was the college kids: us. It took a little time, but I definitely think all those steps were necessary. If we didn't take that step, they would probably not have decided to go with a new group of younger players afterward. And where were those younger players going to come from? From college."

A quick look at the 17-man 1984 Olympic roster, with their birth years alongside, emphasizes the generational aspect at play here:

1984 Olympic Roster

G	David Brcic	1958
G	Jamie Swanner	1961
D	Bruce Savage	1960
D	Jeff Durgan	1961
D	Erhardt Kapp	1959
D	Kevin Crow	1961
D	Gregg Thompson	1960
M	Kazbeck Tambi	1961
M	Angelo DiBernardo	1956
M	Chico Borja	1959
M	Mike Fox	1961
M	Ricky Davis	1958
M	Hugo Perez	1963
F	Jean Willrich	1953
F	Jeff Hooker	1965
F	Amr Aly	1962
F	Steve Moyers	1956

Note the bevy of real-deal veterans on this team: Willrich was 31 at the time, Moyers and Brcic 27. All but Hooker and Perez were born before 1963. That pegged them as Baby Boomers: from another generation. They were indeed seasoned professionals who, in the main, were still approaching their primes. Yet only two members of this team would represent their country at the 1988 Olympic Games in Seoul: Davis and Crow.

As Balboa notes, the Federation would ultimately cut bait on this generation of talent and commit to the next one. That's what American soccer federations, and all federations, do. They groom and assemble teams that reflect distinct generations of talent. Should enough birth years fail to produce, or fail to deliver a critical mass of talent, it's time to start over with a new generation. Many blame the USMNT's failure to qualify for Russia 2018, for instance, on the paucity of frontline professionals born between 1992 and '96. Bruce Arena went with a veteran squad because he was obliged to. Those American pros in their primes back in 2017 couldn't cut the mustard.

Had the "college kids" Balboa cites failed to qualify for *Italia* '90, they, too, would've been cast aside for another, even younger generation of players. That's how the process works. When Team USA took the field in Port of Spain that November afternoon in 1989, not a single member of the 1984 Olympic squad was anywhere to be seen. Not one would make the 1990 World Cup roster, either.

———————

And yet, in the fall of 1984, this mature generation of professional U.S. soccer players wasn't thinking about handing over the national-team keys to anyone, much less a bunch of no-name college kids. Why would they? The late-stage Boomers who composed the Davis/NASL Cohort had, from the beginning of their respective careers, availed themselves of the best professional soccer ever undertaken in this country. The core of this Olympic team had already experienced the crucible of a WCQ campaign, in 1980, and had played together longer — via Team America, via the Olympic effort — than any prior USMNT. Surely they saw nothing before them but opportunity, the best one presented to a U.S. national team since 1969. Here's the main reason why they were so very sanguine: The pending qualification tournament, scheduled to begin in autumn 1984, didn't include the one team they knew they couldn't beat — WC host and archnemesis Mexico, *hands down* the best team in the Confederation. No one else in CONCACAF inspired even half as much respect or fear.

Neither did the USSF require a primer on the opportunity at hand. That fall of 1984, post Olympics, the USMNT put forth a lukewarm-but-winning performance in a preliminary, two-legged CONCACAF qualifier against the Netherlands Antilles: 0-0 in Willemstad, followed by a 4-0 victory in St. Louis. Thereafter, the Federation lined up a credible series of friendlies to prepare the Nats for the penultimate CONCACAF qualifying group, slated for the spring of 1985. The Federation deserves credit for putting together an altogether respectable six-game fixture list at this crucial moment in the World Cup cycle. Results were decent: home victories over El Salvador and Colombia, followed by a 4-0 drubbing in Guatemala City and a less shameful 2-1 setback in Mexico City. The series concluded with a pair of draws against Ecuador. All of these games took place between Oct. 9 and Dec. 2, 1984.

Future U.S. captain Mike Windischmann got his first taste of senior play that fall of 1984. The competition impressed him. Squad administration did not.

"We used to get paid a per diem, and Blazer would give us our checks a month later," he recalls, referring to then-USSF secretary Chuck Blazer. "It wasn't like, 'Here's your bonus.' They just didn't pay us — and the tabs got higher and higher as this stuff piled up. You had to wait a long time to get your money, but at least it wasn't like the situation with the Albany Capitals [in the A-League, 1988], where you had to run to the bank and cash that check right away. If you didn't, they'd bounce it on you."

THE WORLD CUP QUALIFIERS SCHEDULED FOR April and May 1985 brought with them enormous pressure, the natural byproduct of such high stakes. Everything depended on qualification for Mexico '86. The most productive mindset, for U.S. players, would have been laser-focused concentration on the impending qualification crucible. By Christmas 1984, however, NASL had officially entered its death throes. Those in the know, including the players, could see their primary means of employment would likely *not* be in place for 1985, no matter what happened with World Cup '86 qualifying.

That November, as the 1984 NASL playoffs concluded, the San Diego, Minnesota, New York and Chicago franchises revealed they had been successfully poached by the Major Indoor Soccer League. NASL pressed on, junking the winner-take-all Soccer Bowl in favor of a best-of-three Soccer Bowl Series wherein the Chicago Sting swept the Toronto Blizzard. The clinching victory, the final NASL match ever played, took place at Toronto's Varsity Stadium before a crowd of 16,842, on Oct. 3, 1984. Four months later, in early February 1985, just seven clubs bothered to attend a last-ditch organizational meeting. When only two franchises proved willing to put down a deposit guaranteeing participation, three more NASL teams jumped to MISL, and the curtain came down.

Once again, as it had the winter of 1968-69, NASL's economic and administrative failures dealt American World Cup hopes a terrible blow. Once again, and for the first time since 1966, there was no legitimate first-division, outdoor soccer league operating in the United States.

"Most of us had obviously grown up only playing outdoor soccer, and when the NASL folded, reality hit hard," Bliss observes. "Like, what are we gonna do when we graduate? No one had a resume big enough to get to Europe really. That was honestly not even on the radar. It was grim. We were like, what *are* the realistic options for us?"

Tab Ramos' situation was typical. He had been drafted by the hometown Cosmos his senior year in high school. He went off to N.C. State in August 1984, fully expecting to do a year or two of college before jumping straight to NASL. Yet after his freshman season in Raleigh, there was no NASL. "What else is there to say, other than it was where we all wanted to play someday?" Bruce Murray asserts. "In the moment, I've just arrived at college, and, in that sense, I was playing at the level I was supposed to. But obviously, we were all thinking, 'What's gonna happen when this college thing is through?'"

"We thought the dream was over," Tony Meola remembers. "We were gonna be stuck playing at The Courts for the rest of our lives."

For the older, fully professionalized generation of senior USMNT players, the impact was no less stark and immediate: no premium employment come the spring and summer, regardless of what happened in the next stage of World Cup qualifying. *Lord knows* NASL had its flaws, but it had also been the best league, with the fattest paychecks in the land. For 17 years, its quality fluctuated, but it never failed to provide legit first-division futbol across the breadth of North America's two largest countries. Without it, there was only MISL, the second-rate American Soccer League, and a handful of regional backwaters.

U.S. participation at Mexico '86 might have redeemed this sad state of affairs. By securing final passage, the absence of NASL would not cut nearly so deeply. Perhaps the Federation would put the national team in residence, as it had done, after a fashion, with Team America during 1983 — as it would specifically do come 1988. A long-awaited breakthrough might burnish American soccer with an entirely new sheen. Maybe a new league, with a new TV contract, to capitalize on all that nationwide, World Cup-related exposure.

Everything depended on qualification for Mexico.

———•—•———

Three more friendlies in early 1985 concluded World Cup preparation. A 1-1 draw with Switzerland in Tampa prefaced home-and-home defeats to a rapidly improving Canadian side, one of two likely foes in final CONCACAF qualifying, should the Americans advance that far. Late in January of 1985, Windischmann headed back to Adelphi University on Long Island for the spring semester of his junior year — because going back to college straight from their national soccer team camps was something elite American soccer players did in the Eighties. Two weeks later, when the pay phone rang in his dormitory, he learned that he'd landed a spot on Panagoulias' match roster. "*Hey, Windy, you got a phone call!* That's how I found out," he remembers. "I was amazed. Being that young and playing with Ricky Davis and all those guys was unbelievable. It was my dream."

On May 15, the money matches commenced, and the U.S. looked more than ready. Chico Borja and Mark Peterson scored in a 2-1 away victory over Trinidad and Tobago. Indirectly, this victory further settled the squad. Durgan and Davis had been at odds since the latter had jilted Team America. After Durgan was beaten for T&T's lone goal, Panagoulias pulled him off at halftime and sent Paul Caligiuri out in his place. Durgan would never play for his country again.

Four days later, in the second leg versus T&T, Caligiuri — like Windischmann, still a college student, at UCLA — scored the only goal in a 1-0 victory at Murdock Stadium on the campus of El Camino Community College in Torrance, California. If pin-laden voodoo dolls of Caligiuri are still hanging today from darkened rafters in various Port of Spain drinking establishments, one could hardly blame the needle-wielders.

The four games that spelled the Americans' World Cup fate in 1985 — home-and-home ties with Costa Rica and T&T — all took place in the span of 16 days, another bit of fallout from the NASL's untimely demise. CONCACAF scheduled matches according to various countries' league schedules, and the U.S. had no league. As a result, these four crucial matches were essentially squeezed into the calendar once everyone else's league schedules had concluded.

While a tad CONCACAFkaesque, this tightly packed timetable seems to have suited the U.S. just fine. Panagoulias and his side next traveled to Costa Rica on May 26 and produced their finest performance in years: a 1-1 draw before a hostile crowd in Alajuela. Duke University sophomore John Kerr Jr. — the former Montgomery Pinto, who had billeted in Tom Wadlington's house — equalized just before halftime, after the U.S. had fallen behind in the 42nd minute. His goal held up. The vital away point gave the Americans 5 from a possible 6. The USMNT required only a draw in the rematch, at home against Costa Rica, to advance.

Only a draw.

Unfortunately for an entire generation of footballers, the U.S. failed to score on home turf, the infamous confines of Murdock Stadium. The visiting *Ticos* advanced, 1-0. This grim result didn't differ all that much from all the previous losses, the eight decisive defeats that had foiled every attempt since the inception of World Cup qualification tournaments in 1953. More than any other, however, this one stung. With NASL dead and buried, it was hard to see beyond the abyss, to where American soccer might go from this bleak new low.

And so, the finger-pointing began. It continues to this day.

Historical perspectives on this crushing World Cup dismissal — the last of its kind until 2017 — tend to center on the Federation's choice of venue and the crowd that showed up there on May 31, 1985. The 11,800 fans in attendance that afternoon were largely unsupportive, because they were largely Costa Ricans, who were thrilled to watch their *Ticos* steal the game and progress toward *their* country's first-ever World Cup qualification. "I was the left back in that game; it was definitely a Costa Rican crowd," Windischmann reports. "We were just attacking and attacking, but it was like playing *in* Costa Rica. Of course, we were used to that by then. If we played in the U.S. or in El Salvador — anywhere but St. Louis — it was all the same. It was normal for us. But it was a Costa Rican *town*. Why would the Federation pick El Camino Community College in California — you don't think there are gonna be Costa Ricans there? Another hard lesson learned."

The man in charge of home-venue selections during this qualifying series: Federation secretary Chuck Blazer, who served as chairman of the International Games Committee. In 2014, he would be indicted as part of the FIFA bribery scandal, the one that also brought down FIFA general secretary Sepp Blatter. Twenty-nine years prior, it was Blazer who reckoned that playing this match at a sold-out Murdock Stadium would be a good idea.

However, upon examination, the loss, the blame and the fan context prove far more complicated than the bottom dollar.

After all, the U.S. had played at Murdock just 12 days prior, the home victory against T&T. Attendance: 6,115. One could plausibly argue these SoCal surroundings were both familiar and propitious. What's more, as Windischmann notes, the U.S. was well acquainted with playing home games that felt like away games. If the Yanks could draw with Costa Rica in Alajuela, as they had just five days earlier, surely they should have delivered a comparable performance, and result, on home soil.

Windischmann, who would captain the Nats five years later in Italy, was not yet 21 in the spring of 1985. In the maelstrom of a single soccer match, he says, anything can go wrong. And everything *did* go wrong that day in Torrance. The same fate, he adds, could have befallen any group of players, almost anywhere, regardless of who was making noise in the stands, or not.

"We were very confident at that stage, headed into that game," he reports. "And we could not have played a better game, to be honest. Except for not scoring. Basically, one mistake. We couldn't get that tying goal. I'm sure you've been in those games: Someone scores the first goal and you're hitting the post, the crossbar. The goalkeeper is making crazy saves and you just can't get that tying goal. Costa Rica had to win, on the road, and all we needed was a draw. When we went to T&T in 1989, all *they* needed was the tie, and we went there having to win . . ."

The ill-fated 2017 USMNT similarly required *only a draw* at Trinidad and Tobago. Just one point, and its place at Russia 2018 would have been secured.

"Sometimes being in that position, where you don't *have* to win, isn't the best situation," Windy asserts. "We had a lot of great players on that '85 team, but we couldn't get the goal. To me, in a game like that, the crowd doesn't affect what happens. It was just one of those things where they scored the early goal and we just couldn't get the equalizer."

Windischmann tells us all we need to know about this notorious match. From 90-plus minutes of anguish, however, two moments still resonate.

First, front and center: the goal. Without the 1989 success in Port of Spain, and the ensuing 30-year run of successes, this tally might live even larger in the annals of American soccer infamy. U.S. keeper Arnie Mausser ventured out of his goal in the 34th minute to lay his fists on a free kick served from the flank by Costa Rica's Jorge Chevez. Mausser didn't make contact, and the ball did what no ball should ever do in the box: It fell to earth. In the mad scramble that ensued, the Ticos' Evaristo Coronado converted from close range.

Then, with 70 minutes gone, an ever-more-anxious American side looked to have tied the score when Dan Canter's low, angled drive produced the net-bulge his side had been frantically struggling to achieve. Referee John Meachin awarded the goal, pointing definitively back to the center circle. Ricky Davis ran in to retrieve the ball, as if eager to restart the match and score again . . . But in fact, Davis was hoping to retrieve the ball before anyone noticed that Canter's shot had *not* crossed the goal line between the posts. The spheroid had merely found the side netting and snuck through, into the back of the net. Linesman Robert Allen quickly informed Meachin of his mistake. A goal kick was awarded. The match pressed on.

The U.S. never meaningfully threatened again. This combination of yet another inert offensive performance and a single goalkeeping error closed the book on an entire generation of American soccer players. It also handed Generation Zero control of the senior national team, several years ahead of schedule.

———————

Coronado is an historic, beloved figure in Costa Rican soccer circles, but few remember him for his *Yanqui*-slaying goal in Torrance. In 1985, the *Ticos* themselves were also seeking their first-ever World Cup qualification — but their campaign ultimately fell short as well. Canada qualified from CONCACAF's final group stage later that year, whereupon Coronado would go back to his club, Saprissa, for whom he ultimately made 537 appearances and scored 148 times. For these exploits, he earned the congenial nickname *Evagol*. He also came to be known as Costa Rica's *El Caballero del Futbol* ("Gentleman Footballer"), for his generous spirit and respectful sporting demeanor. He was famous, in fact, for never having earned a red card.

When the next quadrennial arrived, he led the *Ticos* in scoring throughout qualifying, and Costa Rica *did* advance to the World Cup finals, alongside the U.S., for the very first time — but Coronado did not go to Italy. His national team coach, none other than Bora Milutinovic, USMNT skipper from 1991-95, left him off the final roster.

Futbol is just a game, but it can be most cruel.

It is also a game of generational ebbs and flows. Davis' national team career did not end that unfortunate afternoon in Torrance, but it did for most all of his teammates. This cohort of NASL-bred professionals would soon fade into the obscurity of regional leagues, indoor circuits and retirement. In the coming years Davis would play the role of steady, ball-winning elder statesman as younger, oncoming members of Generation Zero coalesced and matured around him. Shortly after the 1988 Olympics, while teaching a gym class at his kid's grammar school, he blew out a knee and missed all of the ensuing WC qualification campaign. His new national team coach, Bob Gansler, left him off the roster for *Italia* '90.

The World Cup dreams of both Ricky Davis and Evaristo Coronado effectively ended on the same afternoon, inside Murdock Stadium. "It was as if this game had represented the lost opportunity of my entire generation of players," Davis told journalist Will Parchman in 2013. "This was it. There wasn't going to be an opportunity down the road. It was gone."

HERE'S A CURIOUS THING: I HOLD in my mind's eye no real picture or meaningful sense of any players in the Davis/NASL Cohort, except for Davis himself, and perhaps a very young Hugo Perez. In this respect, I suspect I speak for the vast majority of American soccer fans 57 years of age and younger. I've just allotted several thousand words to explaining why U.S. fans never had the chance to familiarize themselves with

David Brcic's face, Steve Moyer's gait, or Jamie Swanner's capability in tight spaces. They all played in NASL, of course, but the league and its attendant media coverage had sadly waned all throughout the early 1980s before disappearing altogether. These players possessed one last chance at World Cup glory and its broader cultural exposure, only to fritter it away over 90 scoreless minutes in exurban Southern California.

Davis remains the exception because he was the standard-bearing *estadounidense* on the league's best, glitziest, most frequently televised team. The Davis I remember was short, stout, quick and ever boyish. Even in 1984, as a 24-year-old, he looked about 16. There was a reasonably famous poster, among period soccer junkies, that showed Davis lounging on the beach, communing with an actual puma. He had a contract with the German athletic outfitter throughout much of his Cosmos career. But a poster doesn't convey to anyone that he was a ball-winner, a sort of baby-faced, B-grade Claude Makelele, a poor man's N'Golo Kante.

However, as for striker Steve Moyers and defender Dan Canter, whose national team careers ended that afternoon in Torrance? I have no conception of them as players. At all. YouTube clips are few, and they don't help. They remain a *lost* generation, a group of players entirely diminished by the decline and failure of NASL — and then buried in the American soccer subconscious by the failure in Torrance, and the emergence of Generation Zero immediately thereafter.

Here's what I'm getting at: Because this lack of familiarity extends beyond individual players to the 1985 U.S. national team itself, it's terribly difficult to assess this failed qualifying campaign or that single, pivotal performance in Torrance. Did these guys, the Davis/NASL Cohort, merely underachieve? Did they choke? Were they supremely unlucky? Were they poorly managed? How good were the Ticos, *really*? Had they scored to tie the game at Murdock, would the Americans have beaten Canada and advanced to the 1986 World Cup in Mexico?

The on-field combatants themselves — unsurprisingly — willingly take the blame. They're players. They make the fewest excuses, and they are perhaps the most objective when it comes to questions of fair expectations. As Davis himself indicated after the Torrance match, "We can't play much better than that."

When we widen the lens, however, and consult others who were there — the coaches, the attendant media, and especially the older members of Gen Zero who, in many cases, had played *beside* these guys — we gather a fuller picture. We better understand why they did not advance internationally in 1985 and why they were unsuccessful in playing for their country throughout the NASL era. We also begin to get a sense for why Generation Zero *did* prove successful.

Bob Gansler, at this time, was out of the USMNT coaching loop. He was two years into his career with the UW-Milwaukee Panthers, but he knew the Davis/NASL Cohort as a coach, a student of the game and a contemporary evaluator of talent. First, he disagreed with the administrative decision to hire Panagoulias. "I was Walt Chyzowych's assistant when we tried to qualify for the '78 World Cup in Argentina and the '82 World Cup," he says. "We were the Americans — hyphenated Americans: He was Ukrainian-American, I'm German-Hungarian-American or Hungarian-German . . . But I'm American first, and so was Walt. Unfortunately, you still had NASL around in the early Eighties, and Phil Woosnam was still around, and he was of the persuasion that 'we foreigners' could do it better. And obviously there were people in the Federation who thought that, too.

"I think what happened in 1982 and 1986 was, well . . . we forgot about the intangibles. Players bring intangibles. Coaches bring intangibles. If you have a problem when you look at that crest on your chest, if you have a problem figuring out what 'USA' stands for, maybe that's something that's going to be missing in the final outcome and performance. Enough said."

Translation: too many foreign-born coaches wielding too much influence within the national team from 1983-85.

Panagoulias had other detractors, but few players single him out as having held this team back. They found him eccentric, at times unintelligible, but he was not without managerial acumen, in their view. He would ultimately return to Greece and qualify his native country for USA '94. He passed away in 2012, at 78.

I keep coming back to the away leg in Costa Rica five days prior, on May 26, 1985, the Greek's penultimate game in charge. Walking off the field that day in Alajuela, Panagoulias and his charges must have felt they'd done all the hard work. Had the U.S. drawn or prevailed in the Torrance match, if Arnie Mausser hadn't whiffed on that cross, we might view Panagoulias and this generation of players very, very differently. Because Canada, which bested Costa Rica and Honduras for the Confederation's lone World Cup berth, was good but eminently beatable.

Today, Gansler will speculate on such matters only up to a point. He remains a committed believer in evolution when it comes to assessing USMNT stumbles, Torrance included. He has little patience for those who question the speed at which the national team achieved a baseline of technical ability, tactical awareness and winning instinct. It's certainly in Gansler's interest to give Generation Zero — and, by extension, himself — credit for being a special agglomeration of talent, the fabled golden generation, expertly led. However, the coach steadfastly refuses to take that bait.

"What was done at that time was what *could* be done at that time," he says. "During this period, as with previous periods, we were always looking at how we could make it better. But it doesn't happen overnight. Sometimes you go a little off the evolutionary track, sometimes you bog down. But are you trying to tell me that Peter Vermes, Tab Ramos, John Harkes, Paul Caligiuri came out of nowhere? They came out of the system the way it was! Trittschuh, [John] Doyle, Windischmann, Meola and all of them. They were capable. They needed opportunities, and they got more as we went along the way. I disagree with folks who come with, 'Why did it take so long? Why didn't *that* team win?' We're *still* not where we want to be, but we're a helluva lot closer."

Four members of Generation Zero fought their way onto the match roster for Torrance, in addition to the tuneup qualifiers/friendlies. Several more had been in the mix as amateurs before the IOC's decision allowing professionals at the L.A. Olympiad. In short, a bunch of guys from the Class of 1990 played and trained alongside the Davis/NASL Cohort in national team matches and camps conducted throughout 1983, 1984 and 1985. I asked them why the 1985 USMNT never got it done, and why Gen Zero did.

"I got my first taste of the senior national team under Panagoulias, way back then with Mike Fox and Rick Davis," recalls John Stollmeyer. "Maybe it's just me, but almost every national team we ever put together I thought was pretty damned good. The core 15 guys who ultimately played through this period were pretty doggone strong, if you asked me."

Brian Bliss made his national team debut against Ecuador, in late 1984. "Listen, they were good," he says. "I went through five national team coaches and got a cap under five different guys, which is rare, I guess. But I had my first cap with Panagoulias . . . There were mostly old NASL guys involved in the national team at that time. Let me tell you: They could really play. I can't explain the Torrance result. I just can't."

Incidentally, in 10 years representing his country, Bliss would amass only 44 caps — a meager total that boggles the mind. Jeff Agoos is a pretty good comp for Bliss: never a star, but solid and versatile. His USMNT career started in 1988, and he went on to be capped 134 times! "My caps are one of my greatest achievements in a way," Bliss says, tongue in cheek. "When I see guys today with 110 to 120 caps, it amazes me because, you know, we went months and months without playing national team games."

As young players in college or fresh out, Bliss and his contemporaries looked up to the Davis/NASL Cohort as seasoned professionals: the guys they'd been watching on TV, the guys who had ascended to places they wanted and expected for themselves. There was respect for these elders — but Gen Zero saw their shortcomings, too. Because they recognized, better than most, NASL's inherent shortcomings. In the moment, in the spring of 1985, few believed NASL had actually *damaged* American World Cup fortunes. "You'd have thought those guys would have qualified for 1986," says

Steve Trittschuh. "For most of that period, NASL was still around, right? Of course, there was no league at all when the 1990 cycle came around — and *we* qualified. You'd think it would have been the reverse."

But slowly, in the wake of Torrance and the league's collapse, this counter-intuitive narrative acquired purchase.

"Looking back on those guys and that period, NASL was the biggest problem and everybody knew it," Stolly flatly states. "As an American in that period, you didn't have to be one of the 11 best guys to get on the field. At the same time, NASL had all these second-rate European pros taking the minutes."

Windischmann adds another intriguing, broader factor to the mix: "I think indoor affected that team's preparation — coming from outdoor to indoor and back and forth, then trying to do the national team."

By early 1985, NASL had already breathed its last, but its legacy of collapse had been underway for some time. Like rats from a sinking ship, the league's top U.S. players had, in the previous two to three years, started switching over to the Major Indoor Soccer League in earnest — seeking steady pay and match fitness. The U.S. standard-bearer for NASL, Ricky Davis himself, left the Cosmos for the St. Louis Steamers at the close of 1983. Midfielder Mike Fox made just seven appearances for the Cosmos in 1984 before jumping to the Las Vegas Americans for the winter indoor season. Chico Borja joined him there. Forward Mark Peterson played on Team America in 1983 but thereafter latched on with his hometown Tacoma Stars, indoors. Angelo DiBernardo was an established outdoor player with the Cosmos through 1984, but after the Cosmos joined the MISL, he spent the winter prior to WC qualifying playing indoors. Gregg Thompson had, for two years, been splitting time between the Tampa Bay Rowdies (outdoor) and the Minnesota Strikers (indoor). Windischmann's Torrance teammate in defense, Kevin Crow, had also been jumping back and forth between indoor and outdoor, for the San Diego Sockers, since 1983.

In short, eight starters in Torrance — Thompson, Mausser, Crow, Canter, Van der Beck, Davis, Fox, and Hugo Perez — had all played in

MISL over the winter of 1984-85. The remaining three — Kerr, Caligiuri and Windischmann — were still in college and the only ones who trained exclusively outdoors.

"The indoor game hurt us during qualifying, to be honest, because the players and the talent were definitely there," Windischmann says. "They are such different games, such different preparation. After I played that one year of indoor [with the L.A. Lazers of MISL, 1987-88], then going back outdoors to get ready for the Olympics? I couldn't even judge a head ball for a day or two. The fitness is different: We went outside and we were really huffing and puffing. We were like, what the hell is this?

"I understand people were trying to make a living — and in our time it wasn't like we were making tons of money, going back and forth between NASL and MISL. So, you were kinda stuck... I think the underlying issue was indoor soccer affecting our outdoor performance, because the players were definitely there."

—Mike Windischmann

"The first time I got to L.A. and we had an outdoor game, some of these guys [on the Lazers] couldn't even play. But then we went indoors and they were unbelievable! Blocking shots, beating guys, getting assists and looking like great players. In their own right, they *were* excellent indoor players. But once some of them got outdoors, they couldn't deliver. I hate to put names out there, but Mark Frederickson is a good example. Year after year, he was great indoors. An all-star. But once he got outside, he just wasn't as talented. Excellent defender indoors, but not skillful enough outside."

In many ways, Windischmann points out, the NASL minimum had for years obliged many Americans to take their careers indoors. With foreigners occupying so many starting XIs, indoor soccer was where the playing time and money were. When NASL expired altogether, the problems compounded. At that point, even elite Americans had gone indoors.

"I chose not to have an indoor career and tried to stay outdoors," Windischmann adds. "Made a point of it. But I understand people were trying to make a living — and in our time it wasn't like we were making tons of money, going back and forth between NASL and MISL. So, you were kinda stuck. All those guys *had* to go indoor; there was no choice. But going indoor to outdoor and back? I'm sure there were times when these guys [on the 1985 USMNT] were playing indoor and had to go train outdoor with the national team. I think the underlying issue was indoor soccer affecting our outdoor performance, because the players were definitely there."

Bruce Murray agrees — to a point. "It's a great observation by Mike, as usual," he says. "Your fitness is nowhere near what you need it to be, coming out of indoor. That could have been a contributor. But to me, with seasoned pros, they should have qualified anyway. You have a bunch of professionals there; you had NASL. The whole thing was set up for them."

According to *Los Angeles Times* veteran soccer correspondent Grahame Jones, writing the week after Torrance, "Because the United States has rejected the outdoor game and adopted the indoor game, Panagoulias has had to fight to find players. Those he has managed to pry away from reluctant Major Indoor Soccer League teams have come in unprepared to play 90 minutes of hard soccer. They are used to the indoor game, where substitution is unlimited and games are broken into 15-minute segments instead of two 45-minute halves ... And so, the United States will have to wait another four years for another chance. But without an outdoor professional league to provide the players, its chances of qualifying for Italy '90 already seem slim."

———·———

With the passage of time, Davis himself has been extremely forthright in accepting blame for the Torrance result. To this day he remains sober and unsparing in his self-analysis, which provides yet another window on why this 1985 team didn't deliver the World Cup breakthrough U.S. soccer so badly needed.

"When I went and played with the national team, we struggled," Davis told Parchman. "They needed me to do things, and I wasn't it. They needed a goal scorer, and I wasn't that goal scorer. There wasn't a lot of creativity to [my] game. My game was based on physical attributes; I was quick, with a little bit of speed."

For the Cosmos, Davis was a self-described "grunter," a ball-winner who sat on top of the central defenders ball-hawking and destroying the opponent's run of play. For the Nats, because there was no one else, he was obliged to occupy a more central, forward-looking, creative role — one he couldn't credibly fulfill at the international level, even in CONCACAF.

American soccer fans should recognize this positional dynamic, for it's still with us. Landon Donovan is Exhibit A: He was born to play outside midfield at the highest levels of international soccer, as we observed during his stellar-if-truncated stints at Everton, in 2010 and 2012. With the national team, however, he was often obliged to play striker, or a central attacking role behind the strikers, because among the limited choices, he remained the country's best option there. This misfit dynamic plays out in the context of many national teams, of course. However, even a small country like Costa Rica maintains a national league where there are plenty of native players occupying *all* the positions on the field, including central, creative roles. The peculiar evolution of NASL tended to deny American players those positions, those opportunities, those minutes — very much in the way the English Premier League tends to deny native Britons those positions and opportunities today.

Murray is prepared to attribute some portion of the Torrance failure to fate: "Shit happens. Just like 2018. It's CONCACAF. Something can always jump up and bite you."

These are the more nuanced, sympathetic views of the situation. The less accommodating view holds that for all its strengths and professionalism, the 1985 USMNT simply was not good enough. It could not hold serve at home against Costa Rica, a team that would prove unable to best Canada or Honduras in the final stage of qualifying. What's more, the match report reveals something else quite pointed and damning: Three

U.S. collegiates — Caligiuri, Windischmann and Kerr — were all capped for the first time in autumn 1984. All three of them started against Costa Rica on May 31, 1985.

In myriad respects, the Torrance debacle proved a watershed moment for U.S. Soccer because it crystallized for players, coaches and the Federation the lamentable state of its senior national team — a team that many felt was the best USMNT had yet assembled. The qualification failure didn't single out the players alone. The on-field disaster cast doubt on the way those competitors had been professionalized by a league that had just gone out of business. Systemically, the Torrance result exposed the way U.S. internationals had been obliged to follow the money and minutes indoors, only to be called back to play *outdoor* matches that would, sadly, define their places in American soccer history.

With NASL and another major tournament opportunity behind them, the USSF was obligated to move in new directions. This was rock bottom, competitively. Three weeks post-Torrance, the Federation relieved Panagoulias of his duties. Because much of the Davis/NASL Cohort would age out before the next World Cup cycle, these players were free to eke out the remainder of their professional careers indoors.

A year later, when the global futbol community gathered in Mexico, the U.S. Federation turned its lonely eyes to yet another cosmopolitan fiesta taking place just over the border, without them. The Yanks were not missed, not on the field. It's difficult to miss what has not been present since the Truman administration. What's more, this was the *Mundial* of Maradona, the Hand of God, and payback for the Falklands War; of Platini, Lineker and Rummenigge; of emerging Danes, surprising Belgians and inert Canadians. Not everything was sweetness and light. Noon kickoffs, scheduled to leverage prime-time viewing in Europe, subjected competitors to brutal heat indexes. When NBC aired the opener, defending champion Italy vs. Bulgaria, U.S. viewers were treated to commentary from Thai announcers. NBC sportscaster Charlie Jones restored English play-by-play by calling network headquarters in New York City from a press box phone. Collect. The following Sunday, many of the 142 nations expecting transmission of Brazil vs. Spain, live from Guadalajara, failed to receive that feed. Some countries got sound and no picture; others, the reverse. I could go on. TeleMexico eventually sorted things out, but FIFA pooh-bahs, then mulling host nations for 1994, surely thought to themselves, *These Americans are terrible footballers, but they have boatloads of disposable income and they know how to do television.*

Los estadounidenses were indeed treated to more World Cup content in June 1986 than ever before. ESPN broadcast 14 weekday, group-stage matches — always with commentators located back home, in remote U.S. studios. NBC delivered seven weekend matches with in-person, on-location commentary, including a final that drew a respectable 4.1 Nielsen rating. A national ratings point in 1986, the year I graduated college, represented approximately 880,000 U.S. homes. Ours was not a Nielsen home, but that June I did watch each of these games from my parents' house, effectively interrupting, 90 minutes at a time, my first adult job search.

Torrance wasn't quite the end for the Davis/NASL Cohort. That dubious distinction we can attach to a friendly 5-0 drubbing at the hands of England on June 16, 1985, before a smattering of fans (10,145) at the cavernous L.A. Coliseum. The U.S. team sheet reveals a squad in full-on transition, with last hurrahs for a dozen guys who'd never play for their country again. There were minutes for up-and-comers and cameos for guys who went as quickly as they came:

USA: Arnie Mausser (Tim Harris 46'), Kevin Crow, Mike Windischmann, Dan Canter (Michael Brady 54'), Paul Caligiuri, Perry Van der Beck, Ed Radwanski (Steve Snyder 79'), Ricky Davis, Bruce Murray (Jacques Ladouceur 46'), John Kerr (Jeff Hooker 46'), Hugo Perez

World Cup qualification from quadrennial to quadrennial remains an exercise in generation management. We observe that larger truth today in the wake of the USMNT's disastrous failure to qualify for Russia 2018. Under a new coach, Gregg Berhalter, a completely new generation of players is getting its turn. In 1985, the U.S. Soccer Federation, like its counterpart in Costa Rica, witnessed the failure of a particular generation of players, along with the system that created those players. Each country confronted the same regrettable quandary: to keep fishing or cut bait. The Americans went with the latter approach, because they had little choice. An entirely new era — one devoid of first-division, domestic, outdoor soccer — had been foisted upon what remained of the futbol establishment. In most respects, the landscape was demonstrably and unremittingly desolate.

In another sense, however, the fates smiled on Werner Fricker, who had assumed the Federation presidency in late 1984, replacing Gene Edwards. In the wake of the Torrance autopsy, he was handed a slate cleaner than any previous USSF chief had inherited since the mid-1960s. More critically, he could see what Gansler saw — a bumper crop of young talent coming up through the ranks, a crop that had been nurtured via the new ODP/Festival/U-20 apparatus to an extent no previous generation of U.S. players ever had. Here was a thoroughly native footballing generation, America's very first, a cohort completely untainted by the double-edged developmental sword that was NASL.

"Maybe there was something in the water," Brian Bliss says. "You hit the nail on the head there when you said 'golden generation.' In America, those birth years from 1963 to 1967 really were something. We can see that now. The bulk of the guys who went to Italy were all born at that time, they grew up with the game, and they all had the right mentality, maybe had the right coaching, too."

In 1985, Fricker and others at the Federation were not convinced this generation was necessarily golden or providential. There are no certainties when divining these once-in-a-century phenomena, especially in a soccer culture as young and anomalous, as stubbornly exceptionalist as America's. But Fricker & Co. had no choice.

Anomalous is a euphemism, of course, offered up out of politeness. Up to this point, the game's professional culture in America — viewed dispassionately and nearly 40 years on — was not merely peculiar. By 1985, the professional outdoor game in the U.S. was objectively in free fall. It wasn't merely substandard. *It did not exist.* The national team program was only marginally better off: Post-Torrance, the USMNT had failed to reach the World Cup finals nine straight times. And yet, almost in spite of itself, the nation had produced what appeared to be its breakthrough generation. What's more, the powers that be *did* seem to grasp hold of this fact. The Federation had four years to make sure this cohort and its potential were not squandered. New thinking would be required.

This iconic Puma poster graced many a GZ wall during the early 1980s. Ricky Davis' World Cup dreams, and those of an entire generation of U.S. players, were effectively dashed in Torrance, California, on May 31, 1985. *(Arthur J. Klonsky photo)*

U.S. Soccer Federation president Werner Fricker, the man who delivered the 1994 World Cup, was shaped as a player, administrator and dreamer by American soccer's urban/ethnic club experience. After representing his adopted country on the 1964 Olympic team, his United German Hungarians club side (that's Fricker front row, second from right) claimed the 1965 National Amateur Cup. *(Images courtesy of the Fricker family, United German Hungarians)*

7.   *THE PRIMORDIAL SOUP*

The mid-1980s represent a complicated, critical period in the game's modern history on these shores, and yet it can reasonably be viewed today as a nether region in the collective consciousness of American soccer — a sort of darkness before the dawn, largely concealed in a black box. A neater, cleaner, rosier take on this era would perhaps begin with the 1985 debacle in Torrance — yet another deflating, premature coda to yet another failed World Cup qualification campaign. It might conclude four and a half years later in Port of Spain, on the island of Trinidad, just as the "Shot Heard 'Round the World" left Paul Caligiuri's supple left foot. This is indeed how some in the U.S. soccer establishment would prefer we remember things. The truth is just too messy and reflects positively on so few, excepting the players themselves. See here excerpted highlights from this era, according to an otherwise lengthy, exhaustive timeline at USsoccer.com, the official online portal of the U.S. Soccer Federation:

1986 — The Western Soccer Alliance (WSA) kicked off with seven teams . . . At the UNICEF All-Star game in Pasadena, Calif., FIFA officials suggested the USA should bid for the '94 World Cup.

1988 — The ASL [American Soccer League] began play with 10 teams . . . On July 4, the United States was awarded the 1994 World Cup during the FIFA Congress in Zurich.

1989 — Paul Caligiuri scored the biggest goal in U.S. Soccer history since [Joe] Gaetjens' 1950 World Cup goal against England.

Hey, it's just a timeline on a website. We can't expect too much detail or nuance. However, this paper-thin account effectively papers over a 50-month stretch that, in fact, was a sort of primordial soup of movements, trends and evolutions that are vital to our understanding of that match in Port of Spain, to the team that prevailed that afternoon, to the footballing nation we were then, and to the one we've since become.

The on-field avatars of Generation Zero remember this period with visceral precision, and their recollections paint an unflinching picture of a soccer culture not necessarily on the verge of something big. That's the rosy retrospective assumption when it comes to this period, when the mid-Eighties are considered at all. In reality, our soccer culture operated on a knife-edge all through this era of titanic flux and desperation. And you know what? The players from that era don't want the rough edges knocked off for the sake of clean and orderly 21st-century timelines. They want us to know just how freakin' nuts it all was, how haphazard, how recognizably amateurish and retrograde. They want modern American soccer fans to understand how easily it all might have gone awry or come to nothing — were it not for their efforts, their striving, their good fortune, their well-earned if all-too-anonymous role in the history.

"Guys like Walter Bahr and Harry Keough, who helped grow the game and build the game in America, those guys get credit for that, and rightly so," says Brian Bliss, who, during this transitional phase, pursued his chosen vocation in various urban/ethnic semipro circuits, in the ragtag A-League, and even (gasp!) indoors. "Somewhere along the line, though, we hope there's a footnote that sets the record straight. Because we stemmed the tide. Things were not going that great during the mid-1980s. But that's also when that '88-to-'90 squad came together — and that squad played a major role in getting us to where we are today. I don't want to say it's all been swept under the rug, but that story has served mainly as a kind of subtext to what happened in 1994. Not to brag about it, but had we not made the '88 Olympics, or qualified in 1990, who knows what the history would be now."

It's ironic that Bliss should evoke the names of Bahr and Keough, two members of the 1950 U.S. Men's National Team, the squad that stunned England 1-0 during group play at the first Brazilian *Copa do Mundo*. Bahr assisted on the Joe Gaetjens goal that carried the day in Belo Horizonte — the goal referred to in the Federation timeline above. During their competitive primes, however, throughout the 1950s and into the Sixties, Bahr, Keough and Gaetjens never played anything we might recognize as "professional soccer" here in the United States. The national teams they led never qualified for World Cups in 1954 or '58. They played soccer semiprofessionally and without fanfare all through this period, for ethnic clubs based in urban centers sprinkled across a largely soccer-illiterate country. The leagues were regional at best; most served only a particular metropolitan area. The clubs themselves were almost completely local in outlook, except for their participation in American soccer's one enduring national competition: the U.S. Open Cup. All the players, even the stars, held down jobs outside of soccer — to make ends meet and raise their respective families.

Thirty-five years on, once the North American Soccer League had receded from view, it was as if the American futbol landscape had not changed at all since the days of Bahr, Keough and Gaetjens: no national professional league, a paltry soccer consciousness among the general populace, and a national team incapable of qualifying for a World Cup.

Walter Bahr died in 2018 after fathering three sons, all of whom played professional soccer in this country during the late Seventies and Eighties. By 1985, his family should have been celebrated as American soccer royalty, as pillars of U.S. soccer's rich, if anachronistic, history. Instead, the surname "Bahr" is more closely associated with the NFL. Matt and Chris Bahr both played in the NASL, but they earned far more money and fame as placekickers for Super Bowl champions.

In the 21st century, as Bliss asserts, Walter Bahr and Harry Keough have begun to receive their historical due. Gaetjens should likewise be hailed as a folk hero, on the order of other monumental goal-scorers like Paul Caligiuri and Landon Donovan. Instead, he remains a timeline footnote — one who did not live to see the 1980s. Gaetjens returned to his native Haiti in 1957, shortly after Francois "Papa Doc" Duvalier was elected president. Gaetjens was a footballer; he was not politically active, but his two brothers were. By 1957, each had fled to the neighboring Dominican Republic to avoid persecution. On July 8, 1964, two of Duvalier's paramilitary henchmen — known to history as the *Tontons Macoutes* ("Bogeymen") — abducted Joe Gaetjens outside his own front door in Port-au-Prince. He was never seen again. It's estimated that 30,000 people were killed or similarly disappeared during Papa Doc's grotesque, 14-year rule. Gaetjens' murder was not officially confirmed until 1972, the year following Duvalier's death.

———•———

Bliss and his contemporaries remain clear-eyed regarding the pitiable state of U.S. soccer in 1985. Forget the lack of first-division futbol. There was nothing resembling a second or third division, either. The country's shambolic national team program was on hiatus again. The domestic futbol culture had no media mechanism to promote the sport or any administrative mechanism to professionalize the nation's elite young players — to the point where the scions of American soccer legends were kicking field goals for a living. Soccer players have a long history of moonlighting as placekickers. The crossover skill set is obvious. But outright defection was considered adding insult to injury, especially once NASL folded over the winter of 1984-85.

Let's be fair but direct: For the members of Generation Zero, it seemed clear they had inherited a soccer culture in regression. The conditions and opportunities afforded American professionals in 1985, four short years before Caligiuri's famous goal, were commensurate with those on offer in any number of also-ran footballing nations in Africa or Asia at the time — or here in the U.S. during the 1940s or 1950s. The state of affairs, the professional outlook for Bliss and his peers, was that bleak.

"Back then, if you're from the East Coast and it's November through February, what are you doing to stay fit?" Peter Vermes asks rhetorically. "How are you doing it exactly? All of a sudden, it's January and you're taken to Florida to play a qualifier or something — after doing whatever you're doing, in 25-degree weather, somewhere up north. Now you're in 90-degree weather, with humidity. Think about all those things. Then consider the fact that we all had to hold multiple jobs, too, in order to make a living. It was pretty nuts."

With nowhere else to go, Bliss was among those drafted by Major Indoor Soccer League clubs. With no better options, he dutifully went to play for the Cleveland Force, a fly-by-night team in a fly-by-night league. Were this franchise reliably funded, or administered by professional coaches and executives, indoor soccer was still no way to groom world-class outdoor professionals — not in 1985, not in 2005 and not today. Bliss and his contemporaries recognized this reality better than anyone, in the moment. There was nothing to be done about it, however. MISL was the only viable, fully professional option mid-decade.

Come the early 1990s, Bliss played for several clubs in the German *Bundesliga*, where the professionalization of athletes is a social science. Upon his retirement, he committed his work life to coaching and player development. He well understands the role of a technical director, for example, and precisely how young players should be professionalized. Did the Cleveland Force employ a technical director, or any reasonable facsimile thereof, back in 1986-87?

"Um, no. Just a coach and a GM, who kinda did the contracts and dealt with the business side of things," Bliss recalls, his voice dripping with disdain. "It was a bit of a mess. It was a blessing when the club folded, because it forced us all to do something else."

Short of placekicking, "something else" for Generation Zero, from 1985-87, amounted to a combination of soccer camps — where elite, senior national team players served as mere instructors, but *paid* instructors — periodic Federation camps, and ad hoc appearances in regional, semiprofessional ethnic leagues, where the soccer could be very good, but where the pay and level of organization varied wildly. Some swallowed hard and continued to participate in MISL.

Americans are accustomed to progress. They more or less demand it. At this point in time, however, it was obvious to anyone paying attention (and the overwhelming majority of U.S sporting consumers were *not* paying attention) that nothing related to professional outdoor soccer in the United States was improving. There was nothing inevitable about the sport's success here. On the contrary, it wasn't at all clear to the players themselves that *any* next steps toward professionalism and international credibility would be taken any time soon. Nothing set this meager table like the death of NASL in 1984. The void created by its demise, in all these areas, was cavernous. Just think how the American soccer community would look and operate today if Major League Soccer folded its tent tomorrow and simply disappeared. American soccer during the second Reagan administration laid bare, for all to see, just how amateurish, rinky-dink and aimless the sport had become. The promise of NASL over the course of the past 17 years had proved entirely superficial, fleeting or chimerical.

———•——

Starting in 1985, with NASL no longer in the picture and another World Cup qualification down the tubes, the Federation and its cohort of elite young players responded to these degraded circumstances by returning to the game's long-standing American roots: to the so-called ethnic soccer community, the soccer infrastructure that had trained up the likes of Keough, Bahr and Gaetjens. The elite members of Generation Zero quickly recognized that decades-old semiprofessional leagues in cities like New York, Philadelphia, San Francisco, St. Louis, Milwaukee, Los Angeles and Boston represented the only practical outdoor options available to them. Playing for these urban/ethnic clubs proved the single most influential, on-field experience of their young professional lives. Defying all expectation, the ethnic leagues effectively readied them to take on the world.

Administratively, the U.S. Soccer Federation had similarly cast its lot with the middle-aged products of this seemingly outdated, urban/ethnic infrastructure. Federation president Werner Fricker was reared in this footballing environment, as were the next two USMNT coaches hired post-Torrance, Lothar Osiander and Bob Gansler. When the nation's soccer prospects were at their most bleak, these first-generation Americans were the figures who steadied the ship, trained up a viable national team, and led Generation Zero through qualification to *Italia* '90. These were also the so-called "hyphenated Americans" who courted and secured the 1994 World Cup tournament for a country that didn't yet know it wanted or deserved such a thing.

Ultimately, late in the decade, several key members of Generation Zero, seeking the advanced professional development they knew they required, went looking for the ethnic experience at one of its primary sources: Europe itself.

In the meantime, however, young American players of quality — the guys who would definitively change U.S. soccer fortunes forever just four years later — focused on their all-consuming, quietly desperate scrambles for money, technical advancement and competitive minutes, wherever they could find them. In the post-NASL apocalypse of 1985, that meant ethnic soccer in regional leagues centered in cities across the country.

There was another rich irony in this development, of course, for these were the same suburban kids to whom organized soccer had been intentionally delivered, in the early 1970s, by immigrants like John Kerr Sr. in Bethesda, Maryland, and Ruben Mendoza in Granite City, Illinois. Men like the foreign-born fathers of John Harkes, Peter Vermes, John Stollmeyer and Marcelo Balboa, who coached up suburban hotbeds in north Jersey, south Jersey, northern Virginia and Southern California. By 1985, professional but leagueless (and largely clueless about their abilities to play abroad), Generation Zero was obliged to reverse this process — to venture from their native suburbs back into those cities — in order to play viable club soccer. To play *somewhere* competitively worthwhile and out of doors, when not engaged with the still-reeling national team program.

And honestly, what better way to take the edge off that white-bread, suburban veneer than an extended run in America's colorfully urban, thoroughly ethnic leagues, which, in the absence of NASL, were now home to the best outdoor soccer being contested north of the Rio Grande?

"After NASL folded, that was the best option," Mike Windischmann says. "My dream had been to play in NASL, but when I got out of college, it had folded. Perfect timing, right? I played one season indoors, but I consciously tried to stay outdoors, and that's what led me to the Brooklyn Italians, where I got to play with [Andranik] Eskandarian and Hubert Birkenmeier, a lot of really good players. How can you go wrong playing with guys like that?"

The Italians, twice U.S. Open Cup champions during this period, illustrate just how competitive, professional and technically advanced New York's Cosmopolitan League could be. Birkenmeier and Eskandarian (father of Alecko, who played in MLS and made a single appearance for the USMNT) were both former Cosmos, after all — in their 30s, but not completely over the hill. There was money to be made with these clubs. There was fitness to be maintained and on-field savvy to be gained. Most of these club organizations maintained regular practice schedules and reserve squads — full teams of players who weren't quite good enough or old enough to appear for the first team, but who remained under contract or otherwise affiliated with the club. Every MLS club fields a reserve side today; they compete in a variety of leagues that constitute the American professional soccer pyramid.

It's telling that NASL clubs never invested in such things, despite the fact that reserve sides have been de rigueur at European clubs since the 1950s. Even in the 21st century, with three tiers of U.S. pro soccer fully operational above it, the Cosmopolitan League's top two divisions still require maintenance of full reserve squads.

The Cosmopolitan League was formed in 1923 as the German American Football Association (GAFA). Along with the San Francisco Soccer Football League (SFSFL) and other elite metropolitan circuits, GAFA represented the top tier of U.S. soccer for decades prior to 1967, notwithstanding serial but invariably fleeting incarnations of the American Soccer League. The formation of NASL naturally put a serious crimp in the GAFA, SFSFL and their like. It drained urban/ethnic clubs of talent and attention. In 1977, GAFA changed its name to the Cosmopolitan Soccer League, to better represent its multi-ethnic makeup — and perhaps to cleverly play on the New York Cosmos' popularity, then at its peak.

When NASL gave up the ghost in 1984, the Cosmo returned to its place atop the American soccer pyramid — where it would stay, for all intents and purposes, until the launch of MLS in 1996. When U.S. soccer needed them most, these metro leagues, largely ethnic clubs with aging stars and modest resources, took Windischmann and the rest of Gen Zero under their capable wings.

"There were just a ton of talented guys on Brooklyn Italians — former Cosmos, guys from Colombia and all over the world. They were great players," Windischmann remembers. "I think the entire time I played for the Italians, we may have lost twice. Just incredible players. Later on they had Tab Ramos. Harkes played there. That was some quality soccer. I was learning stuff all the time."

When the A-League reemerged in 1988, options for young players of quality naturally increased. But the bottom line did not change all that much. There is widespread agreement that the class of soccer remained quite a bit higher in the Cosmo, the SFSFL, the Luso American Soccer Association (LASA) in eastern Massachusetts and Rhode Island, the New York Greek League, and other ethnically organized futbol associations across the country. The A-League and these various circuits were all similarly semiprofessional. However, while A-League players generally ran to the bank to cash checks of dubious backing, this was never an issue for members of the Brooklyn Italians, or LASA outfits like mine, Greek Sportsmen of Somerville.

"It was all cash," Windischmann reports. "Those guys who ran the club, I'm sure they were betting on games, too."

THERE IS NOTHING QUITE LIKE PLAYING SOCCER for cash money. No one got rich playing urban/ethnic soccer during the 1980s, and winning was always its own sweet reward — but victory *and* a C-note is that much *sweeter*. What's more, the ethnic leagues operated on a highly practical, fully incentivized pay structure: If players wanted to guarantee remuneration for a particular match appearance, they had to win.

A cheerful fellow named Gus with prominent, jet-black eyebrows administered Greek Sportsmen, the LASA club I played for during the late Eighties and early Nineties. Never in the course of three-plus years did I get his last name, but he was definitely Greek through and through. He managed the team, ran practices, and presided over food and drink back at the club on Highland Avenue in Somerville, Massachusetts, a diverse community of some 75,000 located adjacent to Cambridge, across the Charles River from Boston.

But Gus was not the money man. That fellow was a somewhat mysterious figure named Niko, who showed up at most matches but always watched from a safe remove. If there were bleachers, he sat apart from the crowd. At less formal venues, players could see him leaning against his gold Mercedes sedan, always aloof, off by himself. If we happened to win the match, Niko might waltz onto the field, slapping backs, pinching cheeks and distributing crisp $50 bills — $100s if the victim happened to be rival Hellenica, or Italica. If we lost, Niko was gone before the final whistle. One time we surrendered a golden goal to lose a Cup tie — to some Irish team across the Charles, in Brighton — and Niko chased the referee and linesmen to their cars while showering them with all manner of Greek and English invective.

The Brooklyn Italians operated at a higher level. They were, in many ways, the Galacticos of American soccer at this time. Their players were paid regularly, win, lose or draw, according to Windischmann. Greek Sportsmen and most semipro ethnic clubs of this period worked on less formal understandings: win, and in all likelihood you get paid; lose, and you could pretty much forget about any money.

"Most of the time you got paid win or lose, but there were times when you lost and didn't get anything, only a meal back at the club, which, in college, we thought that was pretty great too," reports Bliss, who first partook of the ethnic club scene while attending Division II power Southern Connecticut State. "During my junior and senior years, we'd get on the train in New Haven and truck it down to Mount Vernon, just north of the city, and play games in the Cosmopolitan League. Sometimes we'd practice twice a week, then we'd take the train down on the weekends to play the games.

"But yeah, as a kid, you win a game, you walk out of there with 150 bucks in your pocket — you thought you were a king! I'm sure the NCAA doesn't want to hear that, but that's the way it was. Guys that I knew, when I was a freshman and sophomore, the seniors — Sammi Joseph and Ronnie Basile — these guys were making big bucks at the time, $400 to $500 a game. If they won. That was unheard-of money at the time."

Bliss makes an important point: When NASL folded, several members of Generation Zero didn't *resort* to the ethnic leagues. They simply continued to play there, as most had been doing, to varying degrees, throughout their college careers.

———·—·———

In the spring of 1988, a more formalized brand of outdoor club soccer resumed operations on these shores. The American Soccer League, newly branded as the "the A-League," was restricted to the eastern United States, and Boston was bestowed the honor of a franchise. The Bolts played where the Boston Minutemen had played, where Wellesley High School had claimed the 1980 state title, where Pelé had faced off with Eusébio that unforgettable night in 1975 — good ol' Nickerson Field, on the urban campus of Boston University.

Responses to this new A-League — on the ground, amongst my teammates on Greek Sportsmen and across LASA — were muted to the point of nonexistence. This is somewhat surprising, in retrospect. LASA league clubs were rife with talented players who might well have seen the Bolts as an opportunity to "play up" and participate in a more organized, lucrative setting. Nonetheless, there was no such talk. Nor was there any interaction between LASA and the A-League. The Bolts never entertained our club, or any LASA sides there at B.U. or anywhere else, in any context.

"That's because they'd get beat," says Bliss, who played for the Bolts after spending his first A-League campaign with the Albany Capitals. "I played one year with the Capitals, and the next year I went to Boston to play with the Bolts and Sid Mazzola. But if you went into the Greek league in NYC, the Cosmopolitan Super League in southern Connecticut and New York City, and obviously the LASA league in Rhode Island and Massachusetts, you would find a better squad of 11 guys than a lot of the A-League teams were putting together — because of the experience. A lot of guys [in the ethnic leagues] were foreigners who were still playing, had played previously in Europe or South America. They were a little more savvy about their games.

"That's where I learned to play, to be honest. Cosmopolitan in the fall and the New York Greek league in the spring."

Again, no one got rich playing semipro, ethnic-league soccer in America. Not Harry Keough in the 1950s: not Bob Gansler, Lothar Osiander, Michael Vermes or Werner Fricker in the 1960s: not Bliss, Windischmann or Peter Vermes during the mid-1980s. On either side of the NASL era, however, these ethnic clubs served up the best soccer the U.S. (or Canada) had to offer. And they often did so with a cultural warmth and physical sense of community the Edmonton Drillers or Tulsa Roughnecks could not have hoped to muster.

"Going to see my dad play at the Hungarian Club was a real family affair," Peter Vermes recalls, referring to the club's physical premises in the Somerton neighborhood of northeast Philadelphia. "We'd get there Sunday, before lunch. We'd eat a big meal, watch the reserves play, then the senior team. We'd sit up on the hill, watch the games, and play in between. We'd have dinner, the men would go to the bar, and the kids would dribble soccer balls through the bar all night. I remember it like it was yesterday."

The A-League that launched in 1988 wasn't just substandard from a technical, quality-of-play standpoint. It was damned late in coming. The A-League took shape only after NASL had been gone *four long years* — exactly the period when Generation Zero graduated college and was attempting to professionalize itself. Accordingly, it's difficult to over-emphasize the importance of urban/ethnic clubs to the 1990 World Cup roster and the evolution of modern American soccer.

As a bonus, we suburbanites also learned how to primitively converse — and cuss — in multiple languages.

While LASA rebranded as the New England Luso American Soccer Association in 2001, its makeup remained strongly Portuguese through-out the 1980s. The most important expression to deploy when playing with the guys at Hudson Benfica, for example, was "Aqui!" (Just don't hold your breath waiting for the ball to arrive.) However, there were multiple ethnicities represented from team to team and within individual sides. Because I spent most of my LASA time (1988-91) with Greek Sportsmen of Somerville, I can report that the playfully derisive vernacular of choice among these particular Greek sportsmen was "malaka," meaning *mas-turbator*, although it's useful to translate this term more colloquially as *wanker*, especially in a footballing context. Usage was nearly always playful — "Give me the ball, malaka. You ain't taking that penalty" — offered and received with a smile.

"Skata" means *shit*, and often the team's fluent Greek speakers mixed it with English, as in "Fuck this skata, man." On the field, you made your-self clear with just these staples. If you wanted to stir things up, "Gama stavros sou!" took things up a notch — or two. According to Gus, whom I consulted on the matter, this phrase means, *I fuck your cross*, thereby combining both obscenity and blasphemy. There was also a derivative that incorporated and spoke most poorly of someone's mother — not that I understood or dared utter this epithet in any form. Despite my classical Greek history major and a vaguely Mediterranean complexion, I remained the team's token suburbanite. No way could some fuckin' prep-py, white-bread *malaka* dish out *gama stavros sou* and make it stick.

IT'S CONVENIENT TO BUILD UP THE qualities of urban/ethnic soc-cer during the 1980s while pissing on the dubious legacies of NASL. However, these shortcomings pale beside the Big One: For the 17 years it managed to stay afloat, NASL failed to produce what American soccer needed most: U.S. internationals good enough to qualify their national team for the World Cup finals. However, let's be evenhanded and historically accurate: Up to 1967, the year NASL launched, the on-field talent produced by the United States — largely via regional leagues dominated by semiprofessional, urban/ethnic clubs — hadn't been up to snuff either. That midcentury American squad that stunned England had been *invited* to the tournament down in Brazil. Ditto for America's appearance at the first two World Cups, in 1934 and '38.

Once a formal qualification process replaced this invitational system — beginning with the 1954 event in Switzerland, the first truly official World Cup — the U.S. Soccer Federation discovered its ethnic-club-fed USMNT wasn't up to the challenge. Not even close. Stocked with players "groomed" by GAFA and SFSFL and LASA talent, the national team never qualified. It never even advanced to the final stage of qualifying. U.S. national teams composed of ethnic club talent like Gaetjens, Bahr, Keough, Mendoza, Fricker, Osiander and Gansler couldn't advance past the minnows — the tiny or otherwise second-tier soccer nations that largely populate our "home" confederation: the Confederation of North, Central American and Caribbean Association Football, or CONCACAF.

However, the urban/ethnic soccer community found another way to hugely and positively affect the U.S. soccer environment all those years ago: Before anyone even contemplated an NASL, it was already training up a succession of capable, ambitious coaches and administrators who would lead the Federation and senior men's national team program through the chaotic mid-Eighties and, ultimately, all the way to *Italia* '90. Two appointments were particularly crucial to and illustrative of this influence.

Werner Fricker was named president of the USSF in 1984, replacing Gene Edwards. He was at once a poster child for the American immigrant soccer experience and a hard-nosed administrative visionary. Fricker understood the Federation required radical modernization, or it would risk squandering the toehold soccer had carved in his adopted country.

Fricker was born in 1936, to parents of German and Hungarian descent, in the village of Karlsdorf in what was then Yugoslavia (now Serbia). His family emigrated to the U.S. in 1952 and settled in the Philadelphia area, where Fricker soon hooked up with the United German Hungarians (UGH), a club side he would captain from 1958 to 1969. UGH was an urban/ethnic powerhouse. It dominated play in Greater Philly and claimed the National Amateur Cup in 1965. By then Fricker was a naturalized citizen and a defensive midfielder on the U.S. national team, captained by Bob Gansler, that had tried (but failed) to qualify for the '64 Olympics in Tokyo. Off the field, Fricker would prove an equally potent, energetic force. He presided as club president from 1968 to 1976. He coached its U-16 select team in the United Soccer League of Philadelphia, where he served as league secretary, then president. Not yet 40, he joined the U.S. Soccer Federation executive committee as a vice president in 1975. Fricker was named executive vice president two years later. He ascended to the top spot following the Los Angeles Olympics. The guy was a dynamo.

One of Fricker's first moves as Federation president — undertaken in late 1984, when the entire professional soccer establishment in North America was going to hell in a handbasket — would prove hugely pivotal. Under his guidance, the Federation formally reorganized itself into youth, amateur, and professional divisions. This cleared the way for the subsequent formation of a subsidiary, the United States Amateur Soccer Association (USASA), which, going forward, would count all the various state soccer associations as members. This reorganization also assisted in creating and then formalizing the Women's National Team program, in addition to the Under-20 and Under-17 Men's National Team programs, which were all administered via the new amateur division.

Not coincidentally, this move was essential to convincing FIFA that the USSF had finally been organized along more traditional, practical lines. Modern, national futbol federations are as much about finding corporate sponsors and brokering television rights as they are about developing native talent. With USASA cordoned off from this corporate liaising, the amateur status of member organizations and players was protected. So far as FIFA was concerned, U.S. Soccer was now structured and administratively capable of pursuing and hosting a World Cup.

———•——

This administrative reorganization also finally freed up the Federation to treat its senior national team as a distinct and purely professional entity. U.S. Soccer could thenceforth fund its various USMNT training camps, coaching salaries, exhibition schedules and tournament appearances directly, with funds solicited from corporate partners. Fricker went this route because this is how other federations around the world husbanded funds for *their* senior national teams — from corporate supporters and television broadcast partners. U.S. Federation officials could only dream of the latter in late 1984. No American network was clamoring to broadcast national team fixtures at that time. But Fricker was enterprising and ingenious in this and other forward-looking regards.

"The number of training camps that we had over the course of those years leading up to and through [*Italia* '90] qualifying was incredible. Compare that to qualifying before '86, which probably wouldn't even register on a graph... That, first and foremost, gave us the ability to put together a team that was much more prepared for that competition than any others prior to that."

—*Peter Vermes*

He also recognized how vulnerable NASL truly was in late 1984. These organizational moves enabled the Federation, in the absence of a professional domestic league, to keep the USMNT roster on a sort of loose retainer — paying the players for their national team activities while allowing them to pursue club options domestically, or even abroad. Senior national team players from the mid-Eighties view this shift in Federation priorities — this willingness to spend on retainers, on monthly camps, on travel to and from those camps — as hugely consequential, a turning point in the way U.S. Soccer did business. Early in my conversations with

Peter Vermes, I asked him why Generation Zero managed to qualify for the 1990 World Cup where previous national teams had all failed. He zeroed right in on this organizational change.

"That's a very easy answer: U.S. Soccer made an incredible commitment to achieve that goal," he declares. "The number of training camps that we had over the course of those years leading up to and through [*Italia* '90] qualifying was incredible. Compare that to qualifying before '86, which probably wouldn't even register on a graph. It made sense: Before, they were bringing a bunch of guys together before the game and saying, 'Play the game.' Whereas what we were doing was training camp, two to three weeks long. That, first and foremost, gave us the ability to put together a team that was much more prepared for that competition than any others prior to that."

Bliss concurs, pointing out that "commitment" has a more practical synonym in this context: "Money. I mean, really, it always comes down to money," he says. "You hate to say that, but when you don't have a budget to go on trips and develop players internationally, and you have only the ODP [Olympic Development Program] as a forum to develop players, it's awfully difficult. You need coaches and sponsorships and trainers and physios — and I think all that comes back to money, funding. It dictates how often you can get together and how often you can be in competitive environments."

Fricker did not wave his wand and magically transform the Federation at a stroke. However, during the mid-1980s, members of the USMNT player pool were beginning to sense the groundswell of change. Team USA undertook only two officially sanctioned internationals in 1986 — a pair of February draws with Uruguay and Canada — but it *was* called into a series of camps, all year long, without fail. That was unprecedented, and the move would not have been possible if the Federation had not spent the money to regularly bring everyone together. What's more, this retainer apparatus would not have been possible if a viable, national, outdoor league had been operating at the time.

"It was just more structured starting in 1986 — and needed to be," outside back Paul Krumpe says. "None of us had guaranteed employment and playing opportunities when we went back home. They were giving us money to supplement our situations once we went home."

These national team camps, this concerted effort to spend money on and otherwise prepare a young team for the international stage, served another purpose: They exposed the promising but inexperienced, utterly leagueless members of Generation Zero to their new national team coach, Lothar Osiander. He was already a familiar face to some — and a man whose grounding in the urban/ethnic ecosystem was nearly as deep as Fricker's.

Like the previous two USMNT coaches, Walt Chyzowych and Alex Panagoulias, like his successor Bob Gansler, and like Fricker himself, Osiander was born elsewhere — in Bavaria, just as World War II was breaking out. His family survived the war and in 1958 moved to San Francisco. The young German national (he wouldn't gain U.S. citizenship until 1965) was then enamored primarily of Greco-Roman wrestling, but since Mission High School didn't have a Greco-Roman wrestling team, he turned to soccer. Osiander would subsequently suit up for City College of San Francisco and moonlight with several teams in the semipro, highly ethnic and competitive San Francisco Soccer Football League (SFSFL), whose long history — dating to 1902, it's the oldest continuously operating league in American soccer — is a story unto itself.

The league would eventually produce *Italia '90* players John Doyle and Chris Sullivan. But it was here, in 1966, that Osiander himself was discovered — by University of San Francisco (USF) coach Steve Negoesco, already a local legend for having led SFSFL clubs Olympic, Hakoah and Viking A.C. during the late 1940s and Fifties. Negoesco had taken over the USF program in 1961, a position he held down while coaching the SFSFL's Italian American Club and its myriad youth squads. With Osiander in the side, the Dons would, in 1966, win the first of five national collegiate championships under Negoesco.

Osiander continued to play and coach in the SFSFL through the mid-1970s. To pay the bills, he waited tables at Graziano's, one of the Bay Area's finest Italian restaurants. At 35, his tactical acumen caught the attention of the U.S. Soccer Federation, which hired him to run some West Coast youth camps. With this gig, he hung up his cleats and threw himself into coaching. He continued at Graziano's, though, and eventually became the maitre d'. He would remain in that job throughout his U.S. Soccer tenure, including his stint as coach of the men's senior national team.

Think about that for a moment: The senior national team manager was moonlighting as a maitre d' to make ends meet. As indicated, the professionalization of the Federation did not come at a stroke. Such was the primordial state of things early in the Fricker administration.

Many members of Generation Zero knew Osiander by the time he took over the USMNT in February 1986. He had coached the West Region squad at several Olympic Festivals. (He also found time to lead the San Francisco Greek-American A.C. to the 1985 U.S. Open Cup championship.) True to his Teutonic stock, Osiander was not a cuddly, New Age type. His vibe could be brusque and ornery. As an émigré and a product of the Bay Area's urban/ethnic soccer scene, he was at times put off by the suburban kids now in his charge.

"Our team is too homogenous," he told the Associated Press in the run-up to the 1988 Seoul Olympics. "They're all the same age, all college students, all middle class. They all go to good schools, read the same books, like the same music, probably chase the same type of women. Everything's equal. It's flat as a pancake."

He could be stubborn and dismissive, as well. As U.S. Olympic team coach prior to the '92 Games in Barcelona, he famously said of striker Steve Snow, "If he couldn't score, he'd be sitting on someone else's bench, not mine. He's a cocky little twerp, but he'll get you a goal." He would, in fact, bench the talented Snow during this tournament — a choice that effectively ended Osiander's long tenure with the Federation.

No coach ticks every last box. Destiny never truly shows up to tap a man or woman on the shoulder. Early in 1986, however, Osiander was the right man at the right time. As was Fricker. If the players of Generation Zero were the modern U.S. soccer movement's founding fathers, Osiander and Fricker were two critical framers. Osiander in particular brought to his young charges a much needed solidity and tactical coherence. He proved a welcome pivot from Panagoulias, the mercurial Greek who exited after presiding over yet another World Cup qualification failure in May 1985.

———•••———

The camps Osiander oversaw throughout 1986 relied on remarkably few veterans. It was, as he described, a young, culturally homogenous and thoroughly untested pool of former suburbanites who would begin Olympic qualifying in the spring of 1987. They had all played beside and against each other, sporadically, at various ODP camps, at National and Olympic Sports Festivals, on the U-20 National Team. But it was under Osiander, starting in 1986, that Generation Zero first came together on the same team at the senior level.

"The majority of that group got invited into the senior team in 1986, down in Florida. It may have been in Miami," remembers Krumpe, the defender who had also played alongside midfielder Paul Caligiuri and goalkeeper David Vanole at UCLA. "We played a couple internationals down there, against Canada and, I think, against Uruguay. We did OK, but I remember that's where we got our first taste of Lothar, of senior play and each other. I also remember Pelé came out to meet with us in Florida. *That* was a huge deal – to meet the one soccer hero that, at that time, we all had. Prior to that, I had met the majority of the guys and played with some of them at the Olympic festivals. But it's different when you're all on the same side."

Gen Zero did indeed get to know each other as teammates in several more tournament settings outside the ODP and festival contexts. A handful had participated in the 1983 World Youth Championship in Mexico. Others had played together at the biennial World University Games

— but opinions differ on exactly when. If you've played a few of those tournaments, one roster can blend rather seamlessly with another, especially 30 years down the road.

"Some of the guys were also on the World University teams, whenever those were," Stollmeyer recalls, sorta kinda. "Windischmann and Bliss were our roommates. [Jimmy] Banks was there. A lot of us were at those games together. If you look at the World University Games rosters, there's a big overlap of those players. That had to be 1987, the year we all finished school and we were all still eligible to play. Over in Zagreb, Yugoslavia. To me, that was the first time that this core group was together."

"Personally, I think of that formative moment being the '85 World University Games," Windischmann contends, referring to the competition held that year in Kobe, Japan. "I remember running into a lot of the 1990 guys at those World University Games in 1985: Bliss, Harkes; you know, all those guys."

Windy also points out that it wasn't just the coming together of all these younger players that solidified the team ethos, but also the banishing of most all the older guys: "It was that confidence and belief that kind of knocked the NASL guys out. It was like, 'Hey, we're ready to get going here. Ourselves.' Harkes and Ramos were there early, with me. They had that confidence, too — that we were good enough. We respected the NASL. We grew up with it, but we wanted to shine, too."

Adds Bliss: "I felt like that group of core guys had spent a ton of time together in different ways, whether it was going back to U-16, U-18 regional teams when ODP was huge, even going back to the U-20 qualifications we failed at — in Trinidad, in '85. By 1987, I feel like we had spent three to five years together as a core group, and those are the guys who all made the national team together under Lothar Osiander."

IN LATE SEPTEMBER 1986, THREE SMARTLY dressed men walked inconspicuously through the terminal at New York City's John F. Kennedy International Airport, bound for Zurich. Their briefcases were not secured to their persons by lock and chain, but the contents *were* secret and substantial: the component parts of America's formal bid to host the 1994 FIFA World Cup. All told, the documentation — facts, figures, projections, stadium commitments, government guarantees — ran to some 380 pages. Werner Fricker referred to them as "The Phone Books." The Federation's trio of mules included U.S. Soccer Federation treasurer Paul Stiehl, former Cosmos and NASL media director Jim Trecker, and Rey Post of Eddie Mahe and Associates, the Washington, D.C.-based consulting firm that compiled the application, at a cost of some half a million dollars. Come early October, in Zurich, this delegation would present the U.S. bid in person to FIFA, thus inaugurating another game-changing chapter in the modern history of American soccer.

President Ronald Reagan made a personal request to host the '94 tournament during a Nov. 19, 1987, meeting at the White House with then-FIFA president Joao Havelange. The tournament would be awarded to the U.S. on July 4, 1988. But the origin of this bid stretches back to 1982, when rumors emanating from FIFA HQ first called into question Colombia's fitness to host the 1986 tournament. In the late 1970s, when that South American bid had first been tendered and then accepted, the tournament had included just 16 teams. The field would be enlarged to 24 nations for the 1982 World Cup in Spain. By the time Paolo Rossi had claimed that title for Italy, Colombia clearly did not have the requisite stadium stock or the will to enhance it in time for the '86 *Copa*.

Surely it did not help matters that, also in 1982, the Revolutionary Armed Forces of Colombia (better known by its Spanish acronym FARC — *Fuerzas Armadas Revolucionarias de Colombia*) declared a shift in its paramilitary strategy. Since 1948, the Marxist, agrarian, anti-imperialist FARC movement had battled the Colombian government for hearts, minds and geopolitical control of the country's rural heartland. Enriched in the late 1970s by the cocaine produced there, however, FARC announced at its Seventh Guerrilla Conference in 1982 that it would take the fight to Colombia's urban centers. President Belisario Betancur reached a ceasefire agreement with FARC in 1984, but it didn't last, and by that time a thoroughly spooked FIFA was out the door. FARC would in fact remain a revolutionary, paramilitary force in Colombia until signing a formal truce in 2016.

FIFA would eventually relocate the 1986 tournament to Mexico, of course. However, during 1982-83, several other countries remained in the running to host this event, as Colombia was essentially a dead host walking. That group of potential hosts included the United States. Brazil expressed interest but dropped out early. Canada also put its hand up, and there was casual talk of the U.S. and Canada filing a joint bid — a foreshadowing of what will indeed take place here in North America come 2026, when the U.S., Canada and Mexico will all share hosting duties. In the end, however, only the U.S. and Mexico submitted formal bids for 1986, and FIFA ultimately found the American effort wanting.

"There is a strong desire by FIFA and most people to have the World Cup come to the United States. A lot of people see [the U.S.] as a white spot on the map of soccer in the world . . . They [FIFA] would very much like to see development of soccer in the United States and to see it grow in a very big way."

—Werner Fricker

FIFA is a worldwide organization, but its ethos is distinctly European. Manners and protocol matter, and the U.S., led by then-Federation president Gene Edwards, did not exude that energy or play that game effectively. At all. The '86 bid was just 92 total pages. Then-USSF treasurer Guy DiVincenzo later called it "frivolous, glossy and transparent." It was not delivered or presented in person. More important, it lacked government-visa guarantees that nations in any way hostile to the U.S. would nevertheless be accommodated as guests. Fricker had been involved in this process as the Federation's vice president and World Cup committee chairman. He reported afterward that the '86 bid had projected U.S. ticket revenues at $42 million, more than twice what Spain took in during the 1982 *Mundial*.

Though tantalizing, this estimate was inadequately documented in the bid package itself, which also failed to include stadium guarantees.

The slapdash nature of the American proposal can be forgiven on some levels. It was prepared quickly, as the Colombia situation was in the process of unraveling. The U.S. Federation had never before dealt with FIFA at this rarefied stratum. For these reasons and others — chiefly, the built-in skepticism toward all things relating to American soccer — the bid was pretty much dead on arrival. Mexico, on the other hand, having hosted the 1970 event, remained well versed in all things FIFA. It met all the requirements. In May 1983, at its spring meetings in Stockholm, FIFA formally awarded Mexico its second World Cup in 16 years. "Mexico is a real soccer country," Havelange said at the time. "The United States and Canada are not ready for such a competition."

This was the historical backdrop when Stiehl, Trecker and Post jetted off to FIFA headquarters in Zurich, just three years later, to initiate what amounted to a massive do-over.

———— • • ————

The intervening years, the period between U.S. bids, had not been kind to American soccer fortunes. NASL had gone belly-up, and nothing had replaced it. In Torrance, the national team then confirmed FIFA's worst competitive fears by failing to qualify for World Cup 1986, to the quiet delight of both the Mexicans and Canadians. Several factors relating to America's 1994 candidacy, however, would ultimately outstrip any of FIFA's lingering concerns.

First, it's impossible to minimize the effect the 1984 Los Angeles Olympic tournament had on FIFA specifically, and worldwide soccer ob-servers in general. We discussed this matter in Chapter 6, but here's one more killer piece of data for you: Set aside those 100,000 who attended the gold medal match in Pasadena. The *bronze* medal match pitting Italy against Yugoslavia also drew more than 100,000 to the Rose Bowl. The tournament filled stadiums all over the country, regardless of whether the home team or medals were involved.

"That was unprecedented," *Soccer America*'s Mike Woitalla asserts. "No country had ever done what we did in Los Angeles, filling up huge stadiums like that for Olympic soccer. You'd think they may have drawn for the Germany games, the medal rounds, but you had small countries playing group games and the stadiums sold out! That's how they knew we'd fill the stadiums in 1994."

Remember the American ticket sales estimate, the one contained in the failed 1986 World Cup bid? The one that doubled revenues from *Espana* '82 and was dismissed as fanciful? In light of the Olympic tournament in '84, it was recast as a lowball figure. In FIFA's own report on the L.A. competition, Sepp Blatter, then general secretary under Havelange, had this to say: "FIFA and the world of sports were equally surprised: The Olympic Football Tournament surpassed the keenest hopes."

Fricker himself sensed this change in mood, post-L.A.: "There is a strong desire by FIFA and most people to have the World Cup come to the United States," he reported shortly after the bid was submitted. "A lot of people see the United States as a white spot on the map of soccer in the world ... They [FIFA] would very much like to see development of soccer in the United States and to see it grow in a very big way."

"The only hole in [Havelange's] marketing and television plan was the United States," Harvey Schiller told *The Washington Post* in June 1994, when he was executive director of the United States Olympic Committee, "and he filled it by coming here."

These comments represent, in essence, the economic perspective — and it wasn't without merit. FIFA saw what everyone else had seen, including the founders of NASL: The richest nation on earth, with a population in the hundreds of millions, most of whom knew or cared little for soccer but all of whom (or at least some healthy portion) were ripe for conversion. FIFA's corporate partners couldn't wait to get at this market. In this regard, Havelange didn't care if the American national team wasn't then good enough to win a group game. He didn't care that there was no domestic first-division futbol in place, though the U.S. bid package did pledge to re-establish one by 1990, a forecast and commitment that would miss the mark by six years.

Another salient factor appealing to Havelange & Co.: The U.S. didn't face particularly stiff competition for the 1994 tournament. Morocco didn't have the stadiums, which seemed clear to everyone but the Moroccans. Brazil was then in the midst of a financial crisis, which didn't bode well for stadium construction or the renovations stipulated in its application. Even its most famous native son threw his support elsewhere. "It is important for football to have the World Cup in the United States," Pelé said in 1986. "I love Brazil. Everybody knows that Brazil is in a bad financial situation. In the United States, it would be good for the game because it would change the World Cup. We played in 1970 in Mexico, but soccer doesn't change a thing. If there is a World Cup in Brazil, it doesn't change anything."

Between October 1986 and July 1988, there would be site visits, stadium inspections, and more shuttling back and forth to Zurich. This time, compilation of the myriad bid supplements was carried out with great care and deliberation. There were questions about whether grass could feasibly be installed indoors, directly atop synthetic surfaces, and what role soccer-illiterate U.S. television networks would play in originating broadcast feeds across the globe. All those questions were eventually answered to FIFA's satisfaction.

When the decision did come down — in Zurich, where another USSF delegation had traveled to receive the good news in person — no one in the global federation and confederation community was too surprised. The U.S. earned 10 votes from the FIFA executive committee (what became the executive council in 2016), Morocco seven and Brazil just two. There were lighthearted jokes about the American delegation actually using the word "futbol" and champagne toasts all around. Once the bubbles had dissipated, however, Fricker was quick to shift gears: "We now have the timetable set for us. We do not have the privilege to say, 'We'll do it someday.' We must do it now."

As well as any American could, the Federation president understood the scope of the task at hand — organizing and hosting the biggest sporting event on Earth. What's more, he and his delegation were already fending off questions of on-field competence. The upshot of such speculation was clear: No World Cup had ever been awarded to a country that had not qualified for one. FIFA wasn't about to start now. It had taken a massive leap of faith. The U.S. and its young national team had but one chance to justify that faith — by qualifying for World Cup 1990.

Werner Fricker and FIFA President Joao Havelange show off the World Cup Trophy in July 1988, on the occasion of FIFA awarding the 1994 tournament to the United States. *(Image courtesy of the Fricker family)*

Many of the Americans who competed at *Italia '90* trace their historic run of form back to their '88 Olympic qualifiers with Canada, late in May 1987: Here, U.S. striker Eric Eichmann (left) and defender Paul Krumpe track Dale Mitchell during the first leg of that elimination tie, held in St. John, New Brunswick. (*Images courtesy of Canada Soccer*)

OLYMPIC
QUALIFYING GAME

CANADA
VS
UNITED STATES
SAINT JOHN, NEW BRUNSWICK
CANADA

$12 N.B. AMUSEMENT
CANADIAN TAX INCLUDED

01175

May 23rd, 1987 · Canada Games Stadium
OPENING CEREMONIES — 3:30 P.M.
KICK-OFF — 4:00 P.M.

OLYMPIC
QUALIFYING GAME
CANADA
VS
UNITED STATES
SATURDAY
MAY 23rd 1987
KICK-OFF 4:00 P.M.
CANADA GAMES
STADIUM
SAINT JOHN, N.B.
CANADA

№ 01175

8.   SIGNS OF INTELLIGENT LIFE

(1987)

When Lothar Osiander called the elite members of Generation Zero into their first senior national team camp — his and theirs, in January of 1986 — he delivered a much needed regimentation to the U.S. Men's National Team program. The manager put his young, unseasoned roster through their paces on a monthly basis thereafter, and the team thrived under his tutelage, and in each other's company. Yet here, as Allen Iverson might put it, we're talking about *practice*, mere training. The squad played only two international fixtures in all of 1986, each in early February. Remarkably, despite the team's obvious lack of senior experience, the U.S. Soccer Federation did not schedule another official USMNT match over the ensuing 16 months. When the Americans finally did face a proper international opponent over 90 minutes, in May of 1987, it wasn't a friendly or some exhibition. The stakes were, in fact, enormous: a two-game, home-and-home, do-or-die encounter with Canada, whereby the loser was eliminated from the 1988 Olympic tournament in Seoul, South Korea.

By November 1989, when the USMNT arrived in Port of Spain for its decisive encounter with Trinidad and Tobago, the players weren't quite so young anymore. By that time they'd played dozens of high-stakes matches together, elimination and otherwise. On a visceral level, they *knew* they were good enough to win a World Cup place. That belief first formed in May 1987, against Canada.

"When I think of the 1990 World Cup team," remembers midfielder Brian Bliss, "I go back two years before that, almost three years actually — to the 1987 qualifying group that went to the Seoul Olympics in 1988. The bulk of those World Cup players came off that Olympic squad, and that tournament experience was really cool and very important in its own way. To me, that's when the World Cup team really came together: May 1987."

A quick scan of that **1988 Olympic roster** supports Bliss' recollection and assertion. Fully 13 of the players on the Seoul squad — each the product of a legitimate hotbed — would represent their country at *Italia '90*.

Steve Trittschuh	John Doyle	Kevin Crow
Mike Windischmann	Frank Klopas	Jim Gabarra
Ricky Davis	Brent Goulet	Peter Vermes
Eric Eichmann	Paul Krumpe	John Harkes
John Stollmeyer	Tab Ramos	Bruce Murray
Desmond Armstrong	Brian Bliss	Paul Caligiuri
David Vanole	Jeff Duback	

One can identify vestiges of an earlier era here, in the person of Davis certainly, but also in Duback and Crow, both of whom toiled for the national team during the dark period extending through 1985. At its core, however, this was a new, much younger crop of players who were all recent products of NCAA soccer — save Klopas, who went straight from high school to the indoor Chicago Sting in 1983. They had all played beside and against one another at various Olympic Festivals, U-20 competitions and World University Games. At that point, however, they were only minimally professionalized — to the extent that urban/ethnic leagues, the Major Indoor Soccer League, and the nascent, semipro Western Alliance (formed in 1986) could perform that function. Those who would eventually get gigs overseas had not yet done so.

For head coach Lothar Osiander and the Federation, Olympic qualifying provided the first real opportunity to determine whether this still-emerging squad had the right stuff — the requisite skill and mettle to form the core of a World Cup-worthy unit. If it did not, there were older, more seasoned players, or perhaps an even younger generation, waiting in the wings.

———•·•———

This preliminary stage, fully 18 months ahead of the tournament in South Korea, featured no group play. The objectives were simple: survive over two legs and advance via aggregate score. The opening match was scheduled for May 23 in the maritime outpost of St. John, New Brunswick, Canada — the return fixture a week later at The Soccer Park in Fenton, Missouri, also known as Big Arch Stadium.

So far as the Yanks were concerned, the draw was unfortunate. Only a date with Mexico would have represented a bigger ask. *El Tri* would eventually be banned from these Olympics, and *Italia* '90, for fielding underage players (more on that in Chapter 10). As for the Canadians, they were arguably the second strongest side on the continent at this time, in the entire Confederation. Fresh off their first World Cup appearance — in Mexico, less than a year before — they were flush with professional talent and eager to put a massive hurt on their culturally domineering neighbors to the south.

The International Olympic Committee had first accommodated professional soccer players only in 1984, in advance of the Los Angeles games. This curious decision grew out of a compromise: Only those pros who had not participated in previous World Cups were allowed to represent their countries in Olympic competition. Fortunately for the Canadians, a further compromise still held in advance of the 1988 Summer Games: The FIFA/IOC ruling would apply only to countries from the European and South American confederations. Africa, Oceania, Asia and CONCACAF were exempt.

Accordingly, Canada was free to use all its senior players for Olympic qualifying in 1987, and this cadre of professionals was the country's best ever, although as of this writing the 2022 Canadian National Team is shaping up as a contender. The 1987 Canadian side included the likes of centerback and NASL vet Ian Bridge (Seattle Sounders and Vancouver

Whitecaps); Carl Valentine (top scorer for MISL's Cleveland Force in 1987); a young Alex Bunbury (who'd eventually spend six seasons with Maritimo in Portugal's top flight); striker Dale Mitchell (Portland Timbers legend who retired as Canada's all-time goal leader); midfielders Paul James, Branko Segota and Mike Sweeney; defender Randy Samuel (he of Dutch first-division sides PSV Eindhoven, Fortuna Sittard and FC Volendam throughout the late Eighties and early Nineties; captain Bruce Wilson (276 NASL appearances including a Soccer Bowl with the Cosmos in 1980); and a Canadian Soccer League legend, the Harvard-educated John Catliff. In 2012, the Canadian Soccer Association issued its All-Time Canada XI. Seven players from this golden era made the squad.

Despite this surfeit of talent, and CONCACAF's exemption from IOC eligibility rules, only four of these established stars (Mitchell, Bunbury, Catliff and James) would play in the May home-and-home qualifiers against the United States. Did the Canadians look past the young, unproven Americans? For fully 90 minutes of this tie, the lack of Canadian star power didn't matter a lick. Before a crowd of some 7,000 at St. John's Canada Games Stadium, Mitchell staked the Canadians to an early lead. Stormin' Norman Odinga — then laboring in attack for the surprisingly consequential Edmonton Brickmen — added another crucial tally before the final whistle. His goal meant the U.S. needed a 3-0 victory in St. Louis in order to advance.

Osiander was characteristically forthright in his assessment. "I don't know how you would describe Canada's play but we just sucked," he barked, to the *Toronto Star*. "It was our worst nightmare come true. It was a nervous breakdown, I suppose, or lack of experience, or something."

Krumpe wasn't so puzzled by the performance, then or now. "There were about six of us who came straight from indoor, and we were not game fit for an outdoor match of 90 minutes," he recalls. "The team just didn't perform as a group — and how could we? We were just a bunch of guys thrown together a week beforehand — for an Olympic qualifier. I don't even know if it was a week."

Osiander *had* organized a camp ahead of the match, in northernmost Maine, at the University of Maine at Presque Isle. "We trained there for a week. We also had a moose walk in front of our bus," Bruce Murray says of the most consequential time the USMNT ever spent in the great state of Maine. "They wanted to acclimate us for St. John, I guess. It was beautiful in Maine. But when we went up there, it was 34 degrees with flurries. Then we went to St. Louis and it was 92 degrees!"

These were the first meaningful matches the USMNT played together since the friendlies with Canada and Uruguay in early 1986 — discounting two Marlboro Cup exhibitions contested in Miami against Deportivo Cali and Millonarios, a pair of Colombian club sides, in March 1987. Olympic soccer today is essentially a U-23 tournament. During the late Eighties, however, this was the second most important competition in world football. FIFA considered U.S. qualification for Seoul almost mandatory, to vindicate its pending '94 World Cup site selection. Failing to advance out of preliminary Olympic qualifying would have been disastrous, another in a long string of USMNT embarrassments. Considering all the changes Fricker and Osiander had authored at the Federation thus far, the level of preparation would appear rather casual — and the score reflected as much.

"There was *always* such a limited amount of time to prepare for what were some pretty huge games," contends Krumpe, one of several players who didn't even attend the Maine camp. They headed straight to St. John from their MISL clubs. "And I definitely remember being unusually fatigued after that match in St. John. I remember feeling demoralized. I remember thinking on the way home, 'If we don't win this next game, this whole group is probably gone and — as U.S. Soccer had done in the past — they'll probably bring in a whole new group for World Cup qualifying.'"

Instead, the Americans' discouraging performance in New Brunswick kicked off the best 18 months of Krumpe's young soccer life — a stretch of play that helped make the difference between his national side going to *Italia* '90 and that side staying home.

The defender's four years at UCLA, where he earned a B.S. in aerospace engineering, had overlapped with those of Paul Caligiuri and keeper David Vanole. Their time together had culminated with an NCAA title in the fall of 1985. Just 24 in May 1987, Krumpe had no outdoor gig at the time; outside the ethnic leagues, none of his teammates did. He spent 1986-88 entirely indoors with the Chicago Sting. During the offseason he worked for McDonnell Douglas, "building MD-80s." Krumpe would eventually coach himself, first at his old high school and then at the infamous El Camino Community College, where he watched Caligiuri go 90 minutes in that excruciating 1985 loss to Costa Rica. He assisted at UCLA before landing the head-coaching gig at Loyola Marymount in 1998.

Krumpe scored only once during his USMNT tenure. However, his 24 official caps don't include any Olympic matches, so his two-goal performance in the return leg vs. Canada on May 30, 1987, is easy to lose in the shuffle of time and circumstance. Nevertheless, one short week following the dispiriting setback in St. John, his goals in suburban St. Louis helped carry the day. In fact, they rank with Caligiuri's 1989 goal in T&T as among the most consequential in U.S. soccer history: Krumpe's brace, along with Jim Gabarra's winner, sent the side through, enabled the entire Seoul Olympic experience, jump-started the squad's fortunes over the next 30 months, and laid the foundation for the Modern American Soccer Movement.

"I scored a couple other goals for the national team, but these were for sure the biggest goals of my entire career," he recollects. "And two goals in a single game, especially from right back? That's pretty crazy. On the first one, Chico [Borja] got a ball through, down the right side, and I thought he was going to goal. As right back I was just flying up behind him, in support. But he turned and instead of going toward goal, he turned away and flicked the ball back to me. I love hitting volleys, and the ball bounced once before I hit a left-footer over the keeper, into the top left corner. Definitely the best goal I ever scored as a national team player. Probably ever."

This *golazo* came 20 minutes into a match the U.S. had to win by three in order to advance. Had he left it there, Krumpe's contribution would have been darned significant, "to get us back into the mix early." As it was, he'd add another. Jim Gabarra scored the second-half goal that ultimately put the Americans through, 3-2 on aggregate. Without *this* goal, without their sensational performance that day in Fenton, these guys wouldn't have played the half-dozen additional Olympic qualifiers that shaped the squad and served preliminary notice that this young, unknown team was legit. And they wouldn't have played the Olympic tournament itself in South Korea, where they removed all doubt. Each and every member of Generation Zero I spoke to pointed to this specific match in Fenton as the moment everything changed.

"Pretty remarkable turnaround. A major win," *Soccer America*'s Mike Woitalla confirms. "That was kind of when we could see things starting to happen."

Nutmeg State soccer legend Jim Gabarra made his name at Division III Connecticut College in New London. During the mid-1980s, just up the road at Wesleyan, we were hugely impressed that a fellow product of NESCAC (the New England Small College Athletic Conference) had made such a mark — catching on, as he had, with the Dallas Sidekicks in MISL and then carving out a spot on the national team. Gabarra would stick with the USMNT through qualifying for *Italia '90*, though rarely starting or starring. His final international appearance came in a stultifying 1989 tie with El Salvador, a result that set up the must-win denouement in Port of Spain. Gabarra would go on to play another nine professional indoor seasons. He captained the U.S. national futsal team from 1986-96. Upon retirement, he coached a succession of women's professional clubs. His most recent gig, with the Washington Spirit of the National Women's Soccer League, came to a close in 2018.

Again, goals scored during Olympic qualification matches don't enter the official USMNT record book. But his strike in St. Louis that May afternoon in 1987 rivals Krumpe's in terms of consequence. "He hit an absolute rocket from outside the box!" Krumpe recalls. "I remember seeing this on video afterward [ESPN televised this match; all three goals

226 — GENERATION ZERO

are available via YouTube]. It went through at least one defender's legs — but it was a laser. Canada got taken for two really good goals that day. Nothing to be done about them."

Thanks in large part to the unheralded duo of Krumpe and Gabarra, here the fortunes of U.S. and Canadian soccer began to diverge — but not at all the way anyone might have expected at the time. Once the final whistle blew that afternoon in Fenton, the U.S. embarked on a veritable tear, qualifying first for Seoul '88 and then for *Italia* '90. It would host in 1994 and qualify for every *Mundial* since — until its 2018 misadventure. Canada, on the other hand, took the field in Fenton riding a crest of talent and success. Just a year removed from Mexico '86, the Canadians would not go to Seoul. They have not been back to a World Cup in 35 years. Since making it to the quarterfinals at the '84 Summer Games, they have not qualified for another Olympic tournament. Prior to the 2021-22 qualification cycle, it cannot be said that Canada even competed among CONCACAF's elite.

Back in the mid-Eighties, when Canada was on the upswing, enjoying the fruits of its own golden generation, Bob Gansler and various members of the Federation spent a lot of time defending the way the USSF managed its affairs. Things were not going well, as we've detailed, and more than once Canada was held up as an example of how a secondary soccer nation should attempt to rise through the international ranks. The Canadian national team featured a glut of players playing abroad at that time, mainly in lower/lesser leagues, something that remained true well into the 1990s.

Gansler bristled at the questions he fielded back then. He's got comparable impatience for those who wonder today why exactly the U.S. took so long — 40 years at least — to get its own act together, an act that coalesced that late May day in Missouri. "We all know that Canada qualified for the World Cup in 1986," Gansler says, "but what did Canada achieve, having sent a zillion guys over to second- and third-division teams throughout Europe? . . . Looking back, we can bash ODP, bash college soccer and the lack of a pro league and all this sort of stuff, but those steps helped. Every little bit helped. We kind of built a mosaic here — very different from the approach Canada took — and here was another piece. There are pieces missing yet."

"Gansler is right," adds Brian Bliss, who spoke to me in 2017. "Back in the 1980s, playing over in Europe was supposed to be the answer, the end-all/be-all, but it didn't help the Canadians that much, did it? It's an interesting case study."

THE COMEBACK VICTORY OVER CANADA DIDN'T just clear a path to the Olympics by eliminating the Federation's No. 2 team. "That game in St. Louis sort of catapulted us forward," Bliss contends. "We had to go to St. Louis and win by three goals; that was the job we left for ourselves," John Stollmeyer says, noting that this team had never overcome anything like that before. It had, in fact, played only three official matches together. "So we went to the Soccer Park in St. Louis, scored one, the next goal, and another goal! That was *so* huge. You have to be able to do that sort of thing if you want to achieve anything. We had a confidence going forward because we'd gone and done that."

Here's the on-field XI coach Osiander deployed that afternoon:

David Vanole

Mike Windischmann **John Doyle**

Steve Trittschuh **Brian Bliss** **Paul Krumpe**

John Harkes **Jim Gabarra**

Chico Borja

Bruce Murray **Brent Goulet**

All but Borja, Goulet and Gabarra would make the *Italia* '90 roster, finalized almost exactly three years later. Peter Vermes and Tab Ramos joined this core group from the college ranks in 1988, essentially re-placing Goulet and Borja. Relative youngsters Tony Meola and Marcelo Balboa would not get the national team call until 1989. Paul Caligiuri did not participate in the Fenton match — he was injured during the first leg in Canada.

Still, May 30, 1987 — a Saturday, under the sign of Gemini — was arguably the day the Modern American Soccer Movement was born. The success of this previously untested, extraordinarily young team vs. Canada that afternoon afforded the squad, the coaching staff, and the Federation an enormous jolt of confidence and belief going forward, a jolt they eventually parlayed into a World Cup berth that changed the way their countrymen viewed futbol. Forever.

The events of this momentous match day also allow observers to credibly examine some of the tactics taking shape within Osiander's emerging squad. In the back, we see the beginnings of the reliable four — Trittschuh and Krumpe flanking centerbacks Windischmann and Doyle, who earned his first-ever USMNT cap at Fenton. This unit would more or less endure through *Italia* '90. John Harkes, just off a Hermann Trophy-winning junior year at the University of Virginia, sat beside Brian Bliss in midfield. Bruce Murray ran up front, although "Brent Goulet was the big target for us at the time," Krumpe remembers. "He had some big games for us." Vermes would eventually win Goulet's place, however, and Ramos/Caligiuri would win permanent spots in midfield partnership with Harkes, replacing Borja and pushing the versatile Bliss into a reserve role.

Injuries and form always wreak havoc with "starting XIs," especially over the course of any 30-month national team period. The inimitable Hugo Perez was in and out of this mix here, as were Frankie Klopas and John Stollmeyer. But this is the side that coalesced in the spring of 1987, and the results were eye-opening.

"We got such a huge boost of confidence by getting through that first round. We were like, 'Oh wow, we can do this!'" Krumpe says. "We actually got into a little bit of a groove after that, a run of form. I'm not sure that U.S. Soccer ever had that opportunity before, where they simply got through a round and kept the same group of guys together. We started to blossom. Good things started to happen."

When Olympic qualifying resumed on Sept. 5, 1987, following an entire summer of playing and training together — the Federation having finally scheduled some friendlies — the Americans displayed their newfound swagger for the rest of CONCACAF to behold. They dismantled Trinidad and Tobago back in Fenton, 4-1. (University of Missouri-St. Louis product Ted Hantak came on for Klopas in the 65th minute to score his fifth goal in six games. It would nevertheless be the last USMNT appearance for this briefly prolific but largely unknown striker.) In the return leg two weeks later, the U.S. ground out a 1-0 victory in Port of Spain.

"We had to stay in the locker room for about two hours afterward. It wasn't a locker room really, more of an underground bunker. We had to wait because there were death threats. I remember the bus that finally picked us up — it had bullet holes! There were Uzis in the Jeep escorts in front and behind. That was kind of eye-opening for everyone."

—Paul Krumpe

Yet the real head turner came Oct. 18 in El Salvador, where Osiander's young charges scored the first three goals and cruised to a "comfortable" 4-2 victory. This result clinched qualification for the Olympics, though the Yanks would have to wait until May 25, 1988, to complete the home-and-home with a 4-1 result on home soil. Still, the result in El Salvador made an enormous impression: on potential competitors within the Confederation; on the USSF, which could now negotiate more credibly with FIFA about hosting World Cup '94, having qualified a team for the Olympics; and on the U.S. players themselves. For many of these USMNTers, the trip to San Salvador was their first taste of a senior qualifier in Central America. Winning there amid all the attendant chaos established yet another foundation of self-possession.

"Our game plan was to feel them out for the first 10 minutes or so — to see what formation they were using and so on," Bliss reports. "Then we scored at four minutes and 10 minutes — that was supposed to be the feeling-out period! The fans were stunned. The El Salvador team was stunned. To tell you the truth, we were, too."

Play would eventually be stopped three separate times, as the home crowd grew increasingly annoyed at the dominant, completely unanticipated U.S. performance. An assistant referee was struck by a plastic bottle. Eventually the crowd started lighting seat cushions on fire and flinging them about the stadium. "I think the seat cushions were given out by sponsors as a promotion," Bliss says. "The fans lit them up and turned them into fiery Frisbees! Lothar was a master at preparing us, painting a terrible, scary picture for us of what to expect. But I think we were so naive, the scene in San Salvador didn't faze us. That's how dumb we were. We didn't know better. We thought, 'I guess this is the way it's supposed to be.'"

Adds Krumpe, "When that game started and El Salvador was stringing some passes together, they got the "*Olé!*" chant going. But once we were up 3-0 at halftime, it got ugly. I remember, as a wide player, the ball would roll out of bounds, and I had to look up each time to avoid all the bottles and trash being thrown my way. By that time, the crowd was *Olé*-ing *us* and throwing trash at their own guys!"

CONCACAFkaesque.

"We had to stay in the locker room for about two hours afterward," Krumpe continues. "It wasn't a locker room really, more of an underground bunker. We had to wait because there were death threats. I remember the bus that finally picked us up — it had bullet holes! There were Uzis in the Jeep escorts in front and behind. That was kind of eye-opening for everyone: It was a big deal to leave the country to play these games. And it must have been weird for Hugo."

———•♦•———

Hugo Perez, whom Krumpe, among others, considers "for sure the most talented U.S. player of that decade," scored twice during the October 1987 victory over El Salvador. "I'm not sure how Hugo felt about that game," says Krumpe. "Must have been strange for him, having the fans turn on their own team." Because had his life gone a little differently, it might well have been Hugo's team.

Hugo Ernesto Perez Granados was born in El Salvador to a profession-al footballing father who moved his family to Southern California when Hugo, his eldest son, was 11 years old. The L.A. Aztecs signed Hugo at 19, but he couldn't get the games he needed playing for the Aztecs. He made 20 NASL appearances for the Tampa Bay Rowdies the next season before landing back in SoCal — San Diego, to be precise — in 1983. Perez would star for the Sockers, indoor and out, for the next five years, scoring 29 times outdoors over NASL's final two seasons and a whopping 125 times in MISL. A technical marvel on the ball, the 5'8", left-footed Perez was the poster boy for what many thought to be U.S. Soccer's future: Here was a young player of impeccable Latin heritage, domestically trained, who could hold and distribute the ball in possession, get forward, and score. Few native-born Americans had ever arrived at the professional level (at 19!) with this sort of skill set and flair. Surely, in the years to come, there would be dozens of Hugo Perez-type players to follow . . .

That last bit was wistful sarcasm on my part. Perez looks today to have been something of a one-off. Tab Ramos would emerge, in 1988, with similar skills via his native Uruguay and Kearny, New Jersey. Claudio Reyna, Jersey-born but with an Argentinian dad, would arrive in the late 1990s. But that's about all she wrote in the Dominant U.S./ Latin Midfielder Dept. Despite a continuous stream of immigration from Central and South America, U.S. Soccer has never effectively tapped this rich vein of soccer heritage — not from a development standpoint and certainly not in the specific central/playmaking role.

As for Perez himself, come 1989 he would score two critical goals for his adopted country during World Cup qualifying. Throughout this peri-od, he always gave the same overall impression — to teammates, coaches and opponents alike — as the most skilled player the U.S. had developed. Ever. But he did not make the rosters for *Italia* '90 or Seoul '88. Why not?

"Hugo was a roommate of mine on a bunch of different national team trips," Stollmeyer says. "Was I surprised he didn't make the final Italy roster? Uh, yeah. Absolutely. Especially when some of the other kids were picked and he was not. I was like, 'Really?' I mean, Hugo's not gonna help us and these guys are?"

The answers to Stollmeyer's pointed, rhetorical question are complicated. With an Olympic appearance assured for September 1988 — and *Italia* '90 qualifying set to begin that fall — the next two years of national team duty were essentially mapped out for members of the USMNT, most of whom did not have any club prospects outside of the U.S. But Perez *did* have club prospects, and those — in addition to Federation politics and some terribly untimely injuries — would doom his major tournament aspirations.

In 1988, before Osiander's team traveled to Seoul, Perez was a force. His Sockers won an MISL title and he was named playoff MVP. This performance elicited the attentions of none other than Ajax manager/legend Johan Cruyff, who expressed interest in signing Perez for the Dutch super club. But San Diego wouldn't release him. This prompted a contractual fight that got plenty ugly and would forever tar the 26-year-old Perez, rightly or wrongly, as "difficult." The spat escalated through the summer months prior to September's Olympic tournament in South Korea. Club seasons in Holland and across Europe begin in August. Unsure whether Perez would be with Ajax or not — and unsure whether his national team commitments were further complicating the transfer Hugo sought — Osiander left Perez off the 1988 Olympic roster. Perez went back to San Diego and waited by the phone. The Ajax deal never materialized.

The Perez situation wasn't entirely unique. Steve Trittschuh had European club aspirations, too. They nearly scotched *his* place in the Olympic team. "During Olympic qualifying in 1987, I went over to Scotland and England on trial," Tritt explains. "Just to see if I could do it. I had some connections over there and it went well. But I needed to decide on that or [securing a first team place for] the Olympics, so I had to pass [on a club career in the U.K]. I had gone to Dundee United — this was July — on trial. Then I went down to Stoke City for another trial right after that. Who knows if I could have qualified for a work permit, because at the time there were no Americans over there. It was one of those decisions: You look back and say 'Maybe I should have done this or that.' But I wanted to play in the Olympics."

Perez had the opposite problem: There was considerable demand for his services. The nature and expression of that demand helps explain why he contributed to qualifying efforts for the '88 Olympics and '90 World Cup finals but never played a minute in either tournament. Additional issues made Perez a difficult Olympic selection.

"I think he'd been playing so much indoor, for him it was a matter of covering ground — or not," Krumpe asserts, taking the more tactical tack. "The younger college guys on the '88 team, we didn't have Hugo's technical ability, but we could cover ground if nothing else. Hugo had become an indoor player. That was my impression at the time. So skilled it was unbelievable. But whether he could cover the ground as a midfielder, outdoors? That might have had something to do with it."

By the time Bob Gansler took over from Osiander in early 1989, Perez had recommitted to the outdoor game, having signed with the American Professional Soccer League's Los Angeles Heat. Gansler eagerly deployed him up top — and he would score those two crucial goals to help the U.S. qualify for Italy. But Cruyff and fate would again intervene. The Dutch master remained a fan of Perez and attempted to work a transfer for the American — to Parma in Italy's top flight, *Serie A*. However, the club needed Perez to play in a World Cup in order to justify an Italian work permit. So Perez signed with Red Star in Paris to prepare himself full time — and promptly tore knee ligaments that spring of 1990. At that point, Gansler's decision to leave the most talented U.S. player of his generation off the *Italia* '90 roster was something of a no-brainer.

Post-Italy, Perez — who coached El Salvador's U-23 team during its 2021 Olympic qualification effort and then graduated to the senior national team in July 2021 — would recover from his knee trouble and move to the Swedish first division. He played well for Orgryte IS of Gothenburg, well enough to be named 1991 U.S. Soccer Athlete of the Year. He even cultivated the good graces of new U.S. coach Bora

Milutinovic, who included Perez on the USA '94 roster — and started him in the round-of-16 loss to eventual champion Brazil. Perez was subbed off for Roy Wegerle after 66 minutes, his only minutes of the tournament, his only World Cup minutes ever.

———·•·———

Hugo's October 1987 performance in El Salvador, and those of his teammates, concluded what amounted to an extended American goal- and victory-fest, the likes of which opponents and U.S. soccer fans were not accustomed to seeing: 13 goals in four straight Olympic qualifying victories — 16 in five if we count the final leg against Canada. During its long and largely forgettable history, the USMNT simply didn't win or score with this sort of frequency. Rivals in CONCACAF were accustomed to having their way with the U.S., especially at home. But here was something different: a collection of extraordinarily young Americans, none of whom had been trained up by any league or club structure (the A-League would not launch for another six months, in spring 1988), who appeared to have been blooded and "professionalized" in spite of all this. The kids certainly knew how to win.

The phrase "golden generation" is thrown around somewhat casually in soccer circles worldwide, but it's a genuine phenomenon. What's more, a critical mass of talent in any single country *can* develop seemingly from nowhere. Witness the coming together of Canada's best-ever national teams prior to Mexico '86. Witness the current incarnation up north, which, all of a sudden, includes the extraordinary young attacking talents of Alphonso Davies, Tajon Buchanan, Cyle Larin and Jonathan David.

El Salvador and other CONCACAF opponents during the spring, summer and fall of 1987 were some of the first to recognize what appeared to be an American golden generation in the making. However, these performances also made profound impressions on the U.S. players themselves.

According to Krumpe: "We were like, 'We can go on the road and win these games, too.'" Going forward, they had also developed a home venue — The Soccer Park in Fenton, Missouri — where they felt confident of maximizing a home-field advantage. "That was our most effective home turf," Bliss says.

"Being with the '85 team and not qualifying, being the young guy on those sides, I knew I would be there in the mix for the next cycle," Windischmann contends, inferring that others would not be there. "Ricky Davis and Chico Borja, who played with all the NASL guys, they were getting to the end of their careers. When Gansler chose me for captain [in 1989], I didn't know this at the time, he had told Ricky [Davis], 'We're gonna go with these young guys and Windischmann is gonna be the captain. These guys are hungry. They're coming up.' We respected those older players, but Harkes, Ramos, Bliss and all those guys — we felt like we could play. Qualifying for Seoul proved it. That was so huge.

"I know the history of the national team, and I know that 1950 had been the last World Cup. I've met those guys and got pictures and autographs and such. We really wanted to be the first team to break the drought. We kinda knew we were ready to get it going. The Olympic experience confirmed it. We felt we were ready to go qualify."

TWENTY-FIRST CENTURY U.S. SOCCER FANS MAY not realize it — or wish to contemplate such an unbecoming reality — but for a short time immediately post-NASL, indoor soccer was the American game's dominant professional strain. Indeed, the heyday of MISL took place even as the country's first golden generation of *outdoor* talent began to coalesce. These coincidental facts, these uncomfortable truths, represent yet more indicators of a domestic soccer culture in a worrisome state of inconstancy, if not outright crisis. However, even outdoor purists were obliged to acknowledge that the Major Indoor Soccer League had survived into 1985 and beyond, while NASL had not. The pay wasn't spectacular indoors, but the checks frequently failed to bounce. What's more, the matches were actually on TV at that time, filling late-night space next to competitive lumberjacking on ESPN.

In 1986, MISL's newest expansion franchise, the New York Express, named Ray Klivecka head coach and player personnel director. He had this to say when 1985 Hermann Trophy winner Tommy Kain — the top Express draft pick that winter — chose not to report. "I was counting on Tom this year," Klivecka told the *Chicago Tribune*. "His decision came out of left field. I knew his dream was to be an outdoor pro, but I thought that wasn't in the picture . . . He's losing a year in the MISL, but I told him that if it didn't work out, he could come back, even this year. He's welcome. He has the potential to be a good indoor player. That's where the game is in the U.S., and that's probably where his future is."

Klivecka had a clear business interest in the Express and its fortunes, but he was not some wild-eyed indoor-soccer evangelist. He'd been an outdoor footballer all his life, as an all-American at Long Island University, as an assistant to Angus McAlpine in training Federation youth squads during the late 1970s, as an assistant to Cosmos coach Eddie Firmani for two years. No one knows whether Klivecka honestly preferred the indoor game, or not — but he clearly sensed where the U.S. soccer wind was blowing during the mid-1980s. Better than most, the coaches understood how shaky NASL truly was. When Klivecka had the opportunity to join the ownership group behind the MISL expansion franchise in St. Louis, he jumped at it: The Steamers joined MISL for the 1979-80 season. He would briefly lead the NASL's Rochester Lancers in 1980, but that was his last outdoor gig. He coached the MISL Buffalo Stallions for two seasons before rejoining the Cosmos, in 1984-85, as head coach for their first (and last) indoor season. The following summer, he joined the expansion Express.

So, Klivecka wasn't posturing for the *Tribune* reporter. He was voicing an attitude about indoor soccer — "That's where the game is" — that proved quite pervasive, if not exactly prevailing, in 1986. Having watched NASL fold, having seen no replacement outdoor league forthcoming, a lot of people felt indoor *was* the way forward for soccer in this country.

The Express would eventually help illustrate why they were mistaken.

MISL had awarded the new franchise to financiers Ralph McNamara and Stan Henry, who intended to generate the club's initial operating capital from an issuance of public stock — the kind of market-based, true-believing thing people did during Reagan's go-go Eighties. They had partnered with none other than former Cosmos keeper Shep Messing, who would play goal and serve as the face of the franchise. The Express positioned itself as an all-American response to the New York Arrows, the demonstrably ethnic MISL franchise it replaced on Long Island. Messing had played six winter seasons for the Arrows. He quickly lined up former teammate Ricky Davis, whose Steamers contract had played out. He also recruited former Cosmos Mark Liveric, Hubert Birkenmeier and Andranik Eskandarian.

"The whole plan for franchise success was built around Ricky Davis. Not the greatest player at that point, but the one with the great American-born name, demeanor and name recognition," Micah Buchdahl told the website Fun While It Lasted. Buchdahl was director of public relations for the Express. Incidentally, Fun While It Lasted (funwhileitlasted.net) is an entertaining treasure trove of information about failed sports leagues and franchises of all kinds.

A few days before the media event introducing Davis, "I was told [Ricky] had changed his mind," Buchdahl told the site. "We had announced that we would introduce the top American-born player in soccer. I remember [Express GM] Kent Russell and Shep asking me if it would be a problem if we just said we had meant Kevin Maher. I told them we'd be totally screwed."

By January 1987, not even halfway through the club's maiden campaign, it was all coming apart. Russell and his assistant bailed on the Express first — jumping to the Dallas Sidekicks. Buchdahl, just 24, became acting GM. Then the club failed to pony up $75,000 in player payroll on Feb. 1, 1987, forcing the league to draw down the club's $250,000 letter of credit to cover it. The owners pulled the plug two weeks later, initiating Chapter 11 proceedings. Let the record show the Express finished 3-23. For those three victories, they spent a reported $3 million during just nine months of operation. Buchdahl ended up holding much of the club's office equipment hostage in his aunt's garage — in a failed effort to wangle five weeks of back pay.

"This team should never have been let in," Eskandarian told the *Chicago Tribune*. "I don't think the league is going to last long if it's going to be like this."

⸺•⸺

For Messing, a childhood hero to Gen Zero and one of the highest-profile U.S. players of the 1970s, the Express debacle was an ignominious close to a colorful, eventful career, on-field and off. If there was a better embodiment of "Seventies Boomerdom, Pro Soccer Division" than Shep Messing (born in 1949, Harvard Class of '72), I can't identify him. When something happened during this consequential era of American soccer, Messing was there in the thick of it. Between the pipes for Pelé's two finest seasons in New York (1976 and '77), Messing had also been in goal that fateful spring night in 1975 at Nickerson Field — for the Minutemen. By then, as a U.S. Olympian, he had already experienced firsthand one of the decade's mind-bending tragedies: the kidnapping and killing of 11 members of Israeli's Olympic team during the Munich Games in 1972. This tragic, macabre drama had unfolded just 30 yards down the hall from Messing's dorm room.

"It really forged a greater Jewish identity for myself at that moment than I ever had before," he told *The Guardian* in 2015. "That was a turning point in my life as an athlete — and as a Jew. Words really can't describe it."

Eighteen months later, Messing latched on with the Cosmos. He was promptly kicked off the team for posing nude in *Viva* magazine, for a reported fee of $5,000. Management argued he'd violated the morals clause in his contract; Messing asserted he'd delivered the club more "exposure" than anything in franchise history. He signed with Boston for the '75 NASL season. Pelé arrived in New York at the same time. The Cosmos re-signed Messing a year later, his trademark mop of curly brown hair and pornstache in tow. He cut a figure straight out of *Boogie*

Nights — something even Harvard graduates could pull off during the 1970s, apparently.

Not yet 30, Messing landed with the newly relocated Oakland Stompers in 1978. There he found time to publish his freewheeling autobiography (*The Education of an American Soccer Player*) before joining the Rochester Lancers in '79, his final outdoor season. That was the Express connection: The MISL Arrows of the early 1980s were stocked almost entirely with NASL Lancers. Like so many Boomers, Messing transitioned straight from the self-actualizing Seventies to the hypercapitalist Eighties. It didn't go well, although Messing's expansion misadventures with the Express registered barely a ripple in that era of soccer anonymity, white-collar crime, junk bonds, and savings and loan crises. Come the Nineties, Messing moved seamlessly into the broadcast booth.

As for McNamara, the moneyman behind the N.Y. Express, his firm closed down when the stock market tanked in October 1987. Four years later, New York state revoked his broker's license. In the late 1990s, he surfaced in Florida under the name Ralph DeLuise, operating what proved to be a fake venture capital operation. In 2007, a court found McNamara guilty of racketeering, conspiracy to commit racketeering, communications fraud, grand theft, loan broker fraud and money laundering. He was sentenced to 15 years in federal prison.

———————

The Express went away, but professional indoor soccer never did. While the original MISL folded in 1992, later iterations — including the still-extant Major *Arena* Soccer League — can still be found on the boob tube, live from assorted secondary American cities. During the mid-1980s, when it wasn't clear whether professional soccer would *ever* fly in this country, MISL remained a vital part of the competitive mix. The league offered players not just a bit of cash but fitness and training, even if its brand of fitness and training did not do much for their outdoor preparedness. That disconnect is why Duke striker Tommy Kain jilted the Express and why Mike Windischmann avoided indoor like the plague.

It's why, when MISL's mighty Cleveland Force drafted him straight out of college in 1986, Brian Bliss didn't exactly jump for joy.

"For us guys who had only played outdoor, we deemed indoor soccer a bastardization of the game," Bliss explains, still visibly bristling at the indignity of it all. "But that was our only option to get paid and make a living in the game. So I did sign with the Force. [John] Stollmeyer and Des Armstrong were there, too, and some of the other guys were spread around the league."

Steve Trittschuh graduated from college with Bliss and also went straight into MISL — because what other practical options did he have? "Brian and I are the same age," Trittschuh says flatly. "We had to make decisions."

"Having grown up in St. Louis, playing for the Steamers was the thing to do. They'd pull in 15,000 to 20,000 a game sometimes, and I was like, 'This is what it is — if you're going to play soccer professionally in this country.' It was really the only thing available at the time."

—Steve Trittschuh

MISL wasn't the only entity fueling America's indoor-soccer heyday. Multiple pro leagues operated during the mid- and late-1980s, featuring a range of geographic reach, money and quality of play. Directly below MISL on the U.S. indoor soccer pyramid sat the American Indoor Soccer Association, where Jim Gabarra first caught on as a professional with the Louisville Thunder. In 1986-87, the AISA expanded beyond its original Midwestern footprint into Pennsylvania, Georgia and Florida. When the Tampa Bay Rowdies first launched an indoor team, it did so as part of the growing AISA.

I was aware of this league because David Slade, a college teammate of mine, played for the AISA's Hershey, Pennsylvania, franchise. "Slado" was a memorable character, a sort of surfer dude whose blond shag haircut and laid-back persona belied his intelligence and his roots in Guilford, Connecticut — hometown of the inimitable Kevin Maher. Slado was probably the best player Wesleyan put forward the last two years I was there: technically excellent, not super fast but big, strong and fearless — the kind of attacking midfielder whose confidence and vision on the ball got better when the standard of opponent got better. I remember running into him in 1989 or thereabouts at some Wesleyan alumni function. He regaled me with stories of his itinerant futbol life in the AISA and his team, the Hershey Impact — surely one of the most unfortunate franchise monikers in American sports history, especially at the height of the AIDS crisis.

I'm not the guy to write it, but the story of MISL, the AISA and U.S. indoor soccer in general deserves a whole separate book — maybe a Triple-A cross between *Ball Four*, Jim Bouton's irreverent baseball classic, and *Loose Balls*, Terry Pluto's stellar, somewhat squalid history of the upstart American Basketball Association. Slado's Impact, for example, came into being thanks to the immortal Larry Samples, a 45-year-old veterinarian from nearby Hummelstown. Samples lined up 20 local investors to make the franchise a reality. The club proved viable for just three seasons, never filling more than half of the 7,200 seats inside Hersheypark Arena (site of Wilt Chamberlain's 100-point game — March 2, 1962; Philadelphia Warriors vs. N.Y. Knicks). In 1991, the AISA rebranded — the National Professional Soccer League would operate through 2001 — and the Impact folded. Much of the roster, according to Slado, simply moved 15 miles west to play for the newly cobbled-together Harrisburg Heat.

We romanticize the ABA, and the AISA, and the NASL, and the old World Football League *because* they failed, of course. For some reason, all these years down the road, their initially grandiose, ultimately hapless dreams add nebulous elements of romance and charm.

But there was something else going on at this time, something more pertinent to our story: In a professional soccer landscape so devoid of outdoor successes, there *was* the inkling, post-NASL, that indoor soccer had the potential to scale, in America specifically. Some believed that perhaps *this* was how the game would finally find a broader U.S. audience, not just live and in person, but on the golden goose of startup requisites: television. This view made some actual sense. A league season contested during the winter months, indoors, meant MISL need not compete with baseball or American football. Goals were more plentiful indoors. No draws, either. The game's hockey-influenced format worked better on television, which was just another way of saying, "The indoor game can be seamlessly jiggered to accommodate commercials, while the outdoor game cannot."

A good portion of this would-be conventional wisdom proved nothing more than speculative marketing perspectives and outright propaganda served up by MISL itself, by league broadcasters, by assorted futbol haters and media contrarians, not to mention soccer impresarios made truly desperate by the grim state of the professional outdoor game in the mid-Eighties. Under their breath, however, in vaguely conspiratorial tones, even staunch backers of traditional outdoor soccer whispered an even more somber point of view: Perhaps American sporting consumers would *never* respond to soccer. In any form. Ever. No one knew for sure whether that heretical belief was accurate. Not in 1986 or '87. But this much seemed obvious: The longer the professional outdoor game remained on hiatus, the more MISL grew in stature. By default.

"At the time," Trittschuh explains, "having grown up in St. Louis, playing for the Steamers was the thing to do. They'd pull in 15,000 to 20,000 a game sometimes, and I was like, 'This is what it is — if you're going to play soccer professionally in this country.' It was really the only thing available at the time."

Bruce Murray never played professional indoor soccer, but he recognizes MISL's prominent, mid-decade role and influence: "MISL came in and rescued things a bit, rescued a lot of careers. Some of those teams were really successful. MISL was actually an incredible option for players and fans. It was big business at that time — in certain cities. Ask Jerry Reinsdorf, the Bulls owner. He said as much during that recent Jordan documentary [*The Last Dance*]. In the mid-Eighties, the Chicago Sting were outdrawing the Bulls by a mile."

Three years and counting from the collapse of NASL, as the young USMNT showed its first signs of life, the overarching prospects for American professional soccer had never been quite so bleak. The new national standard-bearer, the Major Indoor Soccer League, did prove successful in several markets. It was also four short years from folding its own tent. A new outdoor league had been scheduled to launch in 1988, but why would that low-budget venture succeed where NASL had failed?

The hard truth was, there existed during the troubled mid-Eighties no identifiable path forward for professional soccer in the United States, indoor *or* outdoor. The urban/ethnic infrastructure endured. It would always endure. But never would it even aspire to a form of professionalism useful to players, to the Federation, to broadcasters and their corporate partners. As a result, despite the country's first Olympic qualification since 1972, it was impossible to envision how any of these broader professional inadequacies could be overcome. If we had a time machine and traveled back to the fall of 1987, and we informed a gathering of staunch American soccer fans that the U.S. would not only qualify for *Italia* '90 but host the 1994 World Cup as well, they'd look at us stone-faced — then ask what we'd been smoking. If we further informed them that Major League Soccer would celebrate its 25th anniversary in 2021, by which time 31 states would have legalized or decriminalized marijuana, they'd surely dismiss us as cranks.

TOUCHLINE

LARGEST CIRCULATION OF ANY SOCCER MAGAZINE IN THE USA
OVER ••• A MONTH • PAID CIRCULATION 53,000
••• YOUTH SOCCER ASSOCIATION PUBLICATION

JULY 1988

ALL-AMERICAN SUMMER
* USA TO HOST 1994 WORLD CUP
* USA OLYMPIC TEAM HAS SEOUL
* USA/DEPORTIVO CALI IN MIAMI

Non-Profit Bulk Rate
U.S. Postage Paid
Miami, Florida
Permit No. 3404

The summer of '88 witnessed a jump-starting of U.S. soccer fortunes, as the cover of *Touchline* magazine attests. The A-League also launched that spring, under the leadership of Chuck Blazer (pictured above with future boss at CONCACAF, Jack Warner). A year later, 18-year-old Chris Henderson debuted with the Seattle Storm, in the new-ish Western Soccer Alliance. *(Jon van Woerden photos; Storm image courtesy of Chris Henderson)*

9. SHOP WINDOWS, RESTARTS & GRAND TOURS
(OR "HOW TO GET SEEN IN A PRO SOCCER CULTURE GONE UNDERGROUND")

(1987 to '89)

Four times, beginning in the 1920s, soccer impresarios attempted to sell futbol to U.S. sporting consumers using a professional league branded thusly: "American Soccer League." The first ASL launched in 1921 and lasted 12 seasons. The most recent ASL iteration formed in 2014 and expired three years later, in 2017, having failed to achieve viable third-division status in the United States. In between, another American Soccer League took amorphous shape, beginning in the late 1930s. This venture existed in various loose, regional, semiprofessional forms for the next 50 years. During the Eisenhower administration, it clearly existed atop the U.S. professional soccer pyramid. Come the NASL era, it effectively served as U.S. soccer's second division. Throughout its long and circuitous history, it also served up some of the great team names in soccer history: Lusitania Recreation, Brooklyn Hispano, Uhrik Truckers, Pennsylvania Stoners and St. Louis Frogs.

Many of the urban/ethnic clubs discussed in this book participated in this version of the ASL in some way, shape or form. When it folded in 1983, to be followed into the hereafter by the North American Soccer League, urban/ethnic clubs and their regional leagues again took their places atop the U.S. professional outdoor pyramid. However, for all its admirable qualities, ethnic-league futbol remained unsuited to American soccer's most pressing needs during the mid-1980s: the ability to expand, to scale up and cohere, across the breadth of this very large country, into a nationwide first division. These shortcomings were obvious in 1966, prior to NASL's formation. They were identical and equally obvious in 1986, two years after NASL bought the farm.

Into this stew of substandard, outdoor-footballing realities was re-born yet another American Soccer League, in 1988.

It's difficult to assess the impact of the so-called A-League — and the Western Soccer Alliance, its largely semipro West Coast counterpart — all these years later. Neither ever amounted to much. They merged and then fizzled out well before the formation of Major League Soccer in 1996. But they do represent the stouthearted rebirth of "professional" club soccer in America. They provided Generation Zero with games, money, fitness and training, where previously there had been none.

Ultimately, however, the unsatisfactory nature of both leagues forced U.S. players to do something they had been reluctant to do, something most didn't realize they had the capacity to do: go looking for a better class of game, money, fitness and training — overseas.

———•———

The new, late-Eighties version of the American Soccer League, known to one and all as the "A-League," was the brainchild of former Cosmos general manager and NASL executive Clive Toye, the man who brought Pelé to the NASL. U.S. Soccer Federation vice president Chuck Blazer, along with a host of regional Federation officials, all joined Toye in support of the enterprise. They recognized the need to have *something* in place to develop American players — and keep them match fit between U.S. Men's National Team dates — before re-forming a new, fully national, first-division league. Indeed, this "league to be named later" was an outcome soon to be mandated by FIFA's 1994 World Cup agreement with the Federation.

The timing of the A-League's rollout reflects these fundamental realities. In May 1987, while the USMNT was just beginning its 1988 Olympic qualification campaign — and actively courting FIFA — the A-League announced the formation of five franchises. Come the spring of 1988, five more joined the fray and formal play commenced. Blazer served as commissioner. The 10 clubs divided themselves between two divisions: Northern (New Jersey Eagles, Maryland Bays, Washington Stars, Boston Bolts, Albany Capitals) and Southern (Tampa Bay Rowdies, Fort Lauderdale Strikers, Orlando Lions, Miami Sharks, Washington Diplomats).

Brian Bliss would migrate from the Major Indoor Soccer League's Cleveland Force to Albany, where he joined fellow *Italia '90* teammates Mike Windischmann and John Harkes, before finally ending up in Boston. Tab Ramos bounced between the soon-to-fold Miami Sharks and the New Jersey Eagles, where he played alongside Peter Vermes. Steve Trittschuh went to the Tampa Bay Rowdies — a futbol team name that has stubbornly refused to die. It has persisted through multiple leagues, indoor and outdoor, from 1975 to this day.

While all of these future World Cuppers participated in the new A-League, they remained singularly uninspired.

"It kept us going," Bliss says. "We would filter ourselves in and out, depending on the national team schedule. But the level of play was mostly college-type guys, though you had a few leftovers from the NASL, guys on the last legs of their careers. I don't want to say it was 'amateurish' because it wasn't. We were being paid, on a game-by-game basis. But the crowds were small and the level of play was just OK. And let's be real: It was the only game in town."

That game did produce a 20-game regular season in 1988, followed by a championship playoff, wherein the Washington Stars wrested the inaugural title from the Fort Lauderdale Strikers, over two legs. The second, staged at Lockhart Stadium in Fort Lauderdale, drew a crowd of 4,257 hearty, soccer-loving souls. Of course, league soccer in America isn't all about wins or losses, championships or attendance figures. *Ladies and gentlemen, boys and girls . . .* **Meet your 1988 A-League All-Stars!**

G	Winston DuBose	Tampa Bay Rowdies
G	Alan Rough	Orlando Lions
D	Troy Edwards	Miami Sharks

D	Brian Ainscough	New Jersey Eagles
D	Lou Karbiener	Orlando Lions
D	George Lidster	Washington Stars
D	Ross Irwin	Boston Bolts
M	Andy Harrison	Albany Capitals
M	Sonny Askew	Washington Stars
M	Rob Ryerson	Maryland
M	Dirceu Guimaraes	Miami Sharks
M	Steve Powell	Albany Capitals
M	Ray Hudson	Fort Lauderdale Strikers
F	Steve Wegerle	Tampa Bay Rowdies
F	Elvis Comrie	Maryland Bays
F -	Jorge Acosta	New Jersey Eagles
F	Joaquin Canales	Washington Diplomats
F	Teofilo Cubillas	Fort Lauderdale Strikers

The 1988 A-League All-Star Game, also staged at Lockhart, on June 16, was fittingly shambolic. The roster above was necessarily augmented by seven alternates, on account of injuries — and because the All-Stars' opponent was the host, league-leading Fort Lauderdale. Someone found George Best and persuaded him to suit up that day for the Strikers. Washington Stars assistant coach John Kerr Sr. played for the All-Stars. The match went to overtime, 3-3, then penalties. When 10 spot kicks did not determine a winner, the referees declared a draw and whatever remained of the crowd (3,179) went home. Three weeks later, in spite of this underwhelming spectacle, the United States was awarded the '94 World Cup.

Narrow as they can be, all-star rosters or Best XIs *do* tell us who made their marks during a particular league season. It's instructive that we recognize so few names today, aside from NASL veterans like DuBose, Cubillas, Comrie and the incomparable Raymond Wilfred Hudson, whose playing career pales, on these shores, beside his reputation as the Dick Vitale of 21st-century soccer broadcasting. Hudson's manic, bombastic calls on GolTV obscure the fact that he was once a pretty damned good striker. He scored 38 times in 151 appearances for Fort Lauderdale from 1978-83, a stint where, for three seasons, he partnered with *Der Bomber*, the one and only Gerd Mueller. Thereafter, however, Hudson became exactly the sort of NASL "leftover" who, according to Bliss, proved all too common in the A-League. After a goalless 1983-84 season in the *Bundesliga* 2, with SG Union Solingen, Hudson logged four indoor campaigns with MISL's Minnesota franchise. He even did a year in the Canadian League — with the fabled Edmonton Brickmen, alongside Norm Odinga. Only thereafter, fully warmed over, did he show up for the inaugural A-League campaign.

There were dozens of aging, NASL/MISL refugees stocking teams during the first A-League season. That state of affairs naturally hurt on-field quality, while also revealing the paper-thin nature of the North American professional talent pool at this time.

———•·•———

The entire A-League enterprise operated on a shoestring. Payrolls were capped at $75,000 per team. Paltry crowds meant paltry gates, and there would *never* be television money. Nonetheless, during that first campaign, in 1988, A-League commissioner Chuck Blazer managed to pay himself a salary that exceeded any single team's total player budget. Blazer passed away in 2017. *The Guardian* mentioned this salary nugget as part of his obituary, adding, "When he was forced out as commissioner, he took over the presidency of the franchise in Miami, increasing his salary and expenses, while the team drew barely 1,000 spectators per match."

The first two years of the ASL, Vol. III, were replete with fringe characters, from underskilled college products to slightly calcified veterans like Hudson and Comrie to coaches desperate to make their own marks and keep the cash flowing between indoor postings. It was fitting that Blazer, the most CONCACAFkaesque figure in the annals of U.S. soccer, presided for a time over the entire ragtag undertaking. Ultimately, however, the A-League proved too small a pond for Blazer, a man of undeniable abilities, appetites and foibles.

When Blazer left the Sharks in 1989, he did so in order to manage Jack Warner's campaign for the presidency of CONCACAF. Upon his election in 1990, Warner — a native of Trinidad, who today is essentially confined to the island nation, as he resists extradition to the U.S. on charges of wire fraud, racketeering and money laundering — appointed Blazer general secretary of the Confederation. From this perch, the two deftly set about gathering power, prestige and riches on behalf of CONCACAF, the U.S. soccer establishment, and themselves.

Fans and detractors alike tend to fixate on Blazer's propensity for self-dealing business practices — and his physical appearance, which, once he'd gone grey and bearded, suggested a cross between Santa Claus and Dickens' Ghost of Christmas Present. But they also tend to gloss over the progress the man enabled. Blazer enjoyed a 17-year stint on the FIFA board of directors, the first such term served by an American in 50 years. In that role, he was a powerful force both for the greater U.S. soccer good *and* his own aggrandizement. With Chuck Blazer, it's important to always discuss one alongside the other. For example, as the lead television negotiator for the Miami-based CONCACAF, he was widely known as "Mr. 10 Percent," for the millions he skimmed from TV and sponsorship deals. And yet, he *did* play an enormous role in promoting and shaping public consumption of the game in U.S. markets following USA '94. According to former Major League Soccer commissioner Doug Logan, Blazer "brought [U.S.] soccer into the modern television age almost single-handedly."

Blazer controlled and clearly cooked the books for Warner & Co. As such, it's difficult to detail or reckon his legacy without considering that of his mentor, who was implicated in a half-dozen separate corruption scandals before his 2015 indictment. That same year, even FIFA saw fit to ban Warner — for 28 years a FIFA executive committee member — from all futbol-related activities worldwide. For life.

Because Blazer had access to CONCACAF's accounting practices, the Confederation ended up paying for his private residences in the Bahamas, Miami and New York City's Trump Tower, where he kept his cats. He was reported to have claimed $21 million in personal compensation from the

Confederation between 2006 and 2011. And yet, Blazer generated enormous income for the Confederation, as well. It was he, not Warner, who transformed it from an international guppy dominated by Mexico into a hugely profitable and influential confederation, with the United States and its vast, lucrative media market at its core.

The guy proved an authentic character *and* rainmaker, who just happened to exhibit a weakness for embezzlement. He was known to tool around Manhattan on a mobility scooter with his pet macaw, Max, perched on one shoulder. According to *The Sunday Times*, "The bird had an eccentric story of its own. At some point in Blazer's past an ex-wife had departed, taking the parrot with her. By the time she returned it a year later, she had trained it to spout abuse. Blazer kept the bird in a gilded cage in his sumptuous Manhattan penthouse office, and complained that his business meetings were often interrupted by the bird squawking: *You're a dope.*"

The Falstaffian Blazer also proved something of a rat. It was largely his testimony that enabled the FBI's 2015 indictments of multiple FIFA figures — the legal actions that ultimately led to Sepp Blatter's resignation, and the enduring understanding that Qatar had purchased outright the 2022 World Cup. His was quite a life, 1945 to 2017 — a *Boomer* life, it must be said. Blazer would never have cut so wide a footballing swath had his son not started playing youth soccer in 1976. Shortly thereafter, he was running the Eastern New York State Soccer Association. Blazer enjoyed the good life, eventually. But he paid his dues within the Federation, as well. "When I was playing ODP, guess who was driving the van for the East Region coach: Chuck Blazer," Bruce Murray recalls. "That had to be 1981. He was driving the van and Sunil [Gulati, president of the Federation, 2006-2018] was picking up towels! A lot has been written about Chuck. But he always had a big smile on his face."

In 1984, none other than Pelé endorsed Blazer's candidacy for USSF international vice president, a posting that got the ball rolling. By 1994, he had founded a company in the Cayman Islands through which he would funnel all the kickback money to come. For 17 years he lived high on the hog, before the FBI confronted him on the streets of New York City. (It was a sidewalk, actually. He was riding his scooter, with Max.) Blazer would eventually plead guilty to 10 counts of racketeering, money laundering, wire fraud and tax evasion. Gulati replaced him on the FIFA board of directors. Two years later Blazer was dead, at 72. Such a sad and squalid coda should perhaps not obscure or diminish such an eventful footballing life, the most ambitious ever forged by an American Soccer Dad.

----·--·----

By year two, 1989, A-League franchises couldn't pay players enough to keep them with the club full time. Accordingly, they held down jobs outside of soccer, or worked youth soccer camps, or made cameo appearances in the ethnic leagues. Members of the USMNT did likewise, in addition to training with the national team. This absence of dedicated club affiliation and training hurt the on-field product, naturally.

"The old saying is, you're not going to get any better by training and playing no games, but you're also not going to improve by just playing games and not training," Bliss observes. "We would come into Albany sometimes — me, Mike and Harkes — on a Thursday, normally not in time to make training. We'd train with the Capitals on Friday, play Saturday, and often we were gone by Sunday morning. Then we're doing nothing for another week."

Bliss is being somewhat diplomatic. It was a shit show.

"You better believe it was," Trittschuh contends. "I played indoor that one season before the Steamers folded. After that, it was the A-League, or nothing . . . A lot of us wanted to go to Europe, myself included, but we didn't quite know how to go about it. Kerr was a popular guy back then. We all wanted to know what happened over there. But you could just feel [the A-League] was not getting that much better, not gaining momentum. Down in Tampa, when I was there, we would train in the afternoon because a lot of guys had jobs in the morning. That's how it was."

Trittschuh touches on another A-League deficiency: In a country so vast, unless players lived in the Northeast or Florida, participation required relocation. For Trittschuh there was added income from the Federation, which covered his travel back and forth from Tampa. For anyone *not* in the national team player pool, however, the prospect of making a couple hundred bucks per game made relocation to play ASL soccer unrealistic. This effectively regionalized and limited the talent pools for each franchise.

For two years post-NASL, there had been no league at all. *That* represented rock bottom. The Western Soccer Alliance, starting in 1986-87, and the A-League, come 1988, represented only meager upgrades. The takeaway here is stark: Had Generation Zero failed to qualify this country for World Cup 1990 — a prospect avoided thanks only to Paul Caligiuri's fabled left foot — it's easy to imagine professional outdoor soccer in America just quietly fading into obscurity.

IN MAY 1985, WHEN NASL WAS CLEARLY DOWN for the count, four independent clubs from the Pacific Northwest banded together to stop the bleeding. They originated a competition called the Western Alliance Challenge Series, whereby FC Seattle, FC Portland, San Jose Earthquakes and the Victoria Riptide (a Canadian side) played a home-and-home schedule throughout that summer and fall. They also scheduled ad hoc matches vs. everyone's northern Alberta darlings, the Edmonton Brickmen. Alliance clubs also faced off with the Canadian National Team, then looking to stay match-sharp prior to final WC qualifying in November 1985. It's instructive to note the concentration of these teams, not merely in the West but the Pacific *North*west, a region where European-style football traditions and fan culture have endured, more or less uninterrupted, since the 1970s.

History pegs Seattle and Portland as perhaps the most sophisticated and enthusiastic futbol towns in the U.S., the heart of a soccer-mad region that spans two states and spills over into British Columbia. All three MLS franchises in this region preserved their respective NASL club names, for example. It's no coincidence that, in the 21st century, the Portland Timbers, Vancouver Whitecaps and Seattle Sounders routinely draw sellout crowds of young, bearded, scarf-wielding, song-singing, drum-beating, flare-lighting, flag-waving supporters. This robust tradition did not come from nowhere, but rather from deep footballing roots. The hotbed of Washington state in particular produced myriad senior players of quality, starting in the 1980s: Jeff Durgan, Mark Peterson, Kasey Keller, Chris Henderson and Brent Goulet. There is history and talent and continuity and deep-seated passion here.

And so, it's no surprise that when American outdoor professional soccer died on the table late in 1984, its heartbeat would first be revived in the Pacific Northwest.

From that one-off Challenge Series in 1985 emerged the Western Soccer Alliance, which scheduled a full-on, home-and-home fixture list for the fall-to-spring, 1986-87 season. To enable this more structured, league-like undertaking, the Alliance added three California clubs — the Hollywood Kickers, Los Angeles Heat and San Diego Nomads — plus one Canadian side. The vaunted Brickmen replaced the Riptide, which had departed at the end of the Challenge Series. WSA clubs came and went, folded and relocated, but modest growth did eventuate. By 1989, when the Earthquakes morphed into the San Francisco Bay Blackhawks, the league featured nine teams in North and South divisions.

The West Coast supported its own urban/ethnic leagues, of course, and the demise of NASL proved a boon to their top clubs, too — just as it proved a boon to clubs in the Cosmopolitan and LASA leagues back East. Starting in 1986, there was a great deal of roster crossover between Alliance clubs and ethnic clubs in Los Angeles and San Francisco, where Wellesley boys Alex Carrillo and Tom Wadlington were both living and playing soccer at this time.

"The SFSFL [San Francisco Soccer Football League] at Balboa Stadium was excellent. I played for a couple teams in that league," Wad remembers. "It was just full of guys who'd been four-year players at Berkeley, at USF (which was a real power back in the day) and Stanford. Plus tons of international guys; players from Italy, France, Spain, England, Africa, all over the world."

San Francisco Greek-American A.C., the club Lothar Osiander coached to the U.S. Open Cup in 1985, was loaded with Cal Berkeley products at this time — a fact Wadlington, a proud Golden Bear, is quick to emphasize. The roster also featured Peter Woodring, who'd make several USMNT appearances in the early Nineties, and did a couple seasons with Hamburg in the *Bundesliga*. Then there was striker George Pastor, who would play serious minutes for Bob Gansler early in the 1989 World Cup qualification campaign. "Pastor was MVP of the league one time," Wad reports. "That Greek-American team won another U.S. Open Cup early in the Nineties [1994]. But here's the thing: The same core of Greek-Americans formed the core of the Blackhawks when they 'joined' the Alliance."

I love the choice of name for this new league entity: "Alliance" conjures up something thrown together in a postapocalyptic soccer culture, which, in the immediate wake of NASL's collapse, it was. The word also evokes radical decentralization — the addition of San Diego and Edmonton meant a maximum travel distance of 1,788 miles, one way! — and a resolute defiance of unnamed, vaguely malevolent forces.

Not insignificantly, WSA expansion in 1986 also meant the addition of Paul Caligiuri — fresh out of UCLA and playing with the Nomads — plus several more elite players who would contribute to future Olympic and WC qualification efforts: defender John Doyle, newly graduated from the University of San Francisco, who patrolled the back line for San Jose starting in 1987; David Vanole and Hugo Perez in Los Angeles; and Brent Goulet with FC Portland. Goulet was still an undergraduate at Portland's Warner Pacific College that first full WSA season. Nevertheless, he led the Alliance in scoring.

However, it was Caligiuri who earned the league's inaugural MVP award. His single, yearlong stint with the Nomads — in combination with UCLA's 1985 national championship — would land him two additional rewards: 1986 Player of the Year honors from the U.S. Soccer Federation, and a place in the 1986 FIFA-UNICEF World All-Star game. This was a

"Europe vs. The Americas" exhibition match played at the Rose Bowl on July 27, 1986, immediately following Mexico '86. Caligiuri's coach? None other than Serbian-born Bora Milutinovic, the USMNT skipper at World Cup '94. More integral to our story: *Bundesliga* club Hamburger SV had a scout there in Pasadena.

"Felix Magath saw him," explains Brian Bliss, whose own livelihood, post *Italia* '90, was enabled by Caligiuri's previous trailblazing in Germany. "Felix recommended him and Paul went off to Hamburg. That would have been 1987. Paul was fortunate to be seen. No one at that time had a resume big enough to get to Europe, really. Eventually you had guys like Bruce Murray and some guys who had double passports — John Kerr, I think. They had gone over on some trials. Some were successful, but most weren't. The rest of us were like, what are the realistic options for us? There weren't many."

"Man, the WSA: That brings me back," recalls a wistful Mike Woitalla, who was then a young staffer at *Soccer America* magazine. "We covered the Alliance big time. That's all there *was* on the professional side back then. A lot of former NASL guys were in those leagues at that time, as well. Alan Hinton and Jeff Durgan up in Seattle, I think. Where else would they go?"

Marcelo Balboa joined the Nomads for three seasons starting in 1987. He'd sign with the WSA's San Francisco Bay Blackhawks in 1990, after the World Cup — his first full-time club gig. The semiprofessional nature of the Alliance, the presence of all these NASL relics, part-timers and college kids, bothered Balboa not in the least. "It was a *great* time, I'll be honest with you," Balboa asserts. "That entire time with Nomads, I was still a student at San Diego State with [Eric] Wynalda. I was on a full [scholarship] ride but I was still working — at Kmart. I also worked at Little Caesars! The Alliance was all we had and we absolutely enjoyed it. As college kids, it was a little taste of being in a professional league . . . We didn't have options to go to Europe, not yet. The options were simple: Finish school, get a degree, and then, if the Western Soccer Alliance was still around, you would try to play there.

"Going from college to signing a [Federation] contract to playing in a World Cup? That opened doors. It also meant other teams, other coaches around the world could see us play! Maybe somewhere else entirely. That was our way out, man. There was no other way out until that time. I mean, where else would anybody see us?"

—*Marcelo Balboa*

"Even after the World Cup, we felt incredibly fortunate to be in the WSA, on the Blackhawks, where we made decent enough money. We were just so goddamned happy to play soccer and be able to *make some money*. We felt blessed! It was the life we all wanted to live. We wanted to play soccer — something we loved and had passion for — and get paid."

The 1989 season proved a mixed bag for both the A-League and the newly renamed Western Soccer League, the separate, coastal poles then constituting what passed for "first division" U.S. club soccer. Attendance remained abysmal. The yearlong *Italia* '90 qualifying schedule naturally drained both leagues of USMNT star power. Yet one man's international duty is another man's opportunity: Chris Henderson joined Seattle's WSL entry that summer, the rechristened Storm, as an 18-year-old.

The two circuits also took a baby step toward formal unification when they organized a championship game on Sept. 9, 1989, in San Jose, California. Nomads, champions of the Alliance, fell 3-1 to the A-League winners, the Fort Lauderdale Strikers. For the first time since 1984, a U.S. club could claim an undisputed, national, professional title.

The regional nature of both the A-League and the WSL was broadened when the two organizations agreed to formally join forces for the 1990 season. Just to make a point — Balboa's overriding point above — a key word was added to their new, joint name: Behold, the American *Professional* Soccer League (APSL). Outdoor pro soccer in the United States had finally scaled up and grown back, just strongly enough to connect the coasts. Sort of. The provincial, low-budget nature of the APSL, of all the franchises and their highly regionalized talent pools, proved an issue that would not go away — not until Major League Soccer launched in 1996.

———·•·———

FIFA's July 1988 decision to bestow World Cup '94 on the United States included all manner of mandates and caveats, yet The Big One remained little discussed in media circles, or anywhere else outside the Federation: The U.S. was obliged to qualify for *Italia* '90 — in order to make USA '94 a reality. "We were told," confirms USMNT keeper Tony Meola. "We knew FIFA and how it operated. The World Cup in '94 sorta hinged on us qualifying for Italy." FIFA also directed the host country to restart first-division futbol prior to the '94 tournament. Seeking that designation for itself, the APSL pressed on through the early 1990s. When formation of MLS was announced in 1993, however, FIFA immediately blessed the new league. Consigned to second-tier status going forward, the APSL went back to the old A-League moniker in 1995. Two years later, it joined forces with the emerging United States Interregional Soccer League. In 2005, this joint enterprise rebranded as the United Soccer League.

When the darkened, post-NASL era had first settled on the land, in late 1984, few of these developments were the least bit imaginable. Four years later, having played through a footballing apocalypse, Generation Zero had come out the other side — into the light. The sort of light that greets weary, steadfast travelers from the end of a tunnel.

"Even though we loved the Alliance, the future was so bleak for us until they got the World Cup and [the Federation] decided to give us all full-time contracts," Balboa explains. "But those contracts were the reason we could no longer really commit to those [APSL] clubs, most of us. The clubs weren't crazy about that, but the opportunity to play in a World Cup — and to get paid as professionals — that made sense to us, as players. Before we left school, we didn't know where we'd go . . . Going from college to signing a [Federation] contract to playing in a World Cup? That opened doors. It also meant other teams, other coaches around the world could see us play! Maybe somewhere else entirely. That was our way out, man. There was no other way out until that time. I mean, where else would anybody see us?"

Balboa, Meola and Wynalda were three of Generation Zero's youngest members. The limited footballing options Balboa describes above — college, followed by the USMNT on retainer — had given way to an entirely new universe of possibilities, beginning in July 1988. As such, these younger guys were perfectly content to play exclusively for the national team right through the Italian World Cup, should the U.S. manage to qualify.

As for their relative elders in the national team program, not so much. Their college experiences were distant memories. They had been desperately seeking viable club gigs for years, some since 1984. Being on some manner of retainer with the Federation had been welcome in 1986, but they couldn't wait around for the APSL to be replaced. These national team players were entering their competitive primes. They were eager to truly professionalize themselves. For them, the obvious limitations of the A-League, the Western Soccer League and the APSL — remunerative, technical and otherwise — would prove the most compelling reasons to get out of Dodge altogether. To go, as Marcelo Balboa maintains, where somebody might see them.

GENERATION ZERO DESERVES CREDIT FOR SO many pioneering steps in the modern history of American soccer, it's easy to overlook the fact that these same Yanks were also the first to play the game professionally in Europe. Nitpickers might take issue with this assertion. Someone like Gerry Baker — Bob Gansler's teammate on the 1969 USMNT, who'd been born to British parents in New Rochelle, New York, but was raised in Motherwell, Scotland, and played all over the U.K. from 1956-1973 — is a technical exception. So are the professionals who, after being naturalized for NASL duty during the Seventies, returned to play in their countries of origin. Even so, the native-born players in Generation Zero were something entirely new and precedent setting. Today, according to U.S. Soccer Federation data, more than 400 American-born professional players ply their trade abroad. In 1985, that number was precisely zero.

Let us not be carried away by false sentiment, however. As Balboa makes plain, those who first undertook their intrepid Euro-quests, starting in the mid-1980s, did so mainly out of self-interest and desperation. Such was the dire, rudimentary state of outdoor professional soccer here at the time.

The first player to touch this glass ceiling was striker Tommy Kain, another New Jersey product — this one from Wall Township, near Asbury Park — who had played in Australia alongside John Stollmeyer on the 1981 U-20 national team. It was Kain's poor luck to graduate from college in the spring of 1986, into a newly denuded outdoor soccer landscape. NASL was gone. Drafted by the MISL's new expansion entry, the New York Express, Kain instead leveraged a personal connection and, as Mark Twain advocated, lit out for the territory.

"They came to me," Kain told the *Chicago Tribune* that summer of 1986. He explained that the father of a friend, Alex Wipperfurth, owned a club in the West German second division, SG Union Solingen — the club that gave Ray Hudson his last European place. "I was going to sign with New York, but then this opportunity presented itself. I weighed the options, and I didn't think the opportunity to play abroad would present itself again."

All true. Kain went over in January of 1986, but coach Rolf Muller was not impressed — not enough, anyway. Soon, though, Muller himself was found wanting: The club fired him that spring. Several older players and their contracts were also jettisoned, and Kain was invited back for pre-season the following summer. The second tryout did not go well, either. Kain picked up a few injuries and didn't play his best; he made the squad but never saw time in an official *Bundesliga* 2 match. He spoke to the *Tribune* in the middle of what was a difficult, ultimately fruitless exercise.

"Believe me, I've had second thoughts three or four times," Kain explained. "When I have a bad day and the coach yells at me in German, I think, *Maybe I should have stayed near home and done better than this.* I know I'm playing badly. It would be harder to accept if I was playing well in practice. I'm frustrated because I've played well everywhere else I've been. Barring anything fantastic here, I'll probably end up going back to New

York, probably for the 1987-88 season. Who knows, maybe even this year. I do plan an indoor career. It's hard here, but I'm learning. I hope others will follow. I'm sure I'm not the best player, but somebody had to be first."

Ray Klivecka, the Express coach, was dispassionate in his assessment of Kain's circumstance, but ultimately dismissive: "His situation is a fluke. Very few Americans have the talent or emotional energy to survive on the other side. They only allow two foreigners on each team, so an American kid is taking a German kid's job. It's not an easy situation."

When Kain did return from Germany in the fall of 1986, he found the MISL Kansas City Comets had purchased his rights. Kain eventually made 128 appearances for KC before retiring in 1991, at 27. Few remember citizen Kain's pioneering role in the making of modern American soccer. Few U.S. players had their dreams extinguished quite so quickly or unceremoniously. Yet even fewer went on to fashion for themselves such an influential presence in the game. Kain went to work for Adidas, eventually rising to director of U.S. operations. Nike lured him away at the turn of the century, and Kain rose there as well: to Nike Soccer's head of global marketing, then to director of sports marketing for all of Nike. In May 2018, he was one of a dozen senior managers who left the company amid what *The New York Times* called "widespread allegations of harassment and discrimination against female employees."

———•·•———

Peter Vermes, he of the square jaw and intense glare, is perhaps Generation Zero's most recognizable on-field face, thanks to his long, successful tenure as head coach of Sporting Kansas City. His teams win trophies (the 2013 MLS Cup and 2017 U.S. Open Cup, for example). SKC's academy system is a model for competing clubs across Major League Soccer. Several players groomed by Vermes and his staff have indeed "graduated" to bigger clubs and contracts in Europe: Gianluca Busio to Venezia following the 2021 Gold Cup, for example. Erik Palmer-Brown went off to Porto, then Manchester City in 2018 (he was out on loan to the French Ligue 1 club

ES Troyes AC at this writing). Vermes and his club are pillars of what the American domestic game has become in the 21st century.

When Vermes was a young and upcoming player himself, however, there was nothing like Sporting KC available to him. That's why he bugged out for Europe at the first opportunity.

Vermes had come into Lothar Osiander's side in the fall of 1987, shortly after scoring 21 times while leading Rutgers University into the NCAA tournament. That winter, with the USMNT firmly fixated on qualification for the 1988 Seoul Olympics, he claimed a starting role. His club prospects were not nearly so bright, however. Vermes had committed to his "hometown" New Jersey Eagles, one of the 10 franchises set to participate in the inaugural A-League campaign come the spring of 1988.

Raised the son of a professional footballer, the young Vermes was already a veteran of the ethnic leagues in New York City and Philadelphia. He wanted more than the U.S. domestic scene could offer at that time. Then, in April 1988, a door opened. "That national team was playing a tournament in France, in Lille, I believe," he says. "I forget if we won or finished second, but I do remember having scored a goal. So I'm coming off the field and this person says my name in Hungarian. My parents are from Hungary; I speak Hungarian. I looked over and didn't know who said it. Then this guy calls out, 'Do you speak Hungarian?' He waved his hand. I said, 'Yeah, I do.' And he says, 'Can I talk to you after you have a shower?' Well, he wound up being this Hungarian guy, an agent based in Belgium. He said, 'Look, I'd love to bring you here to Europe. I know I can get you a couple opportunities to play here.' I said, 'Great, because that's what I'm looking to do. When the Olympics are done, I want to do that.'"

Thirty years on, Vermes' determination to go abroad seems to us something of a no-brainer. Why would *any* of these guys have passed up an opportunity to play abroad — or even just travel overseas for a trial? But the prospect wasn't so simple or straightforward back then.

"We were all so young at the time, so inexperienced," Vermes explains. "I don't think any of us knew what kind of impact we'd eventually have.

Obviously, it's been pretty incredible. But there was inexperience and a lack of vision back then because you're so young and focused on the moment. Doors were opened because of what we did, but most of the time we didn't really understand how or why it was all happening – or not happening."

The opportunity to go abroad, in the spring of 1988, was anything but straightforward. The Federation already kept its core roster on a sort of retainer. After the Seoul Olympics, in the fall of 1988, it formalized and sweetened the arrangement to improve team cohesion and preparation prior to CONCACAF qualification, scheduled for 1989. Running off to Europe and relinquishing this level of security struck some, at the time, as imprudent. Even a bit disloyal. Meanwhile, the A-League, which did launch in April 1988, was billed as a rebirth of first-division soccer in the U.S., and there was implicit pressure on American players to participate.

"There were people on both sides of the aisle," Vermes recollects. "There were some who said, 'You're not going to make it. What are you doing?' At that time, I don't think anyone ever thought that we were cheapening our value, if you will. Because let's face it: We didn't have any value! No one rated us back then, and no one was playing over there at that time. I will tell you, it wasn't the easiest of decisions."

Kain's European tale certainly proved cautionary. Neither could Paul Caligiuri's still-evolving experience in West Germany be held up as a shining example of how to get abroad, stay there, and gain first-team experience, much less first-division experience. The Californian had leveraged his appearance in that 1986 FIFA All-Star exhibition into a tryout with Hamburg. However, he never made a first-team appearance there. He shuttled back and forth between the first team and the reserves. When the club brought in a Russian goalkeeper during the 1987-88 winter break, Cal was sent down to the reserves permanently, as German rosters were still limited to two foreigners per club.

By the time Caligiuri and Vermes went to the Seoul Olympics together, in September of 1988, the Californian had moved to second-division SV Meppen, where he would make 45 appearances through fall 1990. These were the first honest-to-goodness, European league matches played by a born-and-reared American player during the 1980s. However, it was Caligiuri's World Cup 1990 credential, not his time at Meppen, that got him noticed by Hansa Rostock, then a member of the East German first division. Caligiuri helped that club win the 1991 East German championship — and a ticket into the newly unified German *Bundesliga* the following season. Unfortunately, Rostock did not bring Cal along. He signed instead with second-division Freiburg.

By 1988, the lower divisions and secondary leagues of Europe had become something like Major League Soccer is today, according to Vermes. "We're always looking for adventurous players who will fit into our league, who will represent an inexpensive transfer, or a free transfer, at a cheap salary," the Sporting KC skipper says. "European clubs back then said the same thing: 'We can get these guys on a really cheap wage and bring them across.' When you think of MLS today, we've sort of come full circle.

"Ultimately, my whole objective was, as soon as the Olympics were over, I was going to shoot over to Europe and basically go on a tryout tour until I made a team. Fortunately, I had run into that fellow in Lille. So, that was my plan, because I felt the leagues here weren't developed enough. It was not the environment where I could see myself developing as a player."

Shortly after the Seoul Olympics concluded and the U.S. team returned home, Peter Vermes was on a plane to Europe, looking for doorsteps. Thanks to his new Hungarian friend, two tryouts had already been scheduled in Belgium. That was Vermes' understanding. However, his new agent bypassed Belgium and whisked him instead straight to the provincial city of Gyor, home to Hungarian first-division club ETO FC Gyor. There, the young American was under the impression he'd have a couple weeks to train before a formal audition was arranged.

"That first training session, they put a mock scrimmage together," Vermes remembers. "So I played in that, and afterward they offer me a contract. So, my first day I had a tryout — and I hadn't even realized it! I later learned they saw this signing as a marketing deal, where they could say, 'Here's this young American-Hungarian coming back to his roots!' I didn't care: Now I'm the first American player to play Division I soccer in Europe — at that point no one had broken into a Division I club on a regular basis, anywhere.'"

Most European leagues maintained limits on the number of foreigners a team could have on the roster at any one time. Hungary still lay behind the Iron Curtain in the fall of 1988. Persuading foreigners to relocate there was a big ask — and a big break for Vermes. The club's marketing intentions quickly resulted in a no-drama work permit. Vermes was off and running.

Even in its domestic competition, ETO FC Gyor was hardly a title contender. The club's finest moment had come in 1965, when it lost a European Cup semifinal to Eusébio and Benfica. Nonetheless, the club remained a solid midtable side in the Hungarian first division, and Vermes made nine appearances for them that 1988-89 season. He failed to score, alas, but did experience total Gyor immersion. "I actually lived at the stadium. I really and truly did. The stadium was part of an all-encompassing complex, which had seven apartments, one for the caretaker and six more dorm rooms, if you will. I lived there, at the stadium, because it was convenient. I was single and I was there for one thing — to play soccer. I woke up and I was 20 yards from the locker room."

During the summer of 1989, while traveling and training all over North and Central America, attempting to qualify his country for the 1990 World Cup, Vermes' contract was purchased by FC Volendam in the Dutch first division, the *Eredivisie*. In many ways, this Dutch experience revealed the player we remember from *Italia* '90: the athletic yet technical striker who nearly scored to draw his team level with the host nation during the group stage; the player who spent four subsequent years in Spain playing for Figueres; the savvy operator who, in the early years of MLS, transitioned from striker to sweeper because his technique, vision and tackling still got the job done, even when his youthful speed had left him.

More vital to our story, the Volendam version of Vermes was the American player many European sporting directors first laid eyes upon

— and they liked what they saw. European clubs would not invest in serious, systematic scouting of American players until 1996. That's when Major League Soccer launched and Old World clubs could easily observe recognized first-division competition on U.S. soil, mainly via television or tape. But the groundwork was laid nearly a decade before, by Vermes, in Hungary and Holland. *Perhaps*, the scouts imagined, likely for the very first time, *there are others like him.*

———••———

Not every member of Generation Zero who arrived in Europe during the late Eighties got flagged down by an agent. Even fewer got whisked away to meaningful club tryouts in the land of their ancestors. What's more, the Bosman ruling — a European Court of Justice decision allowing players whose contracts had expired to move between clubs and across national borders without transfer fees — wasn't issued until 1995. However, when John Kerr Jr. and Brent Goulet showed up in England in 1987, they did have one thing going for them: Neither was then employed by a first-division club. As a result, English clubs were not obliged to pay transfer fees in order to secure their services. All through this period, the absence of meaningful club football in the U.S. worked very much in the young Americans' favor.

Goulet arrived during the summer of 1987, more than a year ahead of Vermes, fresh off a dominant performance in the Western Soccer Alliance's first full year of play. Tall, dark and handsome, the strapping Goulet cut a dashing and prolific figure at striker throughout 1985, '86 and '87. His collegiate performance, first at Warner Pacific University and then at FC Portland as an amateur, earned him his first two caps in February 1986, under newly installed USMNT manager Lothar Osiander. When Goulet graduated and turned professional, he promptly set the Alliance on fire, leading the league in scoring and earning MVP laurels.

That summer of 1987, he joined rival FC Seattle on a five-game exhibition tour of England — something a Timbers player probably wouldn't get away with today. The trip included a match with AFC Bournemouth, then a member of the old second division. (The modern English footballing pyramid, with its idiosyncratic naming habits — Premier, Championship, League One, League Two — would not take its current form until 1992.) Goulet scored twice on the tour, and Bournemouth were tantalized enough to offer him a contract for the upcoming 1987-88 season. They also finagled a work permit — because goal-scoring has its privileges.

Alas, the Yank never did score for the Cherries. He was summarily loaned out to Crewe Alexandra, where three goals in three appearances were not enough to warrant another deal — not with Crewe or Bournemouth. Goulet would return to the U.S., rejoin the Seattle club, and concentrate on qualifying his country for the 1988 Olympics. For all his goals and far-flung travels, Goulet was named the Federation's 1987 U.S. Soccer Player of the Year, though John Kerr Jr. was surely in with a shout. Indeed, John and Brent's Excellent Blighty Adventures would overlap.

Kerr, the former Montgomery Pinto who back in 1976 had billeted in Tom Wadlington's house on Weston Road, won college soccer's top honor, the Hermann Trophy, that fall of 1986 (teammate Tommy Kain had won it the year before). Kerr chose to spend the next semester, his final days as a Duke student, in England, technically on exchange.

"I went over early. I spent my senior spring abroad, which is sort of un-heard of, but I knew I wanted to play professional soccer and I knew that I wanted to go to England to try my luck," Kerr told the Soccer New England website in 2006. "I knew that I could play amateur soccer in England and maybe get seen while finishing off my degree."

Kerr spent the first half of 1987 playing for Harrow Borough in the Isthmian League, a semipro circuit that covered all of London and much of the country's southeast. The Isthmian represented, at the time, the fifth or sixth tier of English soccer, depending on whom you asked. In 1985, when I played at the University of London, the better players often moonlighted there — and in another semipro league, the GM Vauxhall Conference, known simply as the Conference. The soccer on display in each was very good — good enough that Kerr's performance for Harrow earned him a first-division contract offer, reportedly on the firsthand recommendation of Chelsea FC legend Peter Osgood.

"[Harrow] had been pretty mediocre before I got there, and I scored some goals and was lucky enough to get spotted by Peter Osgood, a big star for Chelsea and a former England international back in the late Sixties," Kerr says. "At the time, he was the youth team coach at Portsmouth, which was being promoted from the second division to the first. He invited me down to play in a reserve team game Portsmouth played against Crystal Palace. Alan Ball was the manager of Portsmouth at the time.

"So I traveled down to Portsmouth by train . . . and we won, 1-0. I scored a pretty good goal. Afterwards I went into the dressing room and Alan Ball offered me a contract there on the spot. He said, 'I want you here at Portsmouth next year.' It was one of the biggest thrills of my life. I thought I had arrived."

In June of 1987, the Tacoma Stars of MISL made Kerr their second-round draft pick. Their timing was as poor as Kerr's had been impeccable. Portsmouth were newly promoted to the English first division. Young Kerr signed with the south coast club, making him the first American ever to play in England's top flight, and the first member of Gen Zero to play first-division football anywhere in Europe. Because he held a dual passport — as the son of British-born footballer John Kerr Sr. — Kerr didn't have to bother with obtaining a work permit.

There's a reason Kerr's historic season isn't better known, however. In terms of performance, it was a pretty mixed bag — beginning with his appearance at Oxford United in August 1987 and ending when he came on as a substitute in a 4-1 loss at Luton Town in March 1988. All told, he made just four league appearances for Portsmouth and two FA Cup appearances. He also endured a three-month loan to fourth-division Peterborough United.

"I wasn't ready for prime time," Kerr says. "What overwhelmed me was the intensity of the game there. You had to perform every day in practice. You couldn't take days off, and there were no slouches out there. There were no easy games. There were no easy practices, no easy sessions, no easy segments in a training session. The intensity was just immense."

In the end, American representation in the uppermost reaches of English football required someone who would start, and score, and prove U.S. players had the skill and mettle to compete there with the suitable intensity — not just in matches but every day, during every session in training. Kerr couldn't make that impression, but John Harkes later proved to be exactly that guy, latching on with Sheffield Wednesday — thanks to the *Italia* '90 shop window — from 1990-93. Many Yanks have since made their mark in the English top-flight, but south Yorkshire folk still talk about Harkes' first goal for Wednesday in 1990, against Derby. Go Google it.

———•+•———

Kerr returned home in the spring of 1988 and ultimately signed with the A-League Washington Stars, a club coached by his father. Like Goulet, he had his eye on a regular national team place, the '88 Olympics and World Cup qualifying. When the summer of 1988 drew to a close, however, Kerr found himself out of Lothar Osiander's mix. He wouldn't go to Seoul.

During the ensuing 1988-89 season, Kerr made the choice to split his time between Washington and England, scoring 13 times for Wycombe Wanderers in the Vauxhall Conference. Gansler, who replaced Osiander in early 1989, called in a host of nearly unknown attacking options throughout 1989 World Cup qualifying, but Kerr never got an opportunity. He was never on the short list for Italy. He would subsequently kick around the lower divisions of England, France and Canada throughout the early 1990s, before the Dallas Burn selected him in the inaugural MLS draft. That was 1996. By then his best on-field days were behind him, though he was a surprise inclusion on the 1995 USMNT that made an improbable run to the *Copa America* semifinals. These were Kerr's final caps following a seven-year, extremely well traveled hiatus — one that would have made a Greek hero proud.

Kerr enjoyed an extraordinary career in soccer, much of it intertwined with that of his lifelong friend and fellow Pinto Bruce Murray. Their careers tracked quite closely: Murray, too, won a Hermann Trophy (1987) and played on the Stars in the new A-League, under John Kerr Sr. Murray harbored the same ambitions — to get seen and develop his game in Europe — but they led him to Switzerland in the late Eighties, not England.

"I had gone to Juventus first," Murray explains. "The U.S. Federation had some Juve connection, and I trained there in Turin [Italy] for six weeks. Then I played well at the ['88] Olympics. Juventus had no place for me, but the Swiss club Luzern took me on, paid me, gave me an apartment. I loved it there, but they were only allowed two foreign players and I was the third. Then Gansler called to tell me the Federation was going to give players contracts, and 'We want you here.'

"I felt my best chance at the World Cup was to come back from Switzerland. The Swiss coach Freidel Rausch took me aside and said, 'Listen, I want you. But I can't play you right now. When they go to three foreigners, you're my guy.' But I told him I had to go. I still wonder if I should have stayed and played there, shuttled back and forth [between Luzern and the national team]. I still don't know if I did the right thing. That's what I regret: never knowing if it was the right thing or not. I was playing great there. Banging in goals for fun. I think I could have had a different professional experience there. But who knows? That's life."

Following the 1988 and 1989 A-League campaigns, Murray twice trained with FC Luzern — the same trans-Atlantic, timeshare approach Kerr had taken. But Murray never managed to gain a place with the 1989 Swiss champions. Eventually he had to make a choice: Try again in the land of Helvetians, or accept the offer of paid residency from the U.S. Federation and help his countrymen earn a place at *Italia* '90. Clearly Murray had the desire to play abroad; he gave it another go in the Nineties with English clubs Stoke City, Millwall and Stockport. In the end, his desire for a roster spot in Italy proved the stronger impulse.

Eric Eichmann, Murray's teammate at Clemson and *Italia* '90, took a similar path. After one season with Werder Bremen's reserves in the

West German third division (1987-88), he returned home in 1989 to play with the Fort Lauderdale Strikers. Attacking midfielder Chris Sullivan did likewise, cutting short his journey through the lower divisions of France — with Joue-les-Tours and Le Touquet AC — to better his chances of making the Olympic and World Cup squads.

Kerr opted to continue alternating between the A-League and the lower leagues of Europe, because dreams are made to be chased. Pursuing this one, however, in this fashion, probably cost Kerr his best shot at a World Cup place. "I agree that John hurt his own chances," Murray admits, with not insignificant resignation. "These were agonizing decisions. Trittschuh and Vermes and Cal and Kerr — they deserve kudos for blazing that trail. But it didn't work out for John. He was so quick, such a solid player. He could really play."

DURING THE LATE EIGHTIES, WHEN THESE various white-bread American boys set out for Europe, they did so having just cut their teeth competing in urban leagues of incredible ethnic diversity. They played for, beside and against Greeks and Italians, Guatemalans and Nigerians, Hungarians and Irish, Germans and Cape Verdeans, Argentinians and Portuguese. When those who ventured abroad returned to the U.S., off they went to play national team qualifiers all over the Caribbean and Central America. Once qualified for World Cup 1990, they decamped for Italy, where many hoped to earn for themselves durable careers playing for European clubs, or maybe South American clubs, in any country that might have them.

It's a big wide world out there. One of the distinguishing things about soccer, specifically, is its ability to reflect back to us just how big and wide that world can be. Once we Americans allowed it to do so.

In talking to *Soccer America* editor Mike Woitalla, I was struck by his contention that in many tangible ways American soccer was actually far more mature in 1987 than anyone realized at the time, thanks in large part to its sprawling network of ethnic futbol clubs and communities.

Yes, the country lacked veritable first-division soccer at that time. Yes, the national team had essentially remained a CONCACAF minnow for much of the previous five decades. But in a country of nearly 250 million people, these diverse and hardy blocs of ethnicity may — in the aggregate — have accounted for 25 to 30 million pretty hardcore, adult soccer fans, sifted however thinly over the nation's vast, largely soccer-indifferent cultural grid.

"I would bet that most people didn't know we had a national team in 1986. People just didn't understand how Diego Maradona could play for Napoli and Argentina. They couldn't get their heads around it... This was the depth of knowledge at the time."

—Jim Trecker

It's not clear to me that FIFA saw the U.S. soccer demographic in this way. The folks in Zurich were laser-focused on the country's long-term potential, the tens of millions of *new* American futbol fans still to be generated, and the financial support of massively rich, U.S.-based, multinational corporations. Nevertheless, this not-yet-mainstream support for soccer in America didn't always remain in the shadows. It showed itself during the L.A. Olympiad of 1984. It showed itself every time a few hundred folks showed up for semipro matches staged throughout the 1980s, far from the suburbs, in the specifically ethnic neighborhoods of Miami, Houston, Milwaukee, Chicago, Long Beach, Baltimore, Philadelphia or Lowell. It also showed itself in the country's youth leagues, high school and collegiate programs, all of which grew at remarkable rates, in terms of participation, throughout the decade.

Qualifying the U.S. national team for a World Cup was the next vital step, and Generation Zero ultimately laid that issue to rest. Yet one additional, psycho-structural problem remained, and it was not insignificant: Throughout the 1980s, the American sporting public did not yet understand the basic nature of international, country-vs.-country team competitions. Until it did, the mainstream could not effectively interpret or get excited about the USMNT, or events like the World Cup.

———•+•———

Jim Trecker grasped this curious issue in the moment. You may remember him from Chapter 7: He was one of the three fellows charged with delivering to Zurich the Federation's bid to host World Cup 1994. Later he managed communications and press operations at that event.

"I would bet that most people didn't know we had a national team in 1986," Trecker told Yahoo! Sports in 2018, adding that Americans didn't yet comprehend how international tournaments were contested. "People just didn't understand how Diego Maradona could play for Napoli *and* Argentina. They couldn't get their heads around it. I'd say, 'Think of it like baseball's All-Star Game. Somebody plays for the Yankees, but for this one day they're going to represent the American League. This tournament is a month of that.' This was the depth of knowledge at the time. People would call me up asking where 'the game' would be played. I had to explain to them that the World Cup was actually 52 games over 30 days."

As I trust we've established by now, American ignorance in this area is partly explained by the country's underdeveloped soccer culture. However, country-vs.-country team competitions didn't compute in *any* sporting context, here in the U.S., because our sporting universe for more than 100 years had remained so strongly domestic and insular in scope.

American football provides the most cut-and-dried example: Apart from Canada, no other nation on earth even plays gridiron, for Chrissakes. As a result, international competition is impossible. Until the late 1980s, the U.S. did not seriously compete internationally in *any* team sport context, outside of the Olympics. Full stop. When it did so, the country mimicked the Olympic model by sending amateur athletes to those competitions. While other countries sent their best professionals to world hockey and basketball championships, for example, the U.S. sent amateur college kids. Prior to the 1990s, the NBA and NHL had nothing to do with these international team competitions.

The baseball example is perhaps more nuanced and instructive. For the better part of a century — from 1870 to 1970 — Americans were not broadly aware that baseball, the game *we* invented, had grown so popular and pervasive in Latin America, the Caribbean and the Far East. It took the full-on internationalization of Major League Baseball — the arrival of foreign players *here*, starting in the 1960s — to show Americans how well and how differently the game could be undertaken by different peoples of the earth. Still, the idea of pitting a U.S. *national* baseball team against those from other nations failed to register with Americans. The World Baseball Classic is the closest thing to a world championship that Major League Baseball has ever attempted. It launched in 2006, expired in 2013, and never rose above exhibition status.

America's attitudes in this regard, prior to 1990, loosely mirrored the patronizing, proprietary way the English looked upon soccer played outside its borders until 1950. That was the year England first deigned to participate in soccer's World Cup. It had skipped the first two tournaments, judging the rest of the world unfit to compete with the English in a game the English had invented. This condescending attitude started to change prior to *Brasil* '50. First, England agreed to participate. Then it lost to the lowly Americans and failed to advance from group play. Another key evolutionary moment arrived in November 1953, when Ferenc Puskas and Hungary visited Wembley Stadium and ran their hosts off the park, 6-3. Suddenly, the English — meaning the country's football establishment and sporting public — were all in on international football.

———— • ————

American ignorance of and indifference toward international team competitions fell away in a very similar fashion. An Olympic bronze medal at the 1988 Seoul Games convinced USA Basketball and the NBA that our best pros should indeed compete at world championships and Olympic Games. As it happened, formation of the NBA Dream Team prior to the 1992 Barcelona Olympiad captivated the American sporting public. It also introduced the country's parochial fan base to this *novel* idea: collecting the best players from across the league to represent the United States and compete against all-star teams representing other countries.

At the time, enthusiasm for the Dream Team and the so-called *Dream Team concept* left many U.S. soccer folks bewildered and exasperated. This process of gathering a country's best professional soccer or basketball or handball players to compete on national teams had been going on for decades. More to the point, soccer enthusiasts in this country had been pimping the merits of this arrangement for years! This *all-star* concept, this country-against-country aspect, is exactly what made and continues to make FIFA competitions like the World Cup so damned interesting!

In any case, here's the larger, more pertinent historical point: Americans didn't understand or appreciate the inherent drama and intrigue of international team competitions until the late Eighties and early Nineties. When they finally *did* get clued in, when they recognized the excitement inherent to the phenomenon, this attitudinal shift proved crucial to the growth and mainstreaming of soccer in the U.S. — because so much of the sport's broad appeal is inextricably bound up in these international, country-vs.-country dynamics.

And yes: The single biggest factor in changing this understanding in America was the fabled Dream Team of Barcelona's Summer Olympiad. Ahead of 1991, when the team was selected (*Sports Illustrated* actually coined the "Dream Team" moniker on its Feb. 18, 1991, cover), this idea that American pros would leave their clubs or franchises to compete for the U.S., as a team, against other countries, was *revolutionary* for American sports fans. Previously, the idea of players representing both club and country simply didn't scan.

This lack of understanding within the insulated American sporting public is precisely why qualifying for the 1990 FIFA World Cup proved so foundational to the growth and expansion of soccer in America. Missing the tournament every four years meant the lightbulb could not go on, in the soccer context, and would not go on, for at least another four.

———•·•———

Here's a further irony: For many Americans today, the World Cup has become the *only* soccer competition that truly matters. Yes, Major League Soccer has grown by leaps and bounds over its two-plus decades. Three women's professional leagues have launched since 1999. However, the U.S. Men's National Team and the U.S. Women's National Team each occupy an *outsized* place in the American soccer tableau, because sporting consumers here initially identified soccer with this country's national teams — first at *Italia* '90, then USA '94 — rather than any of its club teams. Indeed, at the time this country had no prominent, first-division club teams to support, not until MLS launched in 1996.

Fan support is not a zero-sum game. Nevertheless, in America, intense identification with its national team programs, starting in 1990, has often meant less support for MLS and its franchises. This circumstance has been particularly damaging in the women's context, where USWNT exposure and success have essentially starved domestic leagues, even the current National Women's Soccer League, of exposure and success.

What's more, this phenomenon remains peculiarly American. Germans and Chileans and Japanese and South Africans all adore their respective national teams. However, in those three years between World Cups they go mad following their respective domestic competitions, as well. Americans are still developing this infatuation for domestic soccer between quadrennials.

In 1987, ESPN took a flier and covered the hell out of the America's Cup sailing regatta — live from Australia, with cameras hanging from helicopters and embedded in masts. The network, then less than a decade old, remained famished for live content, and here was a compelling storyline: The U.S. had lost the cup in 1983, for the first time in 132 years. U.S. skipper Dennis Conner, not an elite eastern blueblood but a hardscrabble kid from San Diego, was trying to win it back from the dread Australians four years later. A unique sporting drama, to be sure, and one to which Americans, remarkably, started paying attention. Very few Americans gave a damn about sailing in the 1980s. Few give a damn today. Still, in early February 1987, for the fourth and what proved to be the clinching match race between *Kookaburra III* and *Stars & Stripes*, fully 1,889,000 households — almost 2 million! — flipped on ESPN to watch: a 3.4 Nielsen rating, nine times the average for that time slot and the equivalent of what a Duke-UNC college basketball game might then pull on a weeknight. I can't prove it, but I reckon these America's Cup telecasts had a sanguine effect on ESPN's decision to broadcast later USMNT matches: the second leg of the Olympic tie vs. Canada in May 1987, for example, and final World Cup qualification matches throughout 1989.

Did the programmers at ESPN sense a pending shift in the American media zeitgeist, one that mobilized our not-insignificant jingoism? Did a basketball bronze medal in Seoul ultimately enable the mainstreaming of U.S. soccer in the 1990s? It's hard to make these claims in a definitive fashion. U.S. basketball fans had been pining for NBA participation in the Olympics since 1972, when another gold medal went begging. However, looking back and looking closely, we can say this: The 1990 U.S. Men's National Soccer Team arrived at exactly the right time — just when Americans were ripe to recognize how irresistible international team competitions could be.

John Stollmeyer (from left), Steve Trittschuh and Mike Windischmann prior to an August 1988 World Cup qualifier in St. Louis. *(Image courtesy of Mike Windischmann)*

Coach Bob Gansler (at left) and his young charges on the tarmac in Tegucigalpa, Honduras, September 1989. TAN Airlines (Transportes Aereos Nacionales) was merged into SAHSA, another Honduran airline, in 1991. *(Jon van Woerden photo)*

10.   SURVIVE & ADVANCE

B efore I began researching the Modern American Soccer Movement (1970-90) in earnest, I harbored any number of preconceptions about this particular era of U.S. soccer — preconceptions that ultimately proved muddled, half-wrong or just plain mistaken. For example, I had assumed this generation of footballing peers viewed the Major Indoor Soccer League as a sort of welcome way station between the disintegration of NASL in 1984 and the launch of the A-League four years later. Instead, I gathered that elite players widely viewed MISL as the sport's redheaded stepchild, something aesthetically and competitively debased that *also* had a dele-terious effect on one's outdoor skill set. I also presumed the 1990 World Cup qualification campaign did not differ from any of the seven quad-rennial exercises conducted thereafter: a single tournament, beginning with a preliminary round or two — wherein minnows were engulfed by regional heavyweights — and concluding with a final Pentagonal group competition. Time frame: No more than 12 to 14 months.

This description does accurately represent CONCACAF qualification for *Italia '90*. However, this is not the way members of Generation Zero perceived the process — not back then, in the moment, and not today, in retrospect. For this team, qualification for World Cup 1990 extended to nearly three times that duration. It proved a competitive continuum that started in early 1987, in the Canadian Maritimes, and concluded 30 months later on the island of Trinidad, where Paul Caligiuri, according to

Bruce Murray, "saved our ass." Why so long? The 1988 Olympic Games came first, and U.S. players uniformly view this competition — and its own qualification process — as part and parcel of their larger qualification arc. In short, once the team locked into survive-and-advance mode, it never truly disengaged. It couldn't afford to. The tournaments kept coming. With every passing month, the squad improved and the stakes got bigger.

If we lump in the Olympic experience, as Generation Zero does, we must come to grips with exactly what this competitive marathon entailed: the Seoul Olympiad (inclusive of all its qualifiers, conducted mainly in 1987); a steady diet of competitive friendlies unlike anything the U.S. Men's National Team had ever undertaken; an indoor world championship held in January 1989; a U-20 World Cup finals, inclusive of its own controversial, consequential qualifiers; a preliminary round of CONCACAF qualifying held just prior to the Seoul Olympics; and a final Pentagonal round that extended from April to November 1989. It's worth noting that starting in the spring of 1988, every member of the USMNT had — for the first time in their respective careers — begun playing regular club futbol in the A-League, in the Western Soccer Alliance, or overseas.

This unremitting schedule of competitive matches, over the course of 30 months, would have proved onerous for any group of seasoned professionals. But these were not experienced pros. They were early 20-somethings, a year or two out of college, undertaking matches against older, more battle-hardened veterans, with the future of American soccer hanging in the balance. Then, halfway through this emotional and competitive gauntlet, in July 1988, the U.S. learned it would host World Cup 1994.

"That time was really, really intense. As intense as any period I'd ever spend with the national team," says Tony Meola, who would play for his country at three World Cup finals. "I'm not suggesting the level of play was better. It was incredibly intense because we didn't really know what we were doing — what we were getting into. We still didn't really know *how* to qualify, how to win. We kind of figured it out on the fly."

Nevertheless, this frenzied stretch produced the finest collection of international results in U.S. soccer history. The final result, courtesy of

Caligiuri, closed the book on 40 years of failure. Even as they walked off the field in Port of Spain, however, these remained very young men. They grew up very quickly, thanks to living and playing through this remarkable series of events. The battlefield scars are still there to be felt and pondered today.

"We knew the stakes — then the '94 World Cup was awarded!" Mike Windischmann recalls. "There was just a ton of pressure. And we were so young! Going down to that last game at T&T, we were plenty motivated, but a lot of us said to ourselves, 'What's gonna happen if we don't qualify?' There was that feeling all along, to be honest. For all we knew, there might have been another hiatus with the national team program, if we didn't qualify. And even if there weren't a lull, the politics of why the U.S. was even given the '94 World Cup would have come up, too."

As it had prior to Torrance 1985, everything hinged on World Cup qualification. If achieved, first-division soccer would make its triumphant return. The national team would take its rightful place as a regional hegemon. USA '94 would become a coronation, not a tawdry bauble the American economy had purchased. Going forward, everything that came before, all the struggle and irrelevance, would be bathed in the warm light of satisfied retrospection — in other words, the exercise we're undertaking here, in this book.

Here's the flip side: If the *Italia* '90 qualifying campaign had ended in failure, many of soccer's future prospects in America, including the national team careers of all concerned, would likely have been out the window. "I think it's pretty clear that if we didn't qualify for Italy, the Federation would have just started over with a new set of guys, a new team," defender Paul Krumpe contends. "We all knew that — it was hard to ignore."

"As it turned out," Meola adds, "had we given up a single goal in the last four games of World Cup qualifying — in any *one* of those games — we would not have qualified for Italy. A single goal in *any* of those games, we don't go. That's pressure. Knowing myself now, I'm happy all of that pressure came at *that* point in my life — because back then, I didn't fear anything. Not outwardly. It was there. But I didn't acknowledge it. Now

I have far too many fears to deal with! I'd be a wreck, today. But luckily I was 19 and thought I could do anything."

This ability to look past fear is one of those magnificent assets of juvenescence. It's what makes youthful endeavors such poignant, popular objects of retrospection. Today, as 50-somethings, we admire our younger selves all the more for this absence of fear — along with those vigorous young bodies, and what they could once do.

"Let's be honest: We had no business winning in Trinidad that day," the once-19-year-old goalkeeper asserts, snapping the conversation from reverie back to reality. "And so many things happened in order to even get us there. You may need a trilogy, not a single book, to figure all this stuff out and tell the story."

———

Once its coveted Olympic berth had been secured, the U.S. Soccer Federation spent the fall and winter of 1987-88 lining up a host of first-class friendlies — against Colombia, Poland, Chile, Ecuador, Nigeria — to keep the team fresh and better prepare it for Seoul, come September 1988. This roster of opponents was a sign of how things were already shifting. Earlier in the decade, the Federation had struggled to schedule internationals against countries outside of CONCACAF. Olympic qualification changed the equation. Potential opponents from Europe, South America and Africa now had an incentive to play a team that would be competing in South Korea.

Word was also getting around as to where the World Cup '94 might be headed. FIFA made it official on July 4, 1988, an important day for the American soccer community in so many respects, even if it left much of the international footballing world slightly aghast.

"Did it make sense, when we didn't even have a professional league?" Marcelo Balboa asks rhetorically, three decades on. "It didn't make sense. But we knew what FIFA was looking for: an opportunity to grow soccer in a huge country like the U.S. I think it was also the next step in 'We give you the World Cup, but you have to start a real, professional league.' In a lot of different ways, from that moment, wheels started turning and everything started moving in the right direction. It was pretty central to everything we needed to start that league and promote soccer in a country where it was a secondary sport."

Several massive developments made 1988 the most consequential year in the history of American soccer to that point. Let us count the ways:

1. Following Olympic qualification in April 1988, the USSF established a program of grants for national team players, about $25,000 annually. These funds obliged players to make themselves available for a schedule of ongoing USMNT training and competitions. Directly preceding the Olympic tournament itself, the Federation essentially hired the players outright. Those who didn't have club contracts were kept in residence — together, as a unit, on salary, as a club might retain a player in the conventional, binding sense.

2. In the spring of 1988, professional league soccer returned to the United States after an excruciating, four-year absence. Beginning in May, there were finally legit domestic clubs — in the A-League, which grew into the American Professional Soccer League come 1989 — where Generation Zero could train and compete when national team camps and friendlies were not scheduled.

3. World Cup qualification within CONCACAF began its preliminary rounds on July 24, 1988. Then, in September, the suddenly potent USMNT traveled to South Korea for its first Olympic appearance in 16 years.

However, when a country is tapped to host a World Cup, all else is rendered minor in comparison. FIFA's Independence Day announcement made front-page news in *The New York Times*, and in media outlets around the world. The United States of America had, for a century, been uniformly acknowledged as a dead zone on the world futbol map. Now the planet's richest nation was buying in.

———•———

An American *Mundial* had been on FIFA's radar for several years, as early as 1982, when FIFA recognized the need to pull the '86 event from Colombia. Ultimately that tournament went to Mexico. Yet this ill-fated engagement illustrates an important, enduring reality: When it comes to World Cups, FIFA giveth, and FIFA taketh away.

Replacing a host is rare; it has happened just that once. The problem with FIFA is simple: It invariably acts in the best interests of FIFA. If that means pulling an event, it will do so. If that means keeping one in place, in the face of massive moral and geopolitical headwinds, so be it. Labor scandals, protests and calls for replacement have dogged Qatar 2022 from the moment its would-be hosts purchased the event on Dec. 2, 2010. Argentina's *Mundial*, in June 1978, was awarded by FIFA in July 1966. The brutal military junta charitably known as the "National Reorganization Process" seized power in the summer of 1976. French media and academia led calls for a European boycott; Amnesty International joined the cause. Similar widespread remonstration met Russia's annexation of the Crimea in 2014, ahead of their 2018 World Cup. Nevertheless, both competitions went off as planned.

In short, when FIFA got around to awarding USA 1994, there was no *guarantee* the competition would actually take place here. America was obliged to meet administrative milestones. It was obliged to start a national, professional first division ahead of time (although in actuality, MLS did not launch until 1996). The men's national team would automatically qualify for 1994, as was custom — but it would have to qualify on its own merit for *Italia '90*. Something it had never done before.

"We were in France actually playing games and training with Lothar Osiander, prior to the '88 Olympics, trying to get ready, and that's where the announcement was made to us — in a room somewhere," Steve Trittschuh remembers. "We didn't really know the magnitude of it at the time. We were concentrating on doing our own thing. But as we started qualifying, in '89, we kept hearing things: *Hey, if we don't qualify, they're pulling the World Cup from us.*"

By the time Bob Gansler took over for Osiander in early 1989, he'd been around the block several times. None of those rumors surprised him: "Hey, I'm not an ostrich. I never put my head in the sand. And Werner Fricker, I am sure, at one time or another, said something like, 'Hey, you know, it would be a good idea to qualify. It would probably make things a little smoother, as we prepare for '94.' If he didn't say that, he insinuated it. I could read it in his eyeballs. But I didn't discuss it with the players. That's weight that you don't need to put on your team."

Establishment futbol communities elsewhere around the globe understood the potential riches to be had in America, but they nevertheless remained unconvinced that the sport's marquee event could be staged successfully in such a footballing backwater. Accordingly, while the award of USA '94 was made official on July 4, 1988, final delivery remained contingent on the Americans qualifying for Italy. And everyone in the U.S. camp knew it.

"I came late to the process, the last couple months of qualifying, and played the last four games — so I missed the first year of qualifying, basically," Tony Meola recalls. "By that time, the team was so convinced that we would qualify, the talk was never really, 'Oh man, this is a lot of pressure.' It was more, 'These guys are crazy. What are they talking about? That will never happen.' We were still a bit naive in that way. Because there was no question: We knew about the 'contingency.'"

Certain things that are manifestly true nevertheless go unsaid. Officially, America's date with footballing destiny bore no caveats at all. The party line out of Switzerland was officially cut and dried: The 1994 World Cup was America's. No strings attached.

So far as Mike Woitalla is concerned, the L.A. Olympiad back in 1984 should have mooted the contingency and allayed everyone's fears, the players' included. "No country has ever done what we did at the Olympics, filling up stadiums for Olympic soccer," the *Soccer America* editor contends. "You'd think they may have drawn for the Germany games, for the medal round, but you had small countries playing games, and these huge stadiums sold out! That's why they never would have pulled the World Cup, because they knew we'd fill the stadiums."

Unofficially, however, FIFA was not to be trusted. Plain and simple. The deal would not be done until the final whistle blew on that seismic afternoon in Port of Spain, Nov. 19, 1989. "I don't recall anyone ever coming to us saying, 'Hey, you gotta win this game or we'll lose the World Cup,'" Brian Bliss says. "But there was the possibility of that, for sure, because they did award it prior to our actual qualifying — and we had never qualified before."

At that moment in history, how many World Cups had been hosted by nations that had never qualified for one? Zero. How many such nations have hosted them since? *Zero.* Qatar 2022 will be the first.

"In one telephone call, FIFA could have blown it all up and put the tournament in Germany, and I guarantee you those talks were going on at the time, in the backrooms, during 1989 when we were trying to qualify," Bruce Murray attests. "And let's be honest: We went to the very last day! But Paul [Caligiuri] did score. He saved our ass, because all those things were still in play."

FIFA pulled the plug on the Colombians in 1983, just three years ahead of the tournament. Pulling it five years ahead of the '94 event, following a U.S. failure in the Pentagonal, was not just a distinct possibility. It would have been the response many expected. And so, the stakes in 1988-89 were that much higher than anyone outside the halls of USSF and FIFA would have cared to admit.

Today, the rise of U.S. soccer tends to feel like a foregone conclusion. However, take it from those who were there, the guys on the USMNT in 1988-89: At the time, in the moment, within the USMNT itself, the World Cup never felt guaranteed. Nothing relating to American soccer felt that way. Throughout the Eighties, in the midst of competitive, developmental and organizational episodes so crucial to all these future events, nothing felt preordained. Had T&T keeper Michael Maurice managed to parry Caligiuri's famous volley wide of the goal post, preserving the nil-nil draw, an entire generation's worth of sacrifice, progress and perseverance might have gone utterly for naught.

"There's a little added pressure for you," jokes Trittschuh. "I can't say for sure just how much of it was true. No one can. But that was definitely the talk within the team: 'If we don't qualify, they're pulling the World Cup from us.' That was the word on the street. As we started qualifying in '89, we were all hearing these things. The way FIFA works? Are you kidding me?"

————•—•——

The central difficulty in resisting or otherwise objectively examining all this speculation is FIFA's decades-long reputation for double-dealing, bribe-taking, authoritarian kowtowing and money-chasing, which do nothing but invite further conjecture. However, even its critics agree: FIFA possessed clear and vested interests in the U.S. qualifying for *Italia* '90, to avoid another, even higher level of potential scrutiny, criticism, embarrassment, etc. Thus, FIFA did what it could to pave the Americans' way.

When formal qualification was instituted prior to the 1954 World Cup finals, CONCACAF was awarded a single berth, and that's the way things stayed for the ensuing 28 years. When Mexico hosted the 1970 tournament and earned the automatic berth, El Salvador qualified as Confederation champion. *La Selecta* did not score in three group losses to Mexico, the Soviet Union and Belgium. The Haitians qualified in Mexico's place come 1974, but similarly failed to impress in West Germany. They were outscored 14-2 in three group-phase losses. When the field expanded from 16 nations to 24 in 1982, CONCACAF was granted a second berth; El Salvador and Honduras both qualified ahead of *El Tri*, but neither advanced out of their respective groups. In 1986, when Mexico again hosted, one might have expected CONCACAF to maintain its two berths. But no: FIFA granted the host Confederation just one, and Canada claimed it. The Reds likewise failed to register a single goal during three group matches.

All this is to argue that on-field performance at previous World Cup finals did nothing to suggest the Confederation deserved two berths for 1990. Nevertheless, in June 1988 — just *before* the award of USA 1994 — FIFA bestowed upon CONCACAF two berths going forward, not one. To ward off potential criticism and protect their investments in the 1994 tournament, the boys in Zurich stacked the deck for American qualification in 1990 as well as they could.

That said, we should also give FIFA a fair hearing: *Soccer America*'s Mike Woitalla believes all such speculation about pulling the '94 tournament is much ado about nothing. "I don't think FIFA would have pulled the World Cup. I researched the hell out of this issue, but I could never find any real proof," he says. "I remember trying to find out if there was any truth to it, calling Sunil [Gulati, U.S. Federation president from 2006-18, member of the FIFA executive council from 2013-17] and all that stuff.

"I think the larger point is, our failure to qualify would have looked *so bad*. I mean, the idea of it nowadays rings true — you've got all this bullshit about taking the World Cup to Qatar. Back then it was similar: a first-time host country, not considered a soccer country, without a top-tier pro league even. So you had skeptics who said, 'Why should the U.S. host the World Cup?' — not understanding that even back then we *were* a major soccer country. Such a big country with such a diverse population. Even then we had more soccer fans than most countries did. You just had them in pockets, not as part of a national soccer footprint. But the sheer numbers were there. We proved it during the Olympics in 1984."

There also persists a widespread perception amongst U.S. media, international observers, and even USMNT players from this era that FIFA connived to get Mexico banned from World Cup 1990 — thereby further bolstering American chances of qualification. Because with FIFA, nothing can be ruled out.

"We were very fortunate to qualify in '90, and I think the major reason was Mexico being ineligible," admits Paul Krumpe. "People forget that Mexico had used illegal players at the youth level and was unable to be part of the qualification. We kind of snuck in — and a lot of it had to do with the fact that Mexico didn't have the opportunity to play and qualify. We barely got in as it was."

Mexico was in fact banned from *Italia '90, and* the 1989 World Youth Championship, *and* the 1988 Seoul Olympic soccer tournament. However, as much as we might like to heap more scorn on FIFA or venture into retrospective muckraking, that dog don't hunt. In meting out penalties for the use of underage players during multiple youth tournaments, FIFA did lower the boom on Mexico — but *not* to the direct benefit of American qualification.

Still, it's a damned interesting story.

Early that consequential summer of 1988, FIFA determined that Mexico had used overage players during qualification for the 1989 World Youth Championship (later known as the U-20 World Cup), to be held the ensuing winter in Saudi Arabia. "Not their first mortal sin," according to Gansler, who led the U.S. at that tournament. "There was a pattern of that behavior, not to say they were the only ones." Perhaps recognizing the Mexicans as flagrant repeat offenders, FIFA didn't pussyfoot around with the penalty. What's more, the timing helps explain the widespread misconceptions surrounding what would become known as the Cachirules scandal. Here's how *The New York Times* reported on the matter in its July 1, 1988, edition — three days before the '94 World Cup was awarded to the U.S.:

Mexico was banned from all international soccer competition today, including the 1988 Olympic Games in Seoul, South Korea. The Federation Internationale de Football Association, soccer's world governing body, banned Mexico for two years because a Mexican junior team in a recent world championship qualifying tournament used four players who were over the age limit. The severe sanction by FIFA's executive committee means Mexico is out of the soccer tournament at the Seoul Games, for which it had qualified, and is effectively disqualified from the 1990 World Cup. Mexico's replacement in the Olympics and the 1990 World Cup qualifiers will be determined later, FIFA officials said. The Mexican under-20 junior squad was also disqualified from the junior world championship in Saudi Arabia next year. Mexico's berth was awarded to the United States.

All pretty convenient, on the face of things. The U.S. would soon vie for one of two CONCACAF spots at *Italia '90*, not one. Mexico, the Federation goliath, would not be eligible for either berth and would not participate in qualifying, naturally. Its spot at the 1989 youth championship finals — the most important U-20 tournament in world futbol — would instead go to the U.S., FIFA's 1994 World Cup host, a footballing nation largely devoid of international competitive credentials at that stage. The Mexicans, recipients of FIFA largesse at Colombia's expense not five years previous, were now the objects of FIFA's trademark caprice. They're still pissed about it. The Cachirules scandal, as it came to be known, remains a huge deal south of the border, where its effects are similarly misunderstood.

About the name: *cachirul* or *cachirulo* were early 20th-century terms used to describe a patch of ragtag quality used on clothing. In Mexican soccer vernacular, the term came to describe mercenary players, meaning those who aren't really on the team but appear for clubs as ringers — or more commonly as emergency replacements — to avoid a poor result due to lack of warm bodies. Because substitute players commonly used the names of those actually listed on the club rosters, they were said to represent a *cachirul*. Following the 1988 scandal, *cachirul* has become almost exclusively a footballing term in Mexico.

And the Mexican Football Federation (MFF) did get caught red-handed in 1988. Journalist Antonio Moreno broke the story after studying a 1988 MFF yearbook. The players' ages did not correspond to those supplied to CONCACAF prior to qualification for the U-20 World Cup, Moreno reported. The MFF flatly denied the allegation. After Moreno twisted in the wind for a time, other investigating media reached the same conclusion, and the Mexican futbol community erupted in scandal. Eventually, in April 1988, the U.S. Soccer Federation submitted an official complaint to CONCACAF, demanding the case be investigated. When the Guatemalans joined the protest, FIFA had no choice but to act. The justice dispensed proved swift and harsh.

But here's the rub, as it relates to the U.S. and *Italia '90* qualification: When Mexico was banned from World Cup 1990, the final stage of CONCACAF qualification had yet to begin. *El Tri* were already scheduled to play Costa Rica in a preliminary play-in come August of 1988, just six weeks after the sanction was announced. Only one team would advance from that play-in to the final round. Once the Mexicans were banned, the *Ticos* went through by forfeit.

It remains a widely held understanding — in the U.S. and Mexico — that *El Tri*'s ban enabled U.S. qualification. It did not. Not directly. Costa Rica did in fact finish ahead of the U.S. in the final round of CONCACAF qualifying — just as Mexico might have. But only one nation was going to advance from that preliminary tie pitting Costa Rica and Mexico in August 1988. Therefore, FIFA did not load those particular dice in support of American qualification. Logically, Mexico's absence didn't have a direct and meaningful effect on U.S. World Cup fortunes for 1990.

Now, why were the top two teams in CONCACAF, Costa Rica and Mexico, scheduled to face off in a preliminary round where only one could advance? This matchup was certainly of great convenience to the *Yanquis*, who drew the Jamaicans in this preliminary round. Those pairings would have been a CONCACAF matter — not a FIFA matter. However, they were nothing a few million Swiss francs couldn't help arrange . . .

This episode illustrates how easily rumor can congeal into conventional wisdom, at the very least. What's more, this suspected fix provides yet another ripe example of what people are prepared to believe when it comes to FIFA.

Whom did the Mexican absence most obviously benefit?

The 1989 U-20 USMNT certainly reaped some benefit. The Gansler-led squad had failed to advance from the April 1988 CONCACAF qualification tournament. When the Mexicans were banned, the Americans replaced them at the youth championship finals, as the U.S. had finished third behind Costa Rica and *El Tri* in qualifying. The Americans finished fourth in Saudi Arabia. This result made Gansler's career: A month later, the Federation named him coach of the senior national team.

Costa Rica also benefited. Mexico's ban enabled *Los Ticos* to skip this preliminary round. Costa Rica finished atop the final group, the Pentagonal, and advanced to Italy with some ease. Costa Rica in 1989 were a very good side: good enough to reach the round of 16 in Italy, under Coach Bora Milutinovic, then a somewhat obscure Serb who'd finished his playing career in the Mexican league. Costa Rica's performance at *Italia '90* earned Bora the USMNT appointment in 1991 — replacing Gansler.

Mexico benefited not at all, and Mike Windischmann, for one, has little sympathy for the old rival: "When you cheat, you cheat," he says. "I got stung on a youth national team in 1984-85, when we went to Trinidad trying to qualify for the next U-20 World Cup. In the final game against Mexico, we ended up losing 2-1. That summer we found out they were using under-21 players. And that was just *part* of the cheating."

"Make no mistake," Gansler declaims. "Not their first offense."

THE MOST CONSEQUENTIAL ON-FIELD STRETCH IN the history of U.S. men's soccer kicked off on July 24, 1988, with a scoreless draw on a rock-hard pitch in Kingston, Jamaica. This match with the Reggae Boyz represented the first leg of a home-and-home playoff, the aggregate goal winner advancing to the final qualifying group, scheduled to commence hostilities in April 1989. All the remaining CONCACAF combatants were also obliged to play their way through to the final Confederation stage in this way — all but Costa Rica, who skated through on account of Mexico's ban.

Three weeks later, back at the St. Louis Soccer Park, the Yanks displayed the full spectrum of their capabilities. Brian Bliss put his side ahead in the 18th minute, but the Americans didn't lustily pile on as they had during Olympic qualifying. In fact, they got complacent going forward. When Alton Sterling equalized 9 minutes after the interval, the tide turned, and the young Americans swallowed hard. For 15 terrifying minutes, a potential repeat of Torrance — the possibility of not even advancing to the final round of World Cup qualifying — was very, very real. If, in the next 35 minutes, the U.S. could not answer with a second goal, the Jamaicans would have gone through on away goals. And you would not be reading this book.

Enter Hugo Perez, who proceeded to rescue his mates, their World Cup quest and the entire Modern American Soccer Movement. His 68th-minute tally opened the floodgates. Frankie Klopas confirmed the result eight minutes later. The U.S. did advance, but anyone who was *there* that August afternoon in suburban St. Louis remembers this match not for the 5-1 aggregate result, but for those 15 minutes of sheer existential panic. What the Brits colorfully refer to as *squeaky-bum time.*

Within hours of eliminating Jamaica, the Federation signed each U.S. player in the roster pool to more formal personal services contracts. The deals were modest and flexible, allowing for players to be loaned back to the Federation from their A-League and Western Soccer Alliance clubs as needed. Many on the USMNT had graduated college scant years before. These contracts were the first bits of true job security they'd garnered in their brief professional lives.

"These are guys who hardly made any money. That's part of what made this group so special," reveals Meola, who would not join the national team until six months later. When the Federation first stepped up financially that fall of 1988, he was still at the University of Virginia, playing for Bruce Arena.

"If we won a World Cup qualifier, we'd get 350 bucks. I couldn't partic-ipate because I was in college, but that type of payday got my teammates *excited*. We got a per diem on the road — I think it was $25 a day. That was it. These were guys who had to hold second jobs. The league was starting up at the time, the A-League, where you could make a couple bucks. But if we didn't qualify for the World Cup, then what were you gonna do? Some guys had kids and families by that time. This was a really special group of guys who put their livelihoods on the line. It was entirely the allure of playing in an Olympics, a World Cup. For that they sacrificed everything."

The relative job security conferred by the Federation, however mod-est, paid immediate dividends. Just three weeks later, in their Olympic opener at the Civic Stadium in Daegu, the Yanks jumped out to a 1-0 advantage over mighty Argentina — through Mr. Windischmann, of all people. With 11 minutes remaining in the match, the young Americans stood on the cusp of an epic result. Alas, John Harkes, just 19 years old and playing his first senior tournament, gave away an unfortunate penalty. Carlos Alfaro Moreno converted, and the game ended 1-1. A month earlier they were 30 minutes from being jettisoned from the World Cup field by Jamaica on away goals. Now they were trading punches with the world futbol elite.

"I played every minute of the Argentina game and wow — we're up 1-0 with a chance to knock off the guys who won the last World Cup!" Krumpe remembers, the wonder and enthusiasm still welling within him. "The penalty was unlucky. John was such a young player. But wow. We just tied Argentina and nearly beat them. I mean, *Wow*! Then we get the host country and that's the game where Vanole just played out of his mind."

David Vanole had played alongside Krumpe and Caligiuri at UCLA before moving seamlessly into the USMNT starting lineup, in 1986. He held that position through much of 1989, until Tony Meola won the starting job. Vanole never lost his high standing among his teammates, however. Gansler brought a trio of keepers to Italy, Vanole among them. Dino, as he was called, was a big and burly man — not the lithe, rangy type we associate with international keepers today. He ruled his box, and the young American defensive corps trusted him to bail them out. Against South Korea, in Busan, Vanole did that and more, logging his best-ever national team performance in earning the U.S. a scoreless draw.

"I don't know how he made some of the saves he made that day. We honestly could have lost it eight or 10 to nothing. He really saved us," says Krumpe, Vanole's right back throughout the tournament. "So here we are, two games in, and we've picked up a couple points at a *big* competition. It felt like sort of a big deal, to be playing at the highest level and having that kind of success."

It's not kosher to complain about tournament draws before or after the fact, either as a means of managing expectations or as pure sour grapes. So judge the U.S. group in South Korea for yourself: *La Albiceleste* to open the tournament, followed by a date with the host country, and then a group-concluding match vs. the Soviet Union, the eventual gold medal winners. If there were a "group of death" at this tournament, the Americans were assigned to it. Nevertheless, within the team, great excitement flourished. "These were big-time teams, really good," Trittschuh reports.

Little of the building buzz, however, trickled back to America's soccer-loving public, such as it was. NBC televised this Olympiad, but its indifference to futbol and the awkward time difference between Korea and the U.S. allowed only for highlights of the soccer competition. Like most summer Olympics, track & field and aquatics dominated network coverage stateside. These were, after all, the games of Carl Lewis and his Canadian foil Ben Johnson, Janet Evans, Greg Louganis, Matt Biondi, and Florence Griffith-Joyner.

"We used to go to a bar that would stay open for us to watch the games from Korea — on Mexican satellite TV," recalls Woitalla, by then a new Cal graduate and a young *Soccer America* staffer. "It was the Golden Bear on Grand Avenue, a rugby hangout, actually. We knew the owner, so he left the place open for us. And yeah, I think that's when I'd say people started taking notice. They had qualified for the Olympics and did some interesting stuff there. Pretty remarkable, actually."

Back in Daegu, the U.S. needed a result — a draw or victory — in the third group game against the USSR in order to advance to the knockout stage. This proved a bridge too far. Trailing 3-0 by halftime, the Americans eventually went down swinging, 4-2. "I blew out my ankle just before halftime of the Russia game, so I was out," Stollmeyer notes, "but I remember the first goal they scored. Our keeper came out and got caught in no man's land. Then they scored again and that was that."

Adds Krumpe, "If Harkes [didn't] commit that penalty [against Argentina], we *would* have advanced. We didn't get a win in Korea, but we were about as close to advancing as you can possibly get. And the two best teams in the tournament — including the gold medal winner — advanced in our place. Tough group."

For Trittschuh, who had sacrificed career opportunities to chase an Olympic experience, this near-miss proved a satisfying payoff and an auspicious segue to the next challenge. "That was the start for us," Trittschuh says. "From late 1986, our goals were first set on that, really. To go there and actually have some real success? That jump-started us. The crowds in Seoul were unbelievable. The whole experience got us ready for World Cup qualifying the following year."

For Osiander, a few tactical revelations became apparent in Seoul. Peter Vermes, fresh out of Rutgers, hadn't been in the senior national team mix until Osiander saw him play at the 1987 Olympic Festival. During the Olympics proper, he was among the top choices at striker, beside Murray and ahead of Brent Goulet. Further back, Caligiuri proved he was a younger, more dynamic alternative to Ricky Davis at holding midfielder.

"Cal was just like Davis, a holding player who wasn't necessarily there to be creative," argues Krumpe, Caligiuri's teammate since their days at UCLA. "Cal really benefited in having [Tab] Ramos and Harkes in front of him. Ricky Davis was kind of *The Guy*, but for a previous generation. Around this time he handed the mantle over to Cal a little bit. In my opinion. It took a little longer than it could have because Ricky was the captain of our Olympic qualifying team — but he ended up not being on that team that went to Italy."

Bliss has little doubt about the ultimate upshot of the Olympic tournament, along with the summer leading up to it: "We gave a really good account of ourselves in '88, and I think it fueled us to the point that, you know what? This is our chance. There was, I don't want to say 'confidence' or 'arrogance,' but certainly that little bit of swagger. Competing at those Olympics gave us confidence about qualifying for the World Cup. We kind of expected it a little bit, demanded it from one another. It wasn't a pipe dream."

It's ironic that just as the U.S. national soccer team was getting its act together, the Soviet program was poised to disappear. The USSR did indeed claim the gold medal in Seoul. However, with perestroika in full swing and the disintegration of the Soviet Union looming, these '88 Olympic matches were some of the final times Lithuanians and Russians, Ukrainians and Kazakhs, Armenians and Estonians would compete as fellow Soviets — in uniforms bearing that distinctive Cyrillic acronym: CCCP.

The 1980s in America centered around a profound cultural and economic transition toward Reaganism, the diplomatic thrust of which triggered a series of final dust-ups with a sclerotic Soviet Union. The Berlin Wall came down Nov. 9, 1989, 10 days ahead of Paul Caligiuri's "Shot Heard 'Round the World." Formal dissolution of the USSR required several more years. At the 1992 Olympics in Barcelona, former Soviet athletes would compete not for the CCCP but for a so-called Unified Team.

As schoolchildren, we in Generation Zero had sat at our desks watching films of Fifties-era kids ducking and taking cover *under* their desks. These black-and-white images were shared without irony. Throughout the 1970s, the Cold War had seemed very real indeed. Come the early 1980s, however, the stakes and our nation's attendant confrontations with communism felt ever less menacing, perhaps because they arrived packaged for safety in sporting prophylactics: tit-for-tat Olympic boycotts, hockey games and soccer fixtures. While watching the 1984 Canada Cup Series on our shitty, 10-inch, black-and-white television, my college roommate Dennis Carboni conjured a whimsical, alternative translation for CCCP, one suited to these less fractious times: "Communist Country, Communist People." Has a nice ring to it. Shame it never had time to catch on.

Just after New Year's Day 1989, several members of the newly emboldened USMNT traveled to the Netherlands to compete as one of two CONCACAF entries at the inaugural FIFA Futsal World Championship. The tournament proved a propitious if little remembered beginning to a fateful year of international competition.

Futsal is indoor soccer without walls. The word is shorthand for the Spanish *fútbol sala* and/or the Portuguese *futebol de salão*. Either way, the English translation amounts to "indoor football." Futsal remains the preferred version of the indoor game in Europe and South America, which explains FIFA's involvement and sanction, starting with this 1989 tournament. Internationally, the brand of indoor played *with* walls — in the Major Indoor/Arena Soccer League, for example — is known as "minifootball," arena football or fast football. This incarnation of the game is administered by the World Minifootball Federation (WMF), which replaced the *Federacion Internacional de Futbol Rapido,* or FIFRA, in 2013. The WMF, based in Switzerland, has conducted its own world championship since 1997.

The U.S. squad in Holland featured a host of national team stalwarts: Peter Vermes, Eric Eichmann, Mike Windischmann, Tab Ramos, Brent Goulet, Jim Gabarra and Bruce Murray, in addition to assorted NASL and MISL veterans, among them defender Doc Lawson and keeper A.J. Lachowecki. Expectations were low. As the first-ever Futsal World Cup, the event was replete with unknowns. But this American squad nevertheless managed to finish third, bowing out to the hosts, 2-1, in the semifinals. It's difficult to paint this outwardly impressive result as any sort of fluke. The U.S. topped its group, blowing out Italy in the process, 4-1. In the second group phase, the Americans had their way with both Argentina (3-1) and eventual champion Brazil, 5-3. Windischmann potted the game winner in a 3-2 win against Belgium to claim third-place honors.

"We just kept on winning. Just incredible to finish that high," Windy told journalist Michael Lewis in 2020. "Tab Ramos said it: The 1989 team was the most fun we've ever had playing soccer together."

WHEN FIFA BANNED THE MEXICANS FROM the 1989 World Youth Championship finals — scheduled for late January in Saudi Arabia — their direct neighbors to the north filled the vacancy. On its face, this decision doesn't appear to have carried any real import or impact. Not a single player on the American roster would influence senior USMNT fortunes during 1989 or 1990. **The U-20 roster** that traveled to Saudi Arabia is here:

Kasey Keller	Cameron Rast	Mike Burns
Dario Brose	Neil Covone (captain)	Martin Munnelly
Curt Onalfo	Steven Snow	Gerard Lagos
Troy Dayak	Chris Henderson	Oscar Draguicevich
Ben Crawley	Adam Tinkham	Bryan Thompson
Tim Horton	Lyle Yorks	Markus Roy
	Coach: Bob Gansler	

Keller made the 1990 World Cup roster, but only as a third keeper behind Meola and Vanole. He wouldn't see any *Mundial* minutes until 1998. Neil Covone went to Italy with five senior caps, never left the bench, and never again appeared for the USMNT. Chris Henderson enjoyed a long national team career; he made Gansler's Italian roster but did not appear in a match. Mike Burns was a squad player at USA '94 and appeared at World Cup 1998, in France. But he wasn't on the roster for *Italia* '90. Like all these players, Burns, the pride of Marlborough, Massachusetts, was just too young in 1990.

What the 1989 FIFA World Youth Championship *did* introduce to the big stage was the U.S. coach, 47-year-old Bob Gansler. His squad finished fourth at this event, the highest "outdoor" finish achieved by any U.S. men's side in any FIFA event — to this day. He returned home from the Middle East in early February. Two weeks later, he replaced Osiander as coach of the U.S. Men's National Team.

Different cultures have created specific words to describe the unique dominion enjoyed by male soccer coaches. In the United Kingdom, he is a "football manager," though players often refer to him colloquially as "the gaffer." In many Spanish-speaking realms, media hew to the slightly obsequious *el Mister*, while the Germans prefer the more generic *fußballtrainer.*

Gansler's vibe is distinctly German, an academic subject he eventually studied at the postgraduate level. However, he was born in the Hungarian village of Mucsi, where his family owned a vineyard. This southern Hungarian village had been settled by early 20th-century Germans lured there by the offer of free land. After World War II, the entire village was more or less reclaimed by the Hungarian government, which gave its 3,000 Germanic residents three days to clear out. The Ganslers fled to Frankfurt, but didn't feel welcome there either. "While we were in Hungary we were considered Germans, and while we were in Germany we were considered Hungarians," Gansler told the *Los Angeles Times* in 1989. "So we thought that we might as well try to be Americans."

He was 11 when his parents emigrated. They settled in Milwaukee, where, in a textbook example of how immigrant communities form and grow, they joined dozens of other families from their old village. Gansler matured into a poster boy for America's ethnic soccer experience prior to the game's demographic tipping point in 1970. He played on the club team at Marquette University but came of age as a durable defender with Milwaukee Bavarian SC, the urban/ethnic club to which he would devote himself for 14 years, the last five as player-coach.

By the age of 26, Gansler had captained two U.S. Olympic squads, both of which failed to qualify — for Tokyo 1964 and then Mexico City 1968. If we include Olympic and Pan American tournaments, he appeared for the United States 25 times. If we don't, his caps amount to only five. The final two matches were both losses, to Haiti, in 1969, on the doorstep of the 1970 World Cup. When the decade turned, Gansler's brief run with the NASL's Chicago Mustangs was over. He bedded back in with the Bavarians but devoted himself more to coaching. Gansler led his club team to the U.S. Open Cup title in 1976.

Werner Fricker and Bob Gansler were more than contemporaries; they were fast friends and fellow German-Hungarians who played together as naturalized U.S. citizens on the '64 Olympic side. While Gansler went the coaching route, Fricker opted for administration. It was no coincidence that Gansler held various USSF positions starting in 1975: Fricker served as executive vice president of the U.S. Federation from 1975-84. Gansler assisted Walt Chyzowych during the failed qualifying campaigns of 1978 and 1982. In between, he assisted first Chyzowych and then Angus McAlpine with the U-20 national team (1979-82). Fricker brought his mate back into the Federation fold in 1987. For a year, Gansler coached both the U-20s and the University of Wisconsin-Milwaukee Panthers, led by future national team defender Jimmy Banks. He joined the Federation staff full time in 1988.

Gansler's U-20 national team performed more than ably in Saudi Arabia, getting out of its group and beating Iraq in the quarters before dropping a semifinal to Nigeria 2-1 in extra time. Another loss to group foe Brazil in the third-place game, 2-0, left something of a bad taste, but the positives taken from the tourney far outweighed the negatives. Keller proved a sensation, as did Henderson, Burns and striker Steve Snow, an Indiana University product whose professional career would sadly be curtailed by knee injuries. However, the true breakout star was Gansler himself, who demonstrated he could forge a formidable international unit on short notice from disparate parts. Indeed, he elicited superb performances from players who, with the aforementioned exceptions, would never be quite so productive again.

"I've used those guys and that team repeatedly as an example of folks who maximized," Gansler says. "We had some players. To say it was a miracle might be an overstatement. But we had no preparation. Ralph Perez and I picked those guys on a wintry Thanksgiving weekend in St. Louis, doing what we did at that time: watching the four regional teams play [Olympic Festival] games against each other."

When Gansler and his charges returned home, Fricker made a change few saw coming: He replaced his part-time coach, Lothar Osiander, with a full-timer, Gansler. A curious move. Osiander had done so well with his young team in South Korea and prior. Some point to the second leg vs. Jamaica in August 1988, when he picked a hyperdefensive starting XI — then had to bring on Perez and Murray to salvage the entire qualification effort. In early 1989, the *L.A. Times* reported that Osiander had "resigned because he earned more as the headwaiter at a San Francisco restaurant than he did as a part-time coach." I couldn't confirm this by way of Osiander himself. Gansler wouldn't comment on the subject, even all these years later. Fricker is dead. But there is little disagreement about this much: It was Fricker's call, and Gansler was *his* guy.

"Unfortunately, the man you need to talk to is no longer around — that's Werner Fricker. He made that decision," Gansler told me in 2017. "Lothar and I were good friends — we *are* good friends. We speak maybe once a month or so. We worked together before and after qualifying. But it was Werner's decision, and his thinking was, maybe someone else at the helm would give something that he felt was lacking. For sure I respected Werner immensely. And I still have great respect for Lothar. We've talked about it a little bit, but it was one of those things that's out of your hands."

Here's what Fricker saw: a young team about to embark on an all-or-nothing, six-month qualifying campaign that could make or break the future of U.S. soccer. He saw a team that needed a firm hand on the tiller, additional discipline, better organization, a willingness to experiment with player combinations, and a higher standard of tactical preparation. Because so few members of the USMNT had played under him as U-20s — Stollmeyer during the 1981 World Youth Championship in Australia; a few more when Gansler coached the U.S. at the 1987 World University Games in Zagreb — the players weren't quite sure what they were getting in Gansler. This uncertainty dissipated soon enough.

"I think Gansler was about as organized as you could possibly be, which is what we needed to get us to play at this highest level," Krumpe says.

More specifically, Krumpe and his teammates were getting a known quantity in the art of maximizing performance from first-choice players who were nevertheless flawed or unfinished: the exercise he'd undertaken, with success, at the ethnic-club, collegiate and international U-20 levels.

"He's a great organizer," Keller told the *L.A. Times* that winter of 1989, before WC qualification began. "That's what helped us in Saudi Arabia. He knew what the other teams were going to do before they did. I've been with him since he first got hired on the Under-20 team, and he's a lot easier going. When he first got hired, he was anxious to prove himself. He has really relaxed."

A coy comment from Keller — or perhaps an ironic one? None of the three dozen people I interviewed or anything I read ever used the words "relaxed" and "Gansler" in the same sentence. He was a famously no-nonsense taskmaster, in fact, who didn't indulge in or tolerate bullshit in any form. These qualities drew him to the 23-year-old Mike Windischmann, whom the coach tapped to replace Ricky Davis as captain within days of taking over the team.

"Mike was technically talented and extremely aware tactically," Gansler told the US Soccer website in 2020. "He just had those leadership qualities. He did it by example and did it in a quiet, confident manner. He had a calming influence on the field. I don't think his pulse ever went awfully high. He was confident enough to say, 'I can handle this' without being arrogant. He had those qualities that made sense to put him out front."

"I think I had a good relationship with Gansler," Windischmann says, all these years later. "I've got a German background myself; I knew exactly how he was going to be: a disciplinarian. You get used to it, but it sort of fell to me to be the voice of the guys, if they had questions or complaints. One time we were training in East Germany with these two-and-a-half-hour sessions. All the guys were like, 'Hey Windy, go talk to him and tell him the practices are too long.' So I go to his room and say, 'Hey Bob, can I talk to you?' He says, 'Yeah.' 'The guys are worried about being on the field for two-and-a-half hours.' He says, 'OK. Yeah. Tell the players to go fuck themselves.' 'Oh. OK, Bob. I'll tell 'em.' So I get back to the room and they ask me, 'What did he say?' So I told 'em."

During one of my conversations with Gansler, I made the mistake of referring to that 1989 U-20 showing in Saudi Arabia as "*perhaps* the best outdoor result the U.S. has ever achieved in a FIFA event." *Herr fußball-trainer* quickly cut me off: "You've gotta eliminate the word *perhaps*. It *was* our best FIFA result. Still is. Bingo."

In Bob Gansler, the USMNT was also getting a manager whose playing/coaching career had spanned the modernization of the American game.

In our interviews, he came off as clearly proud of his days as a player and a coach. But he was both a realist and a committed incrementalist: a man who appreciated progress and loyalty, but never allowed either one to cloud his judgment as to what his players could do or what they could accomplish within a team context — that day, next week against a wholly different opponent, or next month in a different set of qualifiers. Gansler deftly demonstrated this ability, on behalf of the Federation, prior to Saudi Arabia. He did so again, more or less on the fly, during World Cup qualifying throughout 1989. Then he did it again when choosing his final roster for *Italia '90*.

For John Harkes, deploying this nuanced understanding of personnel was what the coach did best: "He had a keen eye to not just observe the ability of players, but to see the desire of the team you are putting together. That's hard."

When I asked *el Mister* what made him a suitable choice for this particular time, and this particular team, he minced no words: "Back in '68, we were almost all immigrants. There were a couple of guys from St. Louis, Pat McBride and Carl Gentile, who were American-born. The rest of us were second generation. But we were American. If you look at that '90 team, there were a lot of guys who were second, maybe third, but mostly second generation. There were some similar characteristics there.

"When I took over the national team, we said, 'Hey, we've come a long way. We can go a little further.' It wasn't a matter of 'Hey, let's make history, first time in 40 years,' etc., etc. That's Hollywood stuff. I don't believe in the Big Bang theory. What was done at that time was what could be done at that time — always looking at how we could make it better."

One has to admire the grace and candor of Bob Gansler. The first time we spoke, he went out of his way to praise the USSF for its deft allocation of USA '94 money, in ways that helped effectively grow the game in succeeding years. This is the same organization that failed to support his friend, Federation president Werner Fricker, when he sought reelection in 1990 — the same organization that hired Bora Milutinovic to coach the 1991 USMNT after Gansler had chosen, coached and coaxed its predecessor to the country's first World Cup appearance in 40 years. I asked him whether he felt he'd earned the right to coach the national team at World Cup '94: "Damn right I did. But I have to say, I was more annoyed when they formed MLS and I wasn't one of the coaches chosen for the first eight franchises."

This combative equanimity, this frank expectation of loyalty in return for loyalty, begins to illustrate what sort of coach the national team was getting in February 1989, mere weeks before the onset of final qualification matches. This early in the Modern American Soccer Movement, there were no obvious hires. The field of coaching candidates was far too thin, too inexperienced. Did Gansler's success in Saudi Arabia offset all those failures he'd presided over, beside Walt Chyzowych, less than a decade prior? No one knew. Gansler had enjoyed success at the University of Wisconsin-Milwaukee, but collegiate soccer had never produced a national team coach of quality. Not in this country. Not in any country.

As a U.S. player and coach, as both founder and framer, Gansler's career had spanned a vast Dark Age. If nothing else, he brought this context and baggage to the most important competitive test of his life. It didn't take long for his players to learn what Fricker had known for decades: Gansler wasn't afraid to speak his mind, to try new things, to tinker with players and alignments. But his young team also gathered that Gansler's primary concern was the shirt. He chose and deployed players whose allegiances lay not with their coach but with the team, its performance, the result, the U.S. Soccer Federation crest. In this respect, Gansler was and would always remain a company man.

Tab Ramos (from left), Brian Bliss and Marcelo Balboa prior to the opening Pentagonal qualifier: USA at Costa Rica, April 16, 1989. *(Image courtesy of Brian Bliss)*

John Harkes eludes a headlong challenge from Trinidad and Tobago midfielder Maurice Alibey during Match Day 3 of final World Cup qualifying, a 1-1 draw in Torrance, California, on May 13, 1989. *(Jon van Woerden photo)*

11.   A QUALIFIED SUCCESS

Sixteen CONCACAF nations entered Confederation qualifying prior to World Cup 1990, FIFA having rejected Belize due to "outstanding debt." With Mexico banned, Costa Rica, Guatemala, El Salvador, and Trinidad and Tobago joined the United States for the final tournament phase. Each of the top two finishers from this Pentagonal competition — each having played the other four, home and away — would punch their tickets to Italy. By granting CONCACAF a second World Cup berth in July 1988, the Lords of FIFA had done all they could to assist the anointed 1994 tournament hosts. The Guatemalans cleared away another obstacle, upsetting the highly favored Canadians, on away goals during the August 1988 preliminary round. Costa Rica presented a first-class challenge, but no one expected much from the other three combatants. After the Americans' impressive Olympic showing in South Korea, many expected the Yanks to make short work of the group lightweights. John Stollmeyer, Generation Zero's senior statesman, was not one of those people.

"Look: I played in the Youth [U-20] World Cup, the Pan Am Games, the World University Games, the senior World Cup, and I played at the Olympics," Stollmeyer says. "The only international tournament I never played in was the world indoor championship — and that's because, after the Olympics, I had surgery on an ankle. So let me tell you: CONCACAF is a very difficult environment to go play in. We took nothing for granted prior to qualifying. I mean, every nation in every confederation has their crazy places to go play qualifiers, but playing in CONCACAF is a very, very difficult thing."

One might well describe the experience as CONCACAFkaesque.

"I wonder how many other countries around the world, first-world soccer nations, would go down to Central America and do well," Stolly continues. "Not just one game. Go play a bunch of them. Go into Honduras or Guatemala or El Salvador or Costa Rica. Go down to those places and try to play your best, where you go to the sideline and rotten fruit and batteries and all sorts of crap are thrown at you. Go play those games on terrible surfaces, under armed guard — or go back and forth from the stadium *without* those guards — and then come back and tell me, 'Ah, yeah. It's not so hard.'

"The truth is, it's really difficult. Everyone at this level plays hard, but it's a whole different level of physicality, too, completely different. Those guys might be nice people off the field, but on the field they're cutthroat pros playing for the same World Cup chance you are, maybe once in a life-time. Anyone who says otherwise is fooling himself. *Nice little dancers?* Some people talk about Central American footballers that way. That's crazy. It is a lot meaner and tougher than you think, than you can see on TV or in some video session. Sometimes that sort of naiveté is what hurts our young kids going into these environments."

The U.S. contingent showed plenty of naiveté over the next seven qual-ifiers. One reason why: Coach Bob Gansler expanded and experimented with his roster to an extraordinary degree, giving coveted starts and pre-cious minutes to the unknown, untested likes of Phillip Gyau, Ted Eck and George Pastor, mainly in search of goals. At the other end, 20-year-old Tony Meola was handed the starting goalkeeping job in June 1989, hav-ing never played an official international match for his country. Some of Gansler's freewheeling roster moves panned out. Others nearly cost the Americans their place in history.

The 1989 Pentagonal can be neatly divided into a pair of distinct, four-match sections. The first opened with a home-and-home against Costa Rica in April. By month's end, each side had claimed 1-0 victories on home soil. From the U.S. perspective, these were highly creditable results. Prior to the opener in San José, the national team had not played an official outdoor match together since the Olympics. That was the loss to the Soviet Union in September 1988: six months prior, under another coach altogether, Lothar Osiander. *Los Ticos* were widely considered the best side left in the competition. All things considered, the Yanks had fared quite well, despite a boatload of personnel and tactical issues that Gansler, on the job only two months, was attempting to sort on the fly.

"Everyone is entitled to their opinions," Gansler told the *L.A. Times* after his side's April 30 victory over Costa Rica at the Big Arch in Fenton, where the U.S. dominated but could score only once, through Tab Ramos on 72 minutes. "In the first [Costa Rica] game, we didn't play at a fast enough pace. Using basketball terms, it was like we walked the ball up the court every time, even when there were fast-break opportunities. We waited for them to set their defense and we were constantly attacking against 11 players. We solved that in the second game, but we went overboard. We were constantly looking for the fast break or, as we say in soccer, the quick play or counter. We were forcing it. We have to find a happy medium."

See here the match reports from both Costa Rica matches:

Match Day 1: April 16, 1989: Costa Rica 1-0 USA [HT 1-0]
San José, Costa Rica · *Estadio Ricardo Saprissa* (26,271)

Scorer: Gilberto Rhoden 14'

CRC: Gabelo Conejo, Vladimir Quesada, Roger Flores, Enrique Diaz, Hector Marchena, German Chavarria, Carlos Hidalgo, Mauricio Montero, Juan Cayasso, Gilberto Rhoden (Leonidas Flores 81'), Evaristo Coronado

USA: Jeff Duback, Steve Trittschuh, Mike Windischmann, Marcelo Balboa, John Stollmeyer, Brian Bliss, John Harkes, Tab Ramos (Frank Klopas 75'), Bruce Murray, Brent Goulet (Jim Gabarra 80'), Peter Vermes

Cards: Evaristo Coronado [Y 60'] – Tab Ramos [Y 61']

Match Day 2: April 30, 1989: USA 1-0 Costa Rica [HT 0-0]
Fenton, Missouri, USA · Big Arch Stadium (8,500)

Scorer: Tab Ramos 72'

USA: David Vanole, Steve Trittschuh, Mike Windischmann, Marcelo Balboa, John Stollmeyer, Brian Bliss (Jim Gabarra 81'), John Harkes, Tab Ramos, Bruce Murray, Brent Goulet, Frank Klopas (Peter Vermes 42')

CRC: Gabelo Conejo, Vladimir Quesada, Roger Flores, Mauricio Montero, Carlos Hidalgo, German Chavarria (Edwin Salazar 44'), Juan Cayasso, Enrique Diaz, Gilberto Rhoden (Leonidas Flores 66'), Alvaro Solano, Hector Marchena

---

Cards: John Stollmeyer [Y 21'] – Alvaro Solano [Y 70'], Edwin Salazar [Y 73']

Two noteworthy lineup changes (all Match Day reports in this chapter sourced via the Society for American Soccer History) centered on young Marcelo Balboa: Gansler picked him at right back against Costa Rica on April 16 because Paul Krumpe had sustained a left-foot stress fracture during training. Balboa started the first three qualifiers before going down with his own long-term injury: "I was back at college by the time we played that T&T game in November 1989," he points out.

Mike Windischmann was always in Gansler's team, but he did move from a traditional central-defending role to a more sweeping role during these initial group games. John Doyle might have benefited from this, but he didn't play any of the first four qualifiers. He came back into the first team for an August friendly vs. South Korea, and then started two of the last three qualifiers, including the finale against T&T. Jimmy Banks, Des Armstrong, Stollmeyer and Krumpe all started games as part of the back four during qualifying. That's a lot of back-four flux by any standard.

"I don't think we ever went into qualifying with that single group of guys," Vermes remembers. "You gotta remember we had two coaches. Lothar Osiander started it and Bob Gansler finished it. We were still figuring it out, but the way we played really suited our strengths, I think. We put a lot of pressure on Latin styles in Costa Rica, Guatemala and El Salvador. I think we had a good formula to beat them by that time."

By June 1989, this inexperienced group did feel as though it had found something.

"Gansler had not been with us that long," Trittschuh attests. "He had not been through qualifying before; we had not been through World Cup qualifying before. It was all so new, but Gansler dealt with it. It helped him grow as a coach, just as we grew. Costa Rica was good. The first game down there kinda opened our eyes. We lost the game 1-0, but we thought, 'OK. Now we know what to expect.' They were supposed to be the best team in the group. Following that game, we beat them in St. Louis. After that, I think we knew that we could do this. It was just a matter of getting results. We didn't score many goals, but we didn't give up a whole lot of goals either."

For the April 16 opener in Costa Rica, Hugo Perez did not make the trip because of a foot injury. Ricky Davis was left behind to recover from surgery on his right knee. Before the team departed for San José, Davis indicated that he might be ready for the return match two weeks later in St. Louis. In actuality, he wouldn't feature in Gansler's team for the remainder of 1989 — not in qualifiers, not in friendlies, nowhere. The torch had effectively been passed from one generation to the next, even if, with seven crucial qualifiers yet to be played, Davis didn't yet recognize it.

Another consequential detail relating to these spring 1989 qualifiers: Costa Rica and Guatemala had already played their home-and-home matches the month before. The *Ticos* lost the opener 1-0 in Guatemala on March 19 and changed coaches three days later (!). Antonio Moyano, a Spaniard, took over from Gustavo de Simone, a Uruguayan. Moyano managed to steer his new side to a 2-1 victory over Guatemala in the return leg. These two results were something of a shock. Guatemala had eliminated Canada in its preliminary play-in, but few gave the plucky *Chapines* a chance to qualify. Such disregard dissipated quickly following their nerveless March split with the group favorites.

The Americans were unfortunate not to claim maximum points from their next two qualifiers, which were sandwiched around a June friendly with Peru. Trittschuh's superb, Google-worthy goal vs. T&T on May 13, back at Murdock Stadium in Torrance, appeared to give the Yanks a critical victory — and a commanding lead in the group. However, Hutson Charles equalized with two minutes remaining in regulation. That's the way it ended.

Why the Federation would return to Torrance for a match of *any* import, following the qualification disaster of 1985, remains a karmic mystery.

In New Britain, Connecticut, on June 17, the U.S. completed the first phase of Pentagonal matches by claiming all the points against Guatemala — just two points per victory back then. Clemson University can claim much of the credit: Alumnus Bruce Murray opened the scoring on two minutes, and fellow Tiger Eric Eichmann potted the winner after the *Chapines* knotted the score. Another razor-thin result. However, with five points from a possible eight over its initial four games, the U.S. matched the group-leading pace of the Costa Ricans, who started their group schedule early and finished it early. By sundown on July 16 — when they nipped El Salvador at home, 1-0 — *Los Ticos* were done: They had played all eight group matches, claiming 11 points from a possible 16.

Match Day 3: May 13, 1989: USA 1-1 Trinidad and Tobago [HT 0-0]
Torrance, California, USA · Murdock Stadium (10,000)

Scorers: Steve Trittschuh 48' — Hutson Charles 88'

USA: David Vanole, Steve Trittschuh, Mike Windischmann, Marcelo Balboa, John Stollmeyer, John Harkes, Tab Ramos (Jim Gabarra 62'), Bruce Murray, George Pastor (Peter Vermes 46'), Brent Goulet, Frank Klopas

TRI: Earl Carter, Clayton Morris, Dexter Francis, Marvin Faustin, Brian Williams, Floyd Lawrence, Paul Elliot-Allen (Dexter Skeene 62'), Russell Latapy, Hutson Charles, Leonson Lewis, Maurice Alibey (Dwight Yorke 69')

Cards: Dexter Francis [Y 36']

Match Day 4: June 17, 1989: USA 2-1 Guatemala [HT 1-1]
New Britain, Connecticut, USA · Veterans Stadium (10,500)

Scorers: Bruce Murray 2', Eric Eichmann 68' — Raul Chacon Estrada 22'

USA: David Vanole, Steve Trittschuh, Mike Windischmann, Jimmy Banks, John Stollmeyer, Brian Bliss (John Doyle 85'), John Harkes, Tab Ramos, Phillip Gyau (Paul Caligiuri 46'), Bruce Murray, Eric Eichmann

---

GUA: Edgar Ricardo Jerez Hidalgo, Juan Manuel Davila Lopez, Rocael Mazariegos, Victor Monzon, Alejandro Ortiz, Marvin Ceballos Arana, Felix McDonald, Juan Manuel Funes, Julio Rodas Hurtarte, Raul Chacon Estrada, Byron Romeo Perez Solorzano

---

Cards: Eric Eichmann [70'] – Victor Monzon [Y 7'], Raul Chacon Estrada [Y 48'], Juan Manuel Funes [R 86']

Once again, these match summaries tell amazingly detailed stories. Halfway through qualifying, Gansler's team was not in disarray, but his preferred XI remained largely inscrutable. To wit:

✦ Caligiuri, soon-to-be hero of Port of Spain, didn't even appear for the USMNT until halfway through Match Day 4, in New Britain, due to injuries. Meanwhile, George Pastor, a Peruvian-born striker and Cal Berkeley product, started the May 13 match against T&T and played the full 90. Pastor was known to the coach through an Upper Midwest connection: Gansler's tenure at the University of Wisconsin-Milwaukee overlapped with Pastor notching a team-record 174 indoor goals for the Milwaukee Wave of the American Indoor Soccer Association. His outdoor career proved brief but eventful. After making his name with the San Jose Earthquakes and SF Bay Blackhawks in the Western Soccer Alliance, Pastor *debuted* for the national team in that May 13 match. His final appearance came 42 days later, in a friendly against Colombia.

✦ Gansler himself was clearly dealing with striker issues, his side having scored just four times in four matches. In all eight Pentagonal qualifiers, he wheeled through a remarkable number of forwards: Brent Goulet (who was rapidly losing form), Eric Eichmann, Bruce Murray, George

Pastor, Peter Vermes and Frankie Klopas all started matches, as did the little-heralded Phillip Gyau, in the June win over Guatemala. When goals are few, *el Mister* is obligated to run out some new faces. *But Ted Eck?* He actually came on for Murray during Match Day 7, a scoreless tie with Guatemala on Oct. 8. The young and mercurial Steve Snow even got a run-in: 35 friendly minutes vs. South Korea, in August.

"That was the most competitive situation I've ever been in, in my life," Murray asserts, looking back. "To hold your job, day in and day out, when they were bringing in 10 new guys to every camp? Every guy wanted my spot. You were on edge all the time, especially if you hadn't scored in a couple days. It was never an atmosphere where you felt comfortable, and I suppose that was the point. That's one way to get the best out of guys, to always have that competition. I don't know what the other guys told you, but I've never felt so much pressure as then."

✦ The situation was no more settled in goal. Veteran Jeff Duback started the first Costa Rica match; Vanole played the next three. Meola made his national team debut against Peru in the June 4 friendly. After sitting and watching Vanole play the 90 vs. Guatemala on June 17, Meola was handed the job permanently. To sum up, Gansler played two known quantities between the pipes and then handed the job outright to a 20-year-old who'd never played anything but a single friendly for the senior USMNT. "I did come in because of injuries — a slew of injuries, not just one," Meola remembers. "I was pretty much the only healthy guy for a period of time. Then I earned the spot in a couple friendlies leading up to the next qualifier that fall."

In and out of goal, Gansler never chose among entirely healthy options. No gaffer ever does. Neither was he choosing among a raft of battle-tested players who'd competed for the national team before. Nor were his roster options getting regular games in something like Major League Soccer; they settled for the A-League and the Western Soccer Alliance. Still, Gansler proved amazingly bold and resourceful in his experimentation, considering how small and untested the player pool was and how big the stakes remained.

"We still only got together for two weeks out of every month, all through 1989," Trittschuh adds. "I played with the Rowdies to get games in between, and I was among the fortunate ones. Other guys were staying home and training with college teams. That's how it was. And we're talking maybe 30 to 35 guys. That's what Gansler had to choose from. Not a lot."

BY JUNE 18, 1989, THE OPENING four-match qualifying phase was complete. The A-League's second season, and the WSA's third, were each in full swing, providing much of that shallow player pool the opportunity to maintain fitness and play competitive matches. Moreover, the Federation again stepped up to arrange top-class friendlies to maintain unit cohesion and confidence ahead of the final phase, come September. The U.S. beat Peru 3-0 on June 4, in East Rutherford, New Jersey, in a veritable goal-fest. The Americans played very well three weeks later in dropping a 1-0 decision in Miami to a full-strength Colombia side featuring Carlos Valderrama, "El Loco" Rene Higuita, Leonel Alvarez & Co. Less impressive was a 2-1 loss to South Korea on Aug. 13 in Los Angeles.

Despite all the lineups Gansler chose to deploy, the team had started to take on the personae of its coach and team leaders — of which there was no shortage, apparently.

"We had more lieutenants than we had clowns because there was no clowning around with Gansler," Meola says. "He was getting to the World Cup, period. You were either onboard or on an airplane going somewhere else. I also look back at our captain, Mike Windischmann, very much a straight shooter. If he didn't like what you did, it didn't take two seconds for him to let you know. John Stollmeyer out of IU, same thing. Jimmy Gabarra was one of Gansler's guys. All business. He would sit and talk to me about how to eat and sleep like a pro. Tab was a straightforward guy right from the start. In our meetings you could hear a pin drop."

According to Trittschuh, "There *were* some clowns. Harkes is one of the funniest people I've ever met. That guy cracks me up. His impressions! He's got that New Jersey attitude and wit — and his dad's Scottish accent. John could do all the U.K. accents. He did all the coaches, too. He could do a great Coach Gansler impression. I remember when Bora took over; he could do Bora, too."

Did Harkes ever do Gansler *for* Gansler? "Uh, no. No way," Trittschuh insists. "Gansler was not that type of coach."

"There were some free spirits who came in a bit before me," Meola reports. "Harkes, for sure. Eric Wynalda changed the culture a bit — but that was mostly between qualifying and the World Cup. I'd be crazy not to mention David Vanole, who was my competition but became my best friend throughout this process."

Meola's rise proved Vanole's competitive undoing. After losing his starting place in June 1989, Vanole never took the field for his country again, not in a game that mattered. However, he never projected the smallest kernel of resentment, according to Meola, the guy who absconded with his job. Dino remained a charismatic team leader all through 1989. Gansler brought him to Italy based almost entirely on these intangibles.

Vanole played one last professional season post-Italy, with the APSL Blackhawks, before taking on a succession of goalkeeper/assistant coaching positions. This new path began at his alma mater, UCLA. He went on to coach with the U.S. U-20 team, the U.S. Women's National Team, the Washington Freedom (in the old Women's Professional Soccer league), and then with D.C. United and the New England Revolution in MLS. He suffered a fatal heart attack during a family ski vacation in 2007.

"We were roommates," Meola says, his voice getting quiet. "The guy could have made my life so miserable in 1989. Here was a young guy taking his position, his place in the team. He could've approached it many different ways, but he chose to approach it in a way that, well . . . I always say he was the best teammate I ever had."

———————

Despite widespread inexperience, the paucity of goals, and the dizzying array of starting lineups, most everything had gone to plan for the USMNT over the first half of final qualifying. An away loss to Costa Rica in San José? No shame in that, especially when it's followed by five points from a possible six. This solid run of form and fortune extended through Match Day 5, against El Salvador.

Match Day 5: Sept. 17, 1989: El Salvador 0-1 USA [HT 0-0]
Tegucigalpa, Honduras · *Estadio Nacional* (3,700)

Scorer: Hugo Perez 74'

SLV: Carlos Rivera, William Giron, Fredy Orellana, Guillermo Ragazzone, Nelson Rivera, Jose Luis Rugamas, Mauricio Alfaro, Julio Palacios Lozano, Hugo Ventura, Jose Maria Rivas, Joaquin Casales

---

USA: Tony Meola, Steve Trittschuh, Mike Windischmann, Jimmy Banks, John Stollmeyer, Brian Bliss, John Harkes, Tab Ramos, Hugo Perez, Peter Vermes (Eric Eichmann 80'), Bruce Murray

---

Cards: William Giron [Y 21'] – Hugo Perez [Y 81'], Tab Ramos [Y 84'], Eric Eichmann [Y 89']

Close readers and keen geographers might notice this game was played in the Honduran capital, a neutral venue, due to the civil war then raging across El Salvador. Credit *Los Cuzcatlecos* for showing up and playing as well as they did, though the match proved a clumsy, indelicate affair. Played before a tiny crowd in a 60,000-seat stadium, a chippy contest turned downright ugly following the deciding goal from *Senor* Perez. Note the trio of U.S. yellow cards handed out in the final 10 minutes.

"Any time you are successful, whether it's an individual game or a qualifying campaign, you've gotta play well," Gansler says, looking back at the fall of 1989. "But you've gotta have good fortune, whether it's a call or the relocation of a game. You've gotta be resilient no matter what, because you're gonna get kicked in the *derriere* or other parts of your anatomy every now and then."

El Salvador would eventually provide plenty of opportunities for U.S. resilience; it nearly foiled American hopes during the return leg in November. However, its valiant qualifying effort would ultimately succumb to larger forces. After repeated rescheduling on account of civil strife at home, *Los Cuzcatlecos* had been slated to conclude qualifying with home-and-home matches against Guatemala in November. By Nov. 19, when the U.S. played its finale at Trinidad and Tobago, neither Guatemala nor El Salvador had any mathematical chance of qualification. Both fixtures were abandoned.

———•———

Many of the interviews for this book were conducted after October 2017, when Bruce Arena's national team traveled down to Trinidad and Tobago and failed to get the draw it needed to advance to the 2018 World Cup finals, in Russia. Because the U.S. had so recently kicked away this qualification effort, it seemed logical to ask Generation Zero whether, at any point during the 1989 Pentagonal, they feared they'd kicked away theirs. Because following a pair of terrible performances on Match Days 6 and 7, they nearly did.

"Those were the two games that we should have won that we tied instead," Trittschuh contends. "The first game, in Guatemala, was a monsoon. The field was full of water, and we just dominated. We had so many chances on goal, but we couldn't score."

This was the match where Gansler turned to Ted Eck, who came on for Bruce Murray after 74 minutes. Frankie Klopas had already come on for Gabarra, as the U.S. desperately sought a winner. No dice.

Match Day 6: Oct. 8, 1989: Guatemala 0-0 USA [HT 0-0]
Guatemala City, Guatemala · *Estadio Mateo Flores* (8,000)

GUA: Ricardo Piccinini, Giovanny Hernandez, Luis Rodriguez Sandoval, Otto Gonzalez, Victor Monzon, David Gardiner, Adan Onelio Paniagua, Eddy Alburei Suarez, Carlos Enrique Castaneda Mendez, Oscar Enrique Sanchez Rivas, Erwin Almengo

USA: Tony Meola, Steve Trittschuh, John Doyle, Mike Windischmann, Jimmy Banks, John Stollmeyer, Brian Bliss, John Harkes, Jim Gabarra (Frank Klopas 61'), Peter Vermes, Bruce Murray (Ted Eck 74')

"That result was a little disconcerting," recalls Paul Krumpe, whose rehab was progressing nicely, though not well enough to rejoin the team for Match Days 6 or 7. "I didn't travel with the team. Back then U.S. Soccer couldn't afford to fly guys out who were unable to play. The Guatemala match wasn't on TV, and there was no internet back then. Obviously, not a good result there."

According to Bruce Murray, speaking in 2021, "Shit happens" during any qualification campaign, "but especially in CONCACAF." Poor results happen to good teams and bad, especially on the road during monsoon season. The nerves weren't so frayed across the rest of October 1989, even in light of this missed opportunity in Guatemala.

Come sundown on Nov. 5, however, following another nil-nil draw, American nerves grew very frayed indeed.

Match Day 7: Nov. 5, 1989: USA 0-0 El Salvador [HT 0-0]
Fenton, Missouri, USA · Big Arch Stadium (8,500)

USA: Tony Meola, Steve Trittschuh, Mike Windischmann, Desmond Armstrong (Frank Klopas 57'), Jimmy Banks, John Stollmeyer, Brian Bliss (Jim Gabarra 83'), John Harkes, Tab Ramos, Bruce Murray, Eric Eichmann

SLV: Carlos Rivera, Victor Coreas, Jaime Rodriguez, Leonel Carcamo, Miguel Estrada, Marlon Menjivar, Mauricio Cienfuegos, Jose Gomez Garcia, Oscar Arbizu, Carlos Zapata, Jose Maria Martinez

Cards: Mauricio Cienfuegos [Y 85']

At home in cozy and familiar Fenton, Missouri, facing a weakened opponent that arrived stateside with absolutely nothing to play for, the USMNT turned in its worst performance in more than two years. Unlike the scoreless draw at Guatemala, video of this game *does* exist, on YouTube. It's a brief, desultory highlight package, just 3:21 in duration. Nevertheless, it shows viewers everything they need to see: El Salvador was terrible, totally lacking in ambition; the U.S. was all ambition, but only the smallest grade above terrible. All the pressure to qualify, all of the American youth, all of the naiveté in front goal came to a head before 8,500 fans and an ESPN audience.

The nil-nil result quite rightly resulted in outright panic.

"I never felt like we'd blown it, but we really screwed up that game with El Salvador," Murray declares. "We laid an egg against an undermanned opponent — in St. Louis! They had half a team, and we didn't execute. Worst day of my national team career. I missed so many chances. We should have wrapped up the whole thing two weeks before we ever got to T&T."

The U.S. would now have to travel to Port of Spain and *beat* Trinidad and Tobago in its final group game — or everything Generation Zero had worked for, including USA '94, would be wasted.

"The game in St. Louis against El Salvador, well, that was the low point," Trittschuh says. "They were already finished, eliminated! And they sent, like, a backup team — still a professional team, I guess, but not their first-choice team. And we tied that game, too. Same issue: Couldn't score."

Costa Rica's 11 points had already locked up one of the two qualifying spots. The U.S. and Trinidad and Tobago sat together, tied for second, each on nine points. But here again, vexing issues in front of goal came back to cruelly bite the young Americans squarely in the ass. Trinidad had a better goal differential and more total goals. Mathematically, Gansler's team could not make the World Cup finals with a draw. It needed a victory, or everything would go up in flames.

Publicly, *Herr fußballtrainer* insisted he had known all along that qualifying would come down to the last match. The Pentagonal had produced a veritable mother lode of nil-nil draws and one-goal games. Such a closely contested competition, he told the *Los Angeles Times*, was bound to go down to the wire. However, the U.S. players recognized their potentially untenable position. They all knew the situation was desperate. Gansler and the U.S. coaching staff knew it. The meager U.S. media entourage knew it. Everyone in CONCACAF knew it.

"It would be very difficult for the Americans to win in Trinidad and Tobago, but not impossible," El Salvador captain Jaime Rodriguez told

The New York Times after his team's draw in Missouri. "We came here expecting to lose and we didn't."

"We don't have the money like the Americans," said George Kiril Dojcinovski, El Salvador's Yugoslavian coach. Unlike the Americans, who had two weeks of preparation in Fenton prior to the match, Dojcinovski's charges arrived just two nights before, quite late, following a seven-hour layover in Houston. In St. Louis, they stayed four players to a room. "I don't think the Americans were flat," Dojcinovski told the *Los Angeles Times*. "They played the way they can play and El Salvador played the right way against them."

Trittschuh is philosophical all these years later: "Everyone remembers that final game — and that *did* get us some real national recognition at the time. Maybe it was fate."

EVERY LEAGUE, EVERY TOURNAMENT, EVERY confederation has its minnows. Guatemala and El Salvador shouldered the role of Pentagonal lightweights back in 1989. The Salvadorans did not win a match (0-4-2). Guatemala prevailed just once in six attempts. However, both nations maintained active, professional leagues throughout the 1980s, whereas the United States did not. We've made a running joke of exposing this country's substandard club soccer environment in wake of NASL's demise. Yet here, in November 1989, we see why such infrastructure matters: Already eliminated from *Italia* '90, El Salvador sent a B team to Fenton, Missouri. That side included nine players from a single club, Firpo of Usulutan, named for the Argentine boxer — the first Latin American ever to challenge for the world heavyweight title. Winless El Salvador went through four head coaches during final qualifying. Dojcinovski accepted the job twice, in the second and fourth slots. He was tapped the last time — for the Nov. 5 match at Big Arch — only because managing Firpo was his day job, his full-time gig. Yet Dojcinovski and his players, pressed into emergency service, arrived ready to play what, for them, was a meaningless match, under considerable travel duress. They competed and managed a point. A very professional point.

Like the old joke says: If you walk into qualifying group and you can't identify the minnow, it might be you.

Thirty years on, in the mature and fulsome futbol landscape created by Generation Zero, it's difficult to reconcile just how small-time the U.S. soccer culture remained in the fall of 1989 — at this specific point in the narrative, *before the match that changed everything*. The failure to beat or score against El Salvador on Nov. 5 or Guatemala on Oct. 8 is proof enough. Yet it's the smaller details that tend to illuminate and instruct. Paul Krumpe, for example, was nearly recovered from the stress fracture he'd sustained in his foot; he almost made training for Match Day 7 in Fenton against El Salvador/Firpo. But U.S. Soccer didn't fly him out to Missouri from Los Angeles. He watched the game on TV, like I did. "We always played well there — but on TV? Wow. That place looked like a high school stadium," Krumpe remembers, all too accurately. For the record, El Salvador traditionally plays *its* Federation qualifiers at the *Estadio Cuscatlan* in San Salvador. Seating capacity: 54,000. By 1989, tiny El Salvador had twice qualified for the World Cup, in 1970 and 1982.

Or consider Krumpe's rehab. The Federation's preferred specialist, Dr. Bert Mandelbaum, handled his surgery. Thereafter, Krumpe worked two civilian jobs, at McDonnell Douglas and coaching at Cal State Dominguez Hills. The Federation physio staff didn't keep any sort of direct, in-person tabs on its starting right back's progress. Krumpe oversaw his own rehabilitation and fitness recovery — from his parents' house in Torrance. "I would go to my parents' pool and run with a wet vest to protect my foot," Krumpe reports, all these years later.

Two weeks following the Firpo debacle, Krumpe started against T&T in the Pentagonal finale. He went 62 minutes. Heroic? Sure. But consider this corollary: The guy who hadn't played a competitive match in six months and who oversaw his own rehab in his parents' pool was reinserted directly into the starting lineup for the biggest match in U.S. soccer history. This was the abysmal status quo for the most powerful nation on earth, a sporting hegemon in every other respect — but a footballing minnow until its national soccer team proved otherwise.

The U.S. defense had not struggled so mightily in Krumpe's absence. The Yanks experienced one helluva scoring drought throughout 1989, but they hadn't conceded in a qualifier since June. Nevertheless, Krumpe would indeed start against Trinidad and Tobago on Nov. 19. Bob Gansler is nothing if not loyal. He's not a hand-wringer, either.

"My mind doesn't work that way. I didn't feel like we'd blown our chance," the coach maintains. "Sometimes people believe me when I say things like that, and sometimes they don't. This was a one-game situation. I believe my phrase at that time — and I'm full of trite things to say (I don't have brown eyes, so the level doesn't rise quite that high) — but my phrase was always, 'Is it doable? Yep, it's doable.' So let's go ahead and do it. It's one game.

"'Are we capable of winning a game on an island somewhere off the coast of South America?' Yes, we are. So let's go and do it. By the way, T&T had tied us late in our qualifier first leg, and they had no business even being close in that one. It was doable. That's what we fixated on."

Gansler's captain was fully onboard.

"You can't look backward. We let Trinidad score that late goal back in June — you could say *that* lapse put us in that situation," Windischmann speculates today. "All I remember is, we went to train in Cocoa Beach [Florida], and we had a lot of confidence that we were going to go down there and do it. We felt like we were gonna win, and that turned out to be the case. T&T only needed a tie, but you know what? Sometimes it's not good when all you have to do is tie."

Twenty-eight years later, members of the 2017 USMNT traveled to T&T needing only a draw to advance to the World Cup finals in Russia. They lost that match 2-1 — to an opponent with absolutely nothing to play for. In May 1985, the U.S. required only a draw against Costa Rica to keep its Mexico '86 dreams alive. It lost that game 1-0. On Nov. 19, 1989, Trinidad and Tobago needed only a tie to advance . . .

"That specific situation puts a weird sort of pressure on a team — the team needing *only* a tie," Windy explains. "I remember that from '86 qualifying; we were in the same situation against Costa Rica. Then all of a sudden, you're down a goal and panic sets in. It's one of those things. I feel like I was in two games like that. In Torrance it worked against us. In Trinidad it worked in our favor."

One of the enduring broadcast images from the calamitous Nov. 5 draw with El Salvador, in suburban St. Louis, was John Stollmeyer repeatedly launching long throw-ins at the Salvadoran goal mouth, his team desperate for something good to come of just one. Despite the grainy YouTube footage, one could see the frustration on Stollmeyer's face. I could hear it in his voice *still*, during our interviews for this book. You can't win if you don't score, but in its seven previous qualifiers, the 1989 USMNT had scored just five times.

"I honestly cannot tell you, even to this day, how we didn't win those last three games by two, three, four goals apiece," Stolly says. "Maybe it was the pressure of the situation that got to people. I could never understand why we didn't score more, generally. We had more chances. We *created* more chances. I don't blame referees; you don't get calls sometimes, you don't get breaks. We had to find a way to mentally survive it."

Adds Meola, "The team felt at that point that it should have been in the World Cup already. But we dealt with it. Same scenario as The Courts: Win or go home."

"I knew we would play well against Trinidad," Trittschuh recalls. "But in the back of our minds, we all wondered what was going to happen to U.S. soccer if we didn't win — and what was going to happen to us?"

"I don't think there was a lot of belief in that locker room," Murray contends. "We were so young. We weren't sure we were getting another contract [with the national team]. We had to win to survive. I was getting married a week later and I was like, 'How am I going to take care of kids?'"

The two-week camp in Cocoa Beach proved tense. Gansler said all the right things and appeared to believe them. Krumpe's return was a boost. The side *had* played T&T off the park in June. But the goal-scoring conundrum hung over the team like a pall. It had been two months and 196 match minutes since an American had last scored. The man who claimed it, Hugo Perez, was available but would not start against T&T on Nov. 19.

The Federation flew in the Bermudan national team for a friendly, an attempt to present a training opponent that mimicked the quick, athletic team awaiting the USMNT in Port of Spain. The good news: The Yanks scored twice through Doyle and Eichmann. The bad news: Bermuda, another verifiable CONCACAF minnow, scored a goal as well and more than held its own.

"We struggled against Bermuda," Joe Machnik, Gansler's assistant, told *The Guardian* in 2015, "so the media around us was very skeptical. They were writing that we couldn't win."

The Guardian also spoke to John Polis, the Federation's director of communications (1988-93): "There was angst among the press at the time, around the team. *Could we do this on the road?* There were people in the press corps who thought we were going to get thumped."

In August 1989, the Federation named Scott LeTellier president of its 1994 World Cup Organizing Committee. His credentials? The Los Angeles attorney had been intimately involved with the 1984 Olympic soccer competition. As a key aide to Peter Ueberroth, the L.A. Olympic Organizing Committee chairman, LeTellier had worked with FIFA to negotiate the various stadium venues. Three months following his hire, during that fateful week ahead of the all-or-nothing T&T match, LeTellier gave an interview to the *Los Angeles Times*: "I can sense that FIFA is frustrated with us. They think it's very important that the United States be in Italy in 1990. They're looking at what's at stake, for them. Considering the American market, they feel there will be more dollars available for them if the United States qualifies. But just from a sporting standpoint, they can't believe that we may not qualify from the group that we're in. They're saying, 'Mexico's out, there's two berths available, and you still can't qualify? If not now, when do you think you're going to be able to do it?'"

The U.S. entourage arrived at Piarco International Airport, 22 miles east of Port of Spain, late on Nov. 16, three days ahead of the Pentagonal climax, Match Day 8. Despite the Federation's and Gansler's best efforts, they were ill-prepared for what they encountered. By November 1989, 30 months into their long march toward the World Cup, the Yanks had traveled over and over to hostile CONCACAF environments. Never had they seen anything like this, however: thousands of people waiting for their plane, *in the airport,* chanting, "No Way, USA!" Thousands more lined the bus route into Port of Spain, all of them decked out in Soca Warrior red.

"I remember at the airport, as we walked off the plane, we walked into a sea of red — and the music was blaring," Gansler recalls. "All of Port of Spain was wearing red that day. All three days."

Soca is Trinidad and Tobago's signature musical genre, an offshoot of calypso with undertones of soul and funk. The name is derived from how the locals themselves describe it: the soul of calypso. The U.S. contingent had arrived knowing there would be some sort of unofficial welcome "party," but also believing their evening arrival might mitigate the spectacle. Nope. "It was 10 o'clock at night, and there were people lining the road all the way to the hotel," Trittschuh says.

"There were people on the roof of the airport!" Vermes told *The Guardian* in 2015. "It was crazy. You could feel the tension of the occasion. It was us against the world."

The longer the Americans were in the country, the more it became clear that the entire population was determined to make their lives and match preparation miserable. And yet, there was something else the U.S. players sensed amid that oppressive sea of red: The whole of this island nation expected victory. They considered the result a foregone conclusion. The local citizenry had, in essence, already begun celebrating. "They had declared a national holiday the day after the game — to celebrate going to the World Cup!" Murray says.

Adds Krumpe, "They were so convinced they were qualifying, they got all their artists to record World Cup songs and were already playing them on the radio."

Trinidad and Tobago had only declared independence from Great Britain in 1962. The country's over-the-top enthusiasm for the biggest sporting event in its short history was to be expected. On some level, the Soca Warriors themselves surely appreciated such impassioned, countrywide support. On another, however, they most assuredly did not.

"I remember walking out of the tunnel before the game," Vermes says. "You could see the terror in [the T&T players'] eyes. All of the pressure to go to the World Cup that had been placed on them."

Nevertheless, in the 48 hours leading up to the match, the U.S. contingent could not go about its business without encountering locals determined to distract, annoy or otherwise foil their preparation. There was a festivity to the nonstop disturbances, a puckish quality. No one on the American team ever felt physically threatened. There was no need for armed military escorts. Yet the scale of the effort took the Yanks aback. The young team had never before seen anything so openly and pervasively CONCACAFkaesque.

"We get to the field, and it wasn't what we thought it would be; [there were] people in red shirts everywhere. We could hardly train," Meola remembers. "We got to the hotel, and they barely knew we were coming — or acted that way. Sleeping with earplugs because they sent the band to the hotel. Outside our windows, they were going crazy all night. Taking the phones off the hooks because people were calling all night long. It was just everything you could imagine.

"We dealt with it. But back then we didn't even know what food we should be eating. We'd sit there and wait until the trainer would go in and test the food himself. If he didn't get sick, it was good for everyone else! All those things we laugh about now. We bring our own cooks today. All our food was flown over to South Korea [in 2002], for example. It's a different animal now, compared to back then. Bob Gansler had tried to prepare us for all this stuff. He really is one of the smartest men we've ever had in the sport of soccer in this country. But there's a limit to what you can block out."

The Yanks got enough on-field time at the National Stadium to know what to expect come game day: another hard, uneven, Caribbean pitch ringed by a running track. (The 30,000-capacity facility would be re-named in 2001 for sprinter Hasely Crawford, who brought home T&T's first Olympic gold medal.) Gansler kept the workouts brief. The idea of a "closed" training session proved impractical in the prevailing atmosphere.

There was but one respite, the day before the match. John Stollmeyer's father had been born in Trinidad, and much of his extended family still re-sided there. The elder Stollmeyer conspired with his son, with Gansler's permission, to slip a group of players out of the hotel and down to the wharf. "We took about six or seven guys and went out to what they call Monkey Island, just a little island off the edge of Trinidad," Stolly says. "The only way to get there was by boat, but that's where the family had a house. We were allowed to go — on a half-day off. My uncle picked us up with his boat, and we just hung out for a couple of hours. Desmond, Doyle, and I think Tritt and Bliss were there. All my defender guys! I have pictures somewhere . . ."

The morning of the match dawned hot and steamy. Many in the U.S. delegation were invited to breakfast at the U.S. ambassador's residence, where presumably the madding crowd would not trouble them — and the food could be trusted. The setting proved stunning: a mountaintop manse that looked down over the Caribbean on one side — and over the National Stadium on the other. At 11 a.m., four full hours before kickoff, the stands and surrounding plaza were filled to capacity.

MIKE WINDISCHMANN HAS IT SPOT ON: When all you need from a match is a draw, a single point, this precarious expectation can truly mess with a team's head, its motivations, its tactics and its resilience should something go awry. It can mess even more toxically with 30,000 fans all dressed in red and waiting to start their celebrations in earnest — to say nothing of the tens of thousands gathered outside the stadium watching on a Jumbotron, burning spliffs, and quaffing beer and rum-based concoctions under a roasting Caribbean sun.

Match Day 8 proved a sweltering Sunday indeed. Dehydrated and ever more lit, the home crowd wanted desperately to celebrate further — they could hardly *wait* to celebrate further. Work and school had already been canceled for Monday. Trinidad, home to Port of Spain, is by far the country's largest, most populous island. Tobago and 21 additional, even smaller islands complete the nation. By noon on Nov. 19, 1989, the entire archipelago was a veritable powder keg of booze, dope, heat and expectation.

"I've played in stadiums with 80,000 crazy people," Murray reckons, "but I've never witnessed a scene like that, with 250,000 people milling around outside the stadium, all wearing red and watching big screens and partying, as they do down there. It was all very festive, but inside the stadium, it was a nervous atmosphere. Tons of marijuana smoke, like there always is when you play down in Caribbean countries."

"We'd played a lot in extreme heat, but that day was really, really hot," Krumpe adds. "I remember being blown away by the fan situation. I got goose bumps walking onto the field because *everyone* was wearing red. Very intimidating. But I also think it was so hot, and those fans had gotten there so early, there wasn't a lot of atmosphere inside the stadium during the game. Maybe they were tired having been there so long. It was not the home-field advantage they [the T&T national team] might have expected, in my opinion."

Krumpe's corollary informed Windischmann's: It's bloody difficult for a packed stadium to maintain an intensity of support when your team is playing for a tie. Similarly, it's hard to stay disciplined and grind out a draw when 30,000 intoxicated countrymen want something more. "I told our guys before the match: '[T&T] will eventually take chances or make mistakes. That's the opportunity we can expect. That opportunity is *going* to be there,'" Gansler recalls.

The U.S. skipper set his team up conservatively, hoping to capitalize on just such a blunder. His one secret weapon, Hugo Perez, Gansler held in abeyance. The last man to score for the Yanks — in Honduras, against El Salvador, 63 days prior! — had not been fit for the scoreless, rain-soaked draw in Guatemala on Oct. 8., thanks to a groin injury. Four weeks later in St. Louis, he was named to the match roster but did not play.

By the time Match Day 8 got underway, the Americans hadn't scored in more than 200 minutes of open play. Their place at *Italia* '90 required a goal. Perez remained on the bench. Stollmeyer, who joined him there, remembers how the homogenous home crowd felt quiet and remote due to the track circling the pitch: "The biggest thing I remember was the red," he says. "Everywhere. But those stands were far from the field, sort of like an American stadium. There was no moat or fencing, like in Costa Rica, where there's a 15-foot fence with barbed wire on top, just a couple yards off the field. That's not how it was in Trinidad. It was a nervous, quiet crowd, and they seemed weirdly far away."

Caligiuri's wonder strike, so celebrated in the decades to follow, came from nothing. What's more, it developed following 30 minutes of tepid, cautious play from both sides: no clear chances, an unsightly collection of nervous touches, a few shots launched from a preposterous distance, very little meaningful possession. The full game remains available on-line, via YouTube. As any neutral observer will attest, this all-or-nothing match started out as an inelegant bore, but all that changed on 31 minutes. Instantly, the U.S. team was elated, energized, emboldened. "There was no belief until Paul scored — and then there was belief," Murray admits.

The match-winner, the era-changer, truly did arise from nothing, a seemingly innocuous possession in midfield. From the left flank, just over the halfway line, Ramos fed Caligiuri in a central position, some 35 yards from goal. The American expertly sold his defender a move to the right before sharply cutting the ball back to his left. *Presto!* Caligiuri had created a modicum of space — and he didn't wait on the bounding ball.

So far from goal, the U.S. defensive midfielder didn't wait to settle it, either. Didn't even look up for a teammate cutting toward the T&T goal . . .

"Paul just let it fly," Gansler recalls.

"He flicked it over to himself and just hit it," Windischmann reports, seeing it from his central position directly behind Caligiuri. "It was surreal, like, in slow motion. The ball kept going and going and just dropped in."

The uneven, rock-hard pitch had created the bounding ball. Because he took it on the volley, on the laces, the topspin was always going to make it hard for the keeper to handle. Gansler deputy Joe Machnik saw the strike leave Caligiuri's boot, and, midflight, he yelled, "Trouble!"

Machnik had been a keeper by trade — an All-American at Long Island University in 1962. He rose in the sport as a goalkeeping coach. From the sideline that afternoon in Port of Spain, he had noticed the low, late-afternoon sun shining directly into the eyes of T&T goalie Michael Maurice. The match tape bears this out. Maurice later claimed that he never saw the ball leave Caligiuri's foot; two T&T defenders were, in fact, positioned directly in the keeper's sight line. What's more, few of the 30,000 in attendance that day, including Maurice, had expected the American defender to even *attempt* a shot from such range.

J.P. Dellacamera called this game on ESPN alongside Seamus Malin. His simple, no-fuss articulation still holds up after 30-plus years: "A left-footed shot . . . and PAUL CALIGIURI HAS SCORED A GOAL AND THE USA LEAD, ONE-NOTHING!"

It was the topspin that kept the shot on frame. In fact, the archival footage makes one wonder whether Maurice was perhaps positioned too far off his line: Once the ball passed over his outstretched arms, it came nowhere near the crossbar. The ball was curling and dipping so hard, it hit the ground before touching the *side* netting.

"I know my abilities to take those kinds of shots," Caligiuri told *The Guardian* in 2015. "It's a confidence level that you don't think about. . . . I probably broke down the garage door taking shots. As I got bigger and bigger, I got further and further back into the street and eventually on the other side of the street. It wasn't always the case that it hit the garage door. It hit the stucco above it. I literally took the stucco out, dead smack in the middle of the goal, middle of the garage. They had to patch it up . . . I worked really hard on developing my left foot, where I felt comfortable. And it paid off."

"We were all amazed when the ball went in," Vermes says. "It was almost as if, 'Holy cow! We GOT this thing now.'"

Murray saw it the same way: "When Paul scored his goal, we realized, 'You know, we can win this game. We can probably score another one.'"

The Soca Warriors came to the identical realizations, just as quickly. They stood in stunned silence — all but Maurice, who lay crumpled and motionless in the goalmouth. An entire nation of fans went similarly limp and lifeless. Inside the stadium, disbelief quickly devolved into deflation before morphing directly into all-consuming panic. There ain't no bigger buzzkill than panic. The party was over.

———————

"The last hour of the game is a blur," Krumpe reveals. "I remember just trying to keep up with the pace, focusing on doing my job. I remember asking to be taken off after halftime, because I was exhausted. I remember celebrating when it was all over — but that's about all. I was just trying to stay as focused as I could. If we didn't give up a goal, we had a chance. We conceded a goal, we were in real trouble."

On came Stollmeyer for Krumpe, on the hour. The game patterns changed very little: T&T carried the ragged play, such as it was, but neither team could produce another bit of individual skill, that one penetrating pass of quality in the attacking third. After yet another long-distance attempt from the Soca Warriors sailed high and wide, Malin quipped, "As they say in Trinidad, that ball is *behind God's back*. It's an expression to mean it is nowhere to be found. Way off target."

What searching balls T&T did muster, Meola snuffed out high in his box. Mindful of what Maurice had dealt with, Meola donned a baseball cap in the second half to deal with a sun now even lower on the tropical horizon. Nineteen-year-old striker Dwight Yorke, the future Manchester United star who had just signed with Aston Villa, was subbed off after 76 ineffectual minutes. With 10 minutes to play, Russell Latapy nearly barged through the U.S. defense, in on goal. Stollmeyer's hard-but-clean slide tackle saved the day.

Not every U.S. tackle was so pristine that afternoon. Back in the 29th minute, U.S. centerback John Doyle appeared to take Philbert Jones down in the penalty area. Argentinian referee Juan Carlos Loustau was not bothered. No call. "If you go back through the T&T game and look at a few of the calls that were made, I don't know . . . you tell me," says Marcelo Balboa, who watched at home like the rest of us. "Go back and look at that game tape. In a normal game, some of those would have been red or yellow or a penalty. But things went our way — 100 percent, they went our way."

In the dying moments of a match so important, players dared not think, *Italy!* That would have been to tempt fate. Focus was instead maintained on the tasks at hand: the sure trap, the safe pass, the ultrasafe clearance. The mind fixated only on concrete matters: one's marking assignment, everyone else's marking assignments, the referee, his watch, the whistle . . . When that whistle finally made its way up toward Loustau's mouth, everything the players had tried *not* to contemplate rushed headlong into their frontal lobes. But the legs were the first to go.

"Everyone just fell down," Windischmann says. "You either put your hands to your head, or you fell to the ground. Or both! There was shock when that whistle blew, because we were waiting and waiting and waiting. It was: 'Oh my goodness, we are going to the World Cup!' It was unbelievable."

"I guess it was joy," Trittschuh says. "But I remember it more as just a feeling of total relief."

"I just stood still," Caligiuri remembers. "I wanted to absorb the celebration from our players and see the excitement from the nonstarters to the starters, guys laying on the ground, Meola jumping up and down going crazy. I just stood still and absorbed everything until I had a microphone in my face [asking] what it feels like. I don't remember what I said."

———••———

Maintaining a public stance of confidence and determination in the face of potential failure — something one does a bit for the press and public, but mainly for one's teammates — requires an enormous amount of psychic energy. Once that obligation is removed, and the possibility of failure has vanished, the mind goes blank. The body more or less shuts down. In the American celebration, any and all posturing fell away.

On the sideline, Gansler and his staff leaned into a group hug. One by one, they splintered off, wandered onto the field and helped players to their feet. They hugged them, too, and briefly milled about before ushering everyone off the field, down to the locker room beneath the concrete stands. There was no sign of trouble in those stands. The stadium crowd — drained by altogether different mental and emotional processes — slowly shuffled out.

Deep in the bowels of the National Stadium, the U.S. players hugged and wept, sang a little, and celebrated the biggest moment of their young lives. Champagne and cases of Budweiser were produced. Water, too. "It was a sauna in there," Gansler recalls.

According to Stollmeyer, "It was *so* hot down there, so humid. You're trying to drink water along with the champagne and beer. Down in the locker room, we let it all go. We were just in there singing. Pure elation. Some relief, too."

"By the time everybody got back to the hotel, everybody was so exhausted," Trittschuh reports. "We didn't even have a party that night. Everyone just sat by the pool."

"For us," Murray adds, "losing that game would have been such a disaster. All that you see now [in U.S. soccer] is because of what Paul Caligiuri did in Trinidad and Tobago. It's as simple as that, if you want to pin it to one specific moment. The '94 World Cup, MLS. He saved our ass. They should put Paul on a lifetime stipend. Seriously."

His impact *was* immediate. Richard Groff, then a USSF board member and later its treasurer, told *The New York Times* that very night, "We have a game [at] Stanford against the Soviets on Feb. 24. We have sold 25,000 seats. Now we'll sell 50,000. That is an extra quarter of a million dollars, right there." Calls into multinationals regarding potential sponsorship deals would begin the morning of Nov. 20, Groff added. For the record, the match at Stanford ended up drawing 61,000.

Not until later did the ridiculously thin margins of T&T's failure, America's feted qualification, and the entire Pentagonal's extraordinary results come into focus. A single conceded goal in any of the last four games — all nil-nil draws and 1-nil victories — would have kept the Americans from their 10th consecutive World Cup finals. The difference between success and failure was thinner than even this factoid conveys. Eighteen matches were played during the Pentagonal. Sixteen were decided by a single goal or finished in draws. Had group winner Costa Rica conceded an additional goal in any of *its* final four qualifiers, its fate would have depended on the Nov. 19 match in Port of Spain, as well. Goals were so scarce that eight men, none of them American, tied for the group "Golden Boot" as top scorers — each with just two goals apiece! Six Americans were among the 13 players who scored only once. They all shared runner-up honors.

The Man of the Match was one of many who, in the locker room, remained dehydrated and dizzy from exhaustion, overstimulation and wonder. Caligiuri guzzled some water before holding court among the small coterie of U.S. press who'd made the trip south to this small island off the coast of Venezuela.

"Everybody will say I scored the goal," Caligiuri told *New York Times* reporter George Vecsey, long an engaged soccer voice in a wilderness of U.S. media indifference. "But let's face it, this is a team game. We're getting better."

Caligiuri was not much of a talker. He would never prove a voluble or viable spokesman for this team or this generation. No one noticed or much cared prior to this moment in Port of Spain, when everything changed. Going forward, Caligiuri — the veteran of Torrance 1985, the NCAA champion, the first Yank to truly *play* abroad, the man whose goal changed the U.S. game forever — would initially be pressed into this public role. Eventually, it became clear the job of spokesperson simply did not suit him. Any and all comment on the state or future of U.S. soccer was better left to someone else.

George Vecsey could not have known all this, not in the bowels of the National Stadium, and so he did his job. Thoughts on Italy, Paul? "We older players, we believe in competition," Caligiuri answered, a bit cryptically. "We do so well in youth competition. This team can only get better."

What about the goal?

"The game plan was to put the ball on the wings and funnel it toward the goal," Cal explained. He smiled widely. "I went against the game plan."

The veteran sports writer pivoted back to the future his young subject had enabled roughly an hour earlier: What about Italy, the World Cup coming to America, the new professional league soon to be formed? And here Caligiuri *did* speak for his colleagues, succinctly but eloquently: "We just want to play in our own country."

The promise of the Youth Soccer Revolution, the phenomenon that moved Paul Caligiuri and his entire generation of boys and girls to kick soccer balls against garage doors, was precisely this simple and straightforward. They wanted to play soccer *in this country*: in its high schools, at the college level, and then professionally, should they develop the requisite skill. This is the expectation all American athletes harbored as kids in every other sport, save soccer, throughout the 20th century.

Largely through their efforts in Port of Spain, Caligiuri and his teammates would now get that opportunity — during an American *Mundial*, in a proper domestic league, in a footballing nation they built for themselves, and for generations to come. In the blink of an eye.

In another corner of the locker room stood Bob Gansler, nursing a can of beer, listening to the others rave and carry on. When the Federation would choose its coach for World Cup 1994, it looked elsewhere. When MLS designated eight teams and eight coaches for its inaugural season in 1996, Gansler was inexplicably absent. But he *would* take these Americans to Italy. Surveying the sweaty scene beneath the stands in Port of Spain, *el Mister* could not have known what was to come. And so Gansler soaked up the moment, the victory he helped create — lost in his own thoughts some of the time, pausing periodically to accept various congratulations, to hug someone, or to wipe still more perspiration from his brow. To a select few, he would smile and share his gift for wry understatement: "Just another game."

Match Day 8: Nov. 19, 1989: Trinidad and Tobago 0-1 USA [HT 0-1]
Port of Spain, Trinidad · National Stadium (30,000)

Scorer: Paul Caligiuri 32'

TRI: Michael Maurice, Clayton Morris, Brian Williams, Dexter Francis, Marvin Faustin, Russell Latapy, Leonson Lewis, Paul Elliot-Allen (Marlon Morris 60'), Philbert Jones, Dwight Yorke (Dexter Lee 76'), Kerry Jamerson

---

USA: Tony Meola, Steve Trittschuh, John Doyle, Mike Windischmann, Paul Krumpe (John Stollmeyer 61'), Paul Caligiuri, Brian Bliss, John Harkes, Tab Ramos, Peter Vermes, Bruce Murray

---

(Jon van Woerden photo)

February 6, 1990 · Vol. 38, No. 5 · Issue 946

$3.50 at newsstands

SoccerAmerica

America's Window on the Soccer World

ITALIA '90

SOCCER 1990 ON THE GO

(Image courtesy of Soccer America; Jon van Woerden photo, Jennifer Cox artwork)

12. ARRIVEDERCI, AMERICA!

(January to May 1990)

The Missouri city of Kirksville, population 17,530, is the Adair County seat and home to Truman State University, which, until 1996, went by a more geographical moniker, Northeast Missouri State University. Founded in 1857, this rural municipality derives its name from Jesse Kirk, a local tavern keeper who cannily parlayed his provision of food, lodging and whiskey to federal surveyors and railroad types into this small but lasting measure of fame. Early in June 1990, during yet another passive-aggressive engagement with international soccer media in Florence, Italy, U.S. Men's National Team coach Bob Gansler might well have conjured fleeting thoughts of Kirksville, until recently the bucolic training ground for one of his top-choice defenders.

To the larger futbol world, the team Gansler brought to Italy remained a curiosity. They arrived at the World Cup after a 40-year absence, sporting a roster filled with what European journalists believed to be a bunch of college kids. This wasn't exactly true, as Gansler repeatedly attempted to explain. A few were indeed college age; others were fresh out. All were, by this time, young professionals, even if employed by the U.S. Soccer Federation. However, as Gansler was repeatedly obliged to confirm, the United States of America was home to no formal, national futbol league. The North American Soccer League had folded in 1984; the European football press understood this. They also grasped that nothing of substance — nothing resembling the first-division leagues that existed in every country across Europe, no matter how small — had since replaced it. This is what confused the ink-stained wretches in Italy. While minnows arrived at World Cup finals every quadrennial, this peculiar American scenario didn't compute. Hence their decision to label the entirety of Generation Zero a collection of college kids. That reduction made sense to them, whereas the actual narrative — that some labored in obscure corners of Europe, while others played with semipro clubs in ethnic leagues and the nascent, substandard American Professional Soccer League — did not.

Professional leagues aren't a mere vanity, after all. They are vital environments for player development. They represent the default systems by which domestic professionals train, maintain match fitness, and earn money between World Cups. It therefore struck media and much of the international futbol community as ridiculous that the world's lone superpower, its largest economy and dominant culture — the country slated to host the next World Cup! — couldn't be bothered to maintain a legitimate professional league.

And here's where Gansler — his mind perhaps drifting a bit in the face of still more impertinent questioning — might have summoned thoughts of Kirksville, Missouri, and John Stollmeyer, his stalwart and versatile defensive midfielder. Instead of honing his skills ahead of *Italia '90* as part of a professional club team in an established American soccer league, Stollmeyer had essentially trained himself alone, in the agricultural landscape of northeast Missouri.

"I was living in Kirksville because my wife was in med school there," Stollmeyer recalls. "I'd run in the morning — out in the cornfields! — do my morning workout, then hang out around the apartment, train again in the evening. This was my prep for Italy, pretty much all of 1989, before and after we qualified. I'd be in Missouri, and the Federation would fly me in to train prior to matches. I'd catch a five-seater out of Kirksville to Kansas City, then catch a real plane out of town.

"At one point, I'm training down at Northeast Missouri State — against some wall, by myself — and I can see a team over there, a couple hundred yards away. Finally some assistant coach comes over and says, 'Who are you?' At first, I didn't tell him my name or what I was doing — he wanted to know if I was a student there! Because here I am, knocking the ball around with some skill . . . I ended up being a volunteer assistant with the team. I'd play with the scrubs, and we'd beat the starters, the varsity, because nobody could stop me once I got the ball. Anytime those kids were playing, I'd play. *That's* how I got ready for the World Cup. You think [Jurgen] Klinsmann would go for that?"

Stollmeyer spoke with me in 2017, when Klinsmann was still the USMNT *fußballtrainer*. Of course, no latter-day national team coach would brook such freelancing, absence of professionalism, or lack of institutional commitment. Gansler went along with Stollmeyer's nontraditional training regimen because he had little choice. Truth be told, each member of the American team lived his own version of the Kirksville scenario — perhaps nothing so solitary or quixotic as Stolly's, but equally improbable and amateurish so far as the international soccer media was concerned. While Stollmeyer ran through cornfields and schooled actual college kids, Mike Windischmann spent 1989 playing indoors — a soccer milieu he despised and saw as degrading to his skills — for the MISL's Los Angeles Lazers. In between qualifying matches and attendant training sessions, he split time between the Brooklyn Italians in New York City's Cosmopolitan League and the Albany Capitals in the A-League. Brian Bliss played for the Capitals, too, mixing in weekend games with weekday appearances for ethnic clubs and random instructor gigs at youth soccer camps.

These were the finest soccer players in the richest country on Earth. And yet, when they weren't with the national team, their professional situations paled beside those of their counterparts in Italy, in Czechoslovakia, in El Salvador. "As players," Peter Vermes explains, "we always had to figure out how to stay fit when we didn't have a full-time league nor the right environment to train. We had to find a way to be successful."

Gansler knew all this, of course. He may have recognized that it was a compelling back story, catnip to futbol media anywhere outside the U.S. But he shared few of these details with World Cup media, who, to be fair, took special interest in the Yanks and their strange backgrounds because these "college kids" would eventually face the host nation during the group stage. Take it from an old newspaperman: The USMNT back story, warts and all, would have made for great copy. At that time, Italy boasted three daily newspapers devoted entirely to sport. Soccer (or *calcio*, meaning "kick") led all three of those papers every day, even when *Il Mondiale* wasn't taking place across the length and breadth of their country.

Still, the U.S. manager had no interest in playing the role of "today's oddity." He saw no percentage in it. Not for *his* team. Gansler had never been a fan of the press. A lifetime devoted to American soccer — where the media's primary role was posing ignorant questions, punctuated by long stretches of utter indifference — will do that to a guy.

"The question they asked over and over again was, 'Well, do you have a league?' Um, no, we don't have a league," Gansler divulges with a weary smile. "'Well, how do you prepare them?' They kept asking me this, so I kept telling them: A week on, a week off, two weeks on, then a week off . . . And they all said, 'Oh no — you're not telling the truth!'"

There was a measure of admiration for what Gansler and his team had achieved in their unconventional way. The Italian press corps in particular was delighted with Paul Caligiuri's heritage. Tony Meola's, as well. The media generally loves an underdog. It was unquestionably a feat to have qualified this group of players for a World Cup. But there was often a mocking tone to the questioning, too, one tinged with cynicism — for the U.S. was indeed the world's wealthiest nation.

"Will the U.S. have a first-division league by the time it hosts the World Cup in four years?" the writers asked Gansler. "Had Mexico been banned from 1990 qualifying to ensure American qualification? With FIFA, it's not a question whether strings were pulled, but which ones were pulled exactly?"

"When they learned I was American," wrote *Sports Illustrated*'s Michael Mewshaw in June 1990, "many of the Italians I talked to . . . asked how much the U.S. had paid Trinidad and Tobago to lie down and lose its last qualifying match last November, allowing Team USA to play in the World

Cup finals for the first time since 1950. To the Italian mind, the notion that a wealthy nation would buy its way into the World Cup is perfectly logical."

This line of thought is exactly what Gansler heard from European media, explicitly and between the lines. It pissed him off. For the sake of their story assignments, he wasn't about to take the bait and wax poetic about Stollmeyer's road work amid the cornfields of Kirksville, Missouri, or Eric Wynalda's course load at San Diego State, or the odd jobs half his team held down to make ends meet. He wasn't about to further illuminate, for anyone, just how truly bush league American soccer had become post-NASL. If he had, his message to Italian futbol writers would have been yet more succinct and intriguing: *You bastards don't know the half of it.*

————

Three short weeks after the triumph in Port of Spain, the futbol world gathered in Rome for the World Cup draw. The Italians had not hosted since 1934, and they missed no opportunities to accentuate the event's pomp, circumstance and specific Italianate qualities. Actress Sophia Loren, still damned glamorous at 55 but wearing a surprisingly sensible red dress, assisted FIFA master of ceremonies Sepp Blatter in retrieving pingpong balls from the various hoppers, although not before tenor Luciano Pavarotti, fronting a small symphony orchestra, had warmed up the global television audience with a stirring rendition of "Nessun Dorma." This aria, from Puccini's *Turandot*, was already part of the operatic canon. Pavarotti's performance here, however, is specifically credited with taking it to new, broader heights. He and fellow tenors Placido Domingo and Jose Carreras issued a new recording shortly thereafter; it appeared on their bestselling album, *The Three Tenors in Concert*. The BBC cemented the aria's association with world futbol by deploying "Nessun Dorma" as the theme song of its *Italia '90* coverage. Its performance was included in formal ceremonies at the next three World Cups.

The Italians broke new ground with this enhanced level of stagecraft. Where previous draws had been methodical, somewhat solemn affairs marked only by the occasional hopper malfunction (1982), the Italians put on a *show* — one that branded *their* tournament as something specifically and uniquely Italian. Ensuing draws attempted to follow suit, with limited success, resulting in ever-stranger juxtapositions of culture and celebrity. World Cup 1994 in Las Vegas was a sign of things to come, as Franz Beckenbauer, Evander Holyfield and Robin Williams all shared the stage. The 2010 ceremony stands out for sheer star mass: Charlize Theron, David Beckham, F.W. de Klerk, Archbishop Desmond Tutu, Beckenbauer, Michel Platini, Eusébio, Roger Milla — and Nelson Mandela via pre-taped video address.

Back in Rome, once the seeded teams were affixed to the top of each group, it didn't take long for the Americans to learn their fate. Ms. Loren chose "USA" first among the remaining 18 lower-seeded pingpong balls, meaning the Americans were paired with the hosts in Group A, based in Rome and Florence. The completed draw produced no shortage of intriguing storylines to follow: the Argentinians based in Naples, home to Diego Maradona's club Napoli; the English shipped off to Sardinia and the Dutch to Sicily, where their rowdy fans might do no broader damage. If the pingpong balls had placed the U.S. less visibly, perhaps with the seeded Belgians in Verona, as USSF officials had hoped, the young Americans might have come and gone from this tournament quietly, just as the United Arab Emirates and South Koreans did. No such luck.

For their part, the hosts could not have been more pleased. Italian eyes were firmly fixed on the July 8 final: Some 700,000 requests had already been submitted for the 79,571 seats in Rome's *Stadio Olimpico*. Winning Group A would also mean a second-round match there in Rome. Drawing a minnow like the U.S. only made that prospect more attainable.

"Italy is favored, and the Czechs and the Austrians are very capable," Gansler told the assembled media horde. "They have a big edge in experience, but their style of soccer is no stranger to us. At this level there are no poor teams, only good teams and better ones. We're delighted to be here. This is a fantastic experience for us: the excitement, the tension, the level of competition. We need the challenge, we need the experience."

Today, Vermes can say what Gansler and his team knew at the time but could not admit — even to themselves: "We knew down deep inside that it would be an incredible challenge to participate against the European teams. We had developed a style that actually put Central American teams under a lot of pressure. But the makeup of our team *resembled* the European teams — and they were just so much more experienced and sharp and technical. They were superior. Tactically, they were so much more adept. They were just better players. So, for us to come away with a miracle, if you will (like the 1980 Olympic hockey team), it would truly take something special. And you know what? We nearly pulled off something like that."

When Blatter and Loren waved their goodbyes, the U.S. opener was six months away. That first match would be played against Czechoslovakia in Florence on June 10, 1990. Four days later, the opponent would be Italy, in Rome, followed by Austria, back in Florence, on June 19.

American reactions to the draw were almost entirely media driven. This is the Fourth Estate's sober, objective role almost everywhere, of course — everywhere outside England, where sportswriters and broadcasters freely display rooting interests and the over-hyping of English World Cup chances has been raised to high art. But here in the colonies, during the winter of 1989-90, the Shot Heard 'Round the World had yet to influence the currency of barstool banter and watercooler gossip.

The responsibility for getting Americans up to speed fell to the media, and special retroactive commendation should be reserved for folks like Bob Ley at ESPN and George Vecsey at the *New York Times*, whose interest in U.S. soccer was evident before Port of Spain. Although cheering from the press box is frowned upon in U.S. sports media circles, these two guys were clearly excited about finally covering a tournament involving their native country. They weren't alone. Clive Gammon produced some lovely features for *Sports Illustrated* ahead of the event; the magazine's tournament coverage, mainly from Mewshaw and Richard O'Brien, would prove solid and artful. My hometown *Boston Globe* employed a fellow named Frank Dell'Apa on the soccer beat, and he did wonderful work, as I recall.

No such commendation will be awarded to many of Ley's former colleagues, however. The level of snark exhibited on ESPN, especially from the likes of assorted *SportsCenter* hosts, proved gratuitous. Keith Olbermann and Brett Haber topped the list, but there were many others: unrepentant, willfully ignorant, soccer-dismissing Baby Boomers all. Turner Network Television won the right to serve as the sole English-language broadcaster to the U.S. market. It planned to beam 33 live matches into American homes — the most ever. (Spanish-language network Univision broadcast all 52 matches live from Italy.) TNT and ESPN were cable competitors, of course. Even though ESPN had broadcast several 1989 qualifiers, plus 14 matches live from Mexico '86, its on-air personalities had corporate incentives to run down or otherwise slight the 1990 World Cup.

"There was a hostile response to it in the press generally," *Soccer America*'s Mike Woitalla recollects. "In many ways it was phobic. I don't know if it was that soccer was something these cigar-smoking, horse-racing, boxing, baseball guys simply didn't understand, or how much was racist and how much was just making fun of people's names, which I just hate. It's so childish. And then, that kind of just went away, the soccer-bashing. Just disappeared. You rarely see it these days, but back in the Eighties and early Nineties, you had guys writing whole columns making fun of soccer. Today, your typical reporter probably has a son or daughter who plays soccer and is less inclined to mock it."

Here's an example of my favorite, widely held, anti-soccer media trope from this period. It was written by then-*Baltimore Sun* columnist Ray Frager (b. 1957) who, upon learning that ESPN and ABC would broadcast live matches from USA '94, without commercial interruption, had this to say: "What kind of television is this? We all know that only PBS goes without commercials. And we've all known for a long time just how un-American those people are."

Tongue-in-cheek? Probably. Comments like these tend to expose an oversensitivity within the soccer community itself. I readily cop to that charge. Even today, a casual observation or critique (*"You know what this game needs . . ."*) tends to transport some of us back to junior high school, when our devotion required explaining or defending. Nevertheless, we never anticipated that Boomer sportswriters valued commercials so highly.

As Woitalla points out, Gen Zero's own defensiveness has dissipated to the point of nonexistence. As with so many things futbol in America, the tipping point was 1990.

"By then I truly did see the day coming when soccer in America would be huge," Vermes maintains. "Now, I didn't know exactly what that meant at the time. If, back then, you told me Kansas City would be a soccer mecca in the U.S., with 36 sellouts in a row and a soccer-specific stadium and so forth, I never could have understood what that meant. But I always saw the possibilities in this country, and I always felt it was coming. It just never got its respect on a professional level and even more so from a media perspective — because they were so indoctrinated into the three major sport mentality here. It was almost as if it was sacrilegious to mention the word soccer next to those other sports, when soccer was the international game and everyone else played it around the world! It was difficult to fight that fight. But I truly believed the game would find itself here."

SHORTLY AFTER THE WORLD CUP DRAW, in December 1989, the Federation called Gansler's core roster to New York City. Everyone — Gansler, his staff, the administrators, all the players — knew precisely why they'd been summoned, although no one knew exactly what to expect. "We had to sign another contract," Trittschuh explains, "because it was the start of another year."

The team had been retained via annual contracts with U.S. Soccer since 1988, but the 1990 contract would be different. Trittschuh and his teammates had, after all, just delivered to their Federation a literal bonanza: the ultimate prize, the keys to the kingdom, a guaranteed pathway to a World Cup *in the United States*, to a meaningful place at the American sporting table, to a seat at FIFA's global table — things about which the

U.S. soccer establishment had only dared to dream the previous 40 years. Qualification for *Italia* '90 had also earned the perennially cash-poor Federation $1.4 million in guaranteed money from FIFA, or so World Cup '94 Organizing Committee president Scott LeTellier told the *L.A. Times*.

In return, the players were desperate to secure places on the *Italia* '90 roster. They also wanted to *play* at the World Cup, to showcase their skills to clubs across Europe and around the world. These were competitive decisions Bob Gansler would make. From the Federation, the players sought altogether different things: They wanted to be taken seriously and treated as actual internationals, a recurring gripe and a source of tension between U.S. players and their Federation stretching back to 1969. Most of all, they wanted to be rewarded financially for all they had done — for themselves, for the Federation, for American soccer.

Yet this trip to NYC proved to be no bargaining session, as the players quickly discovered.

"They gave us the contracts, and we either signed them or we left. There wasn't any negotiation. They said, 'This is it,'" Stollmeyer remembers. "They knew that we would play for free, ultimately, because it's the World Cup. I mean, who wouldn't? Actually, there might have been some players who would not play for free ... But there were enough of us, even though we were clearly getting screwed, who would play for free. They had us over a barrel."

The Federation invited 16 players to the Upper East Side offices of the law firm then representing the USSF. One at a time, players received the tendered offers. There were no negotiations. Contract values were not uniform; they ranged between $26,000 and $40,000 per year, per player — meaning they were essentially unchanged from the 1989 contracts. No bonuses. Many players balked — at the lowball figures, at the absence of bonuses, at the heavy-handed, arbitrary nature of the exercise. The Federation was unmoved. It gave players until Jan. 14 to sign on the dotted line.

"When we qualified," Stollmeyer continues, "they had told us at the time they would take care of us. When we went in for contracts, it was basically a take-it-or-leave-it deal. That was really disappointing. That led to Caligiuri and those guys holding out, not signing those contracts. Caligiuri and Vanole. There were a lot of hard feelings between the players and the Federation. They were basically saying, 'You're replaceable.' They didn't care. They felt they could put anyone on the field in Italy."

Adds Trittschuh: "A few of the guys did feel they were being bulldozed by the Federation."

Members of the 21st-century U.S. Women's National Team can surely relate to this historical moment. Their serial pay disputes with the Federation, broached in earnest after yet another world title in 2015, also stem from their primary employment arrangements, not with individual clubs but with the U.S. Soccer Federation itself. American male professionals during the late 1980s sought money and security from the Federation precisely because club soccer in the U.S. at that time was so amateurish and impoverished. American female professionals sought Federation patronage for the same reasons — women's club soccer in the U.S. today being a pretty good comp for the men's club scene during the George H.W. Bush administration.

The USWNT settled its compensation suit with the USSF in February of 2022, but the point remains: Federations aren't designed to employ a nation's best footballers 365 days a year. Should one do so, out of necessity, application of the Federation's lopsided bargaining leverage is sure to leave all parties disgruntled when revenues are disbursed. In the men's game, it took the establishment of Major League Soccer to render full-time, annual Federation contracts obsolete. It will take the development of women's club soccer — in North America or, more likely, in Europe — to fully resolve the same issues.

Caligiuri and Vanole were the first holdouts that winter of 1990. Harkes and Meola joined them; curiously, both were given extensions on the Jan. 14 deadline. Harkes had already elicited interest from a then-as-yet-unnamed English first-division side. He argued privately to the Federation that the tryout made his timely review of the contract impossible. Meola's extension went unexplained, and some on the team subsequently viewed these extensions as special treatment. Others saw fit to grouse when Meola, Harkes, Hugo Perez and Tab Ramos received $250 apiece to film World Cup promo spots for TNT. Such internal sniping soon threatened to undermine the two things Gansler's squad had going for it, what had been this USMNT's primary strengths since May 1987: morale and cohesion.

Throughout the tumultuous month of January 1990, the team trained together in San Diego. Gansler, caught in the middle of all this fractious behavior, naturally feared how this dissension might affect his ranks. Fighting the Federation was one thing. Fighting amongst themselves was another. It was well known how close he remained to Federation president Werner Fricker, but Gansler did his best to support the guys, his team. He formed a five-player committee to report and funnel grievances to him so that he might better make their respective cases to the Federation.

Just when it seemed the contract situation was stabilizing — the widespread resentment and four holdouts notwithstanding — out walked the team to practice one late January morning. Gansler was waiting for them, the warm San Diego sun still low in the eastern sky. He approached several players, took one look at their boots and said, "You can't wear those."

———·◆·———

"I was one of the original Puma Three," Paul Krumpe explains. "It was Hugo, myself and Vanole who signed with Puma a whole year before those other guys, in 1988. Here's what the problem was: We had to sign those Federation contracts prior to the World Cup, and if you didn't sign that contract, you were not going to be invited to play on the national team — or so we were told. Adidas had an all-program deal with the Federation: Adidas head to toe. And so, we were not allowed to wear our own brand of shoe at the time."

Personal shoe contracts strike one as unremarkable today. They can change from one season to the next regardless of what sponsorship a club or federation might have struck with an outfitter. In fact, these dynamics

were commonplace back in 1990 as well. "I had my own personal contract with Adidas from back in my indoor days," Stollmeyer recalls. "I
would say it was less than five grand, annually, and all the gear I wanted."

Behold the power of *Il Mondiale*. Puma signed those original three in
'88 because *Italia '90* was approaching, and the Yanks had a chance at
qualifying. What's more, whenever Puma had the chance to poke Adidas
in the eye, it did so. With relish. After Port of Spain, the USMNT was a demonstrably hotter property from a marketing standpoint. With the team's
worldwide exposure assured, Puma swooped in and signed another eight
American players. The German outfitter wasn't doing anything it hadn't
been doing for decades. Puma's epic, internecine struggle with Adidas was
ongoing, and Adidas just happened to sponsor Team USA.

The choice of *internecine* here could not be more literal. Two brothers,
Rudolf and Adolf Dassler, founded the corporate forebear of both Adidas
and Puma in 1919. Their company, Gebruder Dassler, was based in the
small Bavarian town of Herzogenaurach. "Gede," as it was known, thrived
on the strength of its pioneering place in the German sports apparel market, its two-stripe designs and several gold medal performances at the
1936 Berlin Olympics. When Rudolf was drafted into WWII, Adolf stayed
home to oversee Gede's conversion to a military outfitter. Rudolf survived
the war but spent 1946 in an Allied prison camp; when he returned home,
the two started production again, together. Shortly thereafter, however,
everything went terribly wrong. Some alleged that Adolf had turned his
brother in to Allied authorities. Others insinuated that something untoward
went down between Rudolf and his brother's wife. No one knows for sure;
relatives have *never* spoken on the subject. But the fraternal split proved
irrevocable. Rudolf founded Puma in 1947, on the north side of the Aurach
River. Adolf founded Adidas a year later, south of the river. For decades,
Herzogenaurach remained divided along these brand lines, between *pu-
maraners* and *adidasslers*, each sponsoring their own local football clubs,
for example. There existed Adidas pubs and Puma pubs, Adidas families
and Puma families. When meeting on the street, townsfolk developed the
habit of looking down to see who wore what — so they might tribalize

accordingly. The brothers died in the 1970s, and these local idiosyncrasies calmed down. A bit. To this day, both multinational companies remain fierce rivals. They also remain headquartered in Herzogenaurach, *Stadt der Sportfeinde,* "the town of sporting rivals," where the mixing and matching of gear is still considered bad form. Natives wear one brand or the other.

"I think the Puma deal was 10 grand a year," Krumpe says, "and for me that was obviously big money at the time. For a young guy making $30,000 a year as a professional player? 'Hey, here's an additional 10 grand'? That's a big deal. But even more important for me, I had issues with my feet. I had that stress fracture. Puma shoes at the time were wider and more comfortable."

The additional eight Puma signings came to light immediately after World Cup qualifying had concluded, when Puma saw the chance to get some actual exposure via the USMNT *and* stick it to Adidas. "Puma gave us, I think, $10,000," confirms Windischmann, Gansler's captain. "We were approached about signing Puma contracts. They gave us boots, but they gave us equipment, too. At the time, Adidas wasn't giving us stuff like that, so it's kind of hard to say no."

Once the Federation had strong-armed players into those '90 contracts and Caligiuri, Vanole, Harkes and Meola chose to hold out for reasons unrelated to the shoes, the shit really hit the fan. The Puma XI, as they came to be known, argued their case to the Federation. They asked why individual players should not be allowed to supplement their income with shoe contracts of their own choosing. Once again, the Federation listened but didn't budge. So the XI retained an attorney, Howard Weitzman, a prominent lawyer who later represented O.J. Simpson in the early stages of his indictment (which would take place smack dab in the middle of USA '94). Matters deteriorated from there.

"Every time we were in Miami, the lawyers were there fighting the Federation about the endorsement deal," Meola remembers. "Those guys fought the Federation for what seems, today, like nothing. You turn on the TV today, *everyone* is wearing their own shoes. They're the tools of your trade! Not back then, not in 1990. Those guys risked everything, risked throwing away their World Cups. It took the rest of us to tell the Federation, 'Hey, we really need these guys.'"

Throughout this winter of discontent, Fricker took the hard line and never wavered, not on the basic contracts and not on the boots. The U.S. Soccer Federation did not have a surplus of money at this time — it had not been able to parlay its place at *Il Mondiale* into much corporate sponsorship so soon after Port of Spain. Not yet. "When we qualified for the World Cup," Gansler told me, "our Federation president, Werner Fricker, put up his Philadelphia construction company as collateral to back a loan that got us some more money. I finally said to the players, 'This isn't the German federation or the Brazil federation or Argentina. This is *us*.'"

How did these USMNT dissidents even find Howard Weitzman? The short answer is, Paul Caligiuri. He had recently met Shelli Azoff, the wife of music-industry mogul Irving Azoff. She persuaded her entertainment-lawyer friends to help Caligiuri and the team negotiate their contracts and shoe deals. She also persuaded a collection of national team players to perform an original World Cup '90 song, "Victory," and produce an accompanying music video. This is what sports teams did in advance of showcase events back then. While the trifling performance has been preserved for posterity on YouTube, virtually no one saw it in the moment. Which may have been for the best.

"We thought that rap video was gonna catch a wave or something, and people were gonna know us," Des Armstrong told *The New Yorker* in 2014. "But nobody cared. It wasn't like, 'Hey, I saw you in the video, man, that was great!' . . . No one even noticed."

Few outside the national team program noticed the Federation's hard-line stances on contracts and shoe deals, either. However, it made a big and lasting impression within the team. They felt the USSF had promised to compensate them appropriately — only to renege. When players started looking out for themselves financially, via the shoe contracts, the

Federation took that prerogative away, too. In each case, USSF made it clear: Get in line, or risk your place in Italy.

"The first guy they didn't call into training was Vanole," Meola reports. "They said, 'Aw, he's not the same player he was, not good enough for the team anymore.' And I'm like, hold on: Not even two years ago he was voted the best goalkeeper at the Olympics. What's going on here? Then we started to realize what was happening."

"I'll be honest," Marcelo Balboa remembers, "the whole thing freaked a lot of us younger guys out. We didn't know what to do. We were so young. We were thrilled to get free shoes. Adidas was the Federation sponsor, so we kinda just sat back and played the safe thing — and stayed with Adidas — because we knew we had no pull. We had no rights. But there was real division in that team, at that time."

According to Murray, "The situation was so rudimentary at that time. It really was. The Federation offered contracts. Some guys signed them. Some guys didn't. Some contracts were low. Some were decent. Some had special money attached, and some didn't. Then there were side deals and shoe deals. Everyone was on their own. If you add up what I was making before 1990, when those contracts were offered, I was probably making six figures. But the only way to make it work was *being* on the national team."

Over time, the Federation broke the will of all dissenters, plain and simple. Its position proved too strong. The lure of World Cup participation, to all the players, was too strong. "We all stuck together as a group for a while, until everybody finally went their own way," Trittschuh says. "I wanted to play in the World Cup. What else were we going to do?"

Adds Krumpe: "At my age, without an outdoor pro league to play in, there was no choice but to say 'yes' to the contract. There was a lot of dissension, but at some point you have to decide, 'I'd like to be able to continue to wear these shoes and make this money — but I want to play in a World Cup.' There were sacrifices to be made, including wearing Adidas."

Stollmeyer remains typically direct on the matter: "They knew that we would play for free, ultimately, because it's the World Cup. Even though we were getting screwed, enough of us would have played for free."

The temptation is to read all this and conclude, *Aha! Well, THAT is the reason Hugo Perez and Ricky Davis — two veterans, two longtime Puma guys, two seasoned pros who were accustomed to getting paid for their services on and off the field — didn't go to Italy.*

"I mean, the most controversial thing Bob Gansler ever did was not bring the old pros," Woitalla says, flatly. "He didn't take Hugo Perez! Didn't take one of the best players in the history of American soccer! Used them both in qualifying but not in Italy. He took a bunch of college kids. I still think that's a questionable move — not taking Hugo Perez."

Was that just more fallout from the Puma XI situation? "I don't know," Woitalla answers. "If Gansler wanted Perez he would have been there. He didn't want him. I mean, I like Bob. I respect him. But I think in the end he was just more comfortable with the college kids."

Parsing consequences from the Puma affair tends to produce these juxtapositions of the circumstantial and the actual. However, when all these individual cases are examined on their own, it doesn't appear as if Gansler or the Federation really punished *anyone* for their contract or footwear choices. In the end, even Vanole was brought back into the fold as the *third* keeper, when it would have been awfully easy for Gansler and the Federation to leave him home.

"Vanole was kind of surprised that he was brought to Italy, because he was the last one to sign," Krumpe admits. "And I'm pretty sure there was a provision at the time: If one of your two keepers got hurt, you could make arrangements to bring in a third keeper. But Dino was such a part of the team that Gansler felt it was important to include him on the roster."

I went around and around the Puma subject with all these Gen Zero guys. Often, they echoed each other's thoughts, and that scans: They were all in the same boat, for the most part. What resentment they once held for the Federation seems long ago abandoned. Of course, the USSF staff and board have turned over myriad times since then.

Early in my conversations with each of the players, I made sure to ask whether they felt the '90 team had been overlooked through the years.

This was my contention, and pretty much everyone on the team agreed. However, to my surprise, players returned to that theme when we discussed the Puma XI. "I always point to the sponsorship-driven aspect of it," Stollmeyer told me. "Nike took over in 1998, and Adidas was the primary sponsor prior to that. Nike doesn't want people talking about or showing video of guys running around in Adidas."

Wait — *what?*

"I think that's a big deal, much bigger than people realize," Krumpe explains. "It's just my opinion, but our group doesn't get as much notice because that was an Adidas team. Think about it: Why, when they show clips of national teams in the past, why would Nike want to show anything from '90 or '94 — in those Adidas uniforms?"

Well, those denim uniforms from 1994 were hideous, but point taken.

"They're gonna want to focus on '98 and beyond, when Nike was the primary sponsor," Krumpe continues. "I don't know how much of a deal that is, but I think it does have an impact. We see fewer videos and pictures of those games, less attention is paid to those teams from those eras, because we were wearing Adidas stuff."

Soccer is an exceedingly brand-centric sport. The addition of Nike to the bitter Puma/Adidas rivalry, starting in the late 1980s, only served to ratchet up the competition between brands and increase their demands of fealty from sponsored federations. Still, it had never occurred to me that logos on shirts and shoes might affect the way a particular USMNT is or is not remembered institutionally by a federation, and in turn by a country's soccer-loving citizens.

Bruce Murray remains skeptical: "Sounds like 'two shooters on the grassy knoll' to me. Who knows? I mean, yes: Sponsorship politics does exist at the higher levels. But you're not talking to a guy who's smart enough to address stuff like that. I was just a dummy who could score goals."

According to Marcelo Balboa, going from Puma to Adidas was no worse than later going from Adidas to Nike. "A lot of players got caught in the middle of that, too," he contends. "I remember as a kid, I had a poster of Ricky Davis running down the beach with a damn Puma, you know what I mean? He was a Puma guy already, way back then. Let's be honest, we all looked up to Ricky at the time: the NASL guy, the Cosmos guy, the face of American soccer. I would have thought, as a kid, that Ricky Davis and Hugo Perez were gonna be on that squad."

Did this Puma business play a role in their being left off? I thought he got hurt that spring, playing for Red Star in Paris?

"You know, that's a great question for Bob."

But Gansler also sidestepped the issue. What I learned on that subject, I related in Chapter 10. Clearly, not everyone has made peace with how it all went down that winter of 1989-90.

"To me, there's a lot of hard feelings still, among players, with the Federation," Stollmeyer contends. "You asked earlier, why this generation of guys and not those? Think about Hugo. Why did he not push harder, push all the way through? Well, he was tired of the B.S. Even guys who work now in the Federation, or with the Federation: I bet if you put them behind closed doors with the rest of us, they'd tell you they wouldn't trust those Federation guys as far as they could throw them. I don't. This whole thing, what went on that winter — that the 1990 team is almost *never* talked about: Why? Why is the Federation so quiet about the 1990 team? Maybe it's the Nike thing. But maybe it's also because they treated us so poorly and they don't want that out there. At that time, they had us over a barrel, and that's how they treated us."

IN THE AUTUMN OF 1989, I took a job as sports editor of two midsize daily papers in central Massachusetts, the *Marlboro Enterprise* and the *Hudson Daily Sun*. These two communities both sat on Interstate 495, Boston's outer ring road, a massive semicircle that would eventually accommodate much of the state's burgeoning tech industry. However, this economic transformation had not yet gone down by 1990. When I arrived, Marlboro and Hudson still sat on either side of the Assabet River, each community decaying and in search of reinvention, as former mill towns continue to do across New England.

Just 25 years old, I inherited a 60-something, functioning-alcoholic assistant sports editor, Bob Pryor, who made Keith Olbermann and his Boomer colleagues at ESPN seem positively enlightened about futbol by comparison. We got along well enough. We both loved sports, golf in particular. Our young staff forever baited poor Bob, who at the slightest provocation could be counted on to spout all manner of hair-trigger, ill-conceived, bigoted and sexist philosophies.

At his core, Bob Pryor wasn't a bad guy, but he did embody all the distinctly American pathologies of a late-century-media soccer hater. As I settled into my new job, Caligiuri and the USMNT would soon deliver the Shot Heard 'Round the World. Naturally, I started pulling Associated Press stories on the team and the upcoming World Cup for my sports section, which led with local coverage but included Boston and national coverage, too. Marlboro in particular had gone hog wild for soccer the previous 20 years, as so many communities had. Both high schools were central Mass. powers. Marlboro had already produced a future USMNTer, then-19-year-old Mike Burns. Hudson had its own LASA club, Hudson Benfica, over whom I always made an editorial fuss. Bob rolled his eyes at that coverage but was galled most of all by *Italia '90* content. This brand of generational drama played out in newsrooms across the country that winter of 1990.

Despite my access to everything issued by AP and my craving for all soccer news, I knew nothing of the contract and Puma-related issues then roiling the Italy-bound national team. That soap opera *would* have made great talk-show subject matter that February, when I cold-called producers at the Boston-based Sports Radio Network, one of the earliest attempts at nationally syndicated sports talk. I offered myself up as a soccer expert. Lo and behold, they brought me in over the phone. I appeared half a dozen times that spring to preview the World Cup alongside Neil Roberts, then head soccer coach at Boston University. The radio stint was good fun, although it failed to launch a lucrative career in on-air soccer punditry.

Neither did I know that Tom Wadlington had already made plans to make another pilgrimage, this time to Italy itself, for that summer's tournament.

"So, there was a guy who played soccer with me out in Berkeley; he captained the St. Mary's College team: Scott Wilkinson," Pilgrim Tom explains. "Basically, a full year before the World Cup he came to me and said, 'I know how to order tickets way in advance from the U.S. Soccer Federation, and I'm doing it. If you want in, I'm gonna need 1,200 bucks from you by Oct. 31 [1989] to put the order in.'"

Tom features prominently in these pages because we played soccer together — often two seasons each calendar year — between the ages of 8 and 18. He had been a pretty close friend, if a bit of a frenemy, through junior high school. At Wellesley High, however, we did not hang much at all. When I went off to Wesleyan and he to Berkeley, we had no contact whatsoever for more than a decade. Only in 1995 did we reconnect when business took me to San Francisco. We fell back in immediately and without effort. Wad and I would eventually travel a great deal together, mainly on soccer-themed trips to England. These began when I was researching a feature story for ESPN.com regarding those Yank-laden Fulham FC teams of the early 2000s. Due to his outgoing nature, Pilgrim Tom was subsequently pulled deep into the Fulham vortex. He remains strongly tied to the subculture that revolves, online and off, around Craven Cottage, south London home to FFC since 1896. This highly outgoing nature is something you need to know about the adult Tom Wadlington: Whereas he was always a prickly kid, a provocateur with authority issues, he grew into one of the friendliest guys you'd ever hope to meet. Almost too friendly. You really can't leave the man alone in a pub for more than five minutes, for example, lest he strike up a conversation with some geezer who can't be shaken — so warmly has Tom received him in the space of a single trip to the loo.

Tom's girlfriend at the time ultimately could not make the World Cup trip. With an extra ticket, Wadlington proved an irresistible social force across the breadth of Italy during that summer of 1990. If you happened to be watching Bob Neal and former Falcons placekicker Mick Luckhurst on TNT that afternoon of June 10, just before the USMNT kicked off its tournament against Czechoslovakia, and you saw a young man running back and forth behind the goal, a giant American flag draped about his head and shoulders — well, you're already familiar with Tom's work.

The Italian futbol scene Tom Wadlington and the USMNT encountered in June of 1990, while arguably at its competitive zenith, also suffered from considerable fan disaffection. Most of the 39 killed during the 1985 Heysel Stadium disaster had been Italians, the result of fan-on-fan violence, specifically English-fan-on-Italian-fan violence. Many believe this incident — prior to a European Cup final in Belgium — contributed to the growth of Italy's own population of *ultras*: the right-leaning super fans who express club support through unflagging tribalism, often coupled with violence and intimidation. *Serie A*, the Italian top flight, was chock-full of imported luminaries at this time: Maradona, Ruud Gullit, Marco Van Basten, Frank Rijkaard. It was home to the world's top young players, the not-yet-luminous Claudio Caniggia, Michael Laudrup and Roberto Baggio. It was home to *all* the top Italians — Franco Baresi, Gianluca Vialli and Walter Zenga — plus French icon Michel Platini and three stars from the eventual World Cup winners in 1990: West Germans Rudi Voller, Jurgen Klinsmann and Lothar Matthaus. By any measure, this was the best, richest, most entertaining league in world futbol. Yet attendance at domestic matches had declined in each of the six years leading up to *Il Mondiale*. Crowds for the 1989-90 season in particular were down 500,000 compared to the year prior. Gate revenues dropped $4.6 million. Seventy-four percent of those surveyed nationwide indicated fear of violence had discouraged them from attending matches.

The Hillsborough tragedy, where 97 English supporters had died prior to a 1989 F.A. Cup semifinal in Sheffield, had taken place only the year before. These particular fan deaths were the result of stadium overcrowding and an indifferent security apparatus, not hooliganism. But contemporary press coverage painted a very different, more menacing picture — and Italian fans could read. In the spring of 1990, they could see similar or at least related fan dynamics taking hold in their own domestic soccer culture, and while Hillsborough had taken place clear across the continent, the English, the Dutch, and *their* respective hooligan fan elements were headed their way.

Gansler's team played 13 friendlies that spring of 1990, posting a record of 6-6-1. One match, a 3-2 loss in Berlin on March 28, is believed to be the last competitive home futbol fixture undertaken by East Germany, soon to be absorbed into a unified Germany. For the U.S., highlights included May's 3-1 victory over Poland in Hershey, Pennsylvania, and April's 1-0 loss in Miami against that super-talented Colombia team. Gansler's side had also drawn with Colombia in February. Both performances showed how competent the young Yanks could be when the opponent was Central or South American. Unfortunately, they typically showed none of these efficiencies or capabilities versus classy European sides. The Poland result had given them hope. The final friendly, a 2-1 defeat in Switzerland, did not.

Throughout this pre-tournament schedule, the core of the USMNT remained largely unchanged — save for the addition of collegian Eric Wynalda, who, over the course of that spring, would earn a starting role beside Vermes up top, in attack. When Davis and the injured Perez were left off the final roster, no one could claim surprise. Gansler had stopped playing Davis long before and had stopped relying on Perez in October of 1989.

The Federation gets retroactive credit for assembling so many useful friendlies ahead of this tournament. As for the team's lodgings and base of operations in Italy itself: "It actually kinda sucked," Trittschuh discloses, neatly summing up the team consensus. The 1990 USMNT spent its three World Cup weeks at the Italian Olympic Training Center in Tirrenia, a coastal town 90 minutes west of Florence. Gansler had decided straightaway that he didn't want his young team in Rome — or Florence itself, where two of the team's three matches were scheduled. He wanted no part of an uncontrolled, urban environment, and his discernment on this front proved broadly unpopular.

"We weren't really in a hotel, but in a *compound*," Trittschuh asserts. "There was a soccer field, dormitories with *bars* on the windows, and a place to eat, surrounded by armed guards. That was it. We were there to play soccer. I get it. We were close to Pisa, and we'd go and see the Tower.

But it was a bit of a letdown. It didn't feel like we were at the World Cup. It was a prison camp."

Did anyone at least go for a swim in the Mediterranean? "Not to my knowledge," Stollmeyer reports. "The problem was, we were watching on TV as all these big teams were coming out of all these posh hotels. We were like, 'Why aren't we living like that?'"

Well before 9/11, any time a U.S. athletic contingent traveled to international tournaments, it was presumed to be a potential target for terrorist entities/activities — and that was the Federation's reasonable fear the moment it sobered up after Port of Spain. The fan situation in Italy leading up to the tournament was becoming less savory by the day. Finally, geopolitical tensions were unusually high in the months leading up to *Il Mondiale*. The first Gulf War erupted in August 1990, just three weeks after the West Germans hoisted the trophy.

Gansler and the Federation had originally planned to share the digs at *Centro Tecnico Federale di Coverciano*, the *Azzurri*'s national training center on the northeastern outskirts of Florence. This arrangement was reached at the Italians' invitation. It's not clear whether the hosts reneged on this offer in December, when the pingpong balls determined they'd be playing the Americans in Group A, or in the spring, when they realized just how much security the U.S. team would require — and how much that might affect the *Azzurri*, should both share accommodations in Coverciano. From what Gansler told *The Guardian* in 2015, it sounds more like the latter:

"They said: 'We have an Olympic training center a little farther away in Tirrenia. It's comparable.' We didn't have any money to go out there ahead of time and find out it wasn't comparable. I didn't go out there before, our coaches didn't go out there before . . . Maybe our shortcoming was that we were too trusting when the Italians told us it was comparable. I could have stood there and pitched a fit, but those were the cards we were dealt."

Sounds to me like a man who didn't find out about the switch until pretty late in the game.

"Bob Gansler has admitted it to me that we as a Federation may have made a mistake in terms of where we located ourselves," says Brian Bliss. "The Italians changed plans and we were kicked to the curb. We got a couple nights out [in Pisa]. I don't think anybody tore it up or anything. But it was one of the first times we traveled where we had full-time security. When we left the compound, we had escorts — the *Carabinieri* [Italian national police]. They would send one or two guys with us wherever we went. Obviously, we always traveled in groups of threes and fours — never 18 or 20 guys. We kept it low-key."

Adds Meola, "We didn't feel like we were much involved in the tournament. At least I didn't. We had bars on our windows, and unfortunately, we came to find out later on, we were a pretty big target at the World Cup, as far as threats and things of that nature. We had to be really protected, which meant that we had to be quite secluded from things. You talk about lessons? We learned a lot of lessons in Italy: You have to feel like you're part of the tournament — and we've done that every time since. Somebody had to learn these lessons, and we were the team that learned the lessons."

Trusting the Italians to choose accommodations on your behalf? Lesson learned. Not sending a Federation reconnaissance team to see the new place for themselves? Lesson learned. Secluding young players? That was part of Gansler's meticulous game plan and the Federation's heedful security plan from the start. As for the players' families? Afterthoughts. "Luckily," Krumpe points out, "there was a sponsor who paid for anyone's spouse and family to travel to Italy. That was a nice touch."

On the other hand: "We had very little time with our families, and that was a mistake," Murray reckons. "Now the team will take over an entire hotel. We don't seclude players completely from their families. My family — we had 50 people over in Italy. It was a big celebration, but I barely got to see them."

<hr/>

Gansler and his staff conducted a full week of camp before the Americans opened vs. the Czechs. On the ground, realities in Tirrenia clearly did not match expectations. But this was a hardy group that had

364 — GENERATION ZERO

bunkered in with one another for long stretches of camp in the past, in conditions more austere than these. The lads made the best of it. Mostly.

"I roomed with John Doyle," Trittschuh says, referring to the rangy, blond, Bay Area defender who joined the Swedish club Orgryte IS post-Italy, and later the former East German outfit Vfb Leipzig. "John and I roomed together a lot. When we first arrived, they had a cafeteria, but the food wasn't good, so eventually they found us an Italian restaurant outside — so we had one good meal, once a day. And you know what, it's silly to complain about the training center. That's how it was.

"John was my roommate through all those years, and we were good friends off the field. Which was great, because we kind of knew that either he or I would play in any single game. There were only two matches where we played together, and we won them both: the second Canada match [May 1987] that we had to win in order to continue to the Olympics, and the final game in Trinidad. At the time, we were always man-marking. It was 'You take that guy, and I'll take that guy,' and we'd mark them out of the game. It was cool back then, because you could really kick the crap out of guys and not get carded."

Bliss bunked with Tab Ramos in what became World Cup Central. "Because the rooms were so spartan," Bliss explains, "and on account of the general boredom, Tab and I took tape — I should say, we stole tape from the trainer, because it *was* a valuable commodity — and we put all the groups on the wall. We wrote all the teams in with a Sharpie. After every match we'd change the standings in all the groups, all the goals against, all on the wall of our room. It was probably Tab's idea, and that kind of helped us get through it."

The accommodations were two to a room for all but Krumpe, Caligiuri and Eric Eichmann. "Something happened with Cal and Kasey Keller; they didn't want to room together," reveals Krumpe, who had pulled a groin in Switzerland and was struggling to regain fitness. "I don't know what went down there. So they put another bed in our room, and Cal stayed with me and Eichmann."

"John Stollmeyer was my roommate," Balboa says, "and yeah, it was secluded. But we were both just happy to be there. And let's be honest: We had no clue as to what we were getting into. At the time, we thought we knew. But we did not know."

Nobody knew what to expect of this team, which, to this day, remains the youngest, with the fewest international caps, of any American side ever to qualify for a World Cup. The players didn't know what to expect. The media assembled in Italy were mighty skeptical, but there was no real precedent for a side like the 1990 USMNT. Media back home didn't much care, save the Boomers and cigar-chomping old-timers, who cynically hoped for the worst. Sitting in my Watertown, Massachusetts, apartment, I didn't know what to expect — neither did any of my fellow Americans watching on TV. Neither did Pilgrim Tom, nor any of the Americans inside *Il Stadio Artemio Franchi* in Florence on June 10, 1990. "We had no idea at that point how good the Czechs would be, how good any of the other teams were going to be," Tom maintains. "That was the thing: no idea. We were hoping our guys were good enough to make a game of it. We knew they'd be up against guys making their livings in leagues all over Europe. We knew they'd be better. We didn't know how much better."

At the recently decommissioned Berlin Wall in March 1990, prior to the USMNT's friendly international vs. East Germany, the final match played by the GDR on German soil. *(Image courtesy of Steve Trittschuh)*

Marcelo Balboa (left) and Paul Caligiuri attempt to converge on Italian midfielder Nicola Berti, inside Rome's *Stadio Olimpico*, June 14, 1990. *(Jon van Woerden photo)*

OVER THE RUBICON

Sports media coverage in the United States can be excessive and absurd in its own specifically American ways: the two full weeks of Super Bowl build-up, for example; our maudlin templates for tales of triumph over adversity; the placing of ever more ex-jocks at a desk, for an hour, to engage in utterly meaningless pregame banter. However, three daily newspapers devoted entirely to Italian sport tend to produce a different, peculiarly Italianate brand of excess. Under such microscopic examination, minor injury scares morph into ongoing sagas. Obscure characters become enormous stars — if only for a day or two. Those 15 minutes of fame arrived for Italian national team physician Leonardo Vecchiet late in May of 1990, when he revealed to media that the *Azzurri*'s training regimen would include plenty of pasta, but no sex — for all but two days — during the three-week runup to the World Cup. About the same time, FIFA general secretary Sepp Blatter generated more frivolous, derivative headlines by giving referees the all-clear to *have* sex during *Il Mondiale*, though only between match days.

At long last, come June 8, 1990, the build-up was over.

"I remember pulling up to the stadium in Florence before our first match," Tony Meola says. "About four blocks away, our bus basically stopped. I was sitting with Tab and Harkes and we just sorta looked at each other. It was like, 'Holy shit, man, we're here!' We had one of those card tables between us. We just looked at each other, across the table. Complete silence in the bus. Everyone inside was just checking out the crowd. Today, that stuff would be on Twitter in like five minutes . . . I think we realized right then that this was everything that we had worked for, to get here, to do something like this."

Italia '90 opened with Cameroon's shock victory over Argentina, the holders, 1-0. This staggering result proved the coming-out party for Roger Milla's Indomitable Lions, for African futbol on the big stage, and for Wellesley's Pilgrim Tom, who was there in Milan for the opener, as he was so many places across Italy during *Il Mondiale.*

"So I flew into Milan that morning, met Scott and his girlfriend, and we went to the opening match — the first game open to the public at the *San Siro*, which was brand-new," he says. "Then they went off to Sardinia. They had chosen different games than I did, so I only saw them one more time the entire month I was in Italy. I was on my own, but I met tons of other people along the way."

His extra ticket came in handy as the ultimate icebreaker — as if Tom needed any help. "I would sell it to someone I would meet, someone American or passionate about the game. Every night would involve going to pubs or outdoor cafes near the stadium, where there were always just tons of other soccer fans from all over the world spilling out into the streets. It was really good-natured. Nobody seemed to have a negative view of the U.S., or anyone really. They were kind of amazed we *had* soccer fans who'd spend their money and follow their team around the World Cup. There was trouble with English fans out on Sardinia, apparently. But I didn't see any fighting at all. It just wasn't that tribal. It was just a mad piss-up, day after day."

Back home, the televised matches kept coming, day after day. It was bloody magnificent: American fans had never before been treated to such a smorgasbord of soccer, an entire major tournament's worth, essentially. I tried to lure someone to my flat each day to watch alongside me: my housemate Tom Laverty, my brother Matthew, my friend Dave Rose, my girlfriend at the time, Helen. There was a morning match each calendar day — kickoff at 15:00 Central European Time — followed by a 2 p.m. U.S. Eastern Standard Time match, contested under the lights in

Italy. Folks joined me only once in awhile: They largely kept regular business hours, whereas I, like most newspaper folks, lived like a raccoon; I didn't arrive at the *Enterprise-Sun* offices until 5 or 6 p.m. With or without company, I watched every single match live.

The players had no sense for how, or how many, were watching back home. TNT reportedly averaged nearly a million viewers for the semifinal and final, and something close to that for each match involving the U.S. A midweek college basketball game would pull double that rating in 1990. TNT aired five commercial breaks per half, each 30 to 60 seconds in duration. The cable network claimed to have lost money on the World Cup venture, having paid $7.75 million for the rights. Univision reportedly *made* money, and its commercial model — never leaving live play but instead showing small, graphically simple ads in the corner of the screen — quickly evolved into the industry standard.

The U.S. Men's National Team was more certain about its support in Italy itself. "There were some expats living there in Italy who sorta jumped on the bandwagon a little bit," Bliss recalls, noting that former pro boxer Marvelous Marvin Hagler made the biggest impression. He had undertaken a film career in Italy after his 1987 loss to Sugar Ray Leonard. "Hagler showed up in the locker room after at least one match. But the largest contingent was family, and they sat together. My parents were there. The Harkes and the Meolas, the Ramoses and Windischmanns — they all traveled together."

Renovated prior to the tournament, the *Stadio Artemio Franchi* in Florence, site of the U.S. opener, remained rather intimate. It accommodated just 35,000 fans. Its modest proportions made it easier to pick out fellow Americans in the crowd. "You'd see a flag here and there," Bliss reports. "A pocket of Americans here and there. It certainly wasn't what it is today with Sam's Army, no way."

"We were treated very well," Wad remembers, "but there *was* a sort of amusement at the U.S. and its fans being there. People were nice, the Italians were very nice. But all of us — the Americans and the Italians and all the other international fans — had no idea how good, or rather how bad, the U.S. was going to be. Most seemed pretty impressed that we had made the trip. It was sort of like we were little kids who'd been invited to a grown-up party."

—————•·•—————

The Team USA coaching staff was no less awed by the moment at hand. "It was ultimate stage," Gansler recalls of the instant when his team kicked off against the Czechs. "People ask if we were nervous. I don't know ... We certainly were anxious. One of the things that was thrown at us, at least at the coaching staff, was 'You guys have no experience.' Well, you need to gain that experience yourself. It's not about talking; that will not get the anxiety out of your system. It's about *experiencing*.

"All that said, Czechoslovakia had a lot of internal crisis going into that World Cup. They were in turmoil. I thought from watching their films, through qualifying, that this was the one game to get a result. Maybe I'm conservative in these matters, but a result vs. Czechoslovakia would have been a tie."

John Stollmeyer still isn't buying Gansler's assessments: "I remember our coaches telling us the Czech game was the one where we had a chance to get a result. I thought: 'Really? I don't remember playing any Eastern bloc team that wasn't hard and didn't run our asses off.' People kept saying how big and physical the U.S. team was. Young, yes. And we *thought* of ourselves as big and fit and so forth. But I remember walking out of that locker room — you know how it's done: You come out paired up with the other team — and almost to a man, you look to your right and you were looking *up*! John Doyle is every bit of 6'4", 6'5". Tritt is 6'1", but they [the Czechs] were big, *much* bigger than us."

"That first game," Murray says, "we were not well prepared. Joe Machnik got the scouting report wrong. He told us that physically, we could be dominant in that match. Well, we were lining up in the tunnel to come out, and I'm right next to Tomas Skuhravy. I'm 6'3" and I'm looking up at him — and few more guys."

Windischmann started questioning the team's overall preparation just a few minutes before that: "We were getting ready to come out against

Czechoslovakia, to warm up. They came out first. There were metal steps up to the field. Gansler hears all the metal on the steps — so he makes everyone go back and change to studs. Right then! I was a player who never played in studs, just regular cleats. So we had to go and change to our studs. A crazy little moment to start the tournament, but sorta telling."

Balboa knew he would start this game on the bench. He remembers the pregame a bit more romantically: "I remember driving up to the Czech game, our first game, and we were singing when we got there. We saw our families outside the stadium. We were fired up and ready to go, man."

———————

It's difficult today to view the 5-1 opening loss to Czechoslovakia with anything but a jaundiced eye. The score line was embarrassing, full stop. Gansler and his staff had completely misjudged their opponents, who, as several have pointed out here, were physically bigger, more technically skilled and more tactically flexible. They dominated this match on the ground and in the air, not just foiling U.S. corners but scoring twice on counters that stemmed from U.S. corners. Goals 3 and 4, the latter from Skuhravy, were both near-post headers, something the Americans were little prepared to defend, evidently. When Ivan Hasek made it 3-0 six minutes after halftime, the result was inevitable. Then Eric Wynalda was sent off. Game over.

Gansler's notion that his opponents were competitively "in crisis" proved way off the mark. These were some of the final tournament fixtures for the Czechs and their longtime Eastern bloc-mates, the Slovaks. Their separation was coming in 1992, and divisions had already formed in the team, the staff and the football federation. Nonetheless, they remained a collection of first-class players inordinately keen to make an impression, to latch on post-*Mondiale* with rich clubs in the "West" and cash in after years of playing for pennies on the dollar. Forget their trouncing of the young Yanks. We're talking about a side that went to the quarterfinals and lost to the eventual champions, 1-0.

"You know, they were a very good team," asserts Steve Trittschuh, whose post-World Cup career was made by this game. He latched on with the Czechs' top club, Sparta Prague, in 1991. "The assistant coach of the national team was the coach of Sparta Prague. I got to know a lot of those guys afterward, at Sparta. They said to me later, 'We just played very well that day.' They were playing for contracts to get out of Czechoslovakia.

"Leading up to that match, we watched videos of the Czechs and we thought we could really compete with them. But the way they played [in the WC opener] was just totally different from what I remember seeing on video. This was a freakin' good team . . . We thought we could play with them. That was our mistake. I remember 10 to 15 minutes in, we were knocking the ball around, stringing some passes together, generating some half-chances on goal. Then it sort of fell apart. First goal on the counter, then the penalty, and we're like, 'What happened?'"

Trittschuh remembers things accurately. The U.S. did trade a few punches with its opponent through the first 25 minutes. There were American attempts on goal, even playing 10 vs. 11. Caligiuri's second-half tally was beautifully sprung, by Murray, and finished. Down 3-1, Ramos had a clear, unhurried chance to make it 3-2 on a bounding bit of service from Murray. He skied it over the bar.

Still, this is so much retrospective happy talk. The Americans showed some startling naiveté in this match — enough to worry anyone contemplating their pending date with the Italians in four days' time. To wit: By the time the U.S. had scored — its first WC goal since Joe Gaetjens' winner against the English in 1950 — Gansler's team was down a man. "I remember having a little conversation at halftime with Mr. Wynalda, who was the most skittish of all of us out there," Gansler says. "I told him he needed to watch out because he was being set up to get thrown out." On 52 minutes, baited once more by the savvy Czechs, Mr. Wynalda was in fact dismissed.

"This was a different level for sure from Korea, or the friendlies," Krumpe adds. "However, again, if Wynalda doesn't get thrown out it's a tighter match. We're not going to compete with any European power down a man, even now."

The penalty on 38 minutes, making it 2-0, was not unlucky but rather indicative of a defensive unit out of its depth. Windischmann had collected the ball at the top of his own box, facing his own goal. Instead of first-timing it away, or back to Meola, he wheeled blindly to his right with the intention of booting it clear. Instead he got his pocket picked. He swung through with his left foot as though the ball were still there, clumsily bringing down a man he never even saw.

Amateur-hour defending, plain and simple — and that individual bungle wasn't the end of it. The two near-post headers that made it 3-0 and then 4-1 proved hugely deflating, embarrassing even. A lot can go wrong on corners, especially against a bigger team, but near-post headers are perhaps the easiest threat to take away. "We were a young team, and we self-destructed," Gansler says, summing it up neatly and fairly.

Per usual, Bliss is more expansive and analytical: "It was a tough one. We had spent most of our time with Gansler and that team — in qualifying and friendly matches — trying to play on the break. Counterattack, maybe absorb some pressure. We were fit and pretty good at it, because we had some guys who could run, some guys who could finish, and in Bruce and Wynalda and Vermes, some guys who could bang a couple in here and there. I think we may have overplayed our hands in that Czech game — thinking maybe we could make some waves, do something a little bit different or unexpected. I think we did play with a bit more risk. I don't want to say we ever tried to *pressure* the Czechs, but we opened up the game a bit more than we were used to. And we paid for it."

In fairness, it was Windischmann and his back-four mates — Stollmeyer, Desmond Armstrong and Trittschuh — who were most exposed by these curious, devil-may-care tactics. "Look, I didn't play so hot," Windy admits. "Afterward, as I'm sitting there in the locker room beating myself up, they were like, 'Go upstairs.' I had to go take a drug test. I'm like, 'Oh great. Perfect.'"

Windy and his teammates were young and inexperienced, but they had played tournaments before. They knew what was coming — and

I don't mean the Italians. Gansler made it clear after the match: There would be changes.

Marcelo Balboa, still 22 that Italian summer, would eventually play in three World Cups, but his first appearance came here, against Czechoslovakia, coming on for Stollmeyer after 64 minutes. Chris Sullivan would replace Bruce Murray on 71.

"I was a starter, but I tore my MCL before the tournament," Balboa explains. "I made it back just in time to be included on the roster, and Gansler made it very clear to me — where not a lot of coaches would have. He was going to play the guys who got us there. Out of respect for everything they'd done, they would start. I didn't have a lot of coaches who were so brutally honest. I totally respected that, because I knew where I stood. Those guys had given so many years of hard work. I was fortunate to get on the field, and I started ever since. But I have the utmost respect for that man, as a coach and mentor."

Il Mondiale truly did launch the career of Marcelo Balboa. He started games two and three in Italy, returned home, and joined the SFB Blackhawks in the APSL — his first games as a full-on club pro. Eventually, he moved to the Colorado Foxes before rejoining the USMNT in residence, prior to the '94 World Cup. He spent two years in *Liga MX* thereafter with Club Leon before returning to launch Major League Soccer as a member of the Colorado Rapids in 1996. He retired in 2002, assumed a role in the Rapids front office, and there he remains to this day — coaching in the club's academy, where he can pay the mentor thing forward. Balboa also does television commentary for Fox and Univision. In many ways, his lengthy career is a model for how it's supposed to be done — in the mature footballing nation he helped to forge.

But you never forget your first World Cup moment, right?

"Dude, I don't remember anything!" he says. "I was in shock. You know how it is, when you finally live that dream and get into the game. I'm warming up, couldn't tell you how long or where; I just remember doing it for maybe two minutes and saying, 'I'm ready! I'm ready!' I honestly don't remember much about that game either; the excitement was just so huge. God, it was such an awful day, but such a great day. Terrible result, but the day we stepped on that field after 40 years of not qualifying? That was pretty spectacular."

When your country hasn't qualified in four decades, there are plenty of World Cup debuts to go around. Some are expected, others not. Krumpe's injury, sustained in the team's final tuneup, meant a starting slot for Desmond Armstrong, who produced 90 solid minutes at left back — a feat he would replicate vs. the Italians later that week. Indeed, Armstrong started all three U.S. matches at *Italia* '90, which he cannily parlayed into a place with Pelé's old club, Santos FC, in 1991 — the first American ever to sign a contract and compete in the Brazilian top flight. He returned to the U.S. in '92, eager to secure a national team place for himself at USA '94. However, like many from Gen Zero, Krumpe included, he never gained the confidence of Bora Milutinovic. MLS wanted him: He was the fifth player chosen in the league's inaugural draft. Instead, he opted to retire at age 31.

The National Soccer Hall of Fame welcomed Armstrong in 2012, a fitting tribute to a guy who won a U-19 McGuire Cup national title, starred at the University of Maryland, played in MISL, helped pioneer the A-League, went to the Olympics and then the World Cup. Post-soccer, Armstrong remained active in both coaching and inner-city Christian ministries. In 2018, he founded East Nash Soccer, a premier youth league in his adopted home of Nashville, Tennessee. He also runs the elite Sporting Nashville Heroes, a premier club that is part of the youth development network overseen by Sporting Kansas City. Yet his main futbol concern these days may be the budding career of son Ezra, who spent two years with Danish club Skovshoved I.F. before joining the USL Pittsburgh Riverhounds in 2021.

Gansler's management of his back four proved a study in damage control throughout the *Italia* '90. Armstrong solved one issue, at left back. Against the host country, the coach sat Trittschuh, who took some comfort that friend and roommate Doyle would replace him. The competition for additional places would not be so polite.

WITHIN 24 HOURS OF THEIR RUDE World Cup awakening, the American situation quickly devolved — on two separate fronts. Outside the not-so-friendly confines of their bunker in Tirrenia, Italian fans and the world footballing press began openly speculating about just how many goals the Italians would score against the seemingly hapless Yanks in five days' time. *The Times* of London reported the Americans "were utterly exposed by such Bronze Age devices as an overlapping fullback." The headline in Milan's *Corriere della Sera:* "USA, What a Delusion." Inside the team, the battle for places went from spirited and sporting to desperate and cutthroat.

"We had a big fight that first session. It was Murray and [Eric] Eichmann," Vermes discloses. "It was a melee. Everybody was basically in the goal throwing punches."

Murray saw this coming, but that didn't make him any happier about it: "I felt that Eric had targeted me during training. If he could make me look bad, it would help his cause to get into the next game. So a couple of late hits, and that was it. The gloves were off. I have no problem today with Eric" — his teammate going back to their days as fellow Clemson Tigers — "but it does show the competitive atmosphere within the group."

As John Harkes told *The Guardian* in 2015: "I would have to think Gansler would look at that and think: 'This is good.'"

Sometimes selfishness does serve a team. The American players had been embarrassed the day before. They'd been locked up with each other for two weeks inside Stalag Tirrenia. There *was* a great deal of steam to be let off. But make no mistake: These were minor factors. World Cup opportunities often come but once in a lifetime. The Murray-Eichmann bout and the general disregard for the ongoing health of fellow teammates were all about places in the starting XI going forward.

"Yeah, Eichmann and Murray: Listen, when Gansler told everybody that there were going to be some changes, that flipped the switch," Balboa says. "I know it got me going. Gansler was smart: He opened the door and didn't mention names. 'There's gonna be some changes and we're gonna see what happens' — and we just went after each other like there was no tomorrow. It really was dog eat dog. When he said there would be changes, well, the guys who started? Some of their faces sort of fell, but everybody else in that meeting room — we all lit up, like, 'Shit, this is our chance!'"

Even Balboa's roommate, the wily veteran Stollmeyer, was taken aback.

"Those practices were brutal, just ugly," he says. "There were guys coming out to practice in screw-ins [as opposed to the softer molded cleats or flats that many players prefer in training]. Changes were definitely gonna happen on the field, and practice became a battle. You could see some guys wanted nothing to do with it. Hey, that can happen — but it became angry. It was for real. You had to just go and really bring it, really play. You didn't play molded [cleats] that day."

But Gansler didn't just throw the team red meat and let them fight it out, gladiator style, in the arena. Match tactics would also change. He and his staff had actually settled on another counterintuitive game plan for the Italians. "I thought if we could control the ball against Italy, they'd grow frustrated because the expectation was they would beat us by 10 goals. And that's exactly what happened," Gansler recalls. "I told our guys we are going to defend with two blocks of four, and we're going to hit them on the counterattack."

Murray and Vermes would shoulder a special responsibility, the underappreciated responsibility of strikers leading the line when everyone else is parking the bus: "Bob said, 'You need to hold the ball more,'" Murray recalls. "And we did. Everything came off exactly as planned."

"We had a sequence where we had 23 consecutive passes without the Italian team touching the ball," Harkes says. "To do that, on that stage, is pretty remarkable in itself."

Unfortunately for the USMNT, three full days of practice separated the Czech debacle from the Italy match. Gansler's possession tactics would eventually prove highly effective. However, holding the ball that much longer is exactly *not* what guys want to do when their teammates openly covet their place in the team — and everyone has already been cooped up with these animals for two weeks, under armed guard. Coach Gansler lucked out that only one real fight broke out between Match Days 1 and 2.

As for Eichmann, he never did see the field in Italy. He returned to his club team, the Fort Lauderdale Strikers, and, like so many others post *Italia* '90, failed to impress Bora Milutinovic; he made his last national team appearance against Honduras in 1993. After several indoor seasons, he made 15 MLS appearances for the newly minted Kansas City Wizards — playing for former Dallas Tornado skipper and Kyle Rote Jr. whisperer Ron Newman (Gansler would not take the helm in KC until 1999). Today, Eichmann is back in his native Florida as director of coaching at Boca United, a U.S. Soccer-affiliated development academy.

———•—•———

Meanwhile, outside their dyspeptic, ascetic cocoon, world football was preparing for a goal fest — one that would potentially humble the world's sole remaining superpower. At the press conference between matches, a German journalist asked, "Mr. Gansler, what would be an acceptable number of goals to lose by? Five goals? Six goals?"

"The Italian paper *La Gazzetta dello Sport* was like: 'Can the Italians score 12?'" Murray recalls. "You have to remember the Italians were the best team in the World Cup, according to 90 percent of the people over there. Their lineup was ridiculous."

"Driving into downtown Rome," Gansler says, "people realized who the bus was carrying. They were showing us all 10 fingers. At first, some people thought they were giving us a two-handed wave. But they were trying to indicate the score."

All this sardonic condescension was down to the sour luck of December's draw. Playing in Verona with the seeded Belgians, for example, such public scorn would never have eventuated — no matter how badly the Americans might have been blown out in an alternative opening match. The Yanks would never have been cooped up in Tirrenia, either. Their every movement about the countryside would not have engendered anywhere near the attention, or necessitated the security.

"On the way to Rome, we had helicopters flying beside the bus, literally down low, like five feet off the ground, and another sweeping across the road ahead of us," Murray recollects. "There *was* some threat, apparently, from some terror group — that they were going to do something. So, that was a concern."

Adds Stollmeyer: "There were one or two police cars ahead of us — they all had Uzis, and they made sure they were visible. We had two or three police in back of us, one on each side, and a helicopter above us. The bus never stopped. We would come up to a toll plaza and it would be cleared ahead of time — the bus would never stop going through the tollbooth."

In the Eternal City itself, when the team bus came to intersections, police details took to the streets to ensure the coast was clear before creeping progress was resumed. By this time, Italian citizens had realized exactly who was inside. All along the bus route they greeted the 1990 USMNT with 10-finger salutes.

———

Match Day 2, in Group A, dawned bright and sunny, and while the team was happy to lodge in an international-standard hotel, in downtown Rome, dispositions inside the U.S. camp were grave. After four fierce days of training, "We all sort of hated each other at that point," Balboa remembers. There was also rampant anxiety about the beating they were likely to absorb that evening at the *Stadio Olimpico*, before a worldwide television audience. Esprit de corps was sorely lacking. "On the day of the match," Gansler says, "Joe Machnik came to me saying the guys wanted to have a meeting. Players only. I said, 'Why not?'"

The meeting took place in a hotel ballroom, a few hours before the team boarded the bus for the stadium. Gansler had named his starters already, and there weren't that many changes after all — which darkened the mood even further among those who'd been scratching and clawing all week, looking for a chance to play World Cup minutes. Several senior players spoke, including team captain Windischmann. But Stollmeyer stole the show, to the squad's great benefit.

"Guys were complaining, and I'd just had it with the bullshit," he recalls. "I called out anybody who was whining and moping. Basically I said, 'You know, I'm not in the lineup either. But I've never heard so much whining and moaning and complaining. The heck with playing for this or that — play for us. Quit your fucking whining and let's get after it. We are here for us. Let's just go out there and play.'"

("I just gave you the G-rated version," Stollmeyer admits. "Bliss told me later that I probably set the record for F-bombs in a two-minute speech.")

Doyle stood up and adjourned the meeting with, "Nothing more needs to be said." Gansler, for one, was impressed: "I was pleased to hear those guys did have gonads after all."

———————

"When I walked out of the stadium tunnel in Rome," Bruce Murray told *The Guardian* in 2015, "I found myself standing next to Paolo Maldini [the AC Milan star]. Then I look over to my right, and there's [NFL legends from the Seventies] Franco Harris and Tom Landry! They were sitting in the front row. I was like: 'What the hell is this?' You couldn't miss them. Tom Landry with his fedora. Franco Harris with his beard; he kind of smiled at me. A very surreal scene."

The *San Siro* in Milan had been newly minted for the 1990 World Cup. The *Stadio delle Alpi* in Turin was similarly renovated for the tournament specifically. But there was never a question as to where the Italian national team would be based, or where the final would be played: *Il Stadio Olimpico*, in Rome. Located midway between Italy's north and south — an enormous cultural divide even today — the stadium was built in the 1930s by none other than Benito Mussolini. *Il Stadio dei Cipressi* was rebuilt and expanded for the 1960 Summer Olympiad, an event which itself became a symbol of the nation's unity and rebirth as a republic, after the nightmares of fascism and World War II. The facility had again been renovated just prior to *Il Mondiale*. The estimated price tag for this refurbishment: $65.6 million.

Actual cost: $139.4 million, roughly the same amount Juventus spent to rebuild the *Stadio delle Alpi* from scratch. The new roof in Rome, with its lattice of exposed girders, proved controversial with the Italian public, as well. Environmentalists and aesthetes objected. Fans complained that it obscured views of Monte Mario, the city's highest hill. Local wags dubbed it a "Crown of Thorns."

Italy is much like my native Boston: Corruption and overspending on public works projects offend, but are more or less expected. *Il Stadio Olimpico* remains an asset of the Italian National Olympic Committee. Back in 1990, to recover some of the cost overrun, the committee resolved to harvest and sell squares of the stadium turf to *calcio*-mad Italians. Sadly, this effort, too, proved something of a muddle, as the *Azzurri* eventually crashed out of this World Cup down in *Napoli*, one step short of the final. The public proved largely indifferent to souvenirs of that failure.

Stollmeyer, however, might have invested in such a memento. "The field was just like a putting green — it was spectacular," he says. And credit the renovators with this: The acoustics and ambience in a structure so sprawling proved extraordinary.

"There was a fog of smoke in there. Flags were waving, people singing, and you couldn't hear a guy five yards away," Stolly recalls. "That was one of those surreal moments when I can sit here, right now, and see all the stadium atmosphere all around me, still in my mind, as if it was yesterday. I played in a lot of different places, but that was a highlight. Just a gorgeous environment. People watch these games and think it's easy to play in a setting like that. But it's not. It's *so* loud: the white noise, the singing, the whistles and cheering. It's nonstop and it's deafening."

"You need to talk to Chris Sullivan," Bliss tells me. (I did my best to track down the University of Tampa product — to no avail. Following the World Cup, Sullivan joined Vermes' old club, ETO FC Gyor in Hungary, and later Brondby in Denmark. He's probably best known today for his broadcast work on Fox Sports.)

"I don't want to throw Chris under the bus," Bliss continues, "but he was like a kid in the candy shop before that game. We all tried to play it cool during warmups, but he was so enamored with the Italian team, he was missing every third trap of the ball. Their players didn't come out as a group. They came out one at a time, and each time the place erupted. Earth-shattering noise level. And Sullivan was like, 'Dude, dude, dude! It's Baresi? Did you see Mancini?' 'Yeah, Chris, we saw him. We gotta warm up.' It was almost comical. He was more than a little bit in awe. I think

Murray finally went up to him and said, 'Richie Riehl (our trainer) has a pen. You want to go get some autographs?'"

As kickoff approached, Wadlington had sold his extra ticket and found plenty of new friends inside. "There were more Americans at the Italy game, but not thousands," he says. "Maybe a thousand in all? The stadium was huge, with a track ringing the pitch so you felt further away from the action compared to Florence. The Italians scored early, but after that it was a bit of a stalemate. We were surrounded by Italians. You could tell the crowd was disappointed and becoming sort of embarrassed. They were expecting a blowout."

Italy's 1-0 victory on June 14, 1990, lives on in the U.S. soccer imagination, which speaks to its consequence, but also to just how little lore there was to choose from between 1950 and 1990. In its historical context, the match should be viewed as the end of the beginning — the official public dawn of the Modern American Soccer Movement. In the moment, however, in the immediate context of the American drubbing just four days prior, it made a lasting impression on the Italian and world soccer communities, as well.

On one level, the result should surprise no one, for the *Azzurri* did what they often do: They pressed for the early goal, nicked it, and made it hold up over 90 minutes. This is the stereotypical Italian performance at major tournaments, regardless of the opposition. So much is made of the Yanks' stoic performance and near-equalizer late in the match that folks tend to gloss over the game's only goal. It came on 12 minutes and proved a thing of rare beauty — a lightning-quick but free-flowing build-up that sent Giuseppe Giannini in alone on Meola, thanks to Gianluca Vialli's pitch-perfect dummy, which froze the entire American back four.

For its part, the U.S. did what it had *never* done — what few believed it was capable of doing at this level: As the game progressed, Gansler's side convinced a really good European side that throwing guys forward with impunity — in search of a blowout victory — might not be worth the risk. The reward for its disciplined tactics? The U.S. nearly *did* score

— perhaps should have scored. In these early, meager days of American soccer's modern era, this near-miss passed for success. And so it should.

"If you go back to that film, you will see we had sequences of 12, 14, 18, 20 consecutive touches at a time," Gansler explains. "Everybody's counting touches nowadays. Well, we had some touches in that game. For sure there was a lot of pressure on our Italian hosts, and that played a part, too. I thought we played an awfully good game against Italy. Look, I went a little too offensive against the Czechs. I had Eric Wynalda wide left, and we played a 3-5-2 that was more like a 5-3-2. We switched for the second game, and Jimmy [Banks] played wide left, with Paul Caligiuri wide right. It was much more balanced that way.

"We could have walked out of there with a 1-1 tie. Would that have been a true and fair representation of what happened that night? No. They were the better side, so we could live with a 1-0 defeat."

Considering the game's hallowed reputation here in America, there's a great deal that people *don't* remember about those 90 minutes, the finest the USMNT had played in 40 years, since the Miracle in Belo Horizonte. The Italians missed a first-half penalty. Vialli — nearly unrecognizable to people today due to his full head of hair — sent Meola the wrong way but clanged his bid off the post. A goal there might have opened the flood-gates. Instead, the miss spooked the *Azzurri* and reinforced the tenuous nature of their one-goal advantage.

The U.S. back line, so callow and porous against the Czechs, did heroic duty this night — and Balboa truly came of age. He proved devastatingly quick and sure in the tackle, winning headers, throwing his body around, destroying any attempts the Italians made to play in small, central spaces. He also did next to nothing in furthering Gansler's possession tactics.

"I was allowed to attack the ball anywhere it went. My job was to go get it, disrupt the play, jump, get in everybody's way," Balboa recalls. "There were certain points in that game where I slid forward and ended up playing more of a defensive midfield role. So, at one point, Gansler yells to me, 'Listen: Your job is not to dribble. Your job is to win the damn ball and give it to Tab or Harksy, and that's it. Win it and give it to the two guys who know what to do with it.' So I'm like, 'Rock on!' I was just look-ing to get it off my foot as fast as possible."

The other heroes were Murray and Vermes. It seems counterintuitive, but strikers are key to any pressure-absorption strategy, because they must accomplish two things: continually chase down long, searching through balls and hector opposing defenders, almost always in vain, and then hold the ball up when or if they manage to take possession of a clearance or outlet, thereby giving teammates a chance to counter and join the attack. With Vermes more withdrawn to assist Ramos and Harkes in clogging the Italians' world-class midfield, much of this dirty work was left to Murray. What's more, the former Pinto's willingness to hold the ball in more dan-gerous positions nearly earned the Americans their draw.

"The crowd started to turn on their team in the first half, because we were just hoarding everything," Murray says. "The whole idea was to get it up to me. I would hold it up so we could get some defensive players out. It actually turned out to be a real battle. I watched that film a thousand times, and it's the best game I ever played. Not because I scored, but because I held the ball for the team against two of the best defenders in the world."

———•◦•———

With 15 minutes remaining, Murray reverted to more orthodox strik-ing: "I got fouled. Free kick from 24 yards out. I sent it over the wall, and [Italian goalkeeper Walter] Zenga dove and knocked it down right in the path of Peter Vermes."

Brian Bliss had the best view of anyone. He was standing by the Italian goal, warming up: "Yeah, not to over-personalize, but I was the first guy Gansler asked to warm up. I didn't play the first game. This was just five minutes after halftime, and I'm like, 'Damn! I'm going in!' So I warmed up for the next 42 minutes and never came on, you know? Anyway, when the whistle blew for the free kick, we were right there, warming up on the sideline — we all stopped to watch it being taken. Murray cracked the free kick, Zenga saved it, and Peter went in alone to finish it. Everyone's heart kind of stopped."

Gansler: "Peter's shot was not cleanly taken but goes through the keeper's legs."

Murray: "It hits both of Zenga's ankles."

Bliss: "Then it bounces up and hits Zenga on the ass!"

Murray: "Then it starts spinning on the line — in slow motion. You could see the ball spinning!"

Vermes: "Then it got cleared off the line."

All this happened in an instant, and just as quickly, the moment passed. "I always say one of two things could have happened there," Vermes recalls. "I score that goal and I immediately get signed to play in Italy somewhere. Or I could be where I am today — but I am happy where I am today."

"It was like Caligiuri's goal: a surreal moment going in slow motion," Windischmann adds. "In the moment, I was just hoping that ball would go over the line. That would have been so nice . . ."

There was one last half-chance, but Balboa blazed it miles over the bar from well beyond the 18. Soon, the match was over, and so began the sustained applause — not from the meager American contingent on hand, but from tens of thousands of Italians. No supporters in futbol appreciate a stalwart, highly organized rear-guard action like the Italians. They refer to this tactic colloquially as *catenaccio*, or "the door bolt." And so the 80,000 spectators inside *Stadio Olimpico* applauded the young Americans off the immaculate pitch – half in appreciation, and half to show their own side their mild displeasure.

"All we ever wanted was to finally get a little respect in the world of soccer, and that's the day we earned it," Balboa asserts. "That applause? When we walked out of that stadium? That was a great day."

THE 21ST-CENTURY TEMPTATION IS TO FIXATE on that ball spinning in suspended animation behind Zenga, on the goal line. An equalizer there would have been an even bigger statement, of course, resulting in more than mere baseline respect for these gallant American underdogs.

A tying goal would have kept U.S. hopes to advance out of Group A alive, as well. For a few more days, anyway.

Nevertheless, the legitimate and lasting quality these Americans showed that night in Rome was their determination to bravely hold the ball against a clearly superior opponent, to bide their time through their own ardent defending, waiting for the one opportunity that always comes. This exercise isn't exactly rare, but it does require maturity, practicality and tactical discipline — especially from a young team that had been blown out four days prior. This tactical and technical moxie is what impressed the Italian crowd that June night, 32 years ago.

And it wasn't just the crowd. Next thing you know . . .

"There's a little bit of a commotion, and the Italian team comes into our locker room to shake hands," Murray told *The Guardian* in 2015. "I don't know who the spokesman was, but he said, 'We want you to know that your country should be proud of you.' I've never had that happen in my entire life. These are superstars: Paolo Maldini, Roberto Baggio, Riccardo Ferri. That was incredible."

Windischmann was similarly touched: "The whole Italian team comes in and wants to trade jerseys, which was pretty amazing."

For his near miss, Vermes exchanged game shirts with none other than Franco Baresi, perhaps the finest defender in the world back in 1990, and the man he nearly beat for the tying goal. Krumpe, still nursing the groin that never did heal in time, traded his for the Great Baresi's warmups.

This tradition of trading jerseys is unique to futbol and somehow survives into the modern game, undimmed by money, celebrity and cynicism. Practically speaking, it can only be deployed by professionals: Amateur clubs and individuals don't have the resources to give game jerseys away and replace them willy-nilly. Even so, this tradition remains simple and moving *because* its participants are wealthy pros. There really is no American sporting equivalent to this peer-to-peer expression of respect.

"There was a player that wore No. 6 on the Italian national team. I think it was Ferri," recalls Harkes, who also wore No. 6. "I wanted to change my jersey with him. He was trying to explain that he had promised it to someone else, so he took off his shorts, and I looked at him and thought, 'Well, OK.' So I took off my shorts. I remember walking down the tunnel in my underwear with his shorts in my hand, and I didn't care."

Harkes wasn't the only one. Trittschuh, who sat out the Italy game, encountered the one and only Roberto Baggio in the hallway outside the U.S. changing room. Baggio also sat this match out (as had future coaching legend Carlo Ancelotti). Baggio was a young star in 1990, but not yet a worldwide icon. He wasn't even wearing his game jersey when he happened upon Trittschuh. After an awkward moment, the Granite City native came to the same realization Harkes had.

"I had Baggio's shorts forever, man," Tritt says with a laugh. "It was the coolest thing."

Baggio didn't have his jersey because Bliss got to him first: "I've still got it," he reports. "Some guys lingered a little bit longer on the field. We shook hands with the Italians, congratulated them. But eventually we went down the flight of steps to the tunnel. I was walking with someone from the team, I can't remember who, and we see Baggio. We looked at each other and did the international hand signal for 'You want to exchange jerseys?' So we both stripped our shirts off, shook hands, gave each other a hug, and traded. I've got it somewhere in a bin, in my basement. If I told Sully that, he'd probably come rob me!"

When the U.S. was eliminated from World Cup '94, Tony Meola swapped shirts with his Brazilian counterpart Claudio Taffarel. In 1990, the young American keeper says he didn't have the presence of mind, or the nerve, to approach Zenga, his fellow *portiere*. That's a shame, because his performance against Italy was his best of the tournament, and a sign of things to come.

For several of Meola's teammates, *Italia* '90 was the end of the road. For Meola, it was only the beginning. He captained the USA '94 squad and started all four matches. He rejoined the USMNT as a reserve for its fairytale run to the World Cup quarterfinals in 2002. He competed in MLS from inception (1996) through to its maturation (2006). There were some blips: He spent the immediate post-*Mondiale* period in England trying to catch on with Brighton & Hove Albion, and then Watford, but couldn't get enough appearances to earn a long-term work permit. He parlayed his '94 WC appearance into an ill-fated placekicking tryout with his hometown N.Y. Jets. There is, of course, a long and distinguished history of such synergies. By the mid-Nineties, however, Meola's attempt to cross over in this way struck some soccer purists — an American population newly created and invigorated, in part, by Meola himself — as dated, opportunistic and heretical.

No one can ever accuse Meola of playing things safe. He appeared in a Broadway play, 1995's *Tony n' Tina's Wedding*. He still plays drums in his own band, Mushmouth. He ran his own mortgage company for a time, and coached indoors for a single season, 2015-16, with the NPSL's Jacksonville Armada. Meola was inducted into the National Soccer Hall of Fame in 2012. For Generation Zero, this first native generation of U.S. fans, he was front and center in our soccer consciousness for a long, long time. In many ways, there he remains. Meola was in Russia doing color commentary for FS1 during the 2018 World Cup. He's a regular on SiriusXM FC.

"I don't have one regret about anything that happened in that World Cup," he contends, looking back. "Somebody had to be that team that broke the string of 40 years. It happened to be us, that particular group. But if that's *all* that happened, we wouldn't be where we are today. We had to give people the chance to dream about playing in a World Cup, then the next World Cup, and the one after that. We had to give that education to Americans watching the tournament for the first time. I can't tell you how many people have told me over the years that the '90 World Cup really introduced them to the game, to *world* soccer.

"It took another group of guys to come in and build on the foundation, then another, year after year. I learned that from a U.S. soccer ambassador who said to me once, 'Keep the ball rolling.' That was Walter Bahr, on some trip. I don't remember which one. But I'll take that saying with me forever. *Keep the ball rolling*. That's what we did, and that's what guys today continue to do."

Driving back to Tirrenia from Rome, the U.S. bus was again recognized by locals along the route. Police and helicopter escorts tend to get people's attention. This time, however, Italians on the street clapped over their heads and offered the dauntless young Americans thumbs up. The next day, when several guys left their gated community and ventured into town, still under armed guard, they were surprised to see dozens of light poles flying both the American and Italian flags. *Together.* In the end, the Italians proved marvelous hosts.

Incidentally, there is no blue in the Italian flag. The shade the national team wears, the reason they're known as *gli Azzurri* (the Blues), celebrates the House of Savoy, a royal dynasty that ruled over northern Italy and later the entire Kingdom of Italy, after Garibaldi & Co. coaxed all the various city-states and principalities into a single constitutional monarchy midway through the 19th century. Italy jettisoned its monarchy completely and became a republic after WWII, but the Savoyards were long seen as particularly supportive of republicanism, and so the blue shirts remain.

"Even before the U.S.-Italy game and during all the 10-finger business, the Italian fans themselves were actually quite good-natured," Wad reports. "I'd say that went for nearly *all* the fans I ran into, as well. But everyone took their cues from the Italians. They just love their footy. You'd end up meeting Italians and fans of other teams who spoke English, and we'd just take over the bars, hang out and talk about soccer."

In the end, the Italians were not rewarded for their hospitality and generosity of spirit. The *Azzurri* went out in the semifinals to Argentina, on penalties, in a match that devastated the nation and irrevocably soured the populace on Diego Maradona, their adopted Argentinian son — because tragedy tends to reveal the many shades of any national character. The notorious semifinal was played in Naples. Maradona played his club soccer there at the *Stadio San Paolo*, winning two league titles for Napoli, a perennial doormat he personally transformed by the sheer force of his will and skill. All the same, *El Pibe*'s central role in Italy's World Cup failure created a witch's brew of Italian resentment. "I went to that semifinal; it was an interesting but pretty dire dynamic to watch a man go from legend to villain in the space of three hours," Pilgrim Tom reports.

Once the Argentinians had advanced, the Italian public, along with the entire Italian football establishment, turned on Maradona in ugly, disgraceful fashion. They shamed him with public drug charges and patrimony claims before banning him from domestic league play altogether. They ran the man out of Italy, basically, for the crime of having beaten the *Azzurri* — in the very stadium where most of the Italians in attendance had worshipped him the day before. Asif Kapadia expertly depicts the entire episode and aftermath in his splendid 2019 documentary film, *Maradona.* When the legendary figure passed away in November 2020, Naples tried to make amends. Today, SSC Napoli plays its home matches in the former *Stadio San Paolo* — now renamed *Stadio Diego Armando Maradona.* (Not to be confused with *Estadio Diego Armando Maradona,* home ground of his very first club, the Buenos Aires-based Argentinos Juniors.) A lovely gesture from the Neapolitan community, but awfully late in coming. Clearly, when playing the Italians on their home soil, it's better to lose gallantly.

Halfway through World Cup 2002, I showed up at an Italian-American club in Glen Cove, New York, to catch an early morning broadcast of Mexico vs. Italy, a final group-stage match live from Oita, Japan. I was on Long Island with my family to cover golf's U.S. Open Championship at Bethpage. We were staying with friends, and I could have watched the game there, in my pajamas, but I wanted a more enthusiastic, spirited, communal soccer-viewing experience. As a member emeritus of the Greek Sportsmen's Club of Somerville, and having familiarized myself with like institutions through the years, I reckoned this "hyphenated-American" club would deliver.

Sure enough, two dozen elderly Italian-Americans were there at the crack of dawn, quietly sipping espresso and smoking cigarettes. With 10 minutes gone in the match, a couple of Mexican dudes slipped in and quietly took seats behind me, near the back. A draw would have seen both teams advance — always a tantalizing scenario when cagey sides like the Italians are involved. All was sweetness and light until *El Tri* went ahead in the 34th minute, which prompted smiles but otherwise respectfully muted celebrations from our Mexican friends. Everywhere else inside the club, the grumbles grew louder; the arm waving and recriminations grew more emotional and frequent.

Ten minutes from full time, the Italians drew a free kick in a dangerous, central position 20 yards from goal. Vincenzo Montella and Alessandro Del Piero argued over who would take it. The old Italian men of Glen Cove loudly argued along with them. Montella prevailed, and struck his effort directly into the Mexican wall — at which point the bar erupted in catcalls and several ashtrays were hurled at the television set. When I looked around, our Mexican neighbors had vanished. Two minutes later, Del Piero equalized, peace was restored, and both teams went through to the round of 16. *Forza Italia per sempre!*

⸺•⸺

The Americans' final group game against the Austrians, punctuating two decades of cultural ferment and footballing evolution, proved an odd and ill-tempered study in anticlimax. The loss to the Italians had all but eliminated the Yanks. When Austrian midfielder Peter Artner was dismissed in the 34th minute — for his intemperate tackle on Peter Vermes — the Austrians realized their tournament was over, as well. They required a lopsided victory to compete with other third-place teams, on goal difference. While playing with 10 men, that eventuality was no longer in the cards.

Many had picked the Austrians to advance from Group A, at Czechoslovakia's expense, and go deep into this tournament. Their side brimmed with veteran *Bundesliga* talent. Strikers Toni Polster and Andi Herzog made them a potent offensive force. Even after they dropped the opener to Italy 1-0, many savvy Euro pundits still fancied their chances to go through. But the Czechs shut them out by the same score, and here they were: a man down, essentially eliminated, playing an ever-more-meaningless match with the tournament's least heralded side, in a half-empty stadium.

Conversely, the Americans were highly motivated to get something from this match. They felt the experience and performance against Italy had lifted them to a new place. "Yeah, 100 percent. We went into that game thinking we could get a result. Not thinking — we *knew* we could get a result," Balboa says.

Instead, what should have been favorable circumstances made it plain just how much the Americans and their golden generation had to learn. Gansler set the U.S. up to absorb pressure and counter. Then, all of a sudden, playing against just 10 men, they were handed the keys to this match. Alas, they had no idea how to drive this particular vehicle. "Obviously, we just weren't used to playing that way," says Bliss, who finally got some coveted World Cup playing time in this match, coming on for Caligiuri with 13 minutes remaining. "The team was built to counter and set up that day to counter. You have to deal with those moments. You have to adapt. But we did not."

Instead, the Austrians did the adapting, almost instinctually, as one might expect from a group of such seasoned professionals. *Unsere Burschen* (Our Boys) had plenty to do. Josef Hickersberger's side started this game with three strikers; they had required goals galore in order to advance. Once reduced to 10, they immediately ceded space to the Americans and fell back into a defensive shell. Having deftly made it to halftime 0-0, Polster came off for midfielder Andreas Reisinger. The U.S. made no changes.

Five minutes after the restart, the score was 1-0 to the 10-man Austrians. The U.S. had committed nearly everyone forward to aggressively prosecute a corner kick. When the ball was cleared, Jimmy Banks and Desmond Armstrong failed to gather it — victims of the always comedic and unfortunate *You got it? No, YOU got it!* shtick. Ultimately, Andreas Ogris swept in and got it, racing by them both and beating Meola from 12 yards.

Now the U.S. was chasing a game it should have been controlling. Gansler sent Wynalda on for Banks, but soon Gerhard Rodax made it 2-0 — on *another* counterattack, this one stemming from an American free kick 25 yards from the Austrian goal. "Their two goals were both on the counter," Gansler points out. "That means we were on the throttle. We just couldn't finish."

Yes and no. Gansler's young team had been victimized four times on the counter in the space of 105 minutes during this tournament: the entire Czech game, plus the first 15 minutes after halftime against Austria. Eventually, an inexperienced side responds to that situation predictably: It simply stops going forward — in numbers, in support of one another — for fear of yet another disaster on the counter. One of the most bizarre scenes from this match took place just a few minutes after Rodax made it 2-nil. Vermes broke into space down the left wing. He picked up his head and saw only Murray and Wynalda running anywhere near him. Up a man, the Americans were attempting to attack 3 vs. 6. Vermes responded by waving his teammates forward, animatedly and pointedly coaxing them into an offensive posture. To no avail.

Murray did pull one back on 83 minutes — a fine reward for the miles and miles of committed running he undertook during this World Cup. However, the game was counterintuitively decided the moment Artner was sent off. The U.S. generated a few chances prior to Murray's goal, but the young side simply did not have the tactical acumen to recalibrate in the moment. Scrapping and clawing, then counterattacking to foil an opponent? That approach they knew well enough. But holding the ball against 10 men, knocking it around for 30 minutes, biding their time patiently to wear down a short-handed foe? No clue.

"We didn't know how to finish a game at that point," Balboa admits. "We were a young group, young coaching staff. I mean, you have to take advantage in a World Cup game against 10 men. We just didn't know."

The Austrian match proved a serious buzzkill, but World Cups seldom send even half the participants home happy. For every 10 fans who manage to look past their team's elimination — on account of the pageantry, the camaraderie, the drunken abandon and good times, the tribal gathering of footballing multitudes in a single place, on a single, global stage — there are at least 10 who leave disappointed, disillusioned and hungover. The poor Italians had nowhere to go when their beloved Blues capitulated on home soil. The sour taste lingered for years.

Come July 8, 1990, the West Germans and their fans were the only ones who left Italy entirely fulfilled. Their 1-0 victory in the final, made possible by Andreas Brehme's penalty kick (made possible, in turn, by a referee's decision polemically disputed to this day by Argentinians everywhere), secured the country's third and final World Cup trophy. All future laurels would belong to a reunified Germany — something made real just three months later, on Oct. 3, 1990.

I watched that rather stultifying final in Portland, Maine, in an otherwise deserted bar on Fore Street. My girlfriend Helen and I had been visiting friends an hour north of there, in Damariscotta. On the way back to Massachusetts, we stopped in the Old Port section of the city just in time for kickoff. Looking back from 2022, that World Cup summer of 1990 proved an indubitable hinge moment, that brief period between *the end of the beginning* and the rest of our American soccer lives. But we didn't yet sense that anything had changed. In fact, it took some doing to persuade the barman at Cadillac Jack's to flip the channel over from a meaningless July Red Sox game.

By that time, the on-field avatars of Generation Zero had all returned home to the United States. Some portion of their collective psyche surely appreciated what they'd accomplished. Four years prior, their participation at *Il Mondiale* would have seemed utterly fantastical. But the Austrian match had dampened their mood, and they couldn't get out of Tirrenia fast enough. The Italian dream, harbored by so many American players for so long, became but a memory with remarkable speed. Their increasingly sophisticated eyes were already cast elsewhere: to the next club gig, the next paycheck, the next contract, the next World Cup. Like the Czechs and Slovaks, most of these young Americans viewed *Italia*

'90 not as the cultural tipping point it proved to be, but rather a massive shop window where they might advertise themselves to talent-seeking, cash-splashing clubs all over Europe.

"That was another question they asked me," Gansler recalls from the pre-tournament pressers. "They said, 'How many of your guys do you think could play in Europe, as you don't have a league of your own?' And I said, 'Right now, maybe half a dozen.' I was thinking about Tab and Marcelo and Harksey and Vermes, who had played a little bit over there already. Caligiuri did, too, in Germany, and Bliss right after that. So I told them, 'At least a half a dozen.' I can still hear the laughter."

Top (#19): Chris Henderson's World Cup 1990 game jersey. Right (#15): Roberto Baggio's *Italia* '90 gam e jersey, procured by Brian Bliss, via the time-honored exchange ritual. According to Bliss, "At the time, Baggio was a relatively un-known player. I needed to look up their roster with our assistant coach, Ralph Perez — who received the pre-match roster list — to figure out whose jersey I traded for." *(Images courtesy of Brian Bliss and Chris Henderson)*

Chris Henderson poses beside a World Cup 1990 poster hanging inside South Korea's Suwon World Cup Stadium, in 2018. *(Image courtesy of Chris Henderson)*

EPILOGUES

The long road to *Italia* '90 dwarfed the road home. "We didn't stay very long, maybe two days? Three days max. Then we all went back," Marcelo Balboa remembers. "It was time to move on to the next parts of our lives. Mostly we wanted to know if there would be interest from clubs in Europe. We wanted to explore our options, because once we signed that contract with the Federation, us young guys weren't going back to school. It was all about finding a pro team to go play for."

Balboa, Tony Meola and Eric Wynalda were the only three World Cuppers whose college/amateur careers had been curtailed by those contracts. As it happened, all three would play for the U.S. come the 1994 World Cup. For that reason, their careers are better known to us today. The Chilean club Colo-Colo expressed some interest in Balboa, but no European counterpart followed suit. Immediately post-*Mondiale*, he happily went off to the American Professional Soccer League before rejoining the USMNT — in its Mission Viejo residence, under a new Federation contract and coach — in late 1992. Meola followed much the same path. It was he who served as team captain during USA '94.

Wynalda's tale is similar, though more baroque. He rejoined the San Diego Nomads, by then a member of the APSL, before eventually signing back on with the national team. The striker did get to Europe eventually: In August 1992, the Federation loaned Wynalda to the *Bundesliga* club 1. FC Saarbrucken, for whom the young American scored 34 times in 61 appearances over the course of two-plus seasons. He couldn't keep the club from being relegated, however, come the spring of 1994. After his second World Cup that summer, Wynalda was sold to newly promoted VfL Bochum. There, the goals did not come. He returned to the U.S. in 1996, and from that point, we know his story: MLS star/pioneer, another World Cup in '98, and John Harkes slept with his wife. Wynalda remarried, and since his retirement in 2002, he's been a fixture on Fox Sports and SiriusXM radio. Starting in 2010, he has managed a succession of lower-division U.S. clubs, most recently the Las Vegas Lights of the second-division United Soccer League.

Harkes went from Italy straight to Sheffield Wednesday, where he scored a few goals the English are still talking about. Yet Americans know him best for playing in the '94 World Cup, not playing in the '98 tournament (that whole thing with Wynalda's wife), and helping to make MLS and D.C. United going concerns. Today, he's as interested in the USL's Greenville Triumph SC, where he serves as head coach and sporting director, as in the Scottish Premiership club Dundee United, where his son, Ian Harkes, pursues the family trade.

Tab Ramos likewise needs no extended "Where are they now?" treatment. He remains highly visible, having ably led the U-20 national team before vacating to manage the Houston Dynamo in 2020. The MLS club fired him the following year. However, none of these 21st-century ups and downs diminish what he did during the 1990s. After a year in Spain's second tier at Figueres, alongside Peter Vermes, Ramos spent three seasons in *La Liga* with Real Betis. Following a one-year stint with Monterrey's Tigres UANL, in *LigaMX*, he returned home in 1996 to headline both MLS and the NY/NJ MetroStars, now the Red Bulls. He retired in 2002. Boosted by his first World Cup appearance at *Italia* '90, Ramos' on-field career might be the most decorated of any Gen Zero alum. He would seem well placed to get another shot at coaching glory, perhaps with the USMNT. Vermes, too, is on the short list of potential USMNT coaches, should Gregg Berhalter fail to deliver a World Cup place and performance after the fashion we've come to expect these last 30 years.

When it comes to the skeptical media horde covering *Italia* '90, Bob Gansler enjoyed the last laugh: Fully 12 of the 17 Yanks who logged minutes in Italy would appear in European leagues following the tournament — double the half-dozen Gansler predicted. This yield illustrates Gen Zero's formidable on-field depth — and the extraordinary influence made manifest by the World Cup shop window.

----•-•----

By the same token, when it comes to those who did *not* cement their Q ratings with another World Cup appearance in 1994 or '98, American footy fans might scratch their heads and ask, "Whatever happened to *that* guy?" Take Steve Trittschuh: "I was back from the World Cup, playing for the Rowdies [in the APSL], and U.S. Soccer calls me up. They said, 'Hey, we've got this thing here from Sparta Prague. It's a contract.' I didn't even have to go there and try out! Just, 'Hey, here's a contract.'"

To review: Trittschuh got skewered by Tomas Skuhravy, among other Czechs and Slovaks, during his only appearance in Italy. No observers were more familiar with said skewering than the management at Skuhravy's club, Sparta Prague. No matter. Trittschuh proved a wonderful signing there. Skuhravy fared well, too: Genoa signed him right after the World Cup, and the striker converted 59 times in 164 *Serie A* appearances.

"There were two places I always wanted to play: Germany and Holland. I was thinking maybe Sparta Prague would be a stepping stone," Trittschuh says. "I was reading up about them when I saw they were gonna play in the European Cup! What the Champions League is today. So I was like, 'Let's do it.' I ended up starting every game and becoming the first American to ever play in the European Cup. It was pretty great. Being the first foreigner at the club in 40 years, they treated me unbelievably well. The level of play was good. The European Cup that October [of 1990] was amazing: playing in front of 50,000 people in Moscow. We lost the home-and-home, 2-0 in both legs. But Spartak Moscow ended up beating Napoli, with Maradona, in the next round. It was cool.

"I was in touch with Tab and Peter Vermes, who were both in Spain at the time. When I'd been with Sparta only a month or two, our national team came through and we played Poland, and then Croatia, which I think was the first time [Croatia] had ever fielded a national team. So, *that* was cool. There were still contract guys on the U.S. team, but there were some, like us, who were playing there in Europe. It was really fun."

To close the Trittschuh file, should these bits of trivia ever come up in conversation: first American to play in the European Cup; started in the first game ever contested by the newly formed Croatian national team; started in the last game ever played by the East German national team on German soil. All these milestones took place between May and November 1990.

"It was a great experience. There were scouts everywhere at that time, checking out the Czech players. A Belgian team was interested in me at one stage," he recalls, his voice a bit tinged with regret. "Looking back, not staying over there was one of the big mistakes I made in my career. When the [1990-91] season was finished, that's when Bora [Milutinovic] took over. I had a chance to come back and do another contract with the Federation. I wanted to make an impression on Bora. So that's what I did — and it was probably the worst thing I could have done. Bora just didn't like the way I played, so I never really played a lot for the national team at that time."

Trittschuh did earn a few more caps, but not till Bora left the building. He returned to the Rowdies in 1993; tried but failed to win a place at SVV Dordrecht in the Netherlands; and then came back home and played on five different U.S. clubs, indoors and outdoors. Then, as Major League Soccer dawned, he reunited with Balboa and Vermes for three fruitful seasons in Colorado, starting in 1996. Upon retirement he became an assistant with the Rapids before taking over the United Soccer League's Colorado Springs Switchbacks. Trittschuh served as head coach for another USL franchise, Saint Louis FC, before accepting the post of academy director at St. Louis Scott Gallagher SC, where today he works alongside a pair of fellow USMNT alums: club president Brad Davis and vice president Steve Pecher.

Federation president Werner Fricker, perhaps the single most important figure behind Gen Zero's rise and run to the Italian World Cup — the man who delivered the 1994 World Cup to America — did not last long in his post following *Il Mondiale*. In the fall of 1990, running for reelection, he was soundly defeated by Alan Rothenberg, administrative hero of the '84 L.A. Olympics. Rothenberg promptly hired Hank Steinbrecher as secretary general. Together, they organized USA '94 and proved instrumental in the launch of MLS and organization of the 1999 FIFA Women's World Cup. Their successes make it difficult for many Americans today to even conceive of the U.S. Soccer Federation pre-Rothenberg. Fricker died in 2001, at 65. In 2009, the Federation presented Rothenberg with its highest honor, the Werner Fricker Award. Steinbrecher was similarly feted in 2012.

Once Fricker left the USSF, old friend Bob Gansler recognized his own days were numbered. He led the USMNT on that fall 1990 tour of Europe, but resigned in February 1991. A month later, Milutinovic, who had coaxed Costa Rica to the round of 16 in Italy, won the job.

Gansler was, at the time, quite vocal in defense of the ousted Fricker, whom he felt the Federation had ill-treated. But he wasn't too annoyed or surprised by how his own USMNT tenure drew to a close. Coaching consecutive World Cup cycles is a minefield for any national team manager. However, I think it's fair to say that Gansler was seriously fucking pissed in 1996 when he wasn't tapped to coach one of the original eight MLS franchises. When he *did* get an opportunity with Sporting Kansas City in 1999, he had a point to prove: Gansler's new club hoisted the MLS Cup a year later. He led SKC until he retired in 2006. From Musci, Hungary, to Milwaukee, Wisconsin, from the early days of NASL to the NCAA game, from *Italia* '90 to MLS at the millennium, Bob Gansler lived an extraordinary soccer life. A thoroughly American life. He won the Werner Fricker Award, too, in 2008 — before Rothenberg did.

"I still think Bob Gansler is completely undervalued in where the game is today," Harkes says. "Because of him and his belief and his keen eye for heart, for players and the discipline he gave us (we were a young team), I think he was probably the biggest catalyst of the game in this country."

Bruce Murray agrees: "I don't think Bob was appreciated as much as he should have been. He was a professional manager of the highest order. Very stoic, but a man who had your back. To a lot of people, he came off as an arrogant asshole, closing off locker rooms to the press and such. But to the players who really knew him and he backed? He was the best. He was the kind of manager who'd say, 'Hey, I know you didn't score, but I'm riding you all the way.' You can't ask for anything more, as a player . . . Someone called me recently and told me it was Bob's 80th birthday [July 1, 2021]. So I found his number and we had this great conversation. He told me I was the biggest pain in the ass of his career — but that he loved me."

The Class of 1990 maintains a fierce loyalty to Gansler. Almost everyone I spoke to had a similarly affectionate story regarding his brusque demeanor hiding a heart of gold. Several took issue here or there with the way he may have prepared or chosen a team, but they universally admired his fairness and coaching acumen. And that is precisely what the coach remains most proud of: the roster he selected for Italy. "In the end, when it comes to that 1990 team, what really makes me feel awfully good to this day was that Ralph [Perez] and Joe [Machnik] and I picked the right team. Because we had a chance to pick guys who had the intangibles. They cared. They worked hard. They were conscientious. Just look at how much they all went on to achieve in the game."

This commitment to U.S. soccer applies even to those players Gansler & Co. chose for Italy, but who did not leave the bench. Chris Henderson was 19 in June 1990. Still an amateur, he went back to UCLA, where he won an NCAA title in the fall of 1990, alongside future USMNTers Brad Friedel, Cobi Jones and Joe-Max Moore. Today, after a long MLS career and 79 caps, he's chief soccer officer and sporting director at the MLS club Inter Miami CF. Kasey Keller, just 20 during World Cup 1990, has been a featured pundit on ESPN for years. He might be the most accomplished goalkeeper ever turned out by American soccer.

"I remember doing an interview during a Chicago Mustangs pre-season down in Sarasota, Florida," Gansler recalls. "This had to be 1967. We were owned by the same folks who owned the White Sox (we played at Comiskey Park). These local media folks, they always asked the same question — about being pioneers — and I always had the same answer: It's fun being a pioneer. We did regard ourselves that way. There were obstacles and difficulties and all that, but there was also opportunity. And so, you know, none of us sat around and said, 'Woe is us,' and, 'Why the hell do we not have more?' Instead we said, 'Hey, we have something. Let's make it more.' I tell you what we didn't say: 'We're gonna get through this for the next generation.' No way. We wanted to make it better for ourselves.

"I'll remember forever my teammates at Chicago and the national team at that time. Yeah, sometimes it hurt because you'd have a foreigner playing next to you — or a foreigner in charge — who didn't really trust you very much. We fought that in the Sixties, when our guys went over to Europe in the Nineties. Today even."

When I spoke to Gansler, I tried like the dickens to draw him out on what remains one of my central theses — that all meaningful progress in American soccer really does stem from Port of Spain, thanks to that first generation of soccer natives who took up the game as small children in the early 1970s. What I learned in the course of my conversations is probably clear to the reader by now: Bob Gansler doesn't think in those terms. He's an evolutionist, and a stubborn one at that. He won't be led afield by some cheeky journalist with a narrative to buttress. And God love him for it. The man's personal integrity and his brand of incrementalism have stood him, and his coaching charges, in very good stead.

The U.S. Soccer Federation itself has traveled light-years from the early days of the Fricker administration, when a handful of true believers operated on a shoestring in near total anonymity. Qualification for the 1990 World Cup changed all that. Immediately.

"We used *Italia* '90 as a major publicity platform to demonstrate, to the many skeptics, that we Americans were ready, capable and knowledgeable," recalls Jim Trecker, World Cup 1994 senior vice president/ communications. "We did a news session in Florence and another at *Stadio Olimpico* before the Final, putting our leadership — Werner Fricker, Scott LeTellier, Henry Kissinger — on the world's dais, so to speak, to show that we knew what we were doing. We also brought dozens of leaders from potential USA venues to Italy, entertained them at matches and at the U.S. Ambassador's Residence. The effort was very broad and very successful in increasing interest. We knew the breadth of the 'legitimacy' issue, but we knew we were up to the task and never had a moment of doubt."

On the ambitious-but-sturdy foundation laid by Fricker et al., the Federation soon proved it could win sponsors, bank profits, host marquee international events, pull its weight in fostering its own regional tournaments like the CONCACAF Gold Cup, and wield lasting player-development influence. Funny how things can shift: In certain respects, the Federation has done too good a job. Since 1990, at surprising speed, American soccer has become uniquely and inordinately dependent on its national teams, men's and women's, to grow and foster the sport's broad visibility and fan interest.

We discussed this dynamic at the end of Chapter 9. MLS was not formed until 1996. Two and a half decades later, domestic league play in the U.S. is only now beginning to hold its own and fulfill the vital, time-honored function of holding fan attention between international spectacles like the World Cup. Which is damned ironic. Until 1990, the economic power and insular nature of our domestic sport establishment generally *precluded* American fans from caring about international competitions featuring U.S. national teams, regardless of the sport. The Federation, through Gen Zero, played a crucial role in allowing Americans to be internationalist in this regard. What's more, where the U.S. *does* compete internationally today, it invariably does so as a hegemon, as the presumed medal-count winner, as the bully on the block. Men's soccer in particular allows the

U.S. to play the role of plucky underdog, where expectations can perhaps be exceeded, not merely met with a shrug.

That said, country and club must complement one another. Gansler recognized early on that hyperfocus on the national team, to the exclusion of domestic soccer, was a dead end: "My takeaway from Italy was, we really needed to get an MLS up and running (a professional league) because a player's evolution in his game comes when he practices with good players and plays against them day to day. *If you don't have a league, you are at the end.*" These italics are mine, because this should be the mantra driving U.S. Women's National Team priorities going forward.

<hr>

If all works of art and commerce are products of their time and place, the reader should know that I started researching this book in 2014, but didn't finish the writing until the pandemic spring of 2020. Several things happened in those six years that significantly affected the finished product. For several years, starting in 2014, the demands of work and family allowed for this book project on a meager level only. Not until March 2020 was I presented with the time and professional latitude (*thanks, clients on hiatus!*) to finish the damned thing. By this time, of course, a lot of relevant shit had gone down. In 2016, for example, Donald Trump was elected Baby Boomer in chief, which nefariously reinforced the generational dynamic I had already begun to detail.

Another important development arrived when the USMNT managed to blow its qualification for the Russian World Cup of 2018: *only needing a draw,* right there on the ever-consequential island of Trinidad. When Bruce Arena's team laid that egg, I was immediately and authorially mortified: My manuscript remained unfinished, but it was littered throughout with references to the USMNT's perfect World Cup qualification record since 1989. *Rewrite!*

The U.S. Women's National Team won another *two* World Cups during this extended gestation period, in many ways eclipsing their male counterparts culturally and igniting a very public pay-equity debate (the USWNT and the Federation settled the resulting lawsuit in March 2022). In social moments, when I would describe my own subject matter, folks would often furrow their brows and say, "Wait, you're writing about the *men's* national team?" *Sorry.* This narrative centers on a 20-year period, 1970 to 1990, when the mainstreaming of soccer in this country finally took place. The USWNT played its first-ever match in 1985. Different story, different book.

To research the relevant history, I reached out to every member of the 1990 USMNT. Some guys never responded. Some emails or phone numbers might have been "bad." I certainly worked a lot harder to get Bruce Murray on the record than Eric Eichmann, because the former played big minutes throughout 1989-90, and the latter did not. Some team members central to the story simply eluded me, despite my best efforts. Paul Caligiuri continues to strike me as a Zelig-like figure who was everywhere during this story, and often got there first. I even went to Southern California in January 2019, plotting to ambush him at the Orange County FC practice facility where he coaches today. But he wasn't there. Nobody was there. He never answered my emails or texts — even those chaperoned by his USMNT teammates, a few of whom kindly vouched for the fact that I wasn't some muckraking stalker. All in vain. Caligiuri remains among the half-dozen guys I never did get to talk to. Note that while Caligiuri is quoted in this book, I cite the media outlet or journalist to whom he spoke on the first reference. This is the style I deployed when quoting any secondary source.

Because I never got the elusive Paul Caligiuri on the record, his teammates were left to speak for him — and about him. They well appreciate the dyke-bursting importance of that fleeting moment in Port of Spain. They unanimously recognize Cal's on-field chops, as well. Not many defensive midfielders get forward and finish like Caligiuri did. Everyone's seen the goal against T&T on Nov. 19, 1989, but you should go Google the clip of his goal against Czechoslovakia, in Italy. Superb.

"Look, Cal was our first superstar, with the commercials and the beach body," says Bruce Murray, the man who orchestrated that Czech goal. "When I got to the national team, early on, right after Torrance, he also welcomed me, and we had a great playing relationship. Such a great athlete — and what a tackler! You did *not* want to get on the wrong side of Paul in the tackle.

"I think some guys maybe grew jealous of him. But there's no way anyone can tell me they don't recognize what Paul Caligiuri's left foot did for U.S. soccer, big picture — and for each of us individually. Check this out: I was getting married after the T&T game. I had a house in Bethesda we wanted to buy. If we didn't win, I didn't know *what* I was going to do. I'd have pulled out of that house deal. Paul saved our ass. That's what he did. I'm indebted to him."

Relational politics within a team are never black and white, especially among American males who compete together as long as these guys did. One thing remains crystal clear, however: When American soccer needed Paul Caligiuri, he showed up. The U.S. played three matches at *Italia '90* and four at USA '94; he went the full 90 in all seven. When MLS launched, Caligiuri was there to provide the new league whatever star power he brought to the table. He retired after 160 appearances for the Columbus Crew and L.A. Galaxy — equivalent to six full seasons of play — and then was inducted into the Hall of Fame beside Windischmann in 2004.

Having coached first the women's team and then the men's team at Cal Poly Pomona, Caligiuri took the helm at the National Premier Soccer League's Orange County FC in 2018. The year before, he surprised more than a few folks by running for USSF president, as part of an eclectic field that included Eric Wynalda, Cindy Parlow Cone and Carlos Cordeiro, who won the election. Cordeiro resigned in 2020 amid fallout from the USWNT pay-equity suit; Cone ascended in his place and was elected to a full term in March 2022. When I chatted with Caligiuri's UCLA teammate Paul Krumpe in 2017, I asked whether he'd been aware of Cal's political ambitions: "No idea."

———•◆•———

Few guys in Generation Zero were as universally respected in the moment as Mike Windischmann, who graciously spent a *lot* of time on the phone with me — enough to explain precisely how the indoor game undermines one's outdoor skills (a certified revelation to me, and I played a lot of indoor). Windy was the captain at *Italia* '90, of course, a call that Gansler made rather arbitrarily, early in his coaching tenure. All these years later, absolutely no one has questioned the wisdom of it.

Windischmann still lives in Queens. He recently left a longtime teaching/coaching position to work at the Teen Center, an NYC Department of Education program for at-risk middle-school kids in the Hollis Queens school district. His Hall of Fame induction arrived well ahead of most of his teammates, because he retired well before they did. Almost immediately after Italy, Windy blew out his knee training for the USMNT's fall 1990 tour through Europe. He stepped away from the sport before he could pursue the tryout he'd lined up with the German side Energie Cottbus.

"I never had a major injury before that," he says, "but I knew immediately I'd torn my ACL. At that time, it was a full year to recover. Now it's easier, six to eight months. It wasn't easy to get those tryouts, either. Now you can basically get one anywhere. Our group sort of broke down those barriers. Energie Cottbus was the team that [Brian] Bliss went to — I was talking with them before I got injured. I had gone over there for two days and was training with them."

Was your German good enough?

"I would have been able to get by."

Readers who have plowed their way through this book should possess a keen understanding of just how many different players participated in the combined '88 Olympic and '90 World Cup qualification campaigns. They should also have a sense for how injury, momentary form and team politics affected rosters and lineups from game to game. That background gives the following stat real heft: When Windischmann stopped playing in 1990, he held the national-team record for the most consecutive USMNT games played (36) and started (33). Those marks still stand. They are unlikely to be broken.

———•———

We Americans naturally view the 1990 World Cup through an especially gauzy lens. While U.S. match results were poor, the event, as we've established, was clearly a gateway event for U.S. soccer: the start of something big. The rest of the footballing world, however, tends to view this tournament as the low ebb of "negative football," an overly defensive, physically cynical, tactically cautious brand of international soccer that prevailed throughout the 1980s. *Il Mondiale* remains the lowest-scoring World Cup competition on record: just 2.2 total goals per game. Both semifinals ended 1-1, each decided on penalties. The final finished 1-0, the lone goal coming from the spot. The competition produced a then-record 16 red cards, including the first-ever dismissal in a final.

These factors proved so glaring and galling that FIFA responded with three consequential rule changes. The first dealt with offside decisions. Up to and including *Italia '90*, an offensive player judged to be *even* with the last defender was ruled to have been in an offside position. Post-1990, *even* with the last defender was considered *on*side.

Second, a new backpass regulation barred goalkeepers from touching the ball with their hands if the ball had been played from a teammate's foot. Modern fans unfamiliar with soccer prior to 1990 have been spared considerable retrospective exasperation. Few things proved more mind-numbing than watching defenders kill time or defuse a high press by blithely passing the ball back and forth with a keeper.

Last, in group-play matches at FIFA competitions, victories would now earn three points, rather than two. This change was instituted to incentivize goals and wins ahead of scoreless or otherwise tactical draws. Eventually, most national football associations also applied this new point system to domestic league standings/tables. The English FA was the first to award three points for a victory in its domestic club competition, way back in 1981. A few smaller footballing nations followed suit during the

Eighties, but no additional major European leagues got onboard until after 1990. FIFA instituted this system across all its competitions starting with the U.S. World Cup in 1994. The German *Bundesliga*, the last major holdout, switched over a year later.

———•—

I felt a real kinship in talking with Brian Bliss. We played against each other back in Connecticut as contemporary college dudes, after all. But he was also chatty and candid and insightful. While he has made his mark in the game (today he's director of player personnel for Sporting KC and has assisted in coaching the U.S. U-20 national team since 2012), Bliss has managed to fly a bit under the radar. Still, few on the 1990 USMNT were more versatile or respected as a player. Immediately post-World Cup, Bliss wanted what all his teammates wanted — the chance to play in Europe — so he spent the next several months working with an agent trying to get a deal. In January 1991, he landed one — with Energie Cottbus in *Bundesliga* 2. Believe it or not, those 13 minutes he logged against Austria in the USMNT's final Italian match made all the difference. "There was no way I would have ended up at Cottbus or anywhere in Germany had I not had the World Cup on my resume — and at least played in a game," Bliss asserts. "The World Cup got you that foot in the door, and I was able to gut it out. You see a lot of guys go to Europe and come right back."

Bliss moved to another *Bundesliga,* 2 side, Saxony's Chemnitzer FC, for the 1991-92 season before settling in with the former East German side FC Carl Zeiss Jena. (The German league absorbed several clubs from the East prior to the 1990-91 season; the country absorbed the whole of East Germany in stages, all through 1990 and 1991.) Bliss would spend four full seasons in Jena, but he never took his eye off the USMNT. Those 13 minutes were not nearly enough for him, and four workmanlike years in Germany had raised his game to new heights. When the U.S. hosted the '94 World Cup, he desperately wanted to be part of it.

"But I hadn't been called into the national team for a couple years," he says. "So I called Sunil Gulati [then a USSF board member], who I have a long relationship with, and said, 'Sunil, what is going on? I play every week; I get good remarks in the *Kicker* magazine. I can't even get called into a random camp for a friendly?' He didn't know anything, but said he'd pass it on to Bora."

Milutinovic, the new USMNT coach, had a brother living in Germany; he was dispatched to Jena to scout Bliss. "So Bora brings me into a December 1993 game with Germany in Palo Alto. I get in somewhere on the hour, and I had a pretty good 35 minutes out there. After the game, Bora says, 'We're going to see each other again.' I'm like, great.

"So the New Year comes, now it's 1994, tournament's only a few months away — I hear nothing. I'm thinking, 'They're not calling me in. OK. Whatever. Gotta live with it.' Then they announce the made-for tour [of friendlies] they always do prior to the World Cup, to get a rhythm going. They lined up Bayern Munich, Kuwait, then Greece in New Haven — and I get called into all three games. As I get called in, they had just dropped a bunch of guys from the Mission Viejo camp: Vermes, Doyle, Dominic Kinnear, Brian Quinn, Des Armstrong, Jeff Agoos. I mean, five of these guys are defenders. I'm thinking, 'Man, I got a great shot here.'

"My club says, 'You can't go to all three games. We're in a pickle over here, fighting to avoid relegation; pick two games.' So I picked the Bayern game in Cleveland on a Wednesday, and Kuwait at Rutgers on a Saturday — then I had to go back. So I get to camp, play those two games, performed pretty well. I think we're at 25 guys at that point; we need to be down to 23 for the final roster. My last night in the hotel in New Jersey, I see Bora. He tells me to have a good flight. I say, 'Hey, any chance you can tell me if I make the final squad or not?' He says, 'I can't tell you that, Mr. Bliss.' Why not? 'Because it's not fair to the others.' I told him I wouldn't tell anyone — I'm getting a plane in 16 hours! And obviously, there's no Twitter back then . . . It would have helped in my decision over the weekend — whether I played, or not, for my club.

"Anyway, I fly back and arrive Friday. The club says they need me to play Saturday; we *are* fighting relegation. I figured I could not take the chance. I couldn't say 'I won't play to avoid injury' because if I don't make the [World

Cup] squad, then I look stupid. So I play. First half, 50-50 tackle, *baboom!* I blow out my knee: third-degree MCL, did the meniscus as well."

Within the week, Bliss was back in the States and under the knife of Dr. Bert Mandelbaum.

"Sometime later, after the World Cup, I ran into Timo Liekoski, Bora's assistant in '94. He says to me, 'Brian, you were in. I'm not telling you that because you want to hear it, but because it's the truth.' I mean, sonofa-bitch . . . That was a bitter one. But that's life. You gotta live with it."

———————

I never did speak with either of the two African-American guys on the *Italia* '90 roster, but it wasn't for lack of trying. One member of Generation Zero — unfortunately, I can't recall exactly who — told me that Des Armstrong had been working on a documentary film project centered on the Shot Heard 'Round the World. He provided Armstrong's cell phone number. I called and texted a few times, but never heard back from the outside back.

When I reached out to Jimmy Banks in 2017, I didn't hear back for a long while. Then I did receive a nice note from him, asking if he could answer my questions by email. By this time it was early 2018. "Sure thing," I wrote back. "Much obliged. See a list of questions attached." I never heard back. Fifteen months later, Banks was dead of stomach cancer. He was 54.

The Federation website posted a splendid feature/obituary on Banks' life in the game. The article led with the fact that Black, footballing athletes were pretty rare where he'd grown up, inner-city Milwaukee. It went on to make clear that Banks' accomplished career was replete with juxtapositions. He played for Gansler at the University of Wisconsin-Milwaukee, which isn't so strange. But the guy never played a minute of professional outdoor soccer thereafter, other than matches with the U.S. Men's National Team. He played six years of indoor with the AISA's Milwaukee Wave and starred outdoors for Gansler's old semipro club, the Bavarians, in Milwaukee. By 1993, he'd called it a career. In Italy, where he roomed with Armstrong, Banks was the beneficiary of Krumpe's injury and Gansler's determination to shake things up after the Czech debacle. Banks started both the Italy and Austria matches, only to be carded and subbed off in both encounters — after 80 minutes vs. the Italians, after 55 in the finale. "Some people thought, 'He played for you in college.' Horsefeathers," Gansler told the U.S. Soccer website in 2019. "That had nothing to do with it. He had 36 appearances with the national team, and for a lot of them I was not the coach. These [appearances] were not gimmes."

Armstrong met Banks when they exchanged jerseys after a National Sports Festival match in Syracuse, New York, during the summer of 1981. The teenagers remained lifelong friends. Des intimated, in the U.S. Soccer feature, that Banks struggled for many years with depression. This may explain his attachment to home, to Milwaukee, and his aversion to a full-on professional soccer life on the road. And Banks did make a good life for himself in his hometown. He coached at the Milwaukee School of Engineering, starting in 1999. After he steadily built the program there, his Raiders qualified for the NCAA Division III tournament in 2014 and 2015 (producing a national player of the year, Logan Andryk, in the process). Banks' three sons — Demetrius, J.C. and Jordan, each of whom played college soccer or beyond — all survive him.

———•——

Mike Windischmann started getting the phone calls toward the end of 2007. Something about a reunion game down in Port of Spain. Then one day he went out for a coffee: "So I run into this guy from the Trinidad and Tobago team, in a Dunkin' Donuts of all places," he says. "I was getting a coffee with my wife. He waves and calls me over. Asks me how I'm doing and whether I'm gonna play in this game down there — just before Thanksgiving 2007. I'm like — 'What? Really?'"

"Desmond Armstrong put it together," Trittschuh explains. "He called and said, 'Would you be interested in this?' Then he called again and said it was off. Then, two or three weeks before Thanksgiving, he calls again: 'It's on. You going?'"

The rematch scheme seemed pretty last minute and somewhat sketchy to most everyone involved. Krumpe — who logged two APSL seasons before retiring, in 1992 — received just a couple weeks' notice.

Talk of being paid preceded talk of sharing gate receipts with the T&T players. Free plane tickets were dangled. This perk morphed into, "Go ahead and buy the ticket. We'll reimburse you." No one knew who exactly had committed and who had not. John Doyle was supposed to have been flown in from San Jose, California, where he worked as GM for the MLS Earthquakes (2008-2016). But his tickets were eventually booked from San Juan, Puerto Rico — a mere 3,126 nautical miles from the South Bay.

"So, he didn't make it," Stollmeyer reports, laughing. "A lot of us connected in Miami — we ran into each other in the airport. That was fun. We're getting a beer and we keep flagging guys down, because we're all flying out to Port of Spain together. Then we recognize some of the Trinidad players coming out of New York, so we sat down with them!"

Only in Port of Spain itself did the situation fully crystallize. Fine accommodations *were* provided, and several commemorative events planned. The glaring problem, however, was one of manpower. Only nine U.S. guys made their way back to T&T that November of 2007: Meola, Windy, Tritt, Cal, Stolly, Krumpe, Eichmann, organizer Armstrong, and Colorado Rapids coach Robin Fraser, who didn't participate in the 1989 original, but did suit up for the USMNT throughout the 1990s.

The T&T alumni, all 20 of them, were more than a bit ready for this reunion match. "Those guys had been playing for a month, month and a half, exhibition games — everything. They were ready for revenge," Windischmann says.

"They'd been stewing over the game a long time," Krumpe adds. "They'd been training a bit together. We sort of threw a team together . . . But what a cool trip that was — to go back to that field, that stadium, and play those guys again?"

The locals encouraged the Yanks to take a couple stand-ins from the embassy, in order to fill out a full team of 11 players. "We told 'em: *We aren't playing like that,*" captain Windischmann recalls.

Stollmeyer was the first to inform me of this reunion match. At this point in the story, during his telling, I could feel a cold sweat developing on the back of my neck. Because there is no more sinking feeling for a

35- to 40-year-old soccer player than showing up for a match — especially an indoor match, say, late on a weeknight, in the dead of winter — and realizing there is just one sub. Or no subs at all. The mature body does not respond well to actual physical exertion on this scale. Without a bench, things can get real ugly, real fast.

"So they do end up flying in a few more guys — from California or somewhere. I don't remember their names," Stolly continues. "So we're *in the locker room* the day of the match, but we all agree we're not coming out 'til we have more guys. Then we hear they've landed and they're on the way to the stadium! Only then did we get ready to play."

The home team prevailed in this hastily made, casually administered rematch, 3-1, a popular result among the few thousand locals who showed up. There were no gate receipts to speak of, but much goodwill was indeed shared — *after* the match, once the Americans had caught their breadth and licked their wounds. "I had torn my ACL and got it fixed, and then had torn it again — and never got it fixed," Windy says. "I played the whole game with that torn ACL. We ended up having only 12 guys. So I wound up playing almost the whole game. I couldn't bend my knee after that!"

"We were exhausted," Stollmeyer confirms. "At halftime, I said to Meola and Krumpe, *Hey if you want to sub me off, that's fine,* and they're like 'No way. We need you to play — just another 15 minutes!' And then I'm about to get subbed, finally, and Desmond is next to me completely cramping up. So he goes off. Then with about 15 minutes to go, Caligiuri goes off and I'm like, *Shit. I gotta play the full fucking 90."*

No one died. Aside from Windy's replacement ACL, there were no major casualties. The match closed with handshakes, hugs and rueful laughter all around. For the crowd and the T&T players especially, a long-awaited catharsis took root and bloomed right then and there. Soccer is that rare human activity that can perform this sort of heavy emotional lifting. It's a bit magical in that regard. Ask anyone who witnessed the *start* of this match.

"So, the opening whistle blows," Windischmann reports, "and just a couple minutes later I send a free kick over. Guess who's there to score the first goal: *Yeah*, Caligiuri. Everybody was stunned. Like, 'Not again!'"

"*Freakin'* Caligiuri," Stollmeyer says, shaking his head. "Ridiculous. They didn't have a lot of people at this game, maybe a few thousand, but they all just go dead silent. Again!! We're on the field laughing at ourselves. Like, this could *not* have happened. Again! But it did. That is the absolute truth."

———•—

Bruce Murray retired from competitive soccer in 1995, in part because a series of concussions forced his hand. Four years later, fellow Montgomery County Pinto John Kerr Jr. assumed head coaching duties at Harvard. By the fall of 2004, Murray had joined his boyhood friend there, as an assistant. That first season together, when the Crimson traveled north to take on the University of Maine in Brunswick, Tom Wadlington and I showed up at the match unannounced. It was Tom's idea. He reckoned there would never be a better opportunity to catch up with our old billet buddies in the flesh.

We set upon the two Marylanders post-match, after Matt Bernal's late goal had earned the Black Bears a 2-1 victory. The visiting coaches weren't thrilled with this result — or the prospect of a dour two-hour bus ride back to Cambridge — but their faces brightened when we introduced ourselves. Soon we were laughing and trading stories about the Italian port city of Tirrenia, the curiously stoic charm of Lothar Osiander, and youth soccer trips up and down the East Coast — trips enabled by our fathers and fleets of Seventies-era station wagons.

I didn't take notes that afternoon. In 2004, the germs of this book were 10 years from forming. Yet much of our subject matter that day has been reprised or touched upon here in some way, shape or form: the 1981 ODP camp where Wad and Bruce had both competed, where Angus McAlpine and his ridiculous accent presided, where George Gelnovatch demonstrated his furtive skills with a fire extinguisher . . . I remember *this* bombshell being loosed in Brunswick: Before landing his gig in Cambridge, Kerr had actually coached at none other than Wellesley High School — under Peter

Loiter, for fuck's sake. While John and I were getting our heads around the unlikely Loiter connection, Tom and Bruce shared stories of Italy, where one 20-something Gen X male roamed freely about the countryside, scalping tickets and "partying like a madman," while the other spent two weeks near Pisa in veritable lockdown, scrapping with Eric Eichmann and frantically preparing for three games his side was destined to lose.

Kerr left Harvard in 2007 to accept the head coaching position at Duke. There he remains. The National Soccer Hall of Fame called Murray in 2011. Today, channeling the spirit of Hubert Vogelsinger, he operates the Bruce Murray Soccer Academy in Darnestown, Maryland. He looks back on the Seventies, Eighties, and his entire competitive career largely without regret. When he and I caught up for this book, he admitted that he didn't honestly believe that Generation Zero's place in history had been usurped by the 1994 USMNT. Unlike several of his 1990 teammates, he couldn't even muster any ill will toward Milutinovic.

"Look, I played and trained and lived with those guys through 1993, when they released me," he says. "I got cut by Bora, who had his own ideas. I definitely think the '94 World Cup *performance* overshadows the 1990 performance. But I don't feel *we* were overshadowed. The reality is, a big part of that group went forward to USA '94. Bora took what we had and added pieces to it."

Murray is spot on. The core of that 1990 team — Harkes, Ramos and Caligiuri in midfield; Wynalda up top, Balboa in back and Meola in goal — formed the core of Bora's 1994 USMNT. Of the five remaining starters, only Alexi Lalas and Cobi Jones were homegrown additions. Earnie Stewart, Roy Wegerle and Tom Dooley were all recruited and naturalized.

"Bora was a brilliant tactician," Murray asserts. "He oversaw that whole traveling circus, as well: That team played a ton of games ahead of that World Cup, all over the world. People don't remember all that, or don't want to admit it. His whole premise was this: We're going to defend the perimeter, from the outside in, squeeze it all in there — and *then*, we're going to turn 'em over. Because Bora saw that we had work rate and pace with Wegerle, Stewart, Cobi Jones and Wynalda. Those guys could really move. From a soccer and historical standpoint, though, you'd have to go with 1990. The team that went to the Olympics in '88, then the World Cup. That team changed everything. We showed this country what soccer was all about."

When we spoke, Bruce also admitted that he didn't remember too many details from our sideline conversation 17 years prior. It was brief, and his mind was elsewhere. "What I *do* remember from that trip was, we lost — and that another assistant, Big Gary Crompton, gave us a guided tour all the way up and all the way home." Crompton, now the coach at Bentley University near Boston, had played centerback for the University of Maine. At least three of his Black Bear teammates — Bob Strong, Dan Noblet and George "Gige" Sherry — were teammates of mine on True North FC during the 1990s, in the Maine Open League. When Murray first joined the Harvard staff, he lived in Needham: Wellesley's next-door neighbor and great soccer rival. Then he moved to Rogers Avenue in Somerville, less than a mile from the flat I occupied a decade before, when playing for the Greek Sportsmen. As a reporter and researcher, it was unmooring but ex-hilarating to have unearthed obscure names from the early modern annals of U.S. soccer history — Manfred Schellscheidt, Dan Canter, Sadri Gjonbalaj — only to hear a long-lost contemporary reel them off and reframe them as part of his own personal journey. The longer our conversation went, the more frequently our narratives intertwined — despite the fact that, save for a 10-minute sideline chat in 2004, we hadn't spoken to each other or communicated in any way since the fall of 1976.

Back on the sideline in Brunswick, Tom and I didn't keep the Marylanders too long. They had a busload of guys waiting on them — the same impatient, sweat-soaked college players we'd all been circa 1984. We said our warm goodbyes and off they went, dragging all manner of gear and ball bags behind them.

INDEX

Italic page numbers indicate photographs.

33333333

Budapest Honved FC, 71
Budweiser Player of the Week, 145
Buffalo Stallions, 236
Bulgaria, 186–87
Bunbury, Alex, 222
Bundesliga, 2, 53, 59, 95, 195, 255, 410
Bundesliga 2, 249, 260
Burns, Mike, 299–301, 357
Button, Dick, 51

C

Cabanas, Roberto, 108
cable television, 1–2, 346
Cachirules scandal, 289–92
Calado, Jorge, *8*
California, 83, 117
California Surf, 86
Caligiuri, Paul (Cal)
  coaching career, 406–7
  collegiate training, 129, 150, 155, 183, 210, 224, 294–96
  European career, 263–64, 271
  injuries, 313
  international career, 256
  Olympic Festivals, 122
  shoe contracts, 353–54
  "Shot Heard 'Round the World," 66, 81, 130, 191
  skill development, 331–32
  USMNT career, 23, 66, 81–82, 124, 129–30, 142, *161*, 173, 180, 186–87, 191, 210, 220, 224, 227–28, 253, 264, 279–81, 286, 296, 313, 330–37, 342, 349–50, 364, *366*, 372, 383, 392, 406–7, 414–17
  WSA career, 255–56
Cameroon, 368
Canada Cup, 297
Canadian National Team, 75, 226–27, 234
  international friendlies, 207
  1984 Olympic Games, 166
  1988 Olympic Games, *218,* 219, 221–22, 225–30, 364
  player development, 253
  World Cup 1974, 58–59
  World Cup 1978, 58–59

  World Cup 1982, 111
  World Cup 1986, 172, 176, 287
Canadian Soccer Association, 222
Canales, Joaquin, 248
Caniggia, Claudio, 360
Canter, Dan, 139, 176–78, 182–83, 187, 418
Cantillo, Ringo, *100,* 109, 139
caps, 75
Carboni, Dennis, 297
Carcamo, Leonel, 319
Caribous of Colorado, *162*
Carreras, Jose, 343
Carrillo, Alex, 125–26, 254
Carter, Earl, 312
Carter, Jimmy, 110
Casales, Joaquin, 317
Castaneda Mendez, Carlos Enrique, 318
Castillo, Edgar, 2
catenaccio (the door bolt) tactic, 385
Catliff, John, 222
Cayasso, Juan, 309–10
CBS, 56, 96
CBS Sports Spectacular, 53
Ceballos Arana, Marvin, 313
Central Americans, 108, 231
Central Connecticut State, 160
Centro Tecnico Federale di Coverciano, 362
Cerritos High School, 102–3
Chacon Estrada, Raul, 313
Chamberlain, Wilt, 241
Championship, The (English), 267
Champions League, 1
Chandler, Peter, 93, 95
Chandler, Timmy, 2
Charles, Hutson, 312
Charles, Toby, 97–98
Chavarria, German, 309–10
cheerleaders, 47
Chemnitzer, FC, 410
Cherundolo, Steve, 83
Chevez, Jorge, 176
Chicago Fire, 89
Chicago Mustangs, 21, 55, 300, 403
Chicago Sting, 171, 220, 224, 242
Chile, 282

E

East Coast Hockey League, 137
East Coast Mafia, 126, 128
Eastern New York State Soccer
    Association, 251
East Germany, 165, 264, 361, *365,* 400
East Nash Soccer, 375
Ebert, Don, 22
Eck, Ted, 308, 314, 318
Ecuador, 170, 282
Edmonton Brickmen, 222, 249, 253-54
Edmonton Drillers, 136
Edmonton Oilers, 136
Edwards, Gene, 163-65, 188, 204,
    213-14
Edwards, Troy, 247
Egypt, 166
Eichmann, Eric
    collegiate training, 150
    European career, 269-70
    indoor career, 378
    USMNT career, 82, *218,* 220, 298,
        312-14, 317-19, 325, 364, 376,
        378, 406, 414, 417
El Camino Community College, 173-76,
    224
Ellinger, John, 122
Elliot-Allen, Paul, 312, 337
Ellis, Jill, 82
Ellis, John, 81
El Salvador
    1988 Olympic Games, 229-30
    2022 Olympic Games, 233
    U-23 national team, 233
    World Cup 1970, 55, 58, 287
    World Cup 1982, 287
    World Cup 1986, 170
    World Cup 1990, 307, 312, 317-21,
        324
endorsements, 350-53
Energie Cottbus, 408, 410
England
    World Cup 1950, 193, 274
    World Cup 1986, 109
    World Cup 1990, 344
English Football Association (The FA),
    46, 81, 409

Enterprise Sun, 369
Eredivisie, 2, 265
Escuela, Chico, 98
Eskandarian, Alecko, 198, 237
Eskandarian, Andranik, 198, 238
ESPN, 3-5, 22, 66, 187, 235, 276-77, 320,
    331, 345-46, 402
Estadio Cuscatlan (San Salvador, El
    Salvador), 322
Estadio Diego Armando Maradona
    (Buenos Aires, Argentina), 390
Estadio Mateo Flores (Guatemala City,
    Guatemala), 318
Estadio Nacional (Tegucigalpa,
    Honduras), 317
Estadio Ricardo Saprissa (San José, Costa
    Rica), 309
Estrada, Miguel, 319
ES Troyes AC, 261-62
ethnic clubs and leagues, 21, 72, 146,
    157, 193, 195-203, 245-46, 252-55,
    341
Etienne, Derrick, Jr., 159-60
Etienne, Fritz, 159
Etienne, Marvin, 159
ETO FC Gyor, 264-65, 381
European Court of Justice, 266
European Cup, 399
European soccer, 2, 86, 197, 259-69
Eusébio da Silva Ferreira, *8,* 12-16, 41,
    344
Evans, Janet, 295
Everett Stadium, 40
Evert, Chris, 43
Everton, 109, 185
exhibition tours, 266-67

F

factory clubs, 78
Fairfax Spartans, 74
family visits, 363, 369
fan support, 37, 54, 276-77
    for CONCACAF, 24
    hooliganism, 360
    hostile fans, 326
    for international competitions, 404
    Italian futbol scene, 360-63, 368,

Lee, Dexter, 337
Lehigh University, 119
lessons learned, World Cup, 363
LeTellier, Scott, 325, 348, 404
Le Touquet AC, 271
Lewis, Carl, 295
Lewis, Eddie, 83, 155
Lewis, Leonson, 312, 337
Lewis, Michael, 110, 298
Ley, Bob, 345
Lidster, George, 248
Liekoski, Timo, 412
Lifton, Robert, 137
Liga MX, 2, 374
linguistics, 46
Liveric, Mark, 41, 93, 109
Liverpool, 41, 109
Llamosa, Carlos, 83
Lockhart Stadium (Fort Lauderdale, FL), 247–48
Logan, Doug, 250
Loiter, Peter, 114–16, 416–17
Long, Stephen, 154
Loren, Sophia, 343–44
Los Angeles, California, 23–24, 215
Los Angeles Heat, 233, 254–55
Los Angeles Lazers, 183, 341
Louganis, Greg, 295
Louisville Thunder, 240
Loustau, Juan Carlos, 333
Loyola Marymount University (Los Angeles), 154, 156, 224
Loyola University (Baltimore), 130, 146, 150
Lucas, George, 31–32
Luckhurst, Mick, 359
Lusitania Recreation, 245
Luso American Soccer Association (LASA), 199–204

M

MacDonald, Duncan, 154
Machado, Mario, 96–97
Machnik, Joe, 325, 331, 370, 379, 402
Mad magazine, 50
Magath, Felix, 256
Eddie Mahe and Associates, 211–12

Maher, Kevin, 160, 237, 241
Maier, Sepp, 28, 61
Major Arena Soccer League, 239, 298
Major Indoor Soccer League (MISL), 22, 131, 135, 166, 171–72, 182–83, 195, 220, 223, 232, 235–43, 279, 298. *see also specific teams*
Major League Baseball, 43, 274
Major League Soccer (MLS). *see also specific teams*
  academy system, 86
  coaches, 155–56
  development of, 2, 6–7, 398, 404–5
  fan support, 1–2, 43–45, 276
  Generation Adidas, 153
  junior club systems, 151
  launch, 4–6, 19, 269, 284, 401
  recognition by FIFA, 258
  shootout format, 104
Major League Soccer Players Association, 74
Makelele, Claude, 178
Makowski, Greg, 22, *100*
Maldini, Paolo, 380, 386
Malin, Seamus, 331
Manchester City, 85, 261
Mandelbaum, Bert, 322, 412
Maradona, Diego Armando, 123, 186, 272–73, 344, 360, 389–90, 399
Marchena, Hector, 309–10
Maresca, Tom, 154
marijuana, 329
Markovits, Andrei, 44–48, 113–14, 147–48, 151, 156
Marlboro Cup, 223
Marlboro Enterprise, 357–58
Marquette University, 300
Marsh, Rodney, 15, 47, 95
Marti, Lucas, 126
Martinez, Jose Maria, 319
Martinez, Roberto, 3–4
Maryland Bays, 247–48
La Masia, 108
Massachusetts U-19 team, 125
Mastroeni, Pablo, 83
Mathis, Clint, 83
Matthaus, Lothar, 360

127–30, 150, 180
European career, 271, 371–72,
    399–400
as fan, 14
height, 370
high school career, 120
indoor career, 240, 242, 252
Olympic Festivals, 122
USMNT career, 82, 220, 227–28, 232–
    33, *277*, 286–87, 296, 309–21,
    324, 328, 333–34, 337, 349, 354,
    361–64, 371–75, 387, 400, 414
youth career, 24–25, 72
Trost, Al, 59, 93
Troyes, 85
True North FC, 418
Truman State University, 339
Trump, Donald, 35, 405
TuS Bechhofen, 106
Tutu, Desmond, 344

U

U-19 tournaments. *see* World Youth
    Championship
U-20 tournaments, 220. *see also* World
    Youth Championship
Ueberroth, Peter, 325
Uhrik Truckers, 245
ultras, 360
Umbro, 61
UNAM Pumas, 109
underage players, 289–92
UNICEF World All-Stars, 191, 255–56
Unified Team, 297
uniforms (kits), 28, 47, 61
    shoes and shoe contracts, 61,
        350–54
    trading jerseys, 94, 386, *395*
    trading shorts, 386–87
United Arab Emirates (UAE), 145, 344
United German Hungarians (UGH), *190,*
    205
United Soccer Association (USA), 55–56
United Soccer League, 108, 205, 258,
    398
United States Amateur Soccer
    Association (USASA), 205

United States Interregional Soccer
    League, 258
University of California, Berkeley, 145–
    46, 254–55
University of California, Los Angeles
    (UCLA), 129–30, 150–51, 155–56,
    210, 224
University of Connecticut (UConn),
    159–60
University of Hartford, 160
University of London, 144
University of Maine, 223, 416, 418
University of Maryland, 150, 375
University of North Carolina (UNC), 119,
    122
University of Portland, 151
University of San Francisco (USF), 150,
    154, 208, 254–55
University of Tampa, 90, 122, 150
University of Virginia (UVA), 120, 127–
    28, 130, 150–51, 155, 228
University of Wisconsin-Milwaukee, 134,
    150, 155, 179, 301, 313, 412
university soccer, 144–45. *see also*
    college soccer
Univision, 346, 369, 374
urban soccer, 20–21, 40, 157, 195–203,
    245–46, 254–55, 271–73
Uruguay, 124, 207, 210
U.S. Men's National Team (USMNT)
    annual contracts, 347–50
    coaches, 125, 142–43, 155, 164, 179,
        196–97, 208–10, 292, 299–305,
        370–71, 398–401
    collegiate training, 151–52, 315
    CONCACAF 1980 roster, *100*
    Copa America 1995, 269
    as Dream Team, 276
    exhibition matches, 223
    family visits, 369
    fan support, 276, 369
    funding, 206–8, 304–5
    Futsal World Cup, 297–98
    geographic spread, 84
    Gold Cup 2010, 24
    golden generation, 234
    home venue, 234–35
    international friendlies, 135–36,

187, 207, 210, 219, 229, 280–83, 315–16, 325, 361, *365,* 411
media coverage, 276–77, 341–43
native players, 109
naturalized players, 84, 93, 105, 109, 205
1964 Olympic Games, *190,* 205
1980 Olympic Games, 109–10
1984 Olympic Games, 142, 165, 167–69
1988 Olympic Games, 5, 127, *161,* 168, 209, *218,* 219–34, 280, 283, 293–97, 418
1992 Olympic Games, 209
personae and culture, 315–16
player development, 137, 143, 145–47, 246, 251, 259, 280, 282–83, 314–15, 340–42
player payments, 57, 111, 206, 283, 293
qualifications, 54, 104–5
regimentation, 219
security, 362–63, 389
sponsorships, 350–53, 356
strikers, 377
tactics, 227, 377
talent, 204
training camps, 206–7, 210, 219–23, 283, 324–25, 340–42, 350, 363–65, 411
U-17 program, 205
U-20 program, 113, 123–27, 155, 205, 210, 260, 280, 291, 298–301, 316, 410
U-20 World Cup, 124–25, 128, 298–302
World Cup 1930, 21
World Cup 1934, 21–22
World Cup 1950, 21–22, 193
World Cup 1970, 55–58
World Cup 1974, 58
World Cup 1978, 58–59
World Cup 1982, 111–12, 134
World Cup 1986, 14, 22–24, 54–55, 130–31, 133–34, 142, 173–82, 185–89, 214
World Cup 1990, 4–6, *7,* 18–19, 66, 70, 81–89, 98, 101, 129, 145, 150–51, 169, 177, 181–84, 188,

191, 219, 235, 255–57, 269, 277, 284, 289–93, 307–18, 326–28, 330–37, 339–65, 367–95, 402, 407, 410, 417–18
World Cup 1994, 102, 105–6, 191, 234, 258, 284–85, 387, 397–98, 407, 417–18
World Cup 1998, 398
World Cup 2002, 83–84, 155, 327, 387–88
World Cup 2014, 3
World Cup 2018, 175, 318, 405
U.S. Olympic Committee (USOC), 87, 164, 215
U.S. Olympic Festival, 88, 122–27, 134, 188, 209–10, 220, 296
U.S. Olympic Team, 125
U.S. Open Cup, 138, 193, 209, 255
U.S. Soccer Athlete of the Year, 233–34
U.S. Soccer Federation (USSF)
  academy structure, 103, 107–8
  administrative organization, 205–8
  amateur division, 205
  camps and clinics, 195, 206–7, 209
  coaches, 94, 124–26, 140
  College Development Program, 158
  evolution, 403–5
  executive leadership, 205, 251–52, 300–301, 407
  Werner Fricker Award, 401
  match-siting strategy, 22–24
  media relations, 57
  NASL partnership, 133
  national team. *see* U.S. Men's National Team (USMNT); U.S. Women's National Team (USWNT)
  player contracts, 347–54
  Player of the Year, 255
  player payments, 111, 170, 283, 304–5, 349, 405–6
  professional division, 205
  publicity, 404
  Soccer Monthly, 67
  spending, 58
  sponsorships, 353–57, 404
  venues, 165
  World Cup 1986 host bid, 213–15
  World Cup 1994 host bid, 211–17,

217, 248, 258, 280–81
World Cup Organizing Committee, 325
U.S. Women's National Team (USWNT), 82, 119, 205
coaches, 120, 316
fan support, 276
history, 406
pay disputes, 349, 405–6
USA Basketball, 274–75
USL Pro, 153
USSR (Soviet Union), 165, 296–97

V

Valderrama, Carlos, 315
Valentine, Carl, 222
Van Basten, Marco, 360
Vancouver Whitecaps, 109, 221–22, 253–54
Van der Beck, Perry, *100,* 109, 139, 182–83, 187
Vanole, David
coaching career, 316
collegiate training, 151, 155, 210, 224
Olympic Festivals, 122
USMNT career, 82, 129, *161,* 220, 227, 294, 310, 312–14, 316, 349–50, 354–55
WSA career, 255
Vecchiet, Leonardo, 367
Vecsey, George, 335–36, 345
Veee, Juli, 93–94, 138
Venezia, 261
Ventura, Hugo, 317
venues, 24
Vermes, Michael, 71–72, 130, 202
Vermes, Peter
A-League career, 247
coaching career, 84–85, 89
collegiate training, 130, 146–47, 150, 154, 158, 180
ethnic club career, 202, 262
European career, 261–66, 271, 400
ODP career, 87, 89–90
professional career, 398–400
training regimen, 194–95, 341

USMNT career, 6, 77, 82, 206, 220, 227–28, 262, 296–98, 309–14, 317–18, 331–32, 337, 345, 361, 373, 377, 384–86, 391–93, 411
youth career, 71–73
vernacular, 203
Veterans Stadium (New Britain, CT), 313
Vfb Leipzig, 364
VfL Bochum, 398
Vialli, Gianluca (Luca), 6, 360, 382–83
Victoria Riptide, 253–54
Villa, Greg, *100,* 139
Viva magazine, 238
Vogelsinger, Hubert (Hubie), 59–65, 80, 97
Voller, Rudi, 360
Vusio, Gianluca, 261

W

Wacky Packs, 62–63
Wadlington, Tom (Wad, Pilgrim Tom), 14, 49, 62, 74, 76, 125–26, 145–46, 254–55, 358–60, 365, 368–70, 382, 389, 416–18
Wake Forest University, 135, 150
Warner, Jack, *244,* 250–51
Warner Communications, 42
Warner Pacific University, 266
Washington, D.C., 83
Washington Darts, 75
Washington Diplomats, 14, 73, 75, 137, *162,* 247–48
Washington Freedom, 316
Washington Spirit, 225
Washington Stars, 74, 247–48, 269
Washington State, 253–54
Washington State Premier League, *99*
Washington Whips, 56
Weah, Timmy, 108
Webster Schroeder High School (Rochester, NY), 88
Wegerle, Roy, 234, 417
Wegerle, Steve, 248
Weitzmann, Howard, 352–53
Wellesley High School, 114–16, 119, 126, 416–17

Z

X

Y

ACKNOWLEDGMENTS

I'd like to thank the team at Dickinson-Moses for all their good work in preparing this book for publication: project manager Marla Markman, designer Peri Gabriel, and proofreader Wyn Hilty, whose dogged efforts proved rather humbling (I've been spelling the phrase "de rigueur" wrong for 35 years, apparently) but also provided yet another, canny layer of fact-checking. Hat tip to Paul Sochaczewski for first connecting me to this crew. We deployed Associated Press style for *Generation Zero*, and it was instructive for an old newspaper guy to observe that AP style, like everything else in this world, evolves.

On the graphic front, I wish to extend special commendation to photographer Jon van Woerden, who proved so very generous with his spectacular archive. Jon was the official U.S. Men's National Team photographer during 1989 and 1990, but also served in a similar role for the NASL club Fort Lauderdale Strikers from 1978 forward. When it came to the Modern American Soccer Movement, his professional perch proved a front-row seat — and readers of GZ are all the richer for it. I only wish I could have found a way to use some of Jon's epic rock concert imagery from the Seventies. I made a concerted effort to crowd-source many of the photos deployed in this book. Accordingly, in addition to the credits attached to each image herein, I'd like to thank the U.S. Soccer Federation, Canada Soccer, *Soccer America,* the Fricker family, Arthur J. Klonsky and especially members of the 1990 USMNT itself, who coughed up some great, behind-the-scenes stuff from their personal archives. We nearly succeeded in reuniting Roberto Baggio's 1990 game jersey *and* shorts.

This book had plenty of early readers: Lucy D. Phillips, Tom Wadlington, Janet Lee Kahla and Rick Leavitt all plowed through pretty full-scale drafts, and I want to acknowledge their kind, useful efforts here. However, my actual editor, Stephen McDermott Myers — whose U-19 coach, Len Renary, was Shep Messing's roommate on the Cosmos (all things eventually circle back to Shep) — deserves special mention. To the extent the language here has been strengthened and refined, Esteban and his skills as editor, poet, scholar and shaman are responsible. I salute his dedication to and enthusiasm for the project. He and I played soccer together at Wesleyan, where the day I showed up for double sessions, in August 1982, I was immediately saddled with a nickname I didn't much like: Bluto. Because the moniker did fit, physically, and *Animal House* so strongly informed the collegiate zeitgeist at that time, it stuck. My Wes soccer teammates still call me that, though, true to form, Esteban would refine and strengthen it. He soon took to calling me Senator Blutarsky, then Senator, a habit he maintains to my delight into the 21st century.

ABOUT THE AUTHOR

Hal Phillips is an author, journalist and media executive based in southern Maine. *Generation Zero: Founding Fathers, Hidden Histories and the Making of Soccer in America* is his first book-length project. Phillips blogs on all matters soccer at www.genzero.halphillips.net. He posts about the world at-large at www.halphillips.net, and tweets (in fits & starts) @mandarinhal.

A daily newspaper and magazine editor until 2001, Phillips has since contributed feature content to *ESPN FC, Sports Illustrated,* Soccer365. com, *GOLF Magazine, Travel & Leisure, Golf Digest China, Portland Press Herald, Golf Australia, McKellar,* LINKS, *Robb Report* and dozens of other titles worldwide, some of which still exist. He was founder and host of the *Unsightly American Soccer Podcast* from 2009 to 2013, pioneering but effectively pre-dating the podcast movement.

An all-state striker at Wellesley High School in Massachusetts, Phillips played four years of college soccer at Wesleyan University in Middletown, Connecticut, where he double majored in ancient Greek history and modern American literature. He logged three years in the semi-pro, Greater Boston-based Luso-American Soccer Association, before heading north and playing 10 more seasons in the Maine Open League. Since 1997, he has owned and operated Mandarin Media Inc., a media consulting, content- and digital-marketing agency serving golf, travel and property clients across North America, the UK and Asia-Pacific.

Made in the USA
Coppell, TX
08 December 2022